THE AGE OF DECEPTION

THE AGE OF DECEPTION

DECODING THE TRUTHS ABOUT THE U.S. ECONOMY

JAMES DALE DAVIDSON

DELRAY BEACH PUBLISHING
55 NE 5th Avenue, Suite 200
Delray Beach, FL 33483
Tel.: (866) 584-4096
Email: www.sovereignsociety.com/contact-us
Web: http://www.sovereignsociety.com

ISBN: 978-0-692-25858-3

Notice: This publication is designed to provide accurate and authoritative information in regard to the subject matter covered. It is sold and distributed with the understanding that the author, publisher and seller are not engaged in rendering legal, accounting or other professional advice or service. If legal or other expert assistance is required, the services of a competent professional advisor should be sought.

The information and recommendations contained herein have been compiled from sources considered reliable. Employees, officers and directors of Delray Beach Publishing do not receive fees or commissions for any recommendations of services or products in this book. Investment and other recommendations carry inherent risks. As no investment recommendation can be guaranteed, Delray Beach Publishing takes no responsibility for any loss or inconvenience if one chooses to accept them.

Delray Beach Publishing advocates full compliance with applicable tax and financial reporting laws. U.S. law requires income taxes to be paid on all worldwide income wherever a U.S. person (citizen or resident alien) may live or have a residence. Each U.S. person who has a financial interest in or signature authority over bank, securities, or other financial accounts in a foreign country that exceeds $10,000 in aggregate value must report that fact on his or her annual federal income tax return, IRS Form 1040. The Foreign Account Tax Compliance Act (FATCA) requires an annual filing along with IRS Form 1040 IRS Form 8938 listing specified foreign assets. An additional report must be filed by June 30th of each year on an information return (FinCEN Form 114, formerly Form TDF 90 22.1) with the U.S. Treasury.

Willful noncompliance of reports may result in criminal prosecution. You should consult a qualified attorney or accountant to ensure that you know, understand and comply with these and any other U.S. reporting requirements.

In Memorium

Lord William Rees-Mogg
(1928-2012)

JAMES DALE DAVIDSON

My name is James Dale Davidson, and over 30 years as a specialist "crisis investor" have taught me to tell things like they are.

My years studying financial collapses have also taught me that it's always the hard working... the savers... the taxpayers... the folks who "play by the rules" that suffer the most.

I'm one of the lucky ones. I've been fortunate enough to escape this crisis without being sucked into the vortex of destruction.

I have since retired from the investment advisory world and began to live the life I always dreamed of.

But I've returned to *Strategic Investment* and *The Sovereign Society* because I refuse to sit idly by while Wall Street's and Washington's incompetence tears apart the lives of decent, hardworking Americans.

I've been warning investors about the dangers of a financial collapse for over 20 years. The first time was in my 1987 book *Blood in the Streets: Investment Profits in a World Gone Mad.* Then I warned about America's dire fiscal trends again in my 1994 book *The Great Reckoning: Protecting Your Self in the Coming Depression.* And now, I have my new book, *The Age of Deception.*

I've spent most of my adult life taking on an over-reaching government. Over the years, I've also helped investors protect their wealth and profit by accurately forecasting some of the biggest political shifts of our time... Events such as the death of the Soviet Union... the fall of the Berlin Wall... the rise of Islamic terrorism... and the more recent bank bailouts.

These predictions were deemed 'impossible' when they were made. (Newsweek even described my forecasts as "an unthinking attack on reason.") But subsequent events have proven me right.

Apart from writing books, I also edit *Strategic Investment*, one of the most successful investment newsletters of its time.

All the best,

James Dale Davidson

James Dale Davidson

"I am an extremely big fan of Jim's writings, which have shaped my thinking about the markets (and the macro world as a whole) perhaps more than anything else."

— Peter Thiel,
Billionaire, Venture Capitalist, and Co-Founder of PayPal

TABLE OF CONTENTS

CHAPTER I

The Neuroeconomics of Denial: Why Most Investors are Blind to Hints of a Coming Collapse

> *"Yet it's clear that there are physical limits to our minds. The consensus on short-term memory, for example, is that most people are limited to retaining just seven items at once, or seven chunks of data — a physical limitation, hard wired into our brains. What if we were similarly hard-wired to effectively manage a limited number of personal relationships? It seems plausible. If memory has a corresponding physical capacity, why wouldn't other functions of the brain?"*

— Mark Sisson, "Are Humans Hard Wired For A Limited Social Circle?"

I begin my analysis of the danger of a coming Dark Age by delving into the interesting question of why everyone does not see this catastrophe looming on the horizon. Why, indeed?

You may even be wondering why it could be useful to you to entertain my unsanctioned vision of a bleak future when it seems so remote from anything that would interest CNBC.

For that matter, I can almost assure you that any member of the editorial board of *The New York Times* would gladly tell you that my warning of a coming collapse is preposterous.

With all the wealth of sources available in the Information Age, is it not wrong-headed of me to propose that the mainstream view could be dangerously wrong?

Let's take up that question. The answer lies not in some peculiar defect of information technology. Rather, it has its origins in prehistory — during the Hunter-Gatherer stage that our ancestors survived before agriculture originated some 10,000 years ago.

Let me explain.

The human experience is at least 250,000 years old. Anthropologists believe that anatomically modern humans initially lived in tight-knit groups of about 150 individuals. However, that seemed to be no more than a random generalization pieced together from excavations of archaeological sites and observation of current Hunter-Gatherer groups — until a little over 20 years ago. Then in 1992, Robin Dunbar, a British anthropologist, had a penetrating insight into the physical basis of the coincidence that primal human tribes were limited to no more than 150 individuals. Dunbar theorized that the number of members in primitive human groups, like the number of members in non-human primate "grooming cliques," is determined by the size of the neocortex region (which is involved in spatial reasoning and conscious thought) of the brain.

By extrapolating from the size of the neocortex for 36 separate species of monkeys and apes, Dunbar could accurately predict the average group size for each of these species. Applying these same extrapolation techniques to humans, he calculated that the maximum "mean group size" for humans was 150, with an "intimate circle size" of 12.

Consider the comment quoted from Mark Sisson at the top of this chapter. Sisson is an expert on the primal dimensions of modern life. He points to the well-supported view about the limitations of short-term memory. This underscores why I am able to predict with a high degree of confidence that your telephone number will have seven variable digits, rather than 17 or 71. Even if you possess an extraordinary, photographic memory that would permit you to recall a 71 digit phone number, your neighbors and others who would be called upon to reach you are in all probability limited to seven digits. That's why almost all telephone numbers on the globe are limited to seven digits. When they stretch to 10 or 11 digits, it is invariably with the addition of area codes and country designations to the unique seven-digit number.

Neuroscientists have other notions about the carryover effects of primal life on contemporary humans. One of these, as we explore below, is not only that the structure of our brains informs the size of the primal human tribe, but it also helps determine our attitudes toward shared perceptions and our willingness to think for ourselves.

Let's face it. Fred Flintstone would not have been able to kill a mastodon on his own. And if he had, through some lucky turn, he would hardly have been able to carry it home by himself. For a quarter of a million years or more, the survival of our ancestors depended upon close cooperation within a tight-knit tribal group of 150 or fewer persons.

Under those conditions, independent or iconoclastic thinking may have been a threat to survival. So at a minimum, we are probably descended from 10,000 to 12,000 generations of anatomically modern human beings for whom thinking independently had negative survival value.

Little wonder then that people today show a strong disposition to trim their opinions to match those of the group. In the bad old days, when survival depended upon hunting mega fauna with a close-knit tribe, having hunters along who thought for themselves could well have led them to act independently at crucial junctures, and thus jeopardize the hunt.

Fast-forward to today, and that could go a long way toward explaining why only a fraction of the educated population of North America (or anywhere else for that matter) is prepared to think for themselves, even where matters of grave importance are involved.

A man who points towards the explanation for this is Gregory Berns, an economist and neuroscientist who holds the Distinguished Chair of Neuroeconomics in the Department of Psychiatry in the Medical School, Emory University in Atlanta, Georgia. ("Neuroeconomics" is the study of how neurobiology places constraints on the decisions people make.) Dr. Berns is the author of "Iconoclast," a book that suggests that the wiring of most people's brains keeps them from thinking independently.

According to Dr. Berns, iconoclastic thinking is a minority trait. Most people were born to gravitate toward team thinking. The brain is hard-wired to conform. He points to a study in which isolated individuals tested on their own determined the correct answer to a question 86% of the time. But when put into a group and told that the group had come to the wrong answer to that question, almost a third of the subjects (31%) abandoned the correct answer in order to conform with the prevailing group opinion.

Or to put it another way, the percentage coming to the wrong answer more than doubled — from 14% to 41%.

This interesting experiment shows more than it might seem at first look. The point is that most people's brains are wired to prefer conforming conclusions.

Presumably, the degree to which the group-think impulse expresses itself depends upon the nature of the group and what is being tested in any given circumstance.

Consider the neuroeconomic dilemma of the citizen contemplating the possible trajectory of the national economy over the next two decades.

What does he know?

He certainly knows the prevailing dogma that the United States is the richest, most successful country on earth. He has a choice between formulating a conforming opinion or veering off in an independent direction — which almost inevitably requires a considerable effort of iconoclastic research and thinking for yourself. This is exactly the setting where the hard-wired bias toward being a team player is most likely to inform expectations.

As a matter of interest, the unwelcome revelations from accountants and actuaries plumbing the books of the U.S. government seem to have had virtually no impact on popular opinion. This is completely contrary to the effect they should have.

A Debt That Will Never be Repaid

Too often, ordinary citizens tend to ignore the logic of double-entry bookkeeping.

In pure logic, the revelation that the U.S. government has unfunded liabilities and debts with a present value of somewhere between $90 trillion and $205 trillion (or almost 1,500% of GDP) implies that Americans, depending upon their specific dealings with the U.S. treasury, could be not the richest people on the globe, but more likely the poorest.

Again, I'm reminded of the charming story that Donald Trump told of himself. A couple of decades ago during the savings and loan crisis, Trump was walking with his girlfriend of the moment on the Upper East Side of New York when the couple encountered a tattered street person begging for alms. Trump shocked his companion by telling her that the street person was worth $1 billion more than he.

"But he doesn't look as though he has a penny," she protested.

"He doesn't," Trump replied.

I am convinced that the neural bias toward conforming opinion goes a long way toward explaining the apparent oblivion of the majority of Americans to the dire fiscal prospects of the U.S. I also think it helps explain the alacrity with which the public seems to accept blatant lies about current economic performance, particularly those that hinge on the mis-measurement and under-reporting of inflation.

Accept it. The U.S. government has been lying to you for decades.

The government and politicians have proven adept at hijacking your in-born inclination to conform your thinking to that of the small tribal group.

In effect, politicians use your primal inclination to trim your opinions to those of the group to manipulate your perceptions of the economy in ways that jeopardize your future.

This was underscored by news reports that politicians in both major parties involved in chronic wrangles over the yawning federal deficit had concurred on steps to save future trillions by further fiddling inflation adjustments on Social Security, and federal pensions. Already, total federal outlays for Social Security are only half what they would have been if inflation were still reported by the same methodology used during the Carter Administration.

In effect, the political establishment has agreed that they can correct what ails the country by compounding the remorseless lies they have already told you.

Don't believe them. Now, more than ever, it is time to think for yourself.

The Income Fraud

The appearance of higher incomes is largely an illusion.

Contrary to the institutionalized pretense of the government, and their lackeys among the Keynesian economists, decades of remorseless government spending out of an empty pocket have impoverished Americans and left most people facing a future they cannot afford.

A major explanation for Obama's re-election in the face of plunging real income is the simple fact that the United States has been so thoroughly impoverished that the only prospect for most of the former middle class facing the future is more income redistribution.

With real wages plunging, it doesn't take a crystal ball to see that most Americans have very little prospect of enjoying a better life if they must pay for it from their own resources.

Consider this frightening fact: 54% of U.S. retirees have less than $25,000 in savings. This amounts to less than their projected out-of-pocket costs for Medicare alone. According to the Employment Benefit Research Institute, Social Security is "the only source of income for one-quarter of current retirees, and the primary source for nearly three-quarters. That dependence will only grow for baby boomers."

Do you wonder why politicians shy away from reducing the unfunded burden of entitlements? Don't.

The inflation lobby has managed to create a situation where the vast majority of Americans have no hope of retirement. And this did not begin with the collapse of Lehman Brothers and the bursting of the housing bubble.

The Slow Decay of America's Middle Class

Let's face it, the American middle class is practically kaput. The average American family has only about $50,000 in savings. And that number is skewed to the upside by the increasingly atypical top 10%.

You almost have to be in the top 10% of the income distribution in the U.S. to live a decent life today. And even that is likely to go away as future Presidents raise taxes on "the rich" to predatory levels. But whether you're a retiree hoping to supplement your income, a wild optimist hoping to retire, or a younger, productive person facing the prospect that much higher taxation and runaway inflation will deprive you of anything you are able to earn, it is time to transcend denial and take a cold, hard look at the situation you face. If you do, you'll see that there is practically no chance for you to enjoy prosperity in the future by going along with the gag.

In historic terms, the situation you face is probably as hopeless as that of the Roman middle-class starting from the time of Diocletian when the decision was made, as described by The Cambridge Ancient History, "to squeeze the population to the last drop."

A ruinous decline in living standards lies ahead in the United States, another case of the decline and fall of a great power that remorselessly overspent the available resources, relying upon predatory taxation and concerted inflation to preserve the state at the expense of the people.

Notwithstanding the pronounced cognitive bias of most people to conform to "group think" and go along with the gag, there is a limit to the malleability of the public when a bankrupt government is dragging its citizens along into bankruptcy as well.

No one knows where the inflection point lies when the government will choose even more overtly despotic forms of repression and control. But I doubt that we're talking about something as far away as 2084.

Why Financial Repression Won't Work

You have heard much since 2010 about "financial repression," the government policy of holding interest rates far below the rate of inflation. This deprives you as a saver of income you would otherwise have received.

To keep abreast of the deterioration of the U.S. government's balance sheet, real interest rates would have to be so far negative that they canceled debt equal to 30% to 40% of GDP annually.

There is a word for that. Hyperinflation.

There is a fine line between "financial repression" and more thoroughgoing repression that limits the freedom of your person as well as that of your money.

The U.S. Government is Closing the Exits

(I wrote this in September 2010 while in Brazil scouting for opportunities in a rare economy that was enjoying robust growth at that time.)…

To illustrate, consider this story — which I well know, as it happened to me. I write from Brazil, where I have been following my own advice by investing my time and money in a more prospective economy.

Knock on wood, I seem to have several fortune making projects on the go. To do this, I've had to send money to Brazil and visit at least 51 times.

My success owes absolutely nothing to the U.S. government. In fact, the overbearing bureaucracy of a repressive surveillance and security state made it extremely difficult for me to make an investment on which I have earned a 1,426% gain to date. (Which is equal to over 5000 years of interest on U.S. treasury bills at their current, invisibly low rate).

As you may know, one of the strong policy thrusts of the Obama administration has been the promulgation of onerous regulations designed to prevent American citizens from creating or maintaining financial assets abroad. These regulations don't make it illegal, per se, for an American to open a foreign bank account. Rather, their aim is to impose regulatory burdens on foreign banks that are so onerous as to make it economically irrational for them to entertain American clients. I have been told by foreign banks that closed my accounts that meeting the regulatory impositions from the US government for permitting an American citizen to hold an account costs $18,000 annually.

A little more than a year ago, I learned to my surprise that Obama is using the same techniques to discourage American banks from allowing their customers to wire money to other jurisdictions. When I attempted to wire funds to support what seemed to be a very prospective investment in Brazil, I was amazed to learn that a bank with which I had been dealing for decades refused to complete the transaction.

Why?

I was told by the president of the bank that regulators had threatened his institution with fines of up to $100,000 for permitting international wire transfers that were not supported by voluminous documentation that the bank had no systems, nor personnel to manage. I was stuck. It certainly was not a question of my proposing to use the money for nefarious purposes.

But my money was getting the same kind of bureaucratic scrutiny before it could travel that you get when you have to take off your belt and shoes at the airport. After much wheedling and cajoling and the patient drafting of long memos to the file, I was finally able to prevail on the bank to proceed with the transfer. As a result, the transaction was gratifyingly profitable.

I don't know whether the bank had to pay a fine or suffer other bureaucratic recriminations for allowing me to conduct business abroad. However, I do know that "financial repression" is edging ever closer to becoming just "repression." Full stop.

This experience made obvious to me that the law in its majesty was making it onerous for anyone but billionaires to do business abroad. In many cases, banks will balk at wiring money abroad for investments unless they make so much profit from handling your account that it will cover the fines and other costly regulatory headaches that they may face from allowing you to exercise your rights. As an entrepreneur.

And it is not just a question of whether they will let you send your money abroad. Don't forget that a big part of successful foreign investment is traveling to other countries, making contacts and realizing opportunities. If you were stuck at home, like an East German pinned in behind the Berlin Wall, you could never launch a fortune making enterprise in Brazil, or any other jurisdiction.

I believe in the not-too-distant future that you will need special dispensation from the government to travel abroad. In fact, the U.S. Senate passed legislation in 2012 to enable the IRS to seize your passport if you owe back taxes. A bill titled "Transportation Research and Innovative Technology Act of 2012" (SB 1813 Sec. 40203), would have given the IRS the power to revoke, limit, and/or deny passports to citizens who owe back taxes.

I also had the pleasure of enjoying a $416,000 tutorial on just how easy it is to have a gigantic tax due to the IRS through no fault of your own. In March 2012, my wallet was stolen. Presumably, that is when some cretin stole my identity and thereafter filed an entirely fictitious tax return with the IRS using my Social Security number.

I suppose he was fishing for a refund. But the return included no details from the various brokerage accounts and banks that file information notices with the IRS. Consequently, I was buried in fines and penalties for "underreporting," which I am still trying to sort out.

If section 40203 of the "Transportation Research and Innovative Technology Act of 2012" had passed the House, I probably would not be in Brazil today. I would have lost the business opportunities I am pursuing now simply because someone stole my identity.

That said, it is not worth delving into the quirks and injustice of this particular piece of legislation, except to note that it illustrates the authoritarian measures the U.S. government will pursue to compel you to do its bidding.

It is almost comically obvious that one of the next steps in the intensification of "financial repression" will be laws to seize part of your retirement assets and forcibly invest them into government bonds, under the guise of "protecting" your retirement.

In my view, it is already "baked in the cake" that U.S. living standards are destined to take another deep notch down. If nothing else, the institution of ObamaCare guarantees that increasing numbers of the formerly middle class will be pushed into part-time employment.

Full-Time Jobs: An Endangered Species?

The coverage for mandated healthcare insurance in Obama's Affordable Care Act kicks in for employees working more than 30 hours a week. Consequently, employers cut hours rather than comply with the mandate to provide costly benefits for workers who exceed the 30-hour threshold.

As a result, many full-time jobs are being converted into part-time work. For example, almost immediately after ObamaCare passed, a Taco Bell in Guthrie Oklahoma announced it "is cutting full-time employees' hours to avoid mandates under the new affordable care law."

National restaurant chains including Applebee's, Olive Garden and Denny's have also joined the parade of employers cutting work hours. It isn't just downscale chain restaurants that are curtailing the workweek. In Ohio, Youngstown State University announced a 29 hour per week mandate — warning employees that they would be fired if they work more than that amount.

News reports indicate that the state of Virginia was trying to force "potentially tens of thousands of public sector employees in the state to work fewer hours so the government can avoid providing them healthcare."

Prior to ObamaCare, the average, full-time employee in the U.S. worked about 39.5 hours weekly, which totals about 2,050 hours a year. And a 2010 study conducted by the Center for American Progress found that many American men born after 1956 considered a 40-hour week to be a "part time" endeavor.

That is probably because it is increasingly difficult for a man with real weekly earnings at an Eisenhower era vintage of $185 (in 1982–1984 constant dollars) to support a family. Still, in his zeal to increase the proportion of Americans that are totally dependent on government handouts, Obama has set in motion incentives that will force many employers to adopt the French workweek.

The Francification of America is Under Way

The "French way" has been to tolerate one of the world's shortest workweeks, with an average of 1,439 hours put in annually, according to an OECD study. That is a little more than 27 hours per week. The results for French work culture were succinctly described by Corinne Maier, who works for a state-owned, French electricity company. She has written a book arguing that the

French attitude to work is to do as little as possible. She says, "The aim is to keep your job without working."

The trouble is that shirking does not pay its way in a competitive world where Turks work almost 50 hours a week and South Koreans only slightly less.

A shorter work week doesn't bode well for the future of U.S. tax rates.

In the 19th century, the famous English economist David Ricardo proposed the so-called "Equivalence Theorem." It holds that consumers will internalize the government's "budget constraint," and recognizing that they will have to pay higher taxes in the future when government increases its liabilities, will put aside savings to pay for the future tax rise.

This may have seemed a reasonable proposition 200 years ago, but today's total U.S. government debt and liabilities are so vast that they comfortably exceed the total GDP of the world. That being the case, there is no way that even the wealthiest taxpayer could make an adequate provision for them.

To me, it would seem more rational to stop acting as if you were a member of a close-knit, primal tribe and declare your cognitive and economic independence.

And get out while you still can.

CHAPTER 2

Obama and The Big Lie

"If you tell a lie big enough and keep repeating it, people will eventually come to believe it. The lie can be maintained only for such time as the State can shield the people from the political, economic and/or military consequences of the lie.

It thus becomes vitally important for the State to use all of its powers to repress dissent, for the truth is the mortal enemy of the lie, and thus by extension, the truth is the greatest enemy of the State."

— Joseph Goebbels, Nazi Minister of Propaganda.

I have been reading "The Folly of Fools: The Logic of Deceit and Self-Deception in Human Life," by Robert Trivers. This writer, who has been described as "one of the brightest minds in evolutionary biology," argues that the human mind is inclined to systematically distort perceptions of reality, and to fool both itself and others. His Darwinian theory of deception and self-deception makes an excellent prologue for understanding the remorseless lies promulgated each month by Barack Obama's Bureau of Labor Statistics (BLS).

The Folly of Fools spells out the biological imperatives that dispose us to be suckers for Obama's lies. But to understand fully the magnificence and audacity of the "big lie" upon which Barack Hussein Obama staked his re-election, we have to go beyond our predisposition to be deceived and revisit the hall of fame of propaganda as curated by Joseph Goebbels, the Nazi Minister of Propaganda.

Let us repeat Goebbels' key statement, in all its vileness: "If you tell a lie big enough and keep repeating it, people will eventually come to believe it."

Trivers' work on self-deception may add perspective about why people are predisposed to embrace certain "big lies," but Goebbels remains the pioneering expert on how governments can build political regimes around some real whoppers.

BS at the Bureau of Labor Statistics

Few "big lies" are bigger and more remote from the facts than the now widely accepted notion that the employment picture in the United States is rapidly improving. As you no doubt know, for several years the BLS has reported "improvements" in the U.S. employment picture.

This fictitious surge in employment not only accelerated a stock market rally, but also touched off some delicious hyperbole among market observers.

What we are really seeing is statistical malarkey.

But the most damning analysis of Obama's manipulation of unemployment statistics comes from certified financial analyst Daniel R. Amerman. In an article titled "Making 9 Million Jobless 'Vanish': How the Government Manipulates Unemployment Statistics," Amerman states:

> "A detailed look at the government's own database shows that about nine million people without jobs have been removed from the labor force simply by the government defining them as not being in the labor force anymore. Effectively all of the decreases in unemployment rate percentages since 2009 have come not from new jobs but through reducing the workforce participation rate so that millions of jobless people are removed from the labor force … When we pierce through the statistical smoke and mirrors and factor back in those nine million jobless… the true unemployment rate is 19.9% and rising not 8.3% and falling."

President Obama has many accomplices in perpetrating the illusion that the unemployment problem in the United States is rapidly improving. He is by no means the only person who seems to devoutly wish that the U.S. employment picture would dramatically improve, putting a sound, robust recovery "just around the corner."

This is an illusion that the last three presidents have helped to create and perpetuate.

The CNBC "booster effect" is widely noted. Either intuitively or from close calculation, most stock market professionals are aware that after a decade of flat returns in most of the major indices, the prosperity of investment banking, per se, is bound to be undermined in a stagnant economy with high and growing unemployment.

The stark and simple truth is the less real wealth that is produced by the younger cohorts of society, the less wealth there will be to support older people after retirement, either through government transfers or from the proceeds of private investments.

Let me suggest as well that, even if you derive high compound returns from following Strategic Investment's portfolio recommendations in high-growth emerging economies, like Brazil, it is still implausible that you would be permitted to keep much of what you earn. This would be especially true in the second Obama administration as he fully institutes financial repression to accompany "the big lie" as a policy response to national bankruptcy.

What is financial repression? It is what happens when a bankrupt government wants to funnel profits from the free markets to its own coffers. During financial repression you can expect caps on interest rates, regulation of cross-border capital movement, and direct lending to the government from pension funds or domestic banks.

Put simply, the U.S. government under Obama has instituted the whole repertoire of policies traditionally associated with financial repression in bankrupt third world countries. This is no accident. It is essential to Obama's plan to make you and other investors pay the staggering costs of his income redistribution programs.

Higher taxes to soak investors are a big part of the Obama plan. For example, the president is now advocating not just a doubling, but almost a tripling of the dividend tax rate to 44.6% — from today's 15% tax rate for high income earners.

An African Economist's Approach to Stealing Your Wealth

Obama appears to have embarked on a mission to fulfill "the dream from his father," an African "economist" who advocated imposing tax rates as high as 100% on the wealthy. According to the elder Barack Hussein Obama, "Theoretically, there is nothing that can stop the government from taxing 100% of income…"

Of course, any dim-witted government official could raise taxes to 100% of income, but what is the incentive to work at all, let alone earn an income sufficient enough to place citizens in the top tax bracket?

And who in their right mind would keep their money in the U.S. if that was the consequence?

More likely, an "economy" of high net worth individuals would move offshore or underground, where Uncle Sam can't trace or tax it.

This benefits no one. Although a simple variable such as logic has never stopped our government from pursuing any flawed idea to its illogical end.

Indeed, raising the top income tax rate to punitive levels happens often enough in America.

During World War I, the top tax rate was raised to about 78% to pay for the significant government spending, which took America's debt-to-GDP from 5% to 25%.

Once the debt was paid off, the top tax rate came back down to a reasonable 25%. But this did not last for a very long time. In the midst of the Great Depression the top tax rate was once again raised to 63% in an effort to control government spending at the time. A few short years later saw Pearl Harbor bombed, and the U.S. entered into another expensive world war.

Our debt-to-GDP steadily climbed to 120% and the top tax rate moved to an extremely painful 94%.

I bring up the past because it reveals exactly what will happen in the years ahead. With a debt-to-GDP north of 100%, our government is going to create a compelling case to tax upper-income individuals to death.

If Obama is as keen on picking your pocket as was his father, the 39.6% top tax rate today will seem like a vacation from the 70% rates you might have to pay tomorrow.

For more details on this, go to the library and borrow a copy of Obama Junior's best-selling book, "Dreams From My Father." I find it telling that Obama frames his dreams in terms of his father, who is obviously something of a Bolshevik.

Comfortable Retirement? Not in America

The promise of a comfortable and dignified retirement so promiscuously made by politicians during the 20th century has outlived its plausibility. And if you look at it carefully, it was never very plausible, given highly reliable population projections that show there will be only two persons aged 16–64 in the U.S. labor force for each person age 65 or older by 2027.

To think that those two workers could be so productive as to generate enough goods and services to support their own families, plus the U.S. government and military infrastructure (not to mention a surplus to repay the tens of trillions of dollars politicians have borrowed from around the globe), as well as one older person between them, always seemed overly optimistic to me.

This is especially true when you take into account the common estimate of financial planners and investment advisers that the coming generations will not only be able to handle this "heavy lifting" but will do it so comfortably that they will be able to accumulate vast capital sums that they will turn over to the Boomers by purchasing real estate and securities that Boomers hope to have accumulated at extraordinarily high prices.

How likely is that?

Something will have to give. Either the retirement age will go up to nearly 80 years, the taxes collected to fund these entitlements increases by a factor of two or more benefits will be drastically cut to keep these programs running within their means.

Either way, what we are being promised today will prove to be nothing more than a mirage as reality sets in.

Be that as it may, financial repression is not merely a synonym for higher taxes. It is more pernicious than that. The main thrust of Obama Junior's plan is not merely to tax a higher fraction of whatever investment income you somehow manage to achieve, it is to prevent you from earning the income in the first place. Financial repression is primarily designed to foreclose your options for investment.

The Insidious Truth About Low Interest Rates

This is obvious with the policy of invisibly low interest rates for savers in the United States. The U.S. government doesn't want you to have the option of earning a real return on money you saved. That would make it harder to finance deficits equal to nearly 9% of the GDP.

A first step toward forcing you to pay a lopsided proportion of the cost of funding a bankrupt government is for the Fed to keep interest rates below the rate of inflation. That way, the "inflation tax" erodes the value of your dollar holdings. If you hold lots of dollars you can expect much of their value to be inflated away.

In order for financial repression to work, it has to be comprehensive, as well as difficult to comprehend. It is necessary for Obama to cut off your options for investing in high-yield securities in growing economies, hence, his drive to stifle cross-border capital movements.

Before Obama, it was never illegal for Americans to invest or live abroad. And it still isn't. It is doubtful that even a Democrat-led Congress would enact legislation to explicitly repress the right of Americans to invest or live anywhere they please.

Obama's plan to impose financial repression on America is not based on laws that explicitly prohibit you from investing or living abroad. He just wants to impose regulations, especially on banks, even non-American banks, that will make it so costly for them to entertain your business that they will refuse to do so — unless you are a multibillionaire whose deposits and invested sums are so gigantic that fees for servicing them would repay the costs of meeting Obama's heavy-handed regulations.

Financial Repression at its Finest

As recently as March 7, 2013, the Obama Treasury released another blizzard of FATCA (Foreign Account Tax Compliance Act) regulations designed to make it difficult for Americans, even those living abroad, to maintain accounts in non-U.S. banks. As one foreign banker described the situation, "After sitting through a three-hour FATCA seminar this week about how the U.S. intends to impose its legislation on the whole world, nothing they do would surprise me."

Under the rules devised by Obama's regulators, banks and other jurisdictions would be obliged to bear heavy regulatory compliance costs in order to open or maintain accounts for U.S. citizens.

The Obama administration has sought to employ heavy-handed banking regulations to sharply raise the costs of such capital transactions. By imposing high regulatory burdens on banks for conducting what are, in principle, simple and legal transactions, Obama will bar all but the biggest and wealthiest investors from investing abroad. As Reinhart suggests, these measures amount to "administrative capital controls."

In other words, Obama is imposing de facto capital controls to keep you from putting your money somewhere beyond his reach.

If Obama has his way and you want to undertake an international, direct investment of $100,000 or even a million dollars, you won't be able to do it. But if your investment size is $10 million, or $100 million, you may still be relatively free. It is far more likely under those circumstances that the bank's earnings from handling your huge account will make it worthwhile for them to shoulder the heavy disclosure, red tape and other requirements that Obama is imposing in his program of financial repression.

How any of this could translate into a "positive" for the economy is beyond my comprehension. I cannot help but see where our government's current policies are tragically taking us: almost certainly to another economic drop that will catch most people off guard.

With what I have shown you here, you have a right to suspect the government is trying to blind you with rose-colored glasses. It wants you to believe the hype that the American economy is not only doing well, but generating substantial jobs which will allow people to once again prosper in our society.

The facts, unfortunately, point to the exact opposite scenario as being true. In the future, the American way of life is going to look drastically different from what we are experiencing today.

CHAPTER 3

The Pinocchio Recovery: How the United States Turned into the Greatest Economic Liar since the Soviet Union

"The official statistics of TS SU (the old USSR Central statistical administration) have exaggerated Soviet economic growth, efficiency and price stability… From the standpoint of official data, the worsening of Soviet economic conditions in the 1980s remained largely invisible; serious long-term problems were admitted, but no crisis… Soviet leaders' reliance on the official statistical record, which blanked out the true picture and shielded them from the necessity to act, explains the uncomprehending complacency with which they ignored the first Law of Holes (if you're in one, stop digging). The upsurge of economic discontent, followed by a turn to terminal disintegration, simply took them by surprise."

— Mark Harrison, "Soviet Economic Growth Since 1928:
The Alternative Statistics of G.I. Khanin"

If you are like most investors, you may puzzle over what investment analyst Mike Larson calls "the greatest disconnect of all time" between the economic fundamentals and the stock market. Floyd Norris points to the same phenomenon in an article published in the October 1, 2010 issue of *The New York Times* (page 3 of the business section) titled "Recession May Be Over, but Consumer Pessimism is Plumbing New Depths." David Rosenberg shows that the view of the American people toward the economy is dramatically disconnected from what would be appropriate for a recovery:

"What really caught our eye was the sub index in the University of Michigan survey that captures 'expected change in business conditions.' Look at this — 123 in January; 107 in August; 101 in September. It averaged 101 in September! In the first quarter of 2009, long before the onset of the 'green shoot' era and amidst a 5% plunge in real GDP, this metric was sitting at 102. This is troubling.

"As far as the coming 12 months are concerned, 64% of respondents reported that they believe that economic conditions will be 'bad,' while only 25% said 'good.' Brother — and people think we're down in the mouth with our forecast. What is disturbing is how the general population is truly throwing in the towel, and not just for the next 12 months. When asked the same question on the economic outlook for the next five years, 58% said 'bad' and just 31% said 'good.'"

What could explain the apparent divorce between the recovering economy and depressed expectations? In fact, the explanation is simple. Many of the statistical indicators that purport to show a recovery are mere confections. Lies.

How the Fed Can Print a Stock Market Rally

Even the robust performance of the stock market in September 2010 is the equivalent of a lie. The market was supported by the infusion of tens of billions of dollars from the Federal Reserve. In effect, the government simulated an economic recovery by monetizing stock market averages — a shocking allegation that is supported by the facts.

Much of the government manipulation of stock prices was meant to have ended with the first installment of Quantitative Easing. But it didn't. A September 28, 2010 article by Graham Summers (Phoenix Capital Research), argues that the "only reason" stocks rallied in September was because the Federal Reserve pumped tens of billions into manipulation of stock prices. The article claims that notwithstanding the Fed's statements that it halted its initial Quantitative Easing (QE) program in March of 2010, and no additional debt monetization occurred between then and the announcement of the "QE lite" program in August, the Fed has continued to "monetize Wall Street's debts EVERY options expiration week since QE 1 purportedly ended. The article continues:

Here's the chart of the Fed's recent actions for those of you who haven't seen this before. Options expiration weeks are in bold.

Week	Fed Action
July 22, 2010	-$8 billion
July 15, 2010	**+$8.6 billion**
July 8, 2010	+$1 billion
July 1, 2010	-$13 billion
June 24, 2010	+$175 million
June 17, 2010	**+$12 billion**
June 10, 2010	-$4 billion
June 3, 2010	+$2 billion
May 27, 2010	-$16 billion
May 20, 2010	**+$14 billion**
May 13, 2010	+$10 billion
May 6, 2010	-$4 billion
April 29, 2010	-$1 billion
April 15, 2010	**+$31 billion**
April 8, 2010	+$420 million
April 1, 2010	-$6 billion

You'll note that the Fed ALWAYS made its largest capital contributions during options expiration weeks. Heck it pumped $31 BILLION into the system in April 2010, just ONE MONTH after it claimed QE 1 ended!

However, since that time the Fed has pumped a total of over $65 billion into Wall Street on options expiration weeks. On non-expiration weeks the Fed either withdraws money or makes small money pumps.

This pattern finally ended in August 2010, when the Fed failed to pump the system on options expiration week. But then again, why bother? The Fed was about to announce its QE lite program in which it would use the interest on maturing securities to purchase Treasuries from Wall Street Primary Dealers via its Permanent Open Market Operations (POMO).

Graham Summers argues that the 18 primary dealers, the "BIG BOYS of finance," including Goldman Sachs, JP Morgan, Bank of America, and others were the primary beneficiaries of the first installment of Quantitative Easing.

Summers notes:

> The Fed bought over one trillion dollars in securities from these firms. Its new QE lite program consists of it using the interest and proceeds from the securities in its portfolio that are maturing to buy Treasuries from the Primary Dealers via … POMO.
>
> In simple terms, the POMO actions allow the Fed to pump money into Wall Street (by buying Treasuries from the Primary Dealers) without DIRECTLY monetizing Treasury debt (the Treasuries had already been issued). The Primary Dealers then take this fresh capital from the Fed and plow into stocks, forcing the sort of ramp job we saw last week on Friday" (September 24, 2010).

Graham Summers is hardly the only one to recognize that the Fed has been manipulating the stock market. For one thing, the September 2010 rally ran completely counter to the flow of funds. The week ended September 22, 2010 marked the 21st sequential outflow of consumer holdings of mutual funds, with $2.5 billion sold, bringing the total year-to-date to over $70 billion. September outflows totaled $16 billion, hardly compatible with the sharp jump in stock indices.

The Obama Administration plays as fast and loose with economic statistics as it does with money. Do you honestly think that if they are prepared to spend trillions out of an empty pocket to fake the appearance of economic recovery that they would have any qualms about faking a few statistics that not one person in a thousand bothers to closely examine?

If you're puzzling over that question, don't bother. They lie remorselessly over just about every headline economic statistic. Some of the biggest lies are reserved for unemployment statistics. One of Obama's clever ploys for reducing unemployment has been to persistently lower the Civilian Labor Force Participation Rate. After averaging around 66.5% for much of the '80s and '90s, it has continuously plunged since January 2008.

Data released over Obama's "recovery summer" of 2010 show that the U.S. adult population that is employed fell to a seasonally adjusted 58.5% in August 2010. It was lowered to 58.5% when the Obamanites engineered a drop in the unemployment rate from 9.7% to 9.5% to support the illusion that vigorous recovery was underway. Under Obama's watch there has been a startling drop off of the employment-to-population ratio (EPOP). If the EPOP were held constant at its 2000 peak of 64.9%, the unemployment rate would be above 14% in August 2010.

A similar brand of statistical fraud has been employed by Obama's Department of Labor in reporting sensitive initial unemployment claims. When announced, the numbers are taken as important current indicators of economic vitality. This is why the Obama Administration has organized a systematic effort to lie to the public about initial claims.

The Unemployment data are not the only economic statistics being distorted by the Obama Administration. A close read of almost any sensitive economic series shows that the numbers are distorted to present a rosier picture than is close to the facts. This is evident in the highly gamed GDP reports.

Barack Obama has taken his economic play book right out of the pages of Pravda. (Or I might more accurately say, the TS SU, the old Soviet Central Statistical Administration that was found to have overstated economic growth in the USSR between 1928 and 1985 by 13-fold.) Under Obama's watch, the U.S. government has replaced the late Soviet Union as the champion fabricator of economic lies in the world. In my view, there are a lot of drawbacks to a policy of lies and government manipulation of stock prices.

You will be paying for them for the rest of your life.

CHAPTER 4

Lies, Jobs, and Dreams

"We live in an amazing world. Everybody has big budget deficits and big easy money, but somehow the world cannot fully employ itself. It is a serious question. We are no longer just talking about a single country having a big depression, but the entire world. If the world cannot employ everyone who is ready and able to work, it raises some big questions."

— Former Fed Chairman Paul Volcker

I wrote this in September, 2010 on a trip in Brazil scouting for opportunities in a rare economy that was enjoying robust growth at that time. What follows are my ruminations from that trip, with a few names changed to protect the innocent…

On the hills overlooking Belvedere, Belo Horizonte's most fashionable neighborhood, high-rise condos are springing up on every buildable lot. There are dozens of them in the works, commanding views of the city and the valleys below. Brazil's current housing deficit is seven million units. That extends across all income levels. Each high-rise sprouting over the skyline contains from 20 to 40 new luxury apartments. Thousands of millionaires have already pre-paid up to three years in advance for three to four bedrooms (plus maid's quarters) at prices ranging from one to five million.

Volcker may be right in suggesting that most of the world is "having a big depression." But when he describes "the entire world," his thinking is clearly limited to the so-called "advanced economies," the only ones that used to matter. As you try to decipher the puzzle of prosperity in a changing world, it is important to recognize that every important economy is not in depression. A few of the rudimentary economies in Africa have enjoyed robust growth, including Zambia, Mozambique, Guinea and São Tomé and Príncipe, along with some less rudimentary ones in South America. I report from the largest economy in South America.

Brazil, the largest economy in South America, is thriving. Following a 9% annualized real advance in Q1 2010, Brazil grew at a more modest 8.8% rate in the second quarter. Meanwhile, it hardly needs emphasizing that this type of growth is a thing of the past in the formerly "advanced" economies.

The economy nearest and dearest to most of us, the United States, grew at a revised annualized rate of 1.6% in Q2, attributable mostly to the $11.3 trillion lent, guaranteed, or spent out of an empty pocket by the Obama Administration.

As I spell out below, there is good reason to suppose that much of the reported growth in U.S. GDP in recent years did not happen as the official statistics suggest. For one thing, there is a massive disconnect between reported GDP and its identical twin, Gross Domestic Income (or GDI). More on that in a minute.

A Pretend Prosperity Built on Government Spending

Another major reason that the so-called "recovery" feels bad is the continued shrinkage of U.S. private sector GDP. If you subtract government spending from the GDP, you can see that there has been no U.S. recovery, just increased federal spending. Consider these numbers for the past decade, stated in millions of 2005 dollars:

Year	GDP	Gov't Spending	Net GDP
2001	$11,371.3	$2,056.4	$9,314.9
2002	11,538.9	2,186.6	9,350.2
2003	11,738.7	2,303.3	9,435.4
2004	12,213.8	2,377.7	9,836.1
2005	12,587.5	2,486.0	10,101.5
2006	12,962.5	2,578.5	10,384.0
2007	13,194.1	2,570.1	10,624.0
2008	13,359.0	2,753.3	10,605.7
2009	12,810.0	3,210.8	9,599.2
2010	13,191.5	3,470.0	9,721.5

Current net private GDP is less than it was in 2004 and, if accurately reported, would probably be at or below 2001's level. As Mike "Mish" Shedlock stated on his blog, "Careful analysis shows that the alleged recovery is nothing more than an illusion caused by unsustainable deficit spending."

I have made no secret of the fact that there is less than meets the eye in the prosperity portrayed in the well-jiggled U.S. economic statistics. In fact, much of this chapter is devoted to detailing the statistical fraud and outright lies that have become standard practice for the U.S. government. It is doing everything it can to hoax what remains of the middle class into believing that the U.S. economy is recovering robustly when it isn't.

The contrast with Brazil, where the economy really was vibrant, is stark. Not only is the U.S. "in a big depression," as Paul Volker says, but in my experience even the minority of Americans who are doing well are not enjoying their success as much as people in Brazil do.

The New York Times reported on October 12, "Call it recession or recovery, for tens of millions of Americans, there's little difference."

> Born of a record financial collapse, this recession… has left an enormous oversupply of houses and office buildings and crippling debt. The decision last week by leading mortgage lenders to freeze foreclosures, and calls for a national moratorium, could cast a long shadow of uncertainty over banks and the housing market. Put simply, the national economy has fallen so far that it could take years to climb back.

It would be hard to overstate the far more buoyant mood in Brazil. It is possible, of course, that my experience of Brazil is prejudiced by the fact that I spend most of my time here with wealthy Brazilians.

How Wealthy Brazilians Spend Their Money

None of them seems harried and stressed the way many of the successful people I know in the U.S. do. They don't spend every waking hour working. Perhaps part of the reason is that Brazilians seem to take a genuine delight in hanging out with their families. Indeed, it is indicative of the greater focus on family that Brazil celebrates "Children's Day" as a national holiday, on a par with Father's Day and Mother's Day.

In the case of Brazilians I know, they entertain lavishly. We have seen them drop millions of dollars on a single party.

Last weekend, I drove out of Belo Horizonte to Moeda, a village in rural Minas Gerais where I was among 300 friends and relatives invited to a barbecue lunch at a country estate. A wait staff in the dozens served a prodigious amount of food and drink.

One thing I've noticed about Brazilian lunches is that they tend to involve one of two excesses apparently designed to hold the guests as far into the evening as possible. In some cases, hosts serve copious quantities of wine, beer, and other alcoholic libations but delay serving food on the supposition that guests might leave after eating.

Presumably, if the lunch never gets started, it can't end. In the more commodious version of this strategy, which we enjoyed last weekend, the hosts keep their guests occupied by serving a huge amount of delicious food.

This particular lunch was followed seamlessly by a full dinner while a live band entertained the guests on the grounds of a house big enough to be a hotel. From this perspective, it seems appropriate that "Moeda" means "money" in Portuguese.

When in the U.S., I spend a lot of time in Palm Beach County, Florida (the only jurisdiction east of the Mississippi with an AAA bond rating), so I have a perhaps equally skewed experience of wealth in contemporary America.

But note that even Palm Beach County is staggering under the weight of real estate woes. Florida realtors reported that banks are repossessing 4,000 homes a month in South Florida. In Palm Beach County alone, 10,385 new foreclosures were filed in the first six months of 2010. The impression I get in Brazil is that it is booming, more so than Palm Beach, with few foreclosures and a lot of people making fortunes. Big ones. The rich in Brazil are really rich.

"A million dollars is nothing."

A pro-U.S. Brazilian tycoon — who keeps a framed copy of the Declaration of Independence on his wall — was quite vocal about the U.S. policy of cheapening the dollar when I spoke with him at our lavish lunch. He stated: "The dollar used to be something. A million dollars used to be something. Today, a million dollars is nothing. The only place it still amounts to anything is the United States. In Brazil today, a million dollars is nothing."

His blatant exaggeration did not strike me as a literal truth — after all, a million dollars is still something. Not what it was, to be sure, but something.

However, this man, although exaggerating, was reporting something important — the devaluation of the dollar in the Brazilian imagination. For many decades, the wealthy in Brazil, as in other parts of South America, tended to measure their success in dollars. Frequently, they actually converted local currency fortunes into dollars and deposited them in Citibank or some similar so-called safe American institution. No longer.

The stark comment that "a million dollars is nothing" hints that the U.S. policy of remorseless spending out of an empty pocket is wearing out its welcome, even among investors who are otherwise pro-American. Brazilian tycoons are no longer thinking in terms of dollars. They are now happy to think in terms of Brazilian real, and they book big profits in their imagination. As I write, the real's exchange value has risen against the dollar for nine weeks in a row.

That did not last.

But one day, perhaps sooner than we think, investors worldwide will begin to act as if the dollar were nothing. The first step toward dumping the dollar is its devaluation in the realm of the imagination. Brazilians, like others around the globe, no longer crave dollars. And when the foreign creditors of the U.S. begin to sell their trillions in U.S. dollar assets, they will be right. A million dollars will be "nothing," much as a million Zimbabwe dollars amount to nothing now. That day isn't here yet, thankfully. But it is coming.

I spoke at length at the barbecue with a wealthy physician who told me that he has taken a "second job." This seemed surprising until I understood what he meant. (The rapidly growing income in Brazil means that people seldomly take second jobs in order to make ends meet, a practice that was, until recently, common in the U.S. — in the days when there were jobs to be had).

In any event, the doctor told me that his "second job" is trading the Bovespa (Bolsa de Valores, Mercadorias & Futuros de São Paulo). The Bovespa has become the world's second-largest stock exchange by capitalization, behind only the Hong Kong Stock Exchange.

Furthermore, the Bovespa now has bragging rights for having staged history's largest public stock offering. The September 24, 2010 Petrobras (Brazil's state-run oil and gas company) secondary stock offering raised $70 billion, almost twice the previous record held by Japanese telecom giant NTT and more than the $60 billion total of all IPOs in all the advanced countries put together. Clearly, there is a lot of action in Brazil's capital markets. And we've been rolling up big profits on Brazilian stocks and bonds.

It is a cliché in the U.S. to say that doctors are seldom successful as investors. Perhaps this unflattering generalization does not apply to Brazilian
doctors. Or if it does, the doctor to whom I spoke is an exception. He entered
into a detailed discussion of his holdings, primarily of Brazilian retailers, upon
which he claimed to be earning returns in excess of 30% a year. He argued
persuasively that the growing Brazilian middle class will expand margins and
grow earnings for such retail companies for many years to come. He is particularly bullish on wine sales in Brazil, said to be growing at a 40% annual rate.

Rapid, real income growth is a big boost to the success of stock investors
as well as wine merchants. Santander Asset Management predicted that the
Bovespa Index would rally above 100,000 in 2011. "Brazil now has a ratio
of two people of working age to every one of non-working age," said Aquiles
Mosca, an executive director at Santander. "Infant mortality is falling. When
this happens, consumption takes off."

From 2000 to 2010, the Bovespa Index went up 400%, while the S&P 500
fell 22% over the same period.

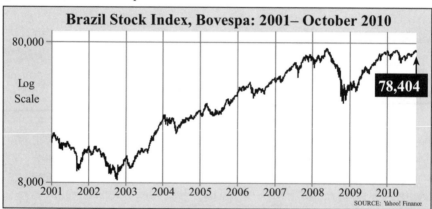

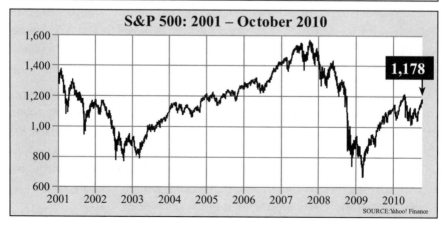

It's not necessary to confine investments to U.S. domiciled stocks. The U.S. government has not become so financially repressive as to prohibit foreign investment — at least not yet.

Brazil's Productive Baby Boomers

On this point, I digress to mention an octogenarian I met, the father of our host, who is a living advertisement for the advantages of not retiring. He owns and manages a large dairy operation that he bought 22 years ago as a hedge against hyperinflation. A broad-shouldered, muscular man in his eighties, if he has aches and pains, they don't affect his movements. His step is as light and limber as that of a man of 30.

He embodies the fact that mandatory retirement is not a Brazilian tradition. It also doesn't hurt that his parents lived to an average age of 101.

Most Brazilians over the age of 65 are still economically active. This makes quite a positive contrast to the formerly "advanced" economies, which have high dependency rates and aging populations. According to the CIA Factbook, the median age in Brazil is 28.9, making its workforce the youngest of any important economy other than India. This also helps explain why Brazilian women tend to be so attractive. Half the women you see in Brazil have not seen their 29th birthday yet.

Consequences of an Old Workforce

By comparison, the median age in other leading economies is a decade or more higher. Most prosperous economies tend to have a "constricted population pyramid," with fewer young people coming along to support a larger number of dependent elderly. Even China's median age, at 35.2 years, is closer to the U.S.'s at 36.8 than to India's and Brazil's. Other notable median ages – Japan: 44.8, Russia: 38.5, U.K.: 39.8, and Switzerland: 41.3. Not coincidentally, the European PIGS countries all have very "constricted population pyramids" with high median ages. Portugal: 39.7, Italy: 43.7, Greece: 42.2, and Spain: 40.1.

Among other influences, these high median ages reflect the liberalization of abortion in Europe a generation ago. This highlights an interesting political subtext in Brazil where abortion is restricted.

Brazil: 2010 Elections

Most Americans are aware that a majority of the elections in the U.S. are held on November 2, 2010. There is probably much less awareness in the U.S. of the elections in Brazil, the first round of which was held on October 3, 2010.

A leading story in that first round of voting is the fact that Dilma Rousseff, the handpicked candidate of incumbent President Luiz Ignacio Lula da Silva's Worker Party, failed to win an outright majority of the votes, necessitating a runoff that she ultimately won on October 31, 2010.

Normally, voters in a booming economy re-elect the incumbent party without question. That didn't happen in Brazil, partly because of what seems a peculiar constellation of alliances between Brazil's growing segment of evangelical Protestants and the environmental movement. Presidential candidate Marina Silva of the Green Party, a Federal Senator and former Environment Minister in Lula's cabinet, is also an anti-abortion, evangelical Protestant.

In the last few days before the October 3rd vote, six million anti-abortion voters switched from Rousseff to Marina Silva, after a campaign by anti-abortion advocates targeted Rousseff for indicating support for liberalizing Brazil's abortion laws. Strangely for a politician in any jurisdiction, "Marina," as she is widely known, said during the campaign that she did not like children.

I am probably not revealing state secrets to tell you that most of the wealthy Brazilians I know are of a conservative bent politically. Indeed, one young lawyer who was quite congenial company and one of the more knowledgeable "foodies" is close to the family of former Minas Gerais Gov. Aecio Neves, whose grandfather was President of Brazil. He was elected Senador of the Republic in 2010.

Although like other Brazilians of privileged backgrounds in Minas, Senador Neves resents the domination of the more moderate of the two major parties, the Brazilian Social Democracy Party (PSDB), by "Paulistas," (factions from São Paulo, Brazil). Neves stuck with it as its 2014 presidential candidate because it represented the best chance for defeating the ruling Workers Party.

Many wealthy and upper middle class Brazilians would like nothing better than to displace Dilma Rousseff with one of their own. In general, they were not big fans of Lula da Silva, whose term as President expired January 1, 2011. They are even less enamored with Dilma, under whose watch the Brazilian economy slowed dramatically as her erratic interventions in the crucial energy market undermined stock prices and reduced the foreign exchange value of the real.

The upper stratum of the electorate mostly supported former São Paulo governor José Serra, the PSDB candidate in 2010. To their delight, Serra surged in the polls going into the 2010 runoff on Halloween. This gave investors looking to divest ahead of a Rousseff victory a favorable chance to do so. Neves proved to be a stronger candidate than Serra, but he failed to win the closest run-off in Brazilian history.

Why the Brazilian Elite Hate Lula and Dilma

I am always a sucker for political gossip, so I listened carefully when one of the younger generation explained their attitude toward Luiz Ignacio Lula da Silva. Although almost everyone was pleased with Brazil's outstanding economic performance during Lula's two terms as president, there is a tendency among the more established factions of Brazilian society to resist the rapid social change associated with and encouraged by Lula. For one thing, he is looked down upon because he speaks the rough Portuguese of a school dropout.

Lula is a man who worked his way up from the bottom. He started his career when he was a child, shining shoes. The Brazilian plutocrats are not as comfortable with that as are the majority of Brazilians.

I got a hint of this informing attitude when our gracious host at the country barbecue chided one of his relatives for having lived in America so long that she no longer thought "like a Brazilian." He said that because she poured him a cup of coffee after a meal. To me, hers was a considerate gesture. But he thought it was "beneath her" to pour coffee, as "that is a servant's job."

The wealthier segment of Brazilians employ servants as a matter of course. If you don't have a cook, a maid, and a driver, you are not successful. This is reminiscent of the situation at the turn of the 20th century in the United States, when some 10% of the U.S. population found employment as domestic servants. Obviously, when lower income Brazilians find their incomes soaring, this creates tensions in domestic employment and points to something of a social revolution. For this and other reasons, the plutocrats who control the commanding heights of Brazilian society have tended to paint as negative a picture as they can of Lula's government.

A generation ago, Brazil was an economic backwater — a gigantic backwater, but a backwater nonetheless — controlled by a few hundred elite families. Brazil is now a world economic power. But, that isn't necessarily a matter of much celebration as you might expect by the old guard who fear they are losing control.

Far from embracing the great economic success that Brazil has enjoyed during Lula's eight years in office, the Brazilian news media have kept up a drumbeat of relentless criticism, portraying Lula's Worker's Party, his colleagues, and relatives as corrupt, and the future of the country dim so long as they remain in charge.

Hence, we have a situation in Brazil that is practically the opposite of that in the U.S. The Brazilian media, controlled by wealthy Brazilians, play down and understate the government's economic accomplishments, while the U.S. media uncritically pound the drums and applaud Obama's supposed achievements, many of which are statistical confections, based on wishful thinking or outright fraudulent reporting.

Note this striking fact: As a result of rapid economic growth, more than 21 million Brazilians rose out of poverty during Lula's presidency. Meanwhile, 5.4 million Americans sank into poverty during Obama's first year in office.

When economies are vibrant, jobs are plentiful and poverty shrinks. Unfortunately, the recent history of job growth in the U.S. does not compare favorably to Brazil's. On the surface, the U.S. lost 115,000 jobs while Brazil gained 15,023,633.

Remember, the U.S. population is 100 million larger than Brazil's, so the U.S. should have created 22,535,449 (one-third more) jobs just to stay even. But the underlying situation is even worse than that.

Statistical Fraud

The Bureau of Labor Statistics has engaged in straightforward statistical fraud under Obama (and many Presidents preceding him), making the U.S. government the world's biggest fabricator of economic fibs since the fall of the Soviet Union.

The recent administrations have played as fast and loose with economic statistics as they did with money. They lie remorselessly, with some of the biggest lies reserved for unemployment figures.

John Williams of Shadow Government Statistics has provided a long-running commentary detailing the various tricks and frauds employed by the government to reduce the headline unemployment rate. To recount all these here would be tedious and turn this into an essay on the further reaches of accounting, as they entail some truly Byzantine statistical manipulation. Yet, to some extent, the Bureau of Labor Statistics actually "comes clean" about these over-statements by releasing various "revisions" that adjust employment down after the numbers are too stale to attract attention.

Here are John Williams's comments on the revisions released October 8, 2010 with the September Jobs report:

> An early estimate for the 2010 benchmark revision… indicated the not-seasonally-adjusted March 2010 payrolls were overstated by 366,000. As the data are re-worked for that estimate, changes will be carried back to the prior revision as of March 2009, as well as carried forward to present reporting. Such suggests that the overstatement of the level of payrolls as of September 2010 reporting is about 550,000 jobs. The formal benchmark revision and restated economic history will be published with the January 2011 employment report, due for release on February 4, 2011.

Statistics, when honestly computed, are subject to random error. But when the mistakes also fall in the same direction, they reveal a systematic distortion.

The unemployment data are not the only economic statistics being distorted by our politicians. A close read of almost any sensitive economic series shows that the numbers are twisted to present a rosier picture than fits the facts.

GDP = GDI (but Not in America!)

This is evident in the highly gamed GDP (Gross Domestic Product) reports. A strong hint that GDP numbers are being tweaked for political reasons is the divergence between GDP and its statistical twin, GDI (Gross Domestic Income) from 2008 to 2010.

In theory, there should be no divergence between GDP and GDI. GDI is merely the other side of the double-entry bookkeeping ledger from GDP. Just as a business that sells products should receive revenue to reflect those sales, so too should GDI closely match GDP. GDI represents the receipts side of the equation when purchasers acquire goods and services.

But guess what? When you compare the two series, GDI is lagging far behind GDP. The reason GDI falls behind is simple. It is an obscure statistical series that no one follows. There is little incentive for the government to go to the trouble of lying about such numbers. Unless you have a perverse hobby of studying national income statistics (or you read Strategic Investment), you would be unlikely to know that the GDI numbers imply that economic growth in the U.S. has been overstated by about two percentage points in the current recovery.

John Williams comments:

> On a quarterly basis, the revised GDI contracted in seven out of the last nine quarters, including two quarters in 2007; the GDP contracted in four out of the last five (and nine) quarters, not including the just-released second-quarter GDP. Note that Q2 GDI has not yet been released.

Barack Obama has taken his economic playbook right out of the pages of Pravda. Under his watch, the U.S. government has replaced the late Soviet Union as the champion fabricator of economic lies in the world. The question is whether this will do him or you any good.

I suspect that disappointment will be the theme of the future. My late father used to quote P.T. Barnum to the effect that "there's a sucker born every minute."

Some will no doubt rally to Obama's support, believing or hoping that the U.S. economy, if not exactly recovering, is at least poised to recover on Obama's program of bailouts, exploding deficits, and printing money (quantitative easing, for the cognoscenti). I doubt it.

In my view, there are a lot of drawbacks to a policy of lies and the remorseless government manipulation of everything. Many of them are already in view. You will be paying for them for the rest of your life. Unless, that is, you find a way out.

If there is a way out, it entails either getting out of the United States (especially if you are young or are on the verge of retirement) and moving someplace where economic prospects are better — or, at the very least, getting your money into the kind of fortune-making companies that are growing in value in Brazil and other parts of the world with vibrant economies.

It is interesting to me that both Barack Obama and Lula da Silva came to office as men of the left. Obama seems to have grown little and clings to the anti-business and anti-market prejudices that he expressed as a candidate. Lula, by contrast, grew in office, and became a strong advocate of Brazilian capitalism. Consider these comments from Lula celebrating the Petrobras share offering:

Never in the history of humanity have we had a capitalization process as big as the one Petrobras is doing here.

It wasn't in Frankfurt, it wasn't in London, it wasn't in New York — it was in São Paulo, in our Bovespa (stock market) that we launched the biggest ever capitalization process in the history of global capitalism. Thank you.

Congratulations to Petrobras, congratulations to Bovespa, and congratulations to the Brazilian people because we have worked to deserve this, to get to this point.

The Brazilian media, along with many of Brazil's plutocrats, may not like Lula da Silva. Again, his Portuguese is far from impeccable. However, he did leave after eight years in office with an 80% approval rating and a legacy of growing prosperity, including 15 million new jobs. His hand-picked successor, Dilma Rousseff, speaks better Portuguese, but seems not to have inherited much of Lula's touch when it comes to economic stewardship.

Obama still has a 40% approval rating, which seems like a miracle to me. But then, the "other shoe" is yet to drop. His legacy will be the sovereign solvency crisis that will bring American living standards tumbling down to a Third World level. Get ready for it.

CHAPTER 5

A Slow, Painful Tutorial in the Predatory Practice of Debtism

*"It ain't what you don't know that gets you into trouble.
It's what you know for sure that just ain't so."*

— Mark Twain

Istanbul, Turkey: I went to this ancient, cosmopolitan city to track the progress of one of the more successful of the many companies I have helped launch. Istanbul, or Constantinople, as it was once known, was more or less the largest city in the world from about 340 AD, when it surpassed the population of Rome, until about 1700, when its 700,000 inhabitants were more numerous than those of London or any city in China. Fast-forwarding to today, the Turks suggest it could once again rank as the world's largest city. If the intensity of its traffic jams are a clue, they may be right.

I went there not to gauge traffic, but to review the progress of Anatolia Minerals, a once tiny figment of my imagination that now has a market cap of more than one billion dollars and will soon be an even bigger enterprise, having announced a big deal (here I quote the headline from Bloomberg on September 8, 2010), "Anatolia to Buy Avoca Resources for C$1 billion."

Quite apart from that, the company has developed a gold property near Ilic, in east, central Turkey that produces between 175,000 and 200,000 ounces of gold annually. With gold trading above $1,200 per ounce, ANO can easily make $100,000,000 a year from its current project.

If you'll permit a personal digression, along with a mixed metaphor, I find it gratifying when one of my "brainstorms" actually becomes a "round-tripper," as a sports-minded investment banker once described a deal that does what you initially hoped it might. Anatolia is one of the good ones. It is just the third company I have had a hand in that reached a market cap of one billion dollars. The other two were "dot-com" companies.

Having thought about it all in retrospect, I now appreciate a seldom-understood dimension in the challenge of optimizing your individual portfolio over your lifetime. You not only need to be shrewd about allocating capital and entrepreneurial effort to the right sectors, you also need uncommon sagacity and/or good luck in adjusting your investments to the waxing and waning of the credit cycle. Here, it is crucial for the stellar success of Anatolia Minerals that its market cap is being lifted by the backwash of the secret takeover of Capitalism by "Debtism."

How Debtism Changed the World

Not to be vain about it, but I probably had a better grasp of the "Big Picture" 20 years ago than all but a few persons on the globe. Working with the late Lord Rees-Mogg, four years before 9/11, we explored this tragic insight on the first page of the preface to the British edition of *The Sovereign Individual*: "...modern society is vulnerable. As vulnerable as the plate glass towers of the World Trade Centre." We correctly anticipated the fall of the Berlin Wall, the collapse of the Soviet Union and failure of the state socialist experiment. It was precisely these insights that led to the founding of Anatolia Minerals, and its stable mates among junior resource companies.

Unlike most other analysts, we did not swallow the conventional wisdom that depressions were a thing of the past that had been superseded by clever manipulation of paper money. We did see that another depression was likely in our lifetime. Further to that, I knew from my eccentric research into past financial crises that they are inevitably bullish for gold.

What I failed to grasp, however, was that the onset of depression would not just entail a cyclical recurrence, but could represent a disastrous transformation of the whole nature of the economy. This was part and parcel of the little-noted transformation of the Capitalist economy of the U.S. and other developed nations into debtist systems.

Why do I call the current economic system debtism rather than capitalism? For the simple and compelling reason that debt, rather than capital, lies at its heart. If you peel back the layers of the onion that shroud the dynamics of the current U.S. economy, you see that capital is no longer central. It is all about debt and the almost desperate angling by the authorities to keep the debt aggregates expanding. All their policies aim toward stimulating private debt expansion. And failing that, their fallback position is to perpetuate bad private debt by transplanting it onto the sovereign balance sheet. If you can't pay your mortgage, it will end up as part of the national debt to be borne in perpetuity (or at least until the government collapses in an orgy of hyper-inflation) by generations of desperate debt slaves.

When Karl Marx criticized capitalist (Kapitalist) mode of production in *The Communist Manifesto* (1848), he focused his attack on capital. According to Marx, the evil of capitalism was that it enabled the owners of capital to extract "surplus value" from workers. While all previous societies had extracted surplus value, capitalism was new in doing so via the sale of produced commodities.

Debtism has trumped capitalism as a mechanism for concentrating wealth. (I say this as someone who has never been an invidious egalitarian.) Inequality of income doesn't particularly bother me, per se. But I think it notable that the movement away from gold-backed (which is to say, "asset-backed" money) to pure paper or fiat money, which is based entirely upon debt, has led directly to an increased concentration of wealth.

You need only look at the dispersion of income in the United States before and after Richard Nixon repudiated the Gold Reserve Standard in 1971. As Kenneth Gerbino pointed out in a June 2010 commentary on his investment management site, the shift from a quasi-asset based money to a pure fiat money, or unalloyed "Debtism," resulted in a drastic loss of income by those who work and save. Gerbino wrote: "The bottom 90% of our citizens went from owning a big piece of the income gains (65%) in the 1960s to being squashed in the 2002 – 2007 period to 11%."

Part of the mechanism by which Debtism impoverishes the masses is due to a transformation of the economy. To outward appearances, the U.S. continued to seem like a free market, capitalist economy. But it changed in subtle ways that advantaged the few at the expense of the many.

The first perversion that arises from fiat money is the substitution of debt for capital as the mother's milk of economic growth. In a fiat system, such as that prevailing in the United States over the past four decades, production is not based upon savings and invested capital. It is spun out of money aggregates that expand as debt grows. Indeed, fiat money itself only comes into existence as debt. Extinguish the debt, and you kill the money supply.

Another hidden expropriation of average people arises from the fact that fiat money devalues earnings. With an asset-backed money, like the gold standard, the price level tends to fall as more goods and services are produced while the money aggregates rise slowly, or not at all. With gold-based money, there is no way to produce a sustained credit expansion. The money supply only expands as a consequence of gold discoveries and increased mine output, or an improvement in the balance of trade that leads to the import of bullion. In short, with a real gold standard, money supply expands very slowly.

Progress Under the Gold Standard, Sort of. . .

Of course, to speak of a gold standard before the Civil War means trading in stylized facts, as the U.S. political system has rarely been hardy enough to sustain the rigors of sound money.

The U.S. banking system then involved the proliferation of note-issuing banks, usually chartered by states, with few or no branch offices. These banks tended to issue far more paper receipts/certificates for gold than their actual gold holdings would permit. Notoriously, note-issuing banks tended to locate their offices in remote corners of states, where it would be costly and inconvenient for customers to travel in order to redeem their notes for gold.

The reality was that the early 19th century gold standard was diluted by the inflationary issue of bank notes that were purportedly redeemable for gold, but actually circulated in generous excess to the underlying bullion. Furthermore, what passed for a gold standard was usually suspended during wars. This led to periods of more pronounced inflation, followed by contractions as credit tightened after the gold standard was re-established.

This happened in the U.S. after the Civil War. During that conflict, on February 25, 1862, Congress passed the Legal Tender Act, which forced Americans to accept paper money at par with gold and silver, thus allowing the government to pay its bills with printed money. After the war, the "greenbacks" were withdrawn from circulation. A long, deflationary phase began in 1873, and lasted until 1896. According to analyst Nikhil Raheja, "During these years, production increased due to excessive savings/investments and high productivity, while the money supply grew at a slower pace, causing a mismatch between the total money available for consumption and the value of products on sale, and resulted in a fall in prices."

I don't see the 19th century fall in prices as a "mismatch" but rather as an example of the free market dynamic at work, in which money tended to grow in value as productivity rose. This made the poor richer, as income they earned grew more valuable. According to economist Murray N. Rothbard, in "A History of Money and Banking in the United States: The Colonial Era to World War II," general prices in the U.S. fell 1% on average each year during that period. Prices fell about 20% over 23 years. Note that, with prices falling as a result of economic progress, a person with stagnant wages grew about 20% richer.

Inflation of Asset Prices Makes the Rich Richer

This was very different to what happens today under the Debtist system of pure credit money, where there is concerted inflation of the money supply as debt proliferates. From 1970 through 2008, the money supply (M-2) in the U.S. skyrocketed by 1,314%, from $624 billion to $8.2 trillion. Meanwhile, real economic goods, the actual things that comprise the good life that people want to buy with money, expanded barely at all. Naturally, prices increased when the dollar was cheapened as the debt orgy proceeded, with each new dollar of debt tending to result in an equivalent increase in the money supply.

If you have been tracking economic statistics with even one eye in recent years, however, you know that consumer prices have not increased by 1,314% in the past four decades. As measured by the government's slanted CPI calculations, you needed $5,549.05 in 2008 to attain the purchasing power of $1,000 in 1970. Obviously, a worker with stagnant wages lost quite a bit of purchasing power. But an even more powerful explanation for the growing inequality of wealth created by the Debtist system becomes clear when you consider which prices were inflated disproportionately by all the trillions in new money borrowed into existence since 1970.

Put simply, the newly created money was put to use funding investment booms in both financial and hard assets. Wall Street analyst Kel Kelly is unusual in looking at this from the perspective of Austrian economic theory. He writes:

> The only real force that ultimately makes the stock market or any market rise (and, to a large extent, fall) over the longer term is simply changes in the quantity of money and the volume of spending in the economy. Stocks rise when there is inflation of the money supply (i.e., more money in the economy and in the markets). This truth has many consequences that should be considered.

Kelly quotes Austrian economist, Fritz Machlup:

It is impossible for the profits of all or of the majority of enterprises to rise without an increase in the effective monetary circulation (through the creation of new credit or dishoarding)... If it were not for the elasticity of bank credit... a boom in security values could not last for any length of time. In the absence of inflationary credit the funds available for lending to the public for security purchases would soon be exhausted, since even a large supply is ultimately limited. The supply of funds derived solely from current new savings and current amortization allowances is fairly inelastic... Only if the credit organization of the banks (by means of inflationary credit) or large-scale dishoarding by the public make the supply of loanable funds highly elastic, can a lasting boom develop... A rise on the securities market cannot last any length of time unless the public is both willing and able to make increased purchases.

Of course, the issue is even more basic than that. Asset booms do not arise solely because banks are prepared to lend funds "to the public for securities purchases." Partly, they are a function of the fact fiat money makes it easier for many businesses to grow in nominal terms and earn a profit. This is a policy that suits the fiscal imperatives of the state. Inflation increases nominal profits and therefore increases tax receipts.

There is probably also a political imperative to ramp up GDP, which happens automatically with inflation. Kelly puts it this way:

A rise in GDP is mathematically possible only if the money price of individual goods produced is increasing to some degree. Otherwise, with a constant supply of money and spending, the total amount of money companies earn — the total selling prices of all goods produced — and thus GDP itself would all necessarily remain constant year after year."

Kelly continues:

If there were a constant amount of money in the economy, the sum total of all shares of all stocks taken together (or a stock index) could not increase. Plus, if company profits, in the aggregate, were not increasing, there would be no aggregate increase in earnings per share to be imputed into stock prices.

In an economy where the quantity of money was static, the levels of stock indexes, year by year, would stay approximately even, or drift slightly lower — depending on the rate of increase in the number of new shares issued. And, overall, businesses (in the aggregate) would be selling a greater volume of goods at lower prices, and total revenues would remain the same. In the same way, businesses, overall, would purchase more goods at lower prices each year, keeping the spread between costs and revenues about the same, which would keep aggregate profits about the same.

Under these circumstances, capital gains (the profiting from the buying low and selling high of assets) could be made only by stock picking — by investing in companies that are expanding market share, bringing to market new products, etc., thus truly gaining proportionately more revenues and profits at the expense of those companies that are less innovative and efficient.

The stock prices of the gaining companies would rise while others fell. Since the average stock would not actually increase in value, most of the gains made by investors from stocks would be in the form of dividend payments. By contrast, in our world today, most stocks — good and bad ones — rise during inflationary bull markets and decline during bear markets. The good companies simply rise faster than the bad.

If you consider the evolution of stock picking as an art during the 20th century, it follows the indicated path of change informed by the changing character of money. Early in the 20th century, when bank credit was far less elastic than at present, analysts tended to recommend stocks based on their dividend yields. As implied by Kelly's argument, there were not many capital gains to be had. The Dow Jones Industrial Average closed at 68.13 on January 2, 1900. It didn't rally decisively above 100 until 1920 — after the inflation engendered by World War I took hold.

Unlike the recent period, when stocks have tended to go public even before they became profitable, and many high-tech companies prided themselves in paying no dividends, in the days before Debtism replaced Capitalism as the organizing principle of the U.S. economy, it was hard to achieve a public listing. Companies could not file a prospectus around a business plan scribbled on the back of a napkin and raise hundreds of millions on the expectation of capital gains as they did during the dot-com boom.

Kelly argues that GDP growth as measured in money and stock market values as reflected by broad indices like the S&P 500 and the Dow Jones Index, rise only as a result of the increase in money caused by the expansion of bank credit. Note that the DJIA went from 809 on January 2, 1970 to 12,800.18 on January 4th, 2008, a gain of 1,582%, even greater than the increase in the (M-2) money supply in that period.

Clearly, a big percentage of the newly created money that was borrowed into existence during recent decades of growing wealth inequality went into increasing stock market values and bidding up other assets, including real estate. Who benefited most from these asset bubbles caused by the hydraulic force of credit expansion working its way through the economy?

Obviously, persons who were already well-off, and had collateral to offer when borrowing money, gained the lion's share of the advantage of access to new credit.

Business owners, managers, Wall Street bankers and stockholders obviously gained more from the asset bubbles inflated by credit expansion than persons with stagnant incomes and no collateral.

Of course, I admit that it is difficult to abstract the impact of pure credit money in distorting the economy. According to Austrian economists, one of the crucial consequences of artificial credit expansion is a dramatic reduction in the efficiency of investment. There is a big surge of mal-investment, which both reduces the productivity of investment and leaves the economy vulnerable to collapse when the credit orgy inevitably comes to an end.

Equally, at first blush, it might not seem credible that rising GDP and escalating stock market indices are entirely epiphenomena of the expansion of bank credit. What of progress and improved productivity? Would they not account for growing wealth in society and stock appreciation?

The answer is "yes" and "no." Without a doubt, real GDP rises when productivity increases and the economy produces more "stuff" that counts in material tallies of the good life. But Kelly's argument is that without artificial credit expansion, society would become richer without an increase in the supply of money. Nominal GDP stays more or less flat, so that progress is reflected in falling living costs, as happened in the 19th century. Therefore, although there would be no explosion in the aggregate amount of profits earned, the real value of each dollar earned in corporate profits would rise.

Then what? A country with sound money in a bankrupt world would stick out like a supermodel in Huntington, West Virginia, widely hailed as America's "fattest city." The value of the sound (or even "semi-sound") currency would skyrocket. The conventional expectation would be that foreign sales for products priced in that currency would shrivel as currency movements raised the real costs of labor and all the factors that contribute to production.

Here you catch a glimpse of another reason that fiat money devalues labor. In a bankrupt world, where every economy is more or less addicted to debt, the central banks are on a "race to the bottom," all trying to make their currencies worth less. By contrast, the mechanism of progress with gold-backed money would be a steady increase in the value of the currency. Nothing of the kind could be tolerated in a Debtist economy.

Witness the continued fulminations of the honorable members of Congress trying to brow-beat the Chinese into making the renminbi yuan worth more in foreign exchange markets. As I originally wrote this, the House Ways and Means Committee met to debate a bill known as the "Currency Reform for Fair Trade Act," that would have authorized the U.S. to slap duties on Chinese goods. Some 150 Congress members sponsoring the legislation were perturbed that the Chinese were buying tens of billions of U.S. dollars every month, thus keeping the value of the dollar from plunging as far as they would like.

"This unfair trade practice translates into a significant subsidy, artificially making U.S. products more expensive, and jeopardizing efforts to create and preserve manufacturing jobs in America," then-House Speaker Nancy Pelosi, D-Calif., said in a statement.

There you see the animating principle of the Debtist economy, namely that Debt should be proliferated as far as possible, and fiat currency depreciated rapidly so as to lower labor and other factor costs, as well as lower the burdens of debt service. Little wonder the poor get poorer with fiat money.

In a better world, sound currencies based on gold would appreciate, rather than depreciate. Nominal GDP and stock market indices would grow slowly or not at all, while real wages and real wealth rose. And no one would mistake Nancy Pelosi for an economist. But note: The fact that she is helping to inform economic policy in the world in which we live underscores an important, informing reason why Debtism replaced Capitalism as the organizing principle of the American economy. Debtism is better suited to the imperatives of politics.

Debtism Helps Politicians Manipulate You

Politicians want to manipulate economies. When they have the "money illusion" at their disposal, they can sell their favors to high bids from many factions angling for advantage in a politicized world. Further to that, the surge in nominal GDP and asset booms that go hand-in-hand with remorseless credit expansion entail great advantages to politicians because they concentrate income and wealth in the hands of a relative few.

Why does this help politicians?

For one thing, notwithstanding numerous pronouncements to the contrary, the impoverishment of the median voter puts him in a position of dependence on politicians. If you achieve financial escape velocity and become independent, it is most unlikely that a politician in Washington, much less in your state capital, will do anything to enhance your solvency or earn your undying gratitude. But it is a very different story if you cannot even put food on your table. Under those conditions, a politician who can extend your access to subsidized food through the food stamp or SNAP program might well hope for a large measure of your gratitude.

Of course, not one voter in a thousand recognizes that the collapse of real income growth is a direct consequence of Debtist monetary policy. It is far more popular to blame "Wall Street" greed and a lack of "regulation." In other words, the prevalent explanations for economic dysfunction circulated by the establishment promise to give politicians more control.

In light of the analysis we have been exploring, the idea that better regulation could have prevented the Great Correction is superficial and stupid. Yes, certain types of regulation that you could imagine might have worked to keep the system from capsizing into collapse. But such regulations would have countermanded what the politicians wanted to see done. For example, can you honestly conclude that the politicians were prepared to authorize regulations that would have stopped the "Sub-Prime" crisis in its tracks? The politicians wanted to expand home ownership. In fact, they instituted specific regulations, like the "Community Re-investment Act" to punish banks that refused to lend large sums to sub-prime borrowers in bad neighborhoods.

Equally, the exaggerated capital gains that arise from a rapid growth of nominal GDP create a lot of wealth that politicians can tap into and leverage for their own purposes. Bill Clinton understood better than Obama that it was in his interest to create conditions under which investors would thrive. My two previous flirtations with billion-dollar companies occurred under Clinton's watch.

They both collapsed for reasons beyond my control, but they provided a tantalizing hint of how really big money can be made "at home in your spare time" in an economy with inflating asset booms. The key is to find or create a company that is right for the current state of the credit cycle.

Another feature of credit-based money that has enabled politicians to more efficiently buy votes is its effect in making it possible to concentrate the costs of government on a small fraction of the population, while spreading benefits to larger voting groups. The inflation of credit leads to higher nominal profits and outsized capital gains for those who are positioned to pocket them. Having helped to fill the pockets of the lucky few, the politicians then help themselves and pick the pockets of the greatest beneficiaries of Debtism. This is clearly illustrated by trends in Pelosi's California. In the 1970-71 fiscal year, before Nixon repudiated the Gold Reserve Standard, the top 10% of California income earners paid a hefty 28.2% of California's Personal Income Tax. By 2006, given the increased concentration of income in the Debtist economy, the top 10% were paying an astonishing 78.5% of California's Personal Income Tax. This enabled politicians to buy votes with money re-distributed from a tiny fraction of the population. The beneficiaries of a whole spectrum of programs, from subsidized education to mental health initiatives, were happy because they were seemingly getting something for nothing.

While this made life for politicians easier so long as the party lasted, it is also high among the reasons that California was broke in 2009. The politicians laid such a high percentage of the tax burden on a small fraction of the population that when the Great Correction began and easy capital gains disappeared, California's finances were devastated. Indeed, California was so dependent on a relative handful of rich persons to pay its bills that if even a few of them moved to Nevada, it threatened to undermine the state's bond rating.

What happened in California is a microcosm of what has happened to the Federal government. California's budget situation was more desperate because the state's personal income taxes were more progressive going into the Great Correction. Also, let's not forget, California's task in borrowing money is more complicated than the Federal government's. California must borrow money that already exists. The Feds can lend themselves cash by creating it out of the clear blue sky.

The U.S. Budget Deficits Would Make Chad Blush

One of the more remarkable failures of the mass media in America has been their silence in reporting the pathetic picture of U.S. federal finances. Notwithstanding the great economic accomplishments by private Americans in building wealth over the centuries, the U.S. government currently finds itself with fiscal ratios so terrible that they have seldom been seen in even the most backward Banana Republics. The U.S. has borrowed (or printed) 55 cents of every dollar it has spent since Lehman Bros. went broke in September, 2008.

Think I am exaggerating? Here were the facts when I originally wrote this essay some years ago. Total net Federal debt issued since September 2008 was $3.351 trillion. Gross individual tax receipts since September 2008 came to $3.185 trillion. Less refunds of $660 billion, the net individual tax take came to just more than $2.5 trillion. Add the corporate receipts of $250 billion, net of refunds, and total net tax revenue came to $2.775 trillion. In other words, the fiscal policy of the U.S. government as of that time was to borrow $0.55 for each $0.45 of tax receipts in the till. It has only gotten worse since then.

This is the kind of deficit spending that has always been associated with hyper-inflation and economic collapse in developing countries, and even in so-called "advanced" countries in the wake of wars.

I have been saying all along that the world's largest economy is fundamentally weak, much weaker than the economic and political establishment pretends. Indeed, I suspect that the U.S. is so weakened it is in peril of collapse.

This may seem incredible in light of the announcement by the National Bureau of Economic Research (NBER) that the longest downturn since the Great Depression ended in June 2009. Yet you should look carefully. I am not alone in thinking that the determination that the recession ended may be politically motivated. Consider this comment by John Williams of Shadow Government Statistics:

> Based on the average of July and August 2010 reporting, versus the average monthly level reported for second-quarter 2010, the annualized rates of quarterly-to-quarter contraction in place at the moment for these series are: housing starts down by 19.9%; new home sales down by 46.0%; existing home sales down by 73.8%; new orders for durable goods down by 1.2%. The rates here are annualized, the same way the GDP is, at an effective compounded annual rate of change. Keep in mind that the home sales contractions were exacerbated by the expiration of tax credit incentives, and the durable goods contraction is before adjustment for inflation. These numbers are on top of the prior week's data, which suggested a quarterly contraction in inflation-adjusted retail sales and slowing quarterly growth in industrial production.

The NBER usually attempts to wait long enough on its timing calls of peaks and troughs in business activity so that they do not get revised. The NBER also does not necessarily wait until a "recovery" regains the prior peak in activity to make its call. That considered, the heavily relied-on nonfarm payroll series likely faces major, near-term downside revisions, with the next benchmark revision's order-of-magnitude to be announced with the October 8th release of September's payroll and unemployment data.

Further, a key factor in determining the end-of-recession timing call was recent GDP reporting. That seems nonsensical, given the extreme short-term unreliability of and regular massive revisions in that series. Such factors lend weight to speculation of political considerations in the timing of this call.

Equally, analyst Dave Rosenberg has some trenchant observations that underscore the fact that the politicians and the media are trying to hoax you into believing that the economy is better than it is. According to Rosenberg:

> By now, based on when the recession ended, we should be at a new high in real GDP (in fact, back to 1947, real GDP is up 4.5% in the first year of recovery). That has happened in every other cycle in the post-WWII — including the 1992 and 2002 periods where recoveries were tepid but not that tepid to prevent real output from attaining new all-time peaks. But as things now stand, real GDP is still 1.3% lower now than it was at the end of 2007 (in fact, getting back to that old peak will likely take another year at the very least). This is what makes this cycle so unusual — steep declines in GDP are typically followed by vigorous recoveries but this time we had the largest decline in GDP since the 1930s and despite unprecedented amounts of monetary, fiscal and bailout stimulus, the recovery has been extremely weak — real GDP growth of 3% is far less than half of what one would ordinarily expect to see coming out of such a deep downturn.
>
> • From the lows in real GDP in June/09, 69% of the recession losses have so far been recouped.
>
> • From the lows in employment in Dec/09, 9% of the recession losses have been recouped.
>
> • From the lows in household net worth in 2009Q1, 28% of the recession losses have been recouped.

- From the lows in wages & salaries in March 2009, 36% of the recession losses have been recouped.

- From the lows in housing starts in April 2009, 7% of the recession losses have been recouped.

- From the lows in home prices in April 2009, 13% of the recession losses have been recouped.

- From the lows in consumer sentiment in November 2008, 27% of the recession losses have been recouped.

- New and existing home sales are at all-time lows — they have never recovered. Hence the label "Great Disappointment" as it pertains to this so-called recovery.

Let's not confuse this cycle with the classic post-WWII recession-recovery phase when downturns were 4 quarter corrections in GDP in the context of what was a secular credit expansion. What we are in today is a totally different animal. The plain-vanilla recession lasts 10 months; the one we apparently completed was 18 months in duration which is far more in line with the cycles that were endured before WWII when recessions lasted an average of 22 months.

I believe that we are ultimately destined to unwind the greatest credit boom in history.

In fact, we are probably facing a worse depression than that of the 1930s, one destined to intensify as governments at all levels exhaust the limits of solvency. It is a process that has begun, and is destined to proceed on its painful path for years to come.

Obama-Style "Prosperity is Just Around the Corner"

This ugly economic reality clashes with political imperatives to suggest that the economy, if not flourishing, will soon flourish. Witness the fact that as we headed into the campaign stage of the 2010 election cycle, President Barack Obama did his best Herbert Hoover imitation. As you probably don't remember, but may have read, Hoover wore out his welcome with the American people by proclaiming, "Prosperity is just around the corner."

Obama is less concise. He says he has taken "the beginning of the first steps to set our economy on a firmer foundation, paving the way to long-term growth and prosperity." You see how politics has improved in the past 80 years. Obama is both walking on the street and paving it at the same time.

Hoover may have been the first president to put a telephone on his desk, but Obama is a pioneer in employing the Internet to tout his economic policies. Instead of an anachronistic promise of "prosperity... just around the corner," Obama launched a website "Recovery.gov" to spotlight tales of recovery. It is far more advanced and interactive than the black and white newsreels of Herbert Hoover speeches.

But contrary to what the Democratic Party and Wall Street shills would have you believe, Herbert Hoover actually had a sounder statistical basis for his claims that prosperity was soon to return than Obama had for his claim to have taken "The beginning of the first steps to set our economy on a firmer foundation, paving the way to long-term growth and prosperity." Hoover not only spoke in more intelligible prose, he did a much better job of combating depression than Obama.

Of course, unless you are a connoisseur of economic footnotes you may not realize that economic recovery after 1929 was arguably more robust under Herbert Hoover than it was under Obama's rule following the 2008 credit collapse.

Contrary to what you may suppose, the depression of the 1930s was not marked by declining quarterly GDP data every single quarter. In fact, the officially recorded downturn in the initial period of depression associated with the stock market crash stretched from the third quarter of 1929 to the third quarter of 1933, almost wholly overlapping Hoover's term. In that initial four-year downturn, from 1929 to 1933, there were no fewer than six — six! — quarterly bounces in the GDP data. The average rate of economic growth in these up-quarters was 8% at an annual rate.

In case you're one of the "Green Shoots" bulls who imagines that politicians and their advisors have learned ever so much more than Hoover and his colleagues knew in 1929, pause and consider. With his trillions in stimulus spending, Obama initially only engineered four quarterly bounces in real GDP, recording an average rate of economic growth of only 3% at an annualized rate.

In other words, while Hoover's economic performance has taken on mythic status as the worst in American history, the bounces off the bottom during the Hoover presidency were more than twice as vigorous as those under Obama.

If you care to read through old *Wall Street Journal* editions or trader's journals from the Hoover era, you see that most people were slow to "get it." They did not see that trying to cushion, postpone or turn back a credit cycle contraction, as Hoover did and Obama tried more recently, only protracts the inevitable period of adjustment.

A depression, unlike a recession of the kind seen 11 times previously since World War II, is not an inventory correction, but a wealth obliterating credit contraction that reduces leverage in the economy and compresses demand. Credit corrections don't yield to sustainable recovery until excess credit is unwound, bad debts are liquidated, and economic demand can be recalibrated on the basis of solvency. Nothing of that kind has happened. To the contrary, total leverage in the U.S. economy has increased since 2008.

You don't need to wonder whether genuine prosperity will be met around any corner towards which Obama is stepping, or on any nearby patch of pavement he is pouring. It is not likely for many years, perhaps decades to come.

This is not a crowd-pleasing realization. Far from it. Denial is a common theme of life at all times in all places. Sometimes, as is the case now, a paradigm shift in conditions leads to a cluster of miscalculations that tend to compound errors of judgment informed by the natural human tendency towards optimism.

Eighty years ago, when Herbert Hoover was a young president trying to turn back the tide of depression, investors repeatedly misread bounces off the bottom and random fluctuations as evidence that a return to prosperity was indeed imminent. Then as now, too many people thought that every "green shoot" was evidence that the economy was about to turn around. Not so.

The most extreme misreading was evidenced in the famous "Sucker's Rally" of 1930 when the market gained 50% on the widespread hallucination that the downturn was poised to end. It wasn't.

Today, under Obama, infatuated investors buy the market on any flimsy hint of underlying economic strength. In fact, markets are moved by minor swings in patently bogus statistics issued by Obama's Administration. As I write, the market has recently undergone a spasm of enthusiasm over a smaller than expected number of new applications for unemployment insurance. Far from signifying an improvement in job prospects, the market-moving number was merely a statistical confection.

John Williams of Shadow Government Statistics explains:

> Unusual volatility in weekly new claims for unemployment insurance,
> likely are seasonal distortions created by unusual and irregular patterns
> of activity in the financially-stressed and largely reorganized U.S. auto-
> motive industry, and from short-lived year-ago stimulus activity.

In other words, the statistical adjustments originally introduced to sharpen
the picture drawn from the data are now confusing it. Williams explains that
the:

> ...large drop in new claims likely resulted from the Department of
> Labor's inability to adjust the weekly data meaningfully for regular sea-
> sonal variations in activity, particularly around holiday periods such as
> Labor Day, and not from a sudden shift in weekly economic activity.

Given the fact that we are deflating the biggest credit bubble in the history
of the world, genuine, sustained recovery won't be arriving soon. While the
markets wax and wane over ticks up and down in an unemployment rate currently at the time of this writing at 9.6%, the bigger picture is totally missed.

Consumption and debt growth have been strongly correlated since 1960.
Rapid debt growth over the last half century allowed consumption to grow
faster than income. Conversely, if households were to go through a sustained
period of deleveraging (retiring debt), then consumption growth would almost
necessarily slow.

Obama's Administration plays as fast and loose with statistics as it does
with money. Do you honestly think that if they are prepared to spend trillions
out of an empty pocket in order to fake the appearance of recovery that they
would have any qualms about faking a few statistics that not one person in a
thousand bothers to closely examine?

Consider that the recipients of long-term unemployment compensation
are only likely to be counted as "unemployed" so long as their payments continue. As soon as their eligibility for unemployment compensation expires,
they magically disappear from the ranks of the unemployed.

Why?

Not because they find jobs. To the contrary. They are dropped from the
labor force entirely. One of the most important statistical gimmicks (read official lies) for disguising unemployment is for the government to drop millions
of persons without jobs from the officially defined "labor force."

There has been an extraordinary fall-off in the employment-to-population ratio (EPOP), because Obama's minions find it harder to fake overall population numbers. They can arbitrarily play games to suggest that those without jobs should not be counted in the labor force. But it is more difficult to fudge census numbers and arbitrarily reduce the population to make the employment picture seem better than it is.

From 2000 to 2010, the graciously defined, "civilian non-institutional population" of the United States has risen from about 211 million in 2000 to about 238 million.

One of Obama's clever ways of reducing unemployment has been to persistently lower the Civilian Labor Force Participation Rate. After averaging around 66.5% for the past 20 years, it has plunged since the credit crisis of 2008.

If the employment to population ratio, or EPOP, were held constant at its 2000 peak of 64.9%, the unemployment rate would be above 14%.

Lies. Lies. Lies. The important point is not to be suckered by reports of Obama's bogus recovery. To keep it in perspective, remember that Obama's remedy for depression has proven only 40% as successful as Herbert Hoover's efforts after 1929. Of course, most Americans are too ill-informed to recognize that the current credit contraction is potentially more devastating than the Great Depression of the 1930s. For one thing, the introduction of Food Stamps and other welfare programs has helped disguise the lines of hungry unemployed people that made such a vivid impression during the Great Depression. Still, according to the government's own statistics, the number of Food Stamp recipients jumped by 20.28% year-over-year to 41 million Americans as of June, 2010 (on its way to an all-time peak of all-time peak of 47.8 million recipients hit in December 2012). The NBER may have determined that a recovery began in June, 2009. But it has come to less than Herbert Hoover's vaunted promise that "prosperity was just around the corner."

This is exactly what should be expected. It will be an effort of many years to mend balance sheets that have been severely stretched to accommodate outsized burdens of debt. As of late 2010, the 55-year mean of Household Debt in the U.S. was 55.4% of GDP. To bring the debt back down to its mean levels implied shedding $6.33 trillion in debt. Hence, the U.S. economy is destined to remain in depression for several years ahead.

Remember, the depression could linger for decades, as it has in Japan, where an epic real estate and stock market bubble collapsed in 1989. Japan still hasn't recovered, in spite of unremitting stimulus packages that involved trillions in deficit spending to build roads to nowhere.

Short of widespread liquidation and bankruptcy to wipe out excess debt in a hurry, there is really no option or magic potion for recovery. During the credit boom, the combination of higher debt and lower saving enabled personal consumption spending to grow faster than disposable income, providing a significant boost to U.S. economic growth. Reversing that means slower than expected growth, as spending lags behind income.

Shedding debt equal to nearly half of GDP implies a much deeper and/or longer contraction than the Great Depression, when the nominal debt of U.S. households declined by one-third. The Japanese de-leveraging involved shedding debt equivalent to 30% of GDP, so the current de-leveraging process in the U.S. looks likely to be one of the more difficult and protracted in history.

CHAPTER 6

Surviving the Obama Depression: Your Future of Blackouts and Shortages as the U.S. Becomes a "Secure Detention Facility"

"The concept of contracts being enforced ended in this country in the fall of 2008 and early in the term of the radical socialist ninny in the White House. They screwed bond holders in the GM and Chrysler deals — broke contracts all over the place. This by our own gobmint. We are now indeed a third world country, where negotiating never ends."

— Rob Wilson, September 3, 2009

Buenos Aires: There is perhaps no better place on earth to contemplate economic decline than in the cosmopolitan city of Buenos Aires, with its somewhat slummy, discount version of European café life that seems to have been distilled from an old post card of Paris or Rome as they might have been on the eve of the Great War.

Buenos Aires is full of Parisian-style patisseries, known here as confiterias, and Roman-style emporias de las pastas frescas artesanales. The city also has Michelin-caliber kitchens, such as La Bourgogne, El Sud, Casa Cruz and Nectarine, where you can eat splendidly for a fraction of what you'd pay in Europe. (For a better view of the culture of fine dining in Buenos Aires see the Argentine Foodie site www.gastronomia-gout.com.ar.)

But economic decline is not just a matter of living well at a discount for those who have managed to retain a smidgen of solvency through eight decades of misgovernment. Decline has a darker side.

In the ultimate expression of recycling, a multitude of cartoneros (literally, "cardboard collectors") prowl the sidewalks of Buenos Aires, pushing unwieldy gray carts made of baling bags on wheels as they deconstruct the city's garbage. This from a *Christian Science Monitor* report:

> Nearly 30,000 "cartoneros" invade the city's neon-laced streets every night pushing handmade canvas carts, overturning garbage cans, strewing trash along the streets and collecting materials that they sell to recycling centers — each on average earning 10 to 15 pesos, about the cost of a large pizza.

As befits a thoroughly politicized economy, the cartoneros have become an officially recognized profession, subsidized by the government to dump trash all over the street and rummage through it for recyclables. The cartoneros hold some of those exciting "green" jobs you keep hearing about.

They also stand as a living refutation of the demagoguery that played so destructive a role in Argentina's past.

Then as now, demagogues claimed that maintaining an open market economy was unacceptable; they had worked up a lusty appetite for "change" during the Belle Époque prosperity. But in those days, demagoguery was not a paying sport. The masses to which demagogues appealed were not permitted to vote in Argentina until high property requirements for the ballot were waived on the eve of World War I. Before the election of 1916, only the richest 10% of Argentine men voted.

When the distribution of ballots is equal but the distribution of economic assets is unequal it is elemental, if seldom acknowledged, that voting will tend toward the equalization of economic assets.

Lake Woebegone Arithmetic

Back when universal male suffrage was introduced, the Argentine elite identified closely with the British upper class. They reasoned that since Britain had experienced more or less universal male suffrage since 1885, that Argentine prosperity could survive adopting it. They reckoned without the world crises that soon disrupted Argentina's economy; Argentina's terms of trade fell by about 50% from 1910 to 1921.

Then as now, one of the issues that most inflamed demagogues was wide income disparities. The old Argentine arguments make an interesting twist on current complaints against globalization. In those days, critics alleged that only the rich benefitted from free trade because they could sell primary prod-

ucts at a high profit that enabled them to afford expensive imported manufactured goods that were beyond the means of the ordinary worker.

Today, after the collapse of the Bubble Epoch, we hear griping about globalization that is the inverse of those old arguments. Anti-globalization critics
fret that free trade hurts the poor because it permits consumers to buy cheaper
manufactured goods, which thereby undercuts the high wages of the ordinary
worker while "the rich get richer."

The moral of the story may be that at any point where the dynamics of
the free economy lead to disproportionate gains, market critics will agitate for
change that involves a lot of political intervention in the economy.

As a "local lady" told Flora Lewis of *The New York Times* in 1990, "All our
grandparents were rich." This smacks of the arithmetic of Lake Woebegone,
where "all the children are above normal." But for Argentines of a certain
class it would have been true. On the eve of the Great War, (World War I),
Argentina had about one-tenth the population of the United States — but
among them were probably more who were wealthy by world standards than
were Americans at that time.

Although precise figures on income distribution in Argentina date only to
the 1930s, there is good reason to believe that the top 1% of Argentines earned
a third or more of national income before export markets collapsed in 1929.

After years of redistribution, quantitative easing and forced industrializa-
tion to achieve "national independence," the sudden spur to exports of grain
and beef caused by World War II raised the percentage of income earned by
the top 1% of Argentines to 26% in 1943. It would have been considerably
higher before the Great War.

The lucky minority of super-rich Argentines were the proprietors of vast
tracks of the Pampas — arguably the most fertile agricultural region in the
world. In many places, the top soil was ten feet deep.

The Argentine pampas make up more than a quarter of a million square
miles — an area larger than France — of which 8.2% of the land titles accounted for 80% of the productive area. As weather conditions in the pampas
permitted two harvests a year, that area was twice as productive as the wheat
growing regions of Canada. This is part of the reason that Argentina vied with
Canada and Australia as the leading destination for British capital before the
Great War.

Like the U.S. today, Argentina was a rich country dependent on foreign capital. In those days, the main source of international capital was the City of London. The staggering cost of the Great War crippled Britain's ability to export capital. Net property income from abroad plunged from 8% of British GNP in 1910 to just 4.5% by 1920. Argentina suffered along with the British capitalists.

During the 1920s, London was still prepared to lend a trickle to Argentina at only 90 basis points above the interest rates on British government Gilts. In New York it was another story: Argentine loans found few takers. The loans that were made were of short duration and at high interest rates of 7%.

As a result of the lack of foreign capital inflows, investments in Argentina declined sharply. And the rapid GDP growth that accompanied high levels of capital accumulation earlier in the century receded. Between 1890 and 1913, the Argentine capital stock had grown by 4.8% annually and then from 1913 to 1929, it grew by only 2.2%. The opportunities for continued expansion of the Argentine economy dwindled correspondingly.

For a Spanish-speaking country, Argentina was thoroughly Anglicized in 1929. In that year, Sir Malcolm Robertson, the British Ambassador to Argentina, said, "Without saying so in so many words, which would be tactless, what I really mean is that Argentina must be regarded as an essential part of the British Empire." He was certainly not wrong. Though as he was widely quoted, it is difficult to parse how much "tact" came into his comments.

In any event, no country suffered more from the decline of the British Empire than Argentina, the only country in Latin America to drive on the left. Wealthy Argentines congregated at the sumptuous Jockey Club in Buenos Aires, conceived as an extravagant version of a London gentlemen's club, with a portrait of the Duke of Wellington positioned at a point of pride over the mantel. Wealthy Argentines, like the Martinez de Hoz family, sent their sons to Eton. And Argentines enthusiastically took up English sports, such as cricket, rugby and polo. There was even a rare Eton Fives court in Buenos Aires. (Eton Fives is the form of handball played at Eton.)

When de-globalization gathered steam as British capital receded after the Great War, Argentina applied for membership in the British Commonwealth to avoid having its exports punished by steep tariffs. The application was vetoed by Canada. Argentina later signed a Commonwealth-like trade treaty with Britain — the Roca-Runciman Pact that gave British goods preferential tariff rates in Argentina. This required Argentines to deposit payment for their export goods with the Bank of England, to be offset against the $2.14 billion of loans Argentina still owed to British creditors.

That treaty notwithstanding, Britain was much more open to free trade with Argentina than was the emerging power of the day, the United States. No doubt, part of the reason was that, unlike Britain, the U.S. economy was competitive rather than complementary to the Argentine. Instead of welcoming Argentine meat, as Britain did, the U.S. imposed import barriers after briefly running a trade deficit with Argentina.

The high tariff policy of the Republicans worsened the situation as the 1921 and 1922 tariff hikes hit Argentina hard, laying prohibitive rates on wheat, corn, meat, wool, hides, flax and sugar. Many Argentine exports had been on the free list; now only two were. Argentina protested. But it got little relief.

When the Great Depression began in 1929, Argentina was the world's leading exporter of wheat, corn, beef, wool, hides, and several other primary products. The Argentine economy was still quite prosperous.

U.S.A.: The Next "Submerging Market"?

Argentines consumed more imported goods per capita than Americans. Argentines also owned more cars per capita than Americans, or indeed, than any other country except Britain. But rather than building on its economic progress to that point, Argentina pioneered the dynamics of the "submerging market," the process through which a once rich economy devolves into poverty and economic retardation.

Like it or not, this is a process destined to engage the attention of Americans, as the United States rapidly adopts the very policies that brought ruin to Argentina.

After 1929, Argentina responded to the Great Depression with a "tremendous growth of statism" — the use of the state to own or guide economic institutions. As a result, the number of government enterprises grew rapidly, as did bureaucracy. What did not grow rapidly was the Argentine economy.

Argentina's example shows how a surge of statism could result in dramatic economic retardation.

Hence the fact that Argentina's politicized economy today has subsidized jobs for cartoneros who live on garbage. It is hard to credit that they enjoy more income, more dignity, a greater chance of advancement or more of anything other than bad odor than even unemployed workers did in the pre-1929 free economy.

Lidia Quinteros, a shoemaker-turned-cartonero and activist, ominously advises Americans, "When a crisis happens in your country, you'll have to do the same thing."

That's what I am afraid of. The crisis has happened, and I fear it is leading the United States in the same direction that Argentina took after the onset of the Great Depression in 1929. At that time, Argentina moved away from an open, free economy that was one of the world's most prosperous, to become a closed, politicized economy, where government rather than the market determined investment priorities.

Of course, all these years later, one could say there is good news. Decay seems to have had some attractive results. For one thing, it seems to have mobilized the desire of women to look alluring. This is something I noticed decades ago as a (temporary) economic advisor in the former Soviet Union.

Before the fall of Communism, the women you saw on the streets there looked as though their deepest desire was to be mistaken for Mrs. Breshnev. Afterward, they all dressed like expensive French whores. As former Governor Mark Sanford of South Carolina could attest, there are some smoking hot women in Buenos Aires.

Steep economic decline, that included a multi-billion-percent inflation and decades of negative compound growth, hit Buenos Aires like an economic neutron bomb, wiping out families but sparing many handsome structures left over from a century ago when Buenos Aires was one of the world's wealthiest cities.

Choosing the Wrong Path

Wherever you turn, there is a lot of faded elegance to be seen. That said, I am not unaware of the fact that one cannot stroll the streets of Buenos Aires without watching one's step. That would be a recipe for breaking a few bones or at least twisting your ankle. You have to be careful not to fall on the broken sidewalks, or tumble over destitute persons lying about, especially sprawled near the doorways to any sort of food establishment.

At night when the confiterias close, the adjacent sidewalks are blocked by crowds of homeless begging for scraps of day-old bread and pastries that would otherwise be thrown out.

From the vantage point of my bathroom window, I can see the courtyard of a crumbling four-story mansion built a century ago by a minor "lord of the Pampas." No homeless here. But the rotting remains of the pergola and the classical 60-degree architectural trellis have been stacked along with dead limbs from a rubber tree and fallen palm fronds to form an incendiary hazard. It looks like the makings of a perfect "bonfire of the vanities."

The derelict mansion next door, like the Belle Époque apartment from which I write, was built when the phrase, "rich as an Argentine" was a self-evident cliché, not an historical curiosity.

In 1929, Argentina was rich. By some accounts it was the fourth richest country per capita — richer than Germany, richer than France and much richer than Japan on a per capita basis. That was a lifetime ago. Today, after eight decades as the pioneer "submerging economy," Argentina has fallen far behind Europe, North America, and Japan.

I suspect that the example of Argentina's steep decline holds lessons for the United States. Like the U.S. today, Argentina entered the Great Depression in 1929 heavily dependent on foreign capital, with highly unequal income dispersion, wide political resentments and lots of what would become bad debts in the banking system.

The path Argentina took out of depression led from bank bailouts to runaway budget deficits, hyperinflation and decades of negative compound growth.

An open, free economy was replaced by a closed system, hobbled by intervention and inward looking strategies after the Great Depression.

Many of these changes were set in motion by a charismatic demagogue, Juan Perón.

The Rise of a Demagogue

Perón burst onto the national scene in September 1930, less than a year into the Great Depression, when he was one of only a few soldiers to organize a military coup that overthrew Argentina's elected government.

A junior officer at the time, he negotiated to become the secretary to the minister of war as his reward for helping plot the successful coup. In that capacity, he had himself assigned to Italy as military attaché, where he took a tutorial in fascism at the feet of Mussolini.

Eventually, Perón returned to Argentina to apply the leadership methods of Mussolini to implement similar fascist economic policies. Perón was driven by his interest in power. He cared little for economics per se, except to use economic grievances to increase his own power, which he did adeptly.

Like Barack Obama, Juan Perón advanced rapidly up the power ladder. He was first Under-Secretary of War, then Secretary of War, then head of the labor department, moving on to become Vice President. (He was part of the military group with General Edelmiro Farrell that ousted President Pedro Pablo Ramírez).

Perón recognized that labor was susceptible to his organization and control. By giving them goodies, he gained their devoted support. Perón used the term descamisados (shirtless ones) to convey his sympathy for the urban and rural working classes and the lower middle class. At political rallies, he would remove his suit jacket and rail against the rich.

Thanks largely to Perón, monetary depredations and predatory taxation wiped out once wealthy families, as the economy of a once-rich country submerged to a lower level of development.

Perón is still a controversial figure in Argentina decades after his death. Although he grievously harmed Argentina's economy, he created many make-work jobs for his supporters in bureaucracy and government-run enterprises.

Recent Argentine presidents are Peronists who have continued his legacy of predatory policies.

Harvard economic historian Alan Taylor argues that "much of Argentina's precipitous decline in relative economic performance can be attributed to deleterious conditions for capital accumulation." In other words, after 1929 it was hard to make money and keep it.

Partly this was because, as Taylor puts it, statist "price disincentives channeled funds away from, rather than toward, those investment activities which are the precursor of growth."

The Perils of Statism

There is no more emphatic example of how government intervention retarded the Argentine economy than the tale of the telephone business, which began auspiciously in 1881.

Until 1929, Argentine telephones were operated profitably by a British-owned company, Unión Telefónica del Río de la Plata Ltd. In 1946, Perón's government bought Unión Telefónica and renamed it Empresa Nacional de Telecomunicaciones (ENTel). ENTel rapidly became a deficit-ridden, poorly administered behemoth. By 1990, prior to being privatized again, ENTel's bloated workforce of 47,000 had been mismanaged under 28 chief executives in the previous 30 years.

The service was then arguably the worst in the world, even worse than the poorest African countries. Argentines had to wait as long as 15 years to obtain a phone line, and then installation cost as much as $1,500.

Unbelievable? Don't laugh.

You can expect similar dysfunctional outcomes in the energy sector in the United States, as the federal government under Obama retreats into an inward-looking import-substitution policy — just as Argentina did under its charismatic demagogue, Juan Perón.

Note that like Obama, Perón had a fascination with cutting edge and doubtful energy projects. In 1951, Perón announced the Huemul Project that he claimed would produce nuclear fusion before any other country.

The project was led by Austrian scientist Ronald Richter. Perón proclaimed that energy produced by the fusion process would be delivered in milk-bottle sized containers, which could be used in airplanes and other vehicles. Success was proclaimed, but no proof was given.

When independent scientists investigated Perón's Huemul Project to provide nuclear fusion in milk bottles, they revealed the project was a fraud.

When Perón took office, Argentina had the world's second largest gold reserves. But these were soon squandered nationalizing industries and funding politicized investments, like the Huemal Project, to provide energy through nuclear fusion.

I fear Obama will do for the all-important energy sector in America what Perón did for telephones in Argentina. In the years to come, I predict that you will look back nostalgically on the days when you could flip the switch and turn on the lights. Obama's energy program, which entails an array of subsidies for extracting sunbeams from cucumbers, could change all that.

Obama's insistence on forcing conversion of U.S. energy production to costly, unproven and unreliable alternative sources, plus the punitive cap-and-trade carbon taxes that lurk in the fine print of his Democrat agenda, will make Al Gore richer; they will certainly make you poorer.

Obama will put you in the business of forecasting rolling blackouts. In the years to come, you won't be able to put aside a freezer full of meat — or even a freezer full of tofu burgers. Your electricity is going to flicker off in erratic blackouts, like it does in Nigeria, Angola, Bangladesh and other Third World hell holes.

Furthermore, the outages will involve constant fears for public health because pumps supplying running water and sewage treatment will be halted. Imagine how your wellbeing will be affected under ObamaCare when power supplies to hospitals fluctuate erratically.

Also, you're not going to enjoy shopping in the America of the future because you'll find that the charming high-school grad who is used to scanning bar codes at the checkout line will take a long time to tally your purchases with pen and paper when the computer system is down.

The American economy will be crippled. Airlines will avoid night travel. And the only source of dependable power will be expensive diesel generators (but we won't want to use them, so as to avoid "global warming.")

How Obama Will Destroy Prosperity

As the U.S. follows the same policy path as Argentina, it will obtain similar results. Perverse policies will destroy prosperity and inspire thinking people to get out, and/or get their money out. This is already happening.

In 2008, more than two million Americans emigrated, marking the first time that net legal and illegal migration will have reduced the population of the U.S.

This is an important inflexion point that will enable Obama to brag that he was the president who solved illegal immigration — by making it unattractive for immigrants and natives alike to live in the United States.

In the future, the government will be more focused on prohibiting people from leaving. As part of this sensitivity, the U.S. government will impose exchange controls to prohibit individuals from escaping.

Soon after, the government will demand that people who had the foresight to take their money out bring it back. Portfolio investments will be the most vulnerable to forced repatriation.

Based on the assumption that governments do the same predatory things over and over again in similar circumstances, it is probably safer to put your money to use buying property abroad rather than acquire only portfolio holdings.

Although the U.S. government will resort to draconian measures to tax the "rich" (and you may be less than delighted to discover that you are "rich" by the elastic definitions they will use), destructive economic policies will diminish tax revenues even as government spending runs amok.

Then you will be destined to see another result pioneered in Argentina.

As economist Mauricio Rojas put it:

> The government couldn't pay its bills, so it tried to inflate them away. The rise in prices between 1976 and April 1991 was an incomprehensible 2.1 billion times. During approximately the same period, per capita income sank by over 25% and the poverty rate among Argentine households soared from 5% to 27%.

Standing in Long Lines

An astonishing result of the inflation was that a billion dollars' worth of Argentine pesos was reduced in value to only 47 cents over 15 years.

Argentina's annual deficits amounted to an average of 14% of GDP — on a similar scale as Obama's budget deficits. The federal government under Obama is now spending nearly 160% of taxes taken in.

Among other consequences of runaway budget deficits and hyperinflation was the virtual disappearance of income tax in Argentina. It shrank to just 1% of GDP as the value of the previous year's income became pocket change by the time taxes were due.

During hyperinflation, the biggest contributor to the Argentine budget were energy taxes. Not coincidentally, these stand to be a major factor in America's future under Obama.

Another predictable consequence as Obama reduces the United States to Third World economic status will be wage and price controls to suppress the evidence of inflation caused by printing money to finance deficits. As implied above, only about 65% of the current U.S. budget is supported by tax revenue. The rest is being spent out of an empty pocket. It will get worse as we follow Obama down the road to fascism.

Runaway deficits eventually lead to runaway inflation. Runaway inflation in a politicized economy leads to price controls, which inevitably lead to shortages… and then to rationing.

Your future in America will involve standing in long lines. Get ready for it.

Argentine-style nostalgia for the "good old days" will predominate in the American imagination as the U.S. follows Argentina into economic retardation.

Of course, the Argentines, like Americans today, were by no means aware that the policies of successive governments were destined to lead to decades of hyperinflation and negative, compound growth. No country ever set out to bring ruin upon itself.

"Smiley-Smiley"

The Argentine leaders who adopted destructive policies in the wake of the last depression thought they were responding with creative solutions in a difficult situation.

They were constrained by the fact that Argentina was heavily dependent on foreign capital. Lacking fiscal resources, they adopted policies remarkably similar to those championed by Obama in the United States today — beginning with a bank rescue plan that set the stage for hyperinflation.

As Morten Roed Sørensen, of Denmark's national bank, observes:

> The recession (the Great Depression) also had political consequences. Government intervention replaced laissez-faire in the field of economic policy…

> Monetary policy also changed. Like many other countries at the time, Argentina used the gold standard, although the exchangeability of banknotes for gold was suspended for long periods (1914-1927 and again, finally, from 1929). In 1931 a decisive step away from the gold standard was taken, as the money supply was from then on increased independently of movements in the central bank's gold reserves.

> From a present-day point of view this was a sensible step, as the recession required an easing of monetary policy. The monetary-policy measures taken by the government and the central bank in 1935 were somewhat more doubtful, although presumably inevitable.

At this point, the government took over all "bad debts" accumulated by the unregulated banking sector during the 1920s and 1930s. In reality, this step was financed via monetary financing and totaled approximately 4 per cent of GDP (della Paolera et al. 1999). This paved the way for the extreme, inflationary monetary policy seen in later periods.

Ominously, the bank bailouts that sent Argentina hurtling toward ruin amounted to a much smaller percentage of GDP than Obama's bank bailouts. According to the Inspector General of the TARP program, these bailouts were nearly 100% of U.S. GDP.

But that is by no means the worst of it.

The most distressing parallel between Argentina after 1929 and the United States today is not the specific policy similarities arising from path dependence of governments undergoing similar solvency crises at the onset of depression. The more worrisome issue is that Obama seems to be precisely the same type of charismatic demagogue as Perón, who imprinted Argentina so negatively with perverse economic policies and fascist dictatorship. He left Argentina in a mess that Obama seems entirely capable of duplicating. As one Argentine critic quipped, "We socialized the losses and exported the profits."

Like Perón, Obama's views are a curious amalgam of radical leftwing notions in a fascist framework. As Jonah Goldberg, bestselling author of "Liberal Fascism: The Secret History of the American Left, From Mussolini to the Politics of Meaning," argues, the big government wing of the Democratic Party is the intellectual heir of Mussolini.

Goldberg suggests that the differences between Mussolini-style fascism and the brand practiced by Obama are stylistic rather than substantive. As per George Carlin on HBO's "Real Time with Bill Maher," "When fascism comes to America, it will not be in brown and black shirts. It will not be with jackboots. It will be Nike sneakers and smiley shirts. Smiley-smiley."

The Narcissus Principle

Of course, a fascist demagogue can be as troubling in Nike sneakers as in jackboots.

I was first alerted to the potential dangers of Obama by prominent Israeli psychologist Dr. Sam Vaknin, who suggests that Obama is a narcissist with much the same personality profile as many dictators.

Dr. Vaknin is a world authority who has written extensively on narcissism. He observes:

> I must confess I was impressed by Senator Barack Obama from the first time I saw him.
>
> At first I was excited to see a black candidate. He looked youthful, spoke well, appeared to be confident — a wholesome presidential package.
>
> I was put off soon, not just because of his shallowness but also because there was an air of haughtiness in his demeanor that was unsettling. His posture and his body language were louder than his empty words.
>
> Obama's speeches are unlike any political speech we have heard in American history. Never a politician in this land had such quasi "religious" impact on so many people.
>
> The fact that Obama is a total incognito with zero accomplishment, makes this inexplicable infatuation alarming. Obama is not an ordinary man. He is not a genius. In fact he is quite ignorant on most important subjects. Barack Obama is a narcissist.

Although I am suspicious of psychobabble, Vaknin is an acknowledged world authority on narcissism. When he talks about the subject, you should listen.

Vaknin says Obama's language, posture and demeanor — and the testimonies of his closest, dearest and nearest — suggest the president is either a narcissist or may have narcissistic personality disorder.

Narcissists project a grandiose but false image of themselves. Among those to whom Vaknin compares Obama are David Koresh, Charles Manson, Mao Zedong, Joseph Stalin, Kim Jong-il and Adolph Hitler.

> All these men had a tremendous influence over their fanciers. They created a personality cult around themselves and with their blazing speeches elevated their admirers, filled their hearts with enthusiasm and instilled in their minds a new zest for life. They gave them hope. They promised them the moon, but alas, invariably they brought them to their doom.
>
> Charmed by the charisma of the pathological narcissist, people cheerfully do his bidding and delight to be at his service. He creates a cult of personality — focused on one thing alone and that is power.

I was particularly struck by Dr. Vaknin's reading of Obama's autobiography.

Obama's election as the first black president of the Harvard Law Review led to a contract and advance to write a book about race relations.

The University of Chicago Law School provided him a lot longer [contract] than expected and at the end it evolved into, guess what? His own autobiography. Instead of writing a scholarly paper focusing on race relations, for which he had been paid, Obama could not resist writing about his most sublime self. He entitled the book "Dreams from My Father." Not surprisingly, Adolph Hitler also wrote his own autobiography when he was still nobody. So did Stalin.

For a pathological narcissist, no subject is as important as his own self. Why would he waste his precious time and genius writing about insignificant things when he can write about such an august being as himself?

Narcissists are often callous and even ruthless and, in the norm, lack conscience. This is evident from Obama's lack of interest in his own brother who lives on only one dollar per month.

A man who lives in luxury, who takes a private jet to vacation in Hawaii, and who has raised nearly half a billion dollars for his campaign (something unprecedented in history) has no interest in the plight of his own brother. Why? Because, his brother cannot be used to increase his power.

A narcissist cares for no one but himself. [...] What can be more dangerous than having a man bereft of conscience, a serial liar, holding an office of great power?

Many politicians are narcissists. They pose the usual threats to others. [...] They are simply self serving and selfish and are prone to passing ill-advised laws.

Obama evidences symptoms of pathological narcissism, which is different from the run-of-the-mill narcissism of a Richard Nixon or a Bill Clinton for example. History shows plenty of evidence that pathological narcissists can be dangerous.

The downside of this is that if Obama's policies turn out to be the disaster I predict, he could prove to be a dangerous demagogue.

All Praise Obama

I predict that by the end of Obama's presidency, Obama will have begun to behave more like Juan Perón at his worst — repressing dissent, nullifying rights and employing bully boys to physically intimidate his critics.

I suspect his behavior will become more dictatorial as it becomes increasingly evident that his extravagant "stimulus" and "bail out" policies have failed to ignite a genuine recovery, and his popularity suffers accordingly.

As former Merrill Lynch economist David Rosenberg points out:

> It is so evident, with fiscal stimulus accounting for 100% of global economic activity this year and an estimated 80% government contribution to world GDP growth in 2010, that this entire recovery is as illusory and artificial as it was in the treacherous 1930s.

When President Hoover's well-intended efforts to turn back the tide of depression failed 80 years ago, he became a widely reviled figure. Luckily, Hoover was a man of wide accomplishment who was not suffering from anything resembling pathological narcissism.

Unlike Hitler, Mussolini, Stalin, Perón and, dare I say, Obama, Hoover did not fancy standing on balconies delivering stirring harangues to multitudes of his enchanted followers. I can't say that I have the same confidence about Obama.

We already know that Obama's administration has undertaken efforts to create "a cult of personality" around Obama that are reminiscent of Juan Perón's efforts to use state power to encourage popular adulation.

I hinted above that I think Obama could prove to be the Juan Perón of the United States. Now couple Dr. Vaknin's warnings about Obama's power hungry personality with the Obama administration's Education Department's proposed mandate to U.S. schools.

The federal government initially wanted schools to assign a project to all children to praise Obama. Those in grades K-6 were to define what Obama has done for them and how they can help Obama. Grades 7-12 were to write how Obama has inspired them, all with posters of Obama and his pronouncements in the classroom.

I don't know how you feel, but I see this as a creepy lesson in fascism that is the equal of anything Juan Perón picked up in his tutorial from Mussolini in the 1930s.

You may think I am joking. But the Education Department's proposed mandate to which I refer is real.

Among the activities the government initially suggested for prekindergarten to sixth-grade students: to "write letters to themselves about what they can do to help the president." Another task recommended that students, immediately after listening to an Obama speech, engage in a discussion about what "the president wants us to do."

The "help Obama" curriculum plan brought sharp criticism from many citizens, including some who complained that classrooms were being used to spread political propaganda. In response, the White House revised the lesson plan that was distributed by the Department of Education.

This is not the only example of the Obama administration using government power and money in outrageous ways to underwrite the Obama program.

Note that a White House official was caught on tape advising hand-picked artists and writers that they could be guaranteed federal grant money if they dedicated themselves to celebrating Obama and his policies. A writer was encouraged to compose a poem celebrating Obama's election as president. And other creative artists were encouraged to create plays, films and music celebrating Obama's health care, energy and environmental policies. Obama voter and filmmaker Patrick Courrielche's account of this attempted manipulation is shown on the "Big Hollywood" blog, where he said:

> I'm not a "right-wing nut job." It just goes against my core beliefs to sit quietly while the art community is used by the NEA and the administration to push an agenda other than the one for which it was created. It is not within the National Endowment for the Arts' original charter to initiate, organize, and tap into the art community to help bring awareness to health care, or energy and environmental issues for that matter; and especially not at a time when it is being vehemently debated.

> Artists shouldn't be used as tools of the state to help create a climate amenable to their positions, which is what appears to be happening in this instance. If the art community wants to tackle those issues on its own then fine. But tackling them shouldn't come as an encouragement from the NEA to those they potentially fund at this coincidental time.

> And if you think that my fear regarding the arts becoming a tool of the state is still unfounded, I leave you with a few statements made by the NEA to the art community participants on the conference call.

"This is just the beginning. This is the first telephone call of a brand new conversation. We are just now learning how to really bring this community together to speak with the government. What that looks like legally? […] Bear with us as we learn the language so that we can speak to each other safely…"

Is the hair on your arms standing up yet?

A Disturbing Discovery

In the future, as Obama's depression policies become about as unpopular as Hoover's were in the Great Depression, you can expect Obama to strike back at his critics, much as Perón did, when he got his thugs to burn down the Jockey Club, repressed newspapers, and enacted the desacato laws (the laws of disrespect) that made it a crime to criticize him.

Obama will be somewhat constrained by the American tradition of respecting civil liberties. But only somewhat. The accumulation of powers in the imperial presidency over many years will give Obama and his true-believing minions ample scope to punish those who withhold support from Obama in the ongoing "emergency." For one thing, the imposition of wage and price controls will give government bureaucrats life and death power over almost every business. By withholding critical supplies from Obama critics, they can impose serious economic harm. Don't forget that the Gestapo not only rounded up Jews and dissidents, it also enforced wage and price controls.

We even know now that the NSA listens to your every phone call and reads your every email. You may already be on some list of dissidents.

Further to that, as clever as Obama is, I would not be surprised if he used health laws under his new system to force people who cause him trouble into involuntary quarantine. News reports already indicate that the government prepared plans to forcibly impress large numbers of Americans into quarantine under the guise of preventing a flu pandemic. Try modifying the word "pandemic" with "Ebola." Does that make the danger more credible?

Here I quote the website Zero Hedge:

Here at Zero Hedge, we are expecting a flock of economic black swans soon, and a pandemic — whether real or hyped — may be part of this flock. An economic collapse will no doubt be triggered soon, and it will be convenient for the political elites to blame the collapse on an external factor, such as a pandemic or a war.

Furthermore, the fall H1N1 pandemic may be a convenient pretext by which dangerous levels of expanding social control can be established by elites which have proven themselves utterly corrupt and morally bankrupt.

That's the bad news. The good news is that Obama has given a speech advising Americans to better prepare for the future that awaits them by saving more. Specifically, the Treasury Series I bonds recommended by Obama to help Americans to increase their savings earned 0.00% as he spoke.

That is the kind of return that will give you some cushion to fall back on when Obama turns the United States into a not-so-original copy of the original "submerging economy," Argentina.

CHAPTER 7

Rome Falls Again: Economic Closure and Financial Repression as the U.S. Faces Bankruptcy

"Collapse may come much more suddenly than many historians imagine. Fiscal deficits and military overstretch suggests that the United States may be the next empire on the precipice. Many nations in history, at the very peak of their power, affluence and glory, see leaders arise, run amok with imperial visions and sabotage themselves, their people and their nation."

— Niall Ferguson, "Rise and Fall of the American Empire"

Slip-Sliding Down the Road to National Insolvency

To most people, the idea that we could be approaching the "End of America" is preposterous. After all, the U.S. has been the world's foremost economy for a century. Almost no one now living can recall a time when any country other than the U.S. was on top of the world.

During much of that time, American workers were by far the most highly paid people on earth. Germans and Belgians, French and British workers all earned less than one third of the typical American income. In 1960, the typical income in Japan was just 1/10th that of Americans. Swedes were exceptional in having attained 45% of the average U.S. wage.

Then in 1971, Richard Nixon repudiated the gold reserve standard. The countdown to national bankruptcy began in earnest as ticking time bombs destined to explode the American Dream were laid and set. The robust income growth that Americans had previously enjoyed came to a screeching halt, while incomes abroad soared.

By 1978, American workers took home 20% less than Swedes and Belgians. Germans and the Dutch also earned a premium over the U.S. income. Japanese income soared from 10% of the U.S. level to 68% in less than two decades.

Of course, it is important to recognize that much of the downward shift in the relative wealth of Americans came from a sharp decline in the exchange rate of the dollar. As William Easterly observed, the unweighted cross-country world average of GDP growth in 131 countries slowed from about 5% in the third quarter of the 20th century to about 3% in the '70s and '80s. During the same time, the worldwide average public debt to GDP ratio rose steeply.

In other words, Nixon's unilateral revision of the world monetary system, scrapping the link to gold, preceded a dramatic drop in world average GDP growth. It also led an even sharper decline in relative U.S. wealth as the exchange value of the dollar plunged.

As I write, 45 years later, the U.S. balance of trade has been in deficit ever since. And the dollar has lost more than 80% of its 1971 value.

Seen in terms of gold, the dollar's depreciation is even more dramatic. At the current price of gold the dollar retains just a little over 2% of its 1971 value in gold.

The Birth of Debtism

While no one noticed it at the time, the shift away from gold in the monetary system to pure fiat money led to debt-driven consumption as the main driver of economic growth. Indeed, when Nixon abolished fixed exchange rates by severing the dollar's link to gold in 1971, the U.S. was the world's largest creditor.

No longer.

The move to fiat money resulted in a wholesale substitution of debt for capital in the U.S. economy. Hydraulic force of the largest, cumulative trade deficit the world had ever seen drove this move.

From 1971 through 2015, the current account accumulated trade deficits of the United States totaled more than $9 trillion. By accounting identity, when the U.S. runs a trade deficit, it necessarily borrows an equivalent sum from foreign creditors.

Four decades of accelerating trade deficits hollowed out the capitalist system in the United States, concentrating wealth among the credit-worthy and eliminating real income growth among average Americans.

The only reason U.S. households have achieved higher real earnings is entirely because of the influx of women into the workforce, which led to two-earner households.

Of course, these data are subject to varying interpretations. Some economists argue that deficiencies in the government's calculation of inflation may exaggerate the fall in real income. No doubt there are such deficiencies... but whether they all tend to exaggerate inflation is more problematic.

We could argue the minutia of real income comparisons. Yet a dramatic change in trend in the early 1970s is indisputable.

For the tens of millions of middle-class Americans classified as "non-supervisory production workers" in government statistics, the post-January 1973 stagnation in real hourly income represents a dramatic departure from the experience of preceding years.

Look at it this way: from 1947, the year I was born, to January 1973, average hourly pre-tax earnings, adjusted for inflation using current methods, grew at an average annual "real" rate of about 2.2%. If real income had continued to grow at that robust rate, average purchasing power would have doubled to more than $40 an hour by 2006. Instead, it stayed around $20.

More often than not the parents of my generation, who expected their children to have more prosperous lives than their own, were disappointed. I was born into the Golden Age of the Middle Class. Then, suddenly and permanently, it ended in February 1973.

When Nixon acted to sever the dollar's link to gold, domestic oil production had just peaked and the United States was the world's manufacturing powerhouse. Factory jobs provided high income for relatively unskilled and less educated people. But the transition away from Capitalism to a Debtist economy accelerated change in everything.

It changed the focus of economic activity in the United States as measured by GDP, from genuine wealth creation to debt-driven consumption.

Unlike a Capitalist economy where profits are based upon actually producing goods that consumers wished to buy in an environment of rising incomes, the Debtist economy enshrines cost-cutting consumption in the face of stagnant or falling incomes.

Americans exploited the dollar's status as the world's reserve currency to borrow trillions through the current account deficit. As "consumers of last resort," Americans borrowed the money to enjoy a higher standard of living than they could afford, and that destined them to be cost-sensitive. As the process unfolded over 40 years, it was only a matter of time until underemployed Americans lined up to buy Chinese-manufactured goods at Wal-Mart.

How Debtism Destroyed the Middle Class

As the U.S. trade deficit mounted, production shifted from the United States to other countries. In time, an ever-greater share of manufacturing gravitated to low wage economies, like China.

Note that labor costs for Chinese manufacturers were a bare chemical trace of those of the United States. The average total labor compensation for a Chinese manufacturing worker was about $1.74 an hour a few years ago, benefits included. Many make far less than that.

Of course, consumers benefited from lower-priced products that came along with the outsourcing of production. And the companies sponsoring such products benefited as well.

For example, the migration of production from the United States to China afforded the opportunity for Apple to create a bigger, more profitable market for its iPhone. It also opened the way to high margins for merchandisers.

The out-migration of industrial production from the U.S. obviously gave a great stimulus for the growth of manufacturing jobs in China, as well as for the global raw materials boom.

For those Americans who lacked the skills to be appreciably more productive than Chinese peasants on an assembly line, the opening of low-wage economies implied the end of the middle class lifestyle. Instead of a broad middle class, where up to 90 million Americans were subsumed together as "non-supervisory production workers" whose prospects improved year in and year out, the prospects of the former middle-class diverged.

The less educated and less skilled segment who worked in the tradable goods sector sank toward poverty. As Edward L. Glaeser, professor of economics at Harvard has shown, population growth in the least educated three-fifths of U.S. counties was less than 3% over the past decade. By contrast, in the one fifth of U.S. counties where more than 21% of adults had college degrees in 2000, growth for the decade was over 13%. A minority of skilled entrepreneurs, along with the highly educated — a total of about 13.2 million persons — became highly successful. They earned more than $100,000 per year.

Another strand of the population continued to enjoy a middle-class lifestyle... but one financed at the general expense. Among those whose skills were not internationally competitive, government employees were exceptional in enjoying growing incomes along with such perks as defined benefit pensions and full spectrum health care coverage.

Unfortunately, as the Romans discovered in the waning days of their empire, it is impossible for government spending to take up the slack in the shriveling private economy on a long-term basis.

For one thing, the resources to fund intervention at the necessary magnitude are not readily available. The weaker the economy becomes, the more tax receipts fall away.

Although it is not widely recognized, real per capita tax receipts in the U.S. had fallen to 1994 levels by 2010. In other words, gross domestic product (GDP) growth over a 17-year period was financed from deficits and debt. In fact, net private GDP has barely budged over the last decade.

While some of the gains in consumption since 1994 were funded on credit cards and through cash-out financing of appreciated real estate equity, the greatest contributor to consumption came from soaring government spending. For the decade since 2001, government spending added more than $31 trillion to GDP.

Pre-Industrial Growth Rates

Note another ominous aspect of the situation: notwithstanding the invisibly low interest rates the Federal Reserve has maintained through the first decade of this century, the national debt compounded far faster than the growth of the net private economy upon which the hope of repayment lies.

GDP minus government spending grew from more than $9.31 trillion in 2001 to more than $9.72 trillion in 2010 — a gain of just 0.043% over a decade. At that truly medieval rate of growth, it would take the Net Private Economy 167 years to double.

That kind of growth rate predates the Industrial Revolution.

Prior to the Industrial Revolution, annual growth rates from 0-1% led to low incomes because they provided too little buffer against the inevitable negative shocks, war, famine and pestilence. This appears to have been true in medieval England, where real farm wages, measured by half century, showed no improvement in the productivity of the economy from 1200–49 to 1600–49.

While growth of the productive economy in the U.S. over the past decade was negligible, the national debt soared from $5.8 trillion in 2001 to more than $17.5 trillion in 2014. That's a gain of 301%.

The burden of the national debt compounded more than 9,000 times faster than the productive economy grew.

Those who find their bearings by looking at the gross GDP numbers to justify a vibrant economy have lost the plot. GDP attributable to government spending, especially deficit spending, is bogus. It is not real prosperity but debt-financed consumption with unpleasant implications for your future.

Why the Wealthy Pay the Most Taxes

The fiscal system of the Roman Empire, like that of the United States, was designed on the premise that the wealthy should pay the state's bills. Nixon's repudiation of gold convertibility helped concentrate the costs of government on the few by incubating asset bubbles.

From 1971 through March of 2010, the base U.S. money supply increased 35 times; but the purchasing power of the dollar only fell by 81.1% as measured by the government's Consumer Price Index (CPI).

If all the fiat money inflation had been reflected in the CPI, the dollar should have lost about 96% of its value.

Instead of pushing up consumer prices, credit expansion disproportionately inflated asset values. The prices of real estate and dot.com companies, to cite two prominent examples, skyrocketed. As a result, wealthy, credit-worthy investors, who got a disproportionate share of the new money created out of thin air, made disproportionate profits and paid disproportionate taxes for the privilege.

For example, three years after the credit crisis that ended the subprime bubble, persons earning $100,000 or more (who comprise a little more than 6% of the population) paid more than 80% of all taxes in California.

Evidently, this still isn't enough.

Are You Ready for Taxes to Double?

The U.S. government is doomed to bankruptcy. Indeed, it is already bankrupt. Never in the history of the world has any government owed as much money as the U.S. Treasury owes today.

As I mentioned to you before, Prof. Laurence Kotlikoff of Boston University, an economics expert in government debt, has calculated that the true indebtedness of the U.S. Treasury is greater than the combined GDPs of all countries.

Yes, it is true that the debts of the United States are denominated in U.S. dollars — a currency that the government can create at little or no cost. But this only means that the dollar is destined to collapse.

If your income and wealth are inexorably tied to dollars, you could be wiped out.

Kotlikoff suggests that the International Monetary Fund (IMF) has already endorsed a remedy — the doubling of taxes in the U.S.

You will find that the IMF has effectively pronounced the U.S. bankrupt. Section 6 of the July 2010 Selected Issues Paper says: "The U.S. fiscal gap associated with today's federal fiscal policy is huge for plausible discount rates." It adds, "Closing the fiscal gap requires a permanent annual fiscal adjustment equal to about 14 percent of U.S. GDP."

The fiscal gap is the value today (the present value) of the difference between projected spending (including servicing official debt) and projected revenue in all future years.

Double Our Taxes.

To put 14 percent of gross domestic product in perspective, current federal revenue totals 14.9 percent of GDP. So the IMF is saying that closing the U.S. fiscal gap, from the revenue side, requires, roughly speaking, an immediate and permanent doubling of our personal-income, corporate and federal taxes as well as the payroll levy set down in the Federal Insurance Contribution Act.

The problem is that any attempt to double taxes would crush the economy. And of course, it is clear that there is little appetite for spending cuts as drastic as would be required to even balance the budget on an accrual basis. As John Williams has calculated, the budget is trillions of dollars out of whack on an accrual basis.

Forget about achieving an appreciable surplus that would retire some of the National Debt. The U.S. government will never repay its debt, except for whatever part of it may be extinguished by inflation. That will come directly out of your hide.

Face it: you are an extra caught in the remake of a bad movie.

Welcome to "The Decline and Fall of Rome, Part II"

The fall of the Roman Empire was an ominous precedent for the destiny of the U.S. We are far poorer than we think. The irresponsible fiscal and monetary policies of our government will make Americans poorer still.

Contrary to what many may naïvely suppose, more energetic efforts to "tax the rich" are likely to result in an even tighter squeeze on those of lower means.

Consider this from an article titled "How Excessive Government Killed Ancient Rome:"

> As the private wealth of the Empire was gradually confiscated or taxed away, driven away or hidden, economic growth slowed to a virtual standstill. Moreover, once the wealthy were no longer able to pay the state's bills, the burden inexorably fell onto the lower classes, so that average people suffered as well from the deteriorating economic conditions. In Rostovtzeff's words, "The heavier the pressure of the state on the upper classes, the more intolerable became the condition of the lower classes." (Rostovtzeff 1957: 430)…

> Although the fall of Rome appears as a cataclysmic event in history, for the bulk of Roman citizens it had little impact on their way of life. As Henri Pirenne (1939: 33-62) has pointed out, once the invaders effectively had displaced the Roman government they settled into governing themselves. At this point, they no longer had any incentive to pillage, but rather sought to provide peace and stability in the areas they controlled. After all, the wealthier their subjects the greater their taxpaying capacity…

> In conclusion, the fall of Rome was fundamentally due to economic deterioration resulting from excessive taxation, inflation, and over-regulation. Higher and higher taxes failed to raise additional revenues because wealthier taxpayers could evade such taxes while the middle class —

and its taxpaying capacity — were exterminated. Although the final demise of the Roman Empire in the West (its Eastern half continued on as the Byzantine Empire) was an event of great historical importance, for most Romans it was a relief.

Of course, Germanic tribes aren't about to pillage the U.S. But you can expect, as suggested in the passage quoted from the Cambridge Ancient History, Volume XI, a Roman-style response as "the menace of state bankruptcy" draws nearer.

You will see a replay of "the fierce endeavor of the State to squeeze the population to the last drop." The amount of squeezing will be prodigious as the U.S. is well and truly insolvent.

The first danger is that government will raise taxes to confiscatory levels... on the wealthy.

Like the original "Alternative Minimum Tax," the new, higher rates will apply at first only to a small segment of the population. But as the continued emissions of new dollars conjured out of "thin air" inevitably devalue the currency, the price level will skyrocket and you will end up earning millions, or even hundreds of millions, of dollars. This would make you one of the "wealthy" to whom the new "taxes on the rich" will apply.

The greatest danger to your living standard therefore is the looming menace of "hyperinflation" and the death of the dollar.

We are approaching what Ludwig von Mises described as "the crack-up boom." He said:

> There is no means of avoiding the final collapse of a boom brought about by credit [debt] expansion. The alternative is only whether the crisis should come sooner as the result of a voluntary abandonment of further credit (debt) expansion, or later as a final and total catastrophe of the currency system involved.

CHAPTER 8

The Imperial Predicament: Sovereign Bankruptcy and the Coming War for Debt

"... When national debts have once been accumulated to a certain degree, there is scarce, I believe, a single instance of their having been fairly and completely paid."

— Adam Smith, "The Wealth of Nations," Volume V, Chapter 3

"As we mark Osama bin Laden's death, what's striking is how much he cost our nation — and how little we've gained from our fight against him. By conservative estimates, bin Laden cost the United States at least $3 trillion over the past 15 years, counting the disruptions he wrought on the domestic economy, the wars and heightened security triggered by the terrorist attacks he engineered, and the direct efforts to hunt him down."

— *The Atlantic*

The announcement of the death of Osama bin Laden underscored the intimate connection between the American empire and financial markets.

Within a week of bin Laden's official demise, the price of silver plunged by one third, gold lost about $80 an ounce, oil fell below $100, and, ominously, copper appeared to break down.

And, notwithstanding the fact that the Federal Reserve has monetized nearly 100% of the federal deficit since 2011, the dollar rallied, and U.S. Treasury yields have remained remarkably low.

Superman may have renounced his U.S. citizenship, but in the cartoon world of U.S. government finance, all news seems to be encouraging to some or most investors.

Apparently, the markets took at face value the demonstration of imperial competence by SWAT teams of Navy SEALs and concluded that this somehow improves the prospects for U.S. solvency.

It almost goes without saying that the official account of bin Laden's death at the hands of U.S. commandos verges on the incredible.

It brought to mind the classic lines spoken by the Joel Cairo character, played by Peter Lorre in the 1941 version of the Maltese Falcon: "I certainly wish you would have invented a more reasonable story. I felt distinctly like an idiot repeating it."

Of course, where "national security" matters are involved, embarrassment over incredible stories is as dated as black and white movies. Consider just the evolving, contradictory briefing points about the firefight in which Osama was allegedly shot dead.

From POLITICO:

> At a Pentagon briefing earlier in the day, a senior defense official said bin Laden used a woman as a human shield so he could fire shots. "He was firing behind her," the official said.

> In another background briefing early Monday morning, a senior administration official also said bin Laden put up a fight. "He did resist the assault force. And he was killed in a firefight," the official said.

> However, during a background, off-camera briefing for television reporters later Monday, a senior White House official said bin Laden was not armed when he was killed, apparently by the U.S. raid team.

> Another White House official familiar with the TV briefing confirmed the change to POLITICO, adding, "I'm not aware of him having a weapon."

In any event, bin Laden was purportedly shot and his body dumped into the Indian Ocean... with no independent witnesses, no public photos or any other evidence of the kind that even the Bolivian Army made available when they laid out the corpse of Che Guevara in a cheap wooden coffin for the media to scrutinize in 1967.

It is remarkable that the highest echelons of the U.S. government are less adept at establishing credibility than the Bolivian Army was 48 years earlier — before the Internet existed to poke holes in what seems to have been a hastily concocted story.

As former Rep. Ron Paul has pointed out, it can only erode credibility when the government announces that bin Laden's identity was conclusively established by DNA tests that would have set world records had they been concluded between the time the raid on the compound in Abbottabad began and his death was proclaimed.

On the other hand, the CIA was rumored to have confirmed Osama's identity by facial recognition.

Obviously, in a curious world where lying is a frequent element of public policy, the official account of bin Laden's demise beggars credibility.

Not the least incredible aspect of the official "bin Laden is Dead!" story is the indictment it implies of the strategic competence of America's multi-trillion dollar national security hierarchy.

Why Did the Government Shoot to Kill?

Look at it this way…

According to their own account, they had a chance to apprehend the world's most wanted terrorist — a man who presumably has more information about Al Qaeda terror threats than anyone else.

If there were ever a man they wanted to take alive and throw into a CIA dungeon for concerted torture, it is bin Laden.

So why would they not arm some of the commandos with tranquilizer guns, so they could subdue bin Laden and whisk him away for interrogation — if they were able to corner him unarmed, as they (sort of) said they did?

There are two troubles with that, of course. One is that the commandos sent after bin Laden were burdened with the "Bounty Hunter's Dilemma." Killing bin Laden entailed the promise of a $25 million bounty.

A similar reward for tranquilizing him may not have been on the table. We don't know the precise terms under which the unit was incentivized.

The other trouble with taking bin Laden alive, of course, is that, if they admitted it, they would have to face Pakistani extradition laws. There would have been raging pressure to bring him to trial, where testimony about his career as CIA operative "Tim Osman" might have proved embarrassing.

And the conditions of his incarceration would have been scrutinized in terms of the Geneva Convention and his human rights.

If bin Laden really were taken alive in that compound on the day of the attack, the U.S. government probably would not have told you about it. He might now be spending his days being water-boarded.

The photos of his corpse may be produced later, after he is killed. (Or after they have had sufficient time to digitally fabricate convincing ones.)

Hence, one reading of the story released on May 1, 2011 is that Osama bin Laden is as a good as dead. As scientists say, his death seems to be "over-determined."

There have been earlier, plausible reports quoting intelligence sources that bin Laden died of diabetes/ kidney failure and/or a "lung infection" at the end of December, 2001.

Earlier reports held that bin Laden was supposedly dying of Marfan's syndrome, a genetic disorder that affects connective tissue, the heart and in his case, the kidneys. He was also reported to have suffered with diabetic nephropathy and Hepatitis C.

If even half of this were true, he would not have qualified for health insurance, even under ObamaCare.

As a resourceful terrorist, however, bin Laden is reported to have acquired a mobile dialysis machine for delivery to his base at Kandahar in Afghanistan in 2000. Bin Laden allegedly needed constant dialysis (every three days) and is said to have been visited by CIA physicians in the American Hospital in Dubai in July 2001.

Fox News reported on December 26, 2001, that bin Laden died, citing a Pakistan Observer report that quoted a Taliban leader who allegedly attended bin Laden's funeral.

Equally, other reports had bin Laden escaping from Tora Bora as 2001 drew to a close. Still, others indicate that the CIA had three opportunities to kill bin Laden during the Bush Administration but, for unknown reasons, did not.

Which of these reports, if any, is true, is anyone's guess, because the whole tale of Osama bin Laden is full of as many distortions as a fun house mirror.

Among the unsubstantiated rumors that imply an alternative history is the interview recorded by former Pakistani Prime Minister, Benazir Bhutto with David Frost of the BBC, which aired in November 2007, shortly before her assassination. Benazir Bhutto says Osama is dead. She tells Frost that bin Laden had been murdered by a man she suspected of wanting to assassinate her. In the following month, she was shot dead.

She may have been mistaken or misinformed about bin Laden's death, but she was not wrong in thinking she was a target for assassination.

These are the footnotes of geopolitics. Markets are moved by the headlines, as you see every time fishy U.S. employment or GDP data are released. Markets get excited about trumped-up jobs numbers created by "trans-statistical" sleight of hand.

Manipulated seasonal adjustments, and/or preposterous guesses about the number of companies that fail or come into existence each month, typically account for the new jobs allegedly created each month. You also hear a lot of hype about temporary hires that don't come close to providing a middle class living for anyone.

But cheer up, the headline unemployment rate is down.

Anywhere you care to look closely, you find confirmation of Ringo Starr's first law of politics, that "everything government touches turns to crap." Examine the data in almost any realm and you see evidence of a gross distortion of the facts. This is especially true in geopolitics.

Bin Laden's role in running Al Qaeda, an NGO (non-government organization) of warfare, made him especially elusive and his story difficult to decipher.

As a sub-state actor, without a specific territory under his command, he could have been anywhere or nowhere. His success depended upon creating confusion.

Equally, who he was, and where he was, were questions the powers-that-be were not always eager to answer accurately.

It is well established, for example, that bin Laden had close ties with the CIA during his stint in Afghanistan fighting the Soviets. In fact, the CIA was apparently the founder of Al Qaeda and bin Laden initially a "figure head" recruited to lead it.

Perhaps part of the reason that bin Laden was chosen was that the U.S. government had plans to convince King Fahd to pay for arms for the Mujaheddin, and having a man from a prominent Saudi family head the effort may have helped open Fahd's purse.

The "War on Terror" was big business. Trillions of dollars were lavished out of an empty Treasury to combat an elusive figure who got his start in clandestine warfare under the sponsorship of the CIA.

When and on what terms his relations with the CIA were terminated remain to be clarified.

With the death of the Soviet Union, the U.S. lacked an obvious enemy to justify expansion of the most costly military enterprise in world history.

That is where Osama bin Laden came in handy. The U.S. needed bin Laden as the embodiment of "the enemy" during the War on Terror.

But the mass uprisings by Arabs longing for middle-class democracy emphasize the fact that fundamentalist Islam, even where it has fanatical adherents, is a minority movement.

Oil for Dollars

The U.S. has long thrown in its lot with repressive regimes that offered oil on favorable terms, along with support of U.S. geopolitical aims.

In 1945, Franklin Roosevelt and Ibn Saud, the first King of Saudi Arabia, concluded a pact securing oil exports in exchange for long-term American support for the Saudi regime. This was later expanded to include an even more crucial arrangement for the expansion and survival of the Debtist economy in the U.S.

In March 1974, U.S. Treasury Secretary Bill Simon signed a secret accord in Riyadh with the SAMA (Royal Saudi Arabian Monetary Authority) to set the framework for a defacto oil-based dollar to replace the gold-based dollar repudiated by Richard Nixon.

Special facilities for the recycling petro dollars were created when Kissinger, the U.S. Treasury, and the New York Fed established the U.S. Saudi Arabian Joint Commission on Economic Cooperation. In return, the U.S. renewed FDR's promise to provide military support for the Saudis and other thinly populated Middle Eastern oil regimes.

You see, the pricing of oil in dollars is central to the arrangements implemented by Henry Kissinger and the late former Treasury Secretary, William Simon, for recycling of the U.S. trade deficit back into American capital markets.

The pricing of oil in U.S. dollars is crucial because the urgent need of the world to purchase oil provides the bid to underpin the U.S. currency.

This makes the dollar worth much more than it would be otherwise. Billionaire Sam Zell estimates that U.S. living standards would plunge by 25% or more if the dollar lost its reserve status.

Put simply, the pricing of oil in dollars preserves a borrowed prosperity in U.S. living standards and keeps the whole global debt kiting operation afloat.

The U.S. can thank this arrangement for the trillions in foreign capital it has received — up to 75% of all global capital exports in recent years.

Seen as a pure investment allocation, it obviously is sub-optimal for the U.S., a mature, slowly growing economy, to be attracting three-quarters of the globe's capital exports.

For example, $1 invested in the S&P 500 on Dec. 31, 1999, was worth just about 90 cents at the end of 2009 — and that includes dividend income.

By contrast, Brazil's stock market was up more than 250% for the decade, and Russia's world-beating performance was up 724%.

The surge of capital that flowed into the U.S. was more a case of the U.S. exploiting the dollar's position as a Reserve Currency than an evidence of rational investment allocation.

Foreign creditors poured money into the U.S. in proportion to the eagerness with which U.S. consumers borrowed money to grab up their goods.

And, of course, every dollar that exporters — like the Chinese — accumulated gave them an additional dollar's worth of incentive to preserve the status of the U.S. currency. They may not have been possessed of neighborly feelings toward the United States, but they didn't want to see their hoard of U.S. dollars become Zimbabwe dollars, as they may have been destined to do.

The tale of bin Laden's apprehension and death is so tangled with loose ends, it is impossible to fathom what interpretation of it the smart money is discounting in the market reaction.

The more cynical among us may wonder whether the spectacular announcement of bin Laden's death was perhaps staged for some larger geopolitical purpose.

For example, it may be a prelude to a spectacular "revenge" attack against the United States that will serve as a pretext for wider military action in the Middle East to stabilize oil supplies.

Why Occupy Iraq?

Some observers have long thought that the Iraq intervention had less to do with combating terror than pre-positioning forces to occupy eastern Saudi Arabia's oil fields in the event of unrest there. Recent news raises the prospect of such troubles sooner rather than later.

The widespread uprisings among the Arab populations in North Africa and the Middle East show that even long-established regimes are vulnerable to being swept away. The stability of Saudi Arabia and the other major oil producers in the Middle East is far from assured.

Another perspective is that, after squandering trillions of dollars trying to chase bin Laden through the caves of Afghanistan, the U.S. government finally got smart enough to stage its own "decisive victory" in the War on Terror.

Even if the Osama death claims are untrue, they establish an efficient and economic basis for winding down the war in Afghanistan.

Ghastly Expense Taxes Empires

The ghastly expense of U.S. military actions in Afghanistan would tax even an empire at the height of solvency.

It taxed the British when the "sun never set on the British Empire" in the late 19th century.

It bled the Soviets who withdrew from Afghanistan shortly before the Soviet Union itself collapsed.

Unlike the British, who confronted the limits of their power a century ago, or even the Soviet Union, whose leaders eventually awoke to the fact that they could no longer afford to occupy Afghanistan, the leaders of the United States today seem oblivious.

But even the Obama Administration must have begun to notice that the ruinous costs of "the War on Terror" are colliding with an intensified fiscal crisis in the United States.

While Bin Laden was a convenient foil for a decade or more, his official demise now opens the door to a different direction in foreign policy.

Speculators, who had bet on oil to continue its surge toward $150 a barrel, had second thoughts after the May 1, 2011 announcement of bin Laden's death.

Commodities in general sold off. Why?

With the end of QE2 looming one month after bin Laden's death announcement, had demand slackened in India, China or Brazil?

Yes, in fact it had.

When QE2 was first introduced, quantitative easing in the U.S. implied quantitative tightening in the BRIC countries and elsewhere in the world where economies are really growing.

China, in particular, saw repeated monetary tightening as inflation surged.

In Brazil, the Central Bank raised rates twice in the first five months of 2011.

As reported in the *Financial Times*:

> The government has been raising interest rates and launching a series of other measures, such as increased taxes on consumer credit and foreign loans, in an effort to cool an economy that analysts say is showing signs of overheating.

Did the death of bin Laden promise a startling improvement in America's balance sheet?

No.

Indeed, even if the official story is taken at face value, the fact that the United States has lavished trillions, not billions, (only World War II cost more) to counteract bin Laden's wicked $2 million 9/11 attack, and the fact that it officially took a full decade to run him to ground underscores a hopeless imbalance in the power equation.

Terrorists and rogue states can wreak havoc at a trivial price compared to what it costs the imperial power to counter them.

Ironically, the rally in U.S. financial assets mirrored that which followed the 9/11 attacks themselves. Post-World War II, international investors have tended to see the dollar and U.S. Treasury obligations as the safest of all investments. Analyzed dispassionately, this no longer makes sense. But it helps explain how the United States contrived to become the world's largest debtor... notwithstanding the fact that the U.S. standard of living has been among the world's highest.

The fact that capital inflows to the United States tend to increase after global security shocks says that the world monetary system is fragile.

No other country boasts capital markets that are as deep and supported by so formidable a security establishment.

Another factor in the attraction of the United States is the fact that the United States was seen as a rapidly growing country through much of the 20th century.

As Harold James argues:

> The ability of the United States to finance its deficits therefore depends on the continued perception that it is a high-growth and high productivity economy and that it is politically and militarily secure. Conversely, the security of the United States depends on the continued inflow of capital, as a sudden adjustment would be unbearably painful and intolerable politically.

Until proven otherwise, markets expect the U.S. to make good on its obligations.

It still has not dawned on the investors of the world that the United States has become a slow growth country where the burden of the national debt compounded, over the last decade, more than 3,000 times faster than the productive economy grew.

U.S.: The Rome of the New Decade

This makes it particularly troublesome that the United States is following in the footsteps of Rome, borrowing against the collateral of its already empty treasury to fight constant, distant wars.

This is a particularly inauspicious time to be an imperial power.

No nation, however wealthy, could afford to lavish a million times more on hostilities than its adversaries do. That is a recipe for bankruptcy.

The power equation has undergone a major reversal from the high water days of European colonialism at the end of the 19th century, as exemplified by the Battle of Omdurman (1898).

In that clash, the British Camel Corps, armed with Maxim guns, killed 10,000 Dervishes, with the loss of only 45 British troops.

Projecting power was a plausible proposition at that time. Not now.

Taking the long view, the welcome U.S. victory over bin Laden exposes the hopeless, bankrupting futility of the U.S. position as the imperial magistrate of the world.

The date of that bankruptcy draws nearer as the incidence of conflict increases.

We previously analyzed the central role of oil both in supplying the motive force for the growth of U.S. prosperity as well as a crucial source of geopolitical conflict. As historian Harold James has observed:

> …when the oil price was low and falling in real terms in the 1950s and 1960s, the availability of cheap energy fueled the growth of international trade but it also made for a lower level of conflict.

> In the 1970s, with the major oil price increases of 1973-74 and 1979-80, the whole trading system was threatened. In the 1980s and 1990s, world trade expanded and trade liberalization advanced with falling oil prices.

As oil prices fluctuate, the result to be expected is more conflict, conflict that is almost bound to embroil the United States.

Note that Adam Smith's comment from "The Wealth of Nations," quoted above, was written in the mid-1770s, on the eve of the Industrial Revolution.

When Smith wrote, annual economic growth was still invisibly meager, under 1% annually.

Under those stagnant conditions, the heavy weight of debt would soon have crushed the economy.

As we have explored elsewhere, however, Europe, led by Great Britain, enjoyed a growth spurt.

This surge in economic growth permitted heavily indebted countries to escape the bankruptcy to which they were otherwise destined.

Now, as we analyzed previously, the growth of the real private economy in the United States has receded to a truly medieval pace. Net of the contribution of debt-financed government spending, net private GDP in the U.S. grew by just 0.043% over the first decade of the 21st century.

At that rate, it would take the private economy 167 years to double.

But it may be even worse than that, as you can see for yourself below. The whole of the "recovery" was based on fiscal stimulus financed by conjuring money out of thin air.

In other words, the deficit spending that has promised ruin for a long time is poised to deliver. As historian Harold James observed, Charles de Gaulle's criticism of the United States delivered almost half a century ago "seems a particularly timeless expression…"

de Gaulle said:

> The United States is not capable of balancing its budget. It allows itself to have enormous debts. Since the dollar is the reference currency everywhere, this can cause others to suffer the effects of its poor management. This is not acceptable. This cannot last.

In "The Death of the Dollar" (1975), two French economists extended Charles de Gaulle's thesis, prematurely comparing the U.S. currency to the hyper-inflated assignat of the French Revolution. They concluded that "the United States, irresponsible banker and corrupt goldsmith, is seriously bankrupt."

They would later be proven right, but their judgment was premature.

In fact, in 1971 when Richard Nixon repudiated the gold reserve system, the U.S. was still earning a very substantial surplus from the post-war buildup of overseas investments.

In 1971, net U.S. foreign income was $7.2 billion to go with a small surplus on services and a negative merchandise trade balance of $2.2 billion.

A recurring theme of U.S. macro policy has been to depreciate the dollar as the U.S. current account gap emerged and widened.

By 1985, when the U.S. Treasury undertook a concerted effort to push down the value of the dollar, the current account deficit had ballooned to $118.155 million, equivalent to 2.8% of GDP.

At that point, the U.S. had become the net debtor it continues to be.

By the first decade of this century, the U.S. was absorbing 75% of world capital exports, as trillions in trade deficits led to foreign borrowing on an unprecedented scale.

Given that Fed monetization exceeded 140% of net treasury debt issuance during QE2, there are reasons to expect severe inflation in the future. As the newly created money used to buy Treasury obligations is deposited into the banking system, we could see surging prices.

In other words, the U.S. Treasury is being financed by Wile E. Coyote, lounging on thin air as he conjures money out of vapors.

And it is not as if the fiscal picture of the U.S. was in any way promising.

The issue that investors tend to miss is that the deficit is not merely a problem of compounding debt, but a symptom of decline and at the same time, a disguise that hides the true weakness of the U.S. economy.

The idea that the U.S. is a rapidly growing economy is based upon extrapolation from old data that was already beginning to gather dust when Studebakers were still being produced.

As John Ross has observed, close review of the record shows that:

> U.S. growth decelerates slowly but perceptibly and continuously. The 70-year annual average growth rate to 2009 (1939-2009) is 3.6%; the 60-year rate (1949-2009) is 3.3%; the 50-year rate (1959-2009) is 3.1%; the 40-year rate (1969-2009) is 2.8%; the 30-year rate (1979-2009) is 2.7%; the 20-year rate (1989-2009) is 2.5%; and the 10-year rate (1999-2009) is 1.9%.

The reality is worse than the picture Ross paints because a large and growing percentage of the GDP growth recorded in the official figures above is based entirely upon the government spending out of an empty pocket.

If you subtract the annual government deficit from GDP data, the decline in growth rates is even more pronounced.

Randy Degner observes, "Since 1980 the number of years with negative GDP growth jumps from 7 to 15, and the average GDP growth rate drops from 2.7% to an incredible MINUS 0.3%."

Perhaps more interesting, though, is how tightly America's economy is correlated with the use of energy... and what that correlation falling apart means to us all.

U.S. Economic Growth Tracks World Energy Output Per Capita

The collapse of U.S. economic growth closely tracks world energy production per capita.

From 1945 through 1973, world energy production per capita grew at a rate of 3.24% per year. U.S. real GDP grew accordingly — at exactly the same average rate from 1945-1973, -3.24%.

Notwithstanding the tripling of the price of oil in 1973 and a further jump after the Iranian Revolution, the growth of energy production per capita from 1973 to 1979 dwindled to an annual average rate of 0.64%. Between 1979 and 2000, energy production per capita declined at an average rate of 0.33% per year, also closely matching the decline in real GDP minus the Federal deficit.

Note that the soaring price of oil has not reversed the decline in energy production per capita, strongly hinting that the barriers to enhanced production are physical, associated with the exhaustion of supplies of the cheapest, most readily extracted oil.

The move toward Peak Oil has already begun to decimate the energy hungry economy of the U.S., where real GDP minus the federal deficit actually has fallen at about the same rate as per capita energy production, 0.3%.

The implications are ominous.

Unless some technology breakthrough comes waltzing over the horizon from nowhere, the dwindling of oil supplies will predictably decrease per capita energy production even further.

If the growth of the productive sector in the United States continues to keep pace (that is to say, wither), you can expect an increasingly deep and semi-permanent depression.

Under such conditions, the most likely political response will be to follow the policies of the last half century to their desperate conclusion.

You can expect politicians to continue to escalate deficits to an ever-greater degree in order to preserve consumption and mask the decline in the productive economy.

The difficulty is that there's not enough loose change in the world to finance deficits even at the current scale, let alone when they double or triple from here.

To maintain a semblance of purchasing power for U.S. currency, the U.S. will have to control oil supplies sufficiently to assure that they remain priced in U.S. dollars.

Given that U.S. authorities have pursued a multi-decade policy of depreciating the dollar, rational owners of oil reserves may be reluctant to continue trading rapidly, appreciating oil for rapidly depreciating dollars.

For example, it is not an insignificant detail in the U.S. intervention to depose Gaddafi in Libya, that he had plans to introduce a gold dinar.

According to a Russia Today news story, Gaddafi was planning to introduce a gold dinar — "a single African currency made from gold, a true sharing of the wealth."

Crucially, he was also planning to price Libyan oil sales in gold rather than dollars.

Remember what happened to Saddam Hussein when he actually shifted Iraqi oil sales to euro pricing? The U.S. invaded, re-priced Iraqi oil in dollars, and promptly converted Iraqi reserves from euros back into dollars.

Tellingly, Saddam's petro euros had appreciated almost 30% against the dollar by June 4, 2003, when the dollar reconversion took place, making the switch all the more urgent from the U.S. perspective.

It was already becoming evident to many in OPEC that the U.S. dollar had seen better days. A more general shift to euro pricing would have undermined the U.S. debt-based economy.

The semblance of prosperity that prevailed during the Dot.com boom and the U.S. Sub-Prime boom was crucially dependent on the continued recycling of the U.S. trade deficit into the U.S. banking system, especially from OPEC countries.

The trillions spent on oil each year constitute a tremendous marginal bid underpinning the demand for dollars.

It is not an exaggeration to say that the pricing of oil in dollars is key to permitting Americans to continue to live beyond their means.

It is also obvious that pricing oil in dollars is not an economically rational act, but one that is dictated by American military power. Therefore, it is not hard to foresee conditions under which the U.S. authorities would employ military force to control the oil.

In effect, the final disastrous collapse of the most protracted credit expansion in history is likely to trigger "a war for debt."

CHAPTER 9

The Twilight of Hegemony: Is Currency Depreciation the Hope for Your Future?

"Key to explosive inflation growth ahead remains a savage sell-off in the U.S. dollar and dollar-denominated paper assets and/or heavy monetization of U.S. Treasury debt by the Federal Reserve. Both factors are likely to come into play in the next year, as an intensified economic downturn — ironically signaled by declining annual real growth in the broad money supply — blows apart projections for the federal budget deficit and related U.S. Treasury funding needs."

— John Williams, Shadow Government Statistics

The April 3rd–April 9th 2010 issue of *The Economist* offered another twist on the happy talk that has tended to obscure the true prospects for the intermediate future of the U.S. economy. In a cover story entitled, "Hope at Last," *The Economist* proclaims that the promising side of the inevitable de-leveraging of the U.S. economy (which as of November 2014 has not yet happened), will be realized as the domestic savings rate soars, and the U.S. learns to "export or die."

To see this prospect as evidence of "hope at last" requires you to take a long view; indeed, perhaps a longer view than many of us have the luxury of indulging, given the normal duration of human life.

To put it in perspective, ask yourself how far the U.S. dollar would have to fall to enable America to run a substantial trade surplus? In 2009, the U.S. trade account was $379 billion in deficit, down from $696 billion in 2008. To achieve a trade surplus of almost $700 billion would apparently require a huge drop in the value of the dollar. And therefore, a concomitant drop in U.S. living standards.

Not to put too fine a point on it, but U.S. living standards are destined to shrink to the point where American wages are no longer at a premium over those in emerging economies. This is the "hope at last" which *The Economist* celebrates.

In my view, it is a long stretch to propose that the U.S. economy will prosper as a major exporting power in the years to come. For one thing, the only example of what becomes of a fading global power casts doubt on the proposition that currency devaluation can convert consumers into dynamic exporters. This certainly did not happen when the British Empire was dethroned as the world's leading economy in the first half of the 20th century.

Remember, the surge in relative income in the United States that resulted in the U.S. surpassing Great Britain as the world's richest economy after a painful transition crisis beginning with World War I was partly an exchange rate phenomenon. The pound was remorselessly inflated to pay the ruinous cost of World Wars I and II.

For a longer perspective, consider this: the number of dollars per pound sterling plunged from $9.97 in 1864 to $4.94 in 1914 to $2.80 in 1950 to $1.29 in 1985. That's an 87% loss of value.

Note that back in 1870, U.K. GDP per capita was about one-third higher than that in the U.S.

But that did not last. The world's former reserve currency, the pound sterling, was depreciated dramatically. In domestic terms, the purchasing power of a pound fell from £1 in 1900 to the equivalent of just 1.5 pence in 1999.

In 1913, on the eve of World War I, The British Empire accounted for 21.1% of global GDP, according to Angus Maddison, former professor at the University of Groningen and Assistant Director of the Economics Development Division for the OECD, in his work, "The World Economy: Historical Statistics."

Coincidentally, this is about equivalent to the U.S. share of world GDP on the eve of the Subprime Crisis, what Reinhart and Rogoff call "The Second Great Contraction," in "This Time is Different: Eight Centuries of Financial Folly."

As you project U.S. prospects going forward, you will not go amiss to put more emphasis on contraction rather than growth. The current structure of the U.S. economy, addled by decades of financialization and credit inflation, is ill-suited to become the equivalent of an Asian tiger and export its way to prosperity.

Why? Because the strength of U.S. manufacturing is in high value products. Notwithstanding the widely noted loss of manufacturing jobs to China in low value products like clothing and consumer electronics, the U.S. reigns supreme in high value products. In terms of the value of goods made, the U.S. produced more than 20% of global manufacturing in 2009, which is about double what China did.

In other words, in terms of our areas of competitive advantage, the U.S. is already an exporting power. But that export advantage has fallen far short of enabling the U.S. to earn its way. The huge trade deficits accumulated in recent decades were associated with a chronic problem: the inability of the U.S. economy to create jobs. The apparent prosperity anchored in U.S. high value manufacturing resulted in only about 400,000 more Americans finding employment from December 1999 to December 2009. The population of the United States grew by about 30 million during that decade.

This underscores the fact that the United States confronts the same dilemma that trapped the United Kingdom in the last century as it fell from world hegemony. In the first place, a wealthy economy will obviously tend to price itself out of low value production before its competitive advantage in high value output. The U.K. began running a trade deficit when it was still the world's leading creditor country because it was cheaper to import food and other consumables than to employ expensive British labor to produce low value products where Britain lacked a competitive advantage.

But then, as now, the fact that the fading power retained an advantage in certain high value production could not guarantee growth in high wage jobs, nor indeed, a growth in employment at all.

In the U.K., a response to the slow growth of employment was widespread net emigration. Between 1870 and 1913, 5.6 million more persons left the U.K. than arrived, mainly to English-speaking settlement countries like Australia, Canada, New Zealand and the United States. There was also significant emigration to British colonies in Africa, with minor flows going to Argentina and India.

In the more recent U.S. case, response to the slowdown in employment growth has been much less fluent. U.S. population growth during the first decade of the 21st century exceeded employment growth by 75-fold, yet until 2008, emigration from the United States remained invisibly small. Public attention continued to focus on the inflow of people coming to the U.S., particularly illegal immigration.

Here it is noteworthy that during the first phase of globalization, economies were far freer than we are today. Migration between countries was mostly a matter of individual choice. With few exceptions, borders were open. Individuals could move more or less wherever they pleased, and leave behind burdensome political obligations simply by departing.

Today, that is no longer true. One of the least free countries in terms of migration is the United States. The government has famously introduced tight border controls that included building of a 670-mile-long border fence along the U.S. border with Mexico.

Notwithstanding these heroic and costly efforts to halt free migration, there is still a considerable flow of undocumented workers across the border with Mexico. These illegal immigrants compete for employment at wage rates that are below the legal threshold of value for on-the-books employment, a fact with at least two important implications: 1) the record of the U.S. economy in generating jobs may not be as bleak as official statistics indicate; 2) the social overhead burden on the U.S. economy has become a considerable impediment to growth. Lots of low value production that has been outsourced to China could probably be profitably pursued in the United States if it were not burdened with the high costs of employment taxes and health insurance mandates designed to guarantee employees higher living standards.

No doubt, the slow growth of jobs and the nil growth of income since 1973 have played a role in intensifying pressures to close off immigration.

This has also figured in the enactment of increasingly draconian restrictions on emigration from the United States. U.S. citizenship carries more fiscal burdens than that of any other country. U.S. citizens alone, among leading economies, must pay U.S. taxes whether they reside in the U.S. or not.

So-called exit taxes, the fiscal equivalent of the Berlin Wall, have been imposed to prevent successful Americans from escaping a lop-sided tax burden in which 73% of income taxes are paid by the top 10% of earners, while the bottom 40% actually receive "refunds," having paid nothing.

With a system so heavily tilted towards income re-distribution, the pressures to close off emigration came naturally. Draconian exit taxes have been enacted to burden emigrants. On the one hand, they require that anyone attempting to resign U.S. citizenship pay capital gains on appreciation of his worldwide wealth, with the possibility that the U.S. would continue to demand tax payments for up to a decade after they quit the United States.

In retrospect, the Imperial system followed by the British Empire at its peak, provided a productive framework for encouraging capital investment and emigration to areas with shortages of capital and skilled workers. This is what Alex Armand referred to in his article "British capital outflows, 1870-1914: a 'global saving need' perspective."

In the period between 1870 and 1914 around 60 million people emigrated from resource-scarce and labor-abundant Europe to resource-abundant countries overseas. The destinations were mainly represented by Argentina, Australia, Brazil, Canada, New Zealand and the United States, not surprisingly also the main destinations of British capital. Moreover, the need for savings came as well from the demographic composition of emigrants: more than three quarters of immigrants who went to the United States were from 16 to 40 years old. In other words, they came mainly from younger generations. This characteristic, generating higher propensities to consume, tied to the low income of the high majority of immigrants can explain the strong need for foreign savings.

The growing number of immigrants, their high fertility and low infant mortality generated fast population and labor force growth in the overseas regions, which in turn created a strong need for imported investment capital. In other words, high dependency rates go a long way toward explaining the need for foreign savings in order to exploit investment possibilities, creating a strong link with British excess of savings. British capitalists profited by encouraging migration to high growth regions, which thereby increased demand for exported capital.

It is a dynamic world, however, and the factors that inform the relative attractiveness of emigration have changed. The U.S. discourages emigration, perhaps because the U.S. is a capital importer rather than an exporter.

There are similarities, as well as differences, in the decline of the British economy as compared to the current decline of the United States. Both economies were running trade deficits prior to the inflexion crisis, although the British paid for their consumption from the profits of the Empire. (The British deficit in merchandise trade was trivial compared to the huge surpluses the U.K. ran in services, such as insurance and transport.)

In contrast to the United States in the waning days of the 20th century, when the American economy came to depend upon a credit-based consumption binge, the U.K. was the major capital supplier to the world in the late 19th century. During this period, the British Empire was arguably a paying proposition. In 1913, overseas income amounted to about 6.5% of British GDP. The profits of the Empire enabled Britain to import more foreign goods for consumption.

In this sense, the U.K. was in a far stronger position than the U.S. today. A century ago, Great Britain was not "living beyond its means." While the U.K. ran an income surplus of 6.5% of GDP, the U.S. since the turn of the century has run a current account deficit of about 6% of GDP. Contrary to the happy talk of *The Economist*, there is little precedent for a happy transition.

The National Bureau of Economic Research (NBER) published a detailed analysis of the U.S. current account deficit titled "Is the U.S. Current Account Deficit Sustainable? And If So How Costly Is Adjustment Likely to Be?" (NBER Working Paper No. 11541) by NBER Research Associate Sebastian Edwards. Edwards provides a detailed analysis that culminates in blunt answers:

> No, it is not sustainable and the adjustment, if history is any guide, is likely to be "painful and costly," causing U.S. economic output, measured as gross domestic product or GDP, to plummet. The results from this investigation indicate that major current account reversals have tended to result in large declines in GDP. These estimates indicate that, on average…the decline in GDP growth per capita has been in the range of 3.6 to 5 percent in the first years of adjustment. Three years after initial adjustment, GDP growth will still be below its long-term trend.

To the contrary, the U.K. did not exploit its status as issuer of the world's reserve currency. The pound sterling was firmly anchored in the gold standard. So long as the gold standard was in place, the U.K. government could not create currency willy nilly.

In the more recent case, the U.S. did exploit its position as the issuer of the world's reserve currency to borrow trillions that facilitated financialization of the U.S. economy.

In my view, the U.S. economy is destined to contract as leverage is subtracted from the system. I believe you will look in vain for rapid growth in the U.S. for the next half century.

The experience in the United Kingdom during the modern world's most recent crisis of hegemony does not encourage optimism about U.S. prospects going forward. While the U.K. entered the transition crisis of a century ago in a far stronger position than that of the U.S. today, British GDP growth slowed to a crawl for about half a century.

U.K. GDP grew at a markedly slower pace than elsewhere after Britain was dethroned as the world's leading economy, possibly because of the U.K.'s gigantic debt burden. It skyrocketed from 24% of GDP in 1914 to 176% ten years later. Over the course of the 20th Century, GDP per capita rose less rapidly in the U.K. than in other major countries. Compared to the four-fold increase in the U.K., per capita GDP rose by 5 1/2 times in Germany and the U.S.A., 6 times in Canada and France, 7 1/2 times in Italy and 14 times in Japan.

The average rate of increase for the British economy over the whole 20th century was 1.4% per annum. However, the average rate in the period between 1900 and 1948 was 0.7% per annum as compared to 2.2% from 1948 to 1998.

In 1870, Great Britain had an income one-third higher than the U.S. In that year, Great Britain generated a GDP per capita of 3.263 expressed in U.S. dollars, while in the same year, the United States recorded a GDP per capita of $2.457.

Falling relative income is associated with large out-migration. Since 1901, more people have emigrated from the U.K. than immigrated. By 1997, a net exodus from the U.K. of 15,600,000 had occurred.

In other words, if the recipe for U.S. recovery is a plunge in consumer spending and a skyrocketing savings rate, then it entails a plunge in living standards.

Prepare for it.

The plan to drive down the value of the dollar suits the U.S. position as the most deeply indebted nation in history. It may be a likely way stop on the road to debt repudiation. But it seems rather a far stretch to characterize dollar depreciation as "Hope at Last."

CHAPTER 10

War and Chaos in the Calculus of Collapse

*"Fascism will come at the hands of perfectly authentic Americans
who have been working to commit this country to the rule of the
bureaucratic state; interfering in the affairs of the states and cities;
taking part in the management of industry and finance and agriculture;
assuming the role of great national banker and investor, borrowing
billions every year and spending them on all sorts of projects through
which such a government can paralyze opposition and command
public support; marshaling great armies and navies at crushing costs
to support the industry of war and preparation for war which will
become our nation's greatest industry; and adding to all this the most
romantic adventures in global planning, regeneration, and domination,
all to be done under the authority of a powerfully centralized
government in which the executive will hold in effect all the powers,
with Congress reduced to the role of a debating society."*

— John T. Flynn, "As We Go Marching" [1944]

My late father advised me not to rely on prejudiced advice. He would say, "Don't ask the barber if you need a haircut." Equally, you would not ask a general whether we need a war.

In "normal" times, the demand for war is low. Only a few revved up young men, entranced by the prospect of becoming heroes, actually yearn for conflict. Indeed, much of history is about the search for narratives that will overcome the rational aversion to slaughter and death that makes war an expensive menace.

Indeed, the word "slogan" derives from "sluagh-gairm" (sluagh = "people" or "army" and gairm = "call" or "proclamation"), the Scottish Gaelic word for "gathering-cry" and in times of war for "battle-cry." The Gaelic word was adopted into English as "slughorn," which became "slogan."

Throughout most of history, battle slogans and war cries were a good deal more succinct than they are now.

The ancient Spartan hoplites went to battle with the war cry, "oupote thanatos," or "never death." It reflected a lifetime of training focused on becoming a fearless warrior, and the expectation that one should fight without fear of death. The Roman and Byzantine Empires used "Nobiscum Deus" (Latin for "God with us") as their battle cry.

When the Normans invaded England at the Battle of Hastings, their battle cry was "Dex Aie!" (Old Norman for "God aid us!") Throughout the Middle Ages, knights and armies invoked God in battle. The favorite war cry of the Crusaders was "Caelum denique!" ("Heaven at last!"). Muslim armies countered with their invocation of Holy War, "Allahu Akbar" ("God is Great.")

To see the equivocal progress of civilization, contrast the Spartan war cry, "never death," with the 20th century war cry of the Spanish Legion, "Viva la Muerte" ("Long live death.")

From Battle Cries to Marketing Themes

That 20th Century nonsense is a bit too stark for the public mood at the moment.

The American military has hired skilled Madison Avenue advertising geniuses to craft what are not battle cries, but rather marketing themes that will fill the ranks with volunteers as cheaply as possible. TV viewers now see 30- and 60-second spots touting the U.S. Navy as a "global force for good."

This is propaganda that pulls out all the stops. Guns blasting on battleships… Sacrifice for country… Red Cross mercy missions… Rescue at sea.

If it is "good," the Navy is involved.

The recruiter's message is a pastiche of patriotism, self-help and recycled themes from "Star Wars."

One way or the other, it all fits a pattern that was well articulated at Nuremberg by the Nazi War Criminal (and world-class expert at manipulation), Reichsmarschall Hermann Goering, founder of the Gestapo, who said:

Why, of course, the people don't want war. Why would some poor slob on a farm want to risk his life in a war when the best that he can get out of it is to come back to his farm in one piece? Naturally, the common people don't want war; neither in Russia nor in England nor in America, nor for that matter in Germany. That is understood. But, after all, it is the leaders of the country who determine the policy and it is always a simple matter to drag the people along, whether it is a democracy or a fascist dictatorship or a Parliament or a Communist dictatorship. ...Voice or no voice, the people can always be brought to the bidding of the leaders. That is easy. All you have to do is tell them they are being attacked and denounce the pacifists for lack of patriotism and exposing the country to danger. It works the same way in any country.

Obama (and before him, Bush) have brought daily proof of Goering's view. They seem to have mobilized majority support for one of the more astounding military campaigns in history.

$2.77 Billion per Al Qaeda and Taliban Operative

My militarized friends believe that every campaign undertaken in the U.S. campaign of ceaseless war is both a mission of mercy and a crucial endeavor to save the freedom of the United States. And if they don't quite swallow that, they believe enough of it that they can no longer be objective about any ridiculous war the politicians who lead the U.S. care to fight. This truth has been put to the test more than once in recent years.

Witness the War in Afghanistan. Its stated objective is "to combat Al Qaeda in Afghanistan" and take down the Taliban. President Obama described the group as a "cancer" in that country, dangerous enough to justify the vast expense of escalating U.S. military involvement there. Yet the head of the CIA admitted that there are only between 50 and 100 Al Qaeda operatives in Afghanistan. And a General estimates some 36,000 Taliban insurgents are active in the country.

Think about that. To combat this small group of terrorists, the United States will ultimately have spent between $4 and $6 trillion.

This is beyond ridiculous. For perspective, our annual outlay to combat a soccer stadium of terrorists is more or less the total annual GDP of the world at the heyday of the Roman Empire (stated in billions of 1990 international dollars.)

Never, in the whole of history, has so much treasure been spent to combat so few. Never has there been so lopsided and unsustainable a power equation on the battlefield. In my view, any time an enemy can force you to spend millions to kill each combatant, he has won. In this case, of course, there is scant evidence of success in combating Al Qaeda and the Taliban.

I would be surprised if more than a few handfuls of Al Qaeda terrorists have been dispatched to paradise, notwithstanding all the trillions lavished on our attempt to speed them to the exits from this world.

Meanwhile, as many as 2,346 Americans died in Afghanistan, and another 20,037 were wounded in action. In other words, not only are we spending millions of dollars per fanatic annually, but we are also losing 10 to 20 soldiers killed in action per fanatic on the ground. These numbers were taken from official U.S. casualty stats as of October 30, 2014.

While the President has promised to move troops out of Afghanistan, the reality is we will likely have troops on the ground for decades to come. And the costs can quickly escalate.

Projecting Power in Afghanistan Never Easy

There are a lot of meanings that can be distilled from the fantastic disproportions of cost to military effectiveness in the U.S. efforts to project power into the remote regions beyond the Hundu Kush.

Firstly, the area has been a graveyard for foreign invaders since antiquity. Indeed, the very name of the mountains, "Hundu Kush" means "Hindu Slaughter," thus memorializing the fate or more than one Indian army that attempted to pass that way. There is no place on earth more remote and inhospitable to projections of power.

It is little-known and hardly remembered today that about 5,000 square miles of Afghanistan comprised a completely anarchic region roughly the size of Connecticut known until 1895 as "Kafiristan," or the "land of infidels."

Until that year, this region was one of the few in the path of expanding Islam that had resisted a millennium of violent efforts to convert its fiercely independent mountain people, who maintained adherence to an animist religion dating to the days of Alexander the Great, who also invaded the territory on his way to India. Indeed, Kafiristan was one of the few sizeable regions anywhere on the globe where people resisted submission to any organized government at all.

In other words, far from being areas traditionally devoted to Islam, at least some big swaths of Afghanistan were as famously resistant to Islam as they were to rule from Kabul. But equally, they were resistant to every innovation of thought and governance that originated after antiquity.

Obama's Third World Fiscal Policy Means ...

Consider this tidbit of national bankruptcy: "Tax and Spend. And Spend," by Nicholas Colas of BNY ConvergEx, published July 16, 2010, points out that all the bulls who pretend the U.S. has been enjoying a genuine recovery ignore the hard evidence collected daily by the U.S. Treasury.

Colas has bothered to read the Treasury footnotes and deciphers the tale they tell. In 2010, the U.S. Treasury collected net tax revenues of $622 billion. In other words, net federal revenue was running at about the levels realized 20 years ago during the first President Bush Administration. (That net revenue was comprised of taxes on individuals of $845 billion and corporate tax receipts of $148 billion, offset by refunds of $371 billion.) During this same period, the Treasury issued $892 billion in incremental debt. In sum, the Treasury borrowed $1.43 for each dollar of net tax revenue collected.

U.S. Solvency Crisis Looms

The run of the United States as a great economy is finished. This "Second Great Contraction" is more than what a Boston investment trust in September 1929 cavalierly described as an "indentation in the ever ascending curve of American prosperity."

That "indentation" now looks more like an inflexion point bending back to earth.

Of course, the adamant Keynesians and Big Government "housecarls" insist that the U.S. can borrow ever so much more than any other country ever attempted to borrow with no ill effects.

According to these infatuated shills, the U.S. is destined to remain great because of all the money it owes. And it owes more than any country, ever. For the last eight years, the U.S. government was borrowing/printing more money than all governments of the world combined.

The magic that Obama has borrowed from Robert Mugabe is the abracadabra of spending out of an empty pocket. But compelling evidence shows that it doesn't work.

Exhibit A is Zimbabwe, where inflation soared to the highest monthly rate in history, at 79,600,000,000% in November 2008.

Exhibit B is Japan, where what was formerly the fastest growing advanced economy went into a coma, following two decades of unremitting stimulus and quantitative easing.

Exhibit C is the U.S.A. In 2010 Eric Sprout spelled out that the actual results of the U.S. stimulus and bailout programs were frightening:

> … The net impact of the stimulus contributions and promises made since 2008 have resulted in a combined budget deficit of close to $2.5 trillion dollars and an incremental net increase in GDP of $200 billion. A $200 billion return for a $2.5 trillion increase in debt represents a terrible return on investment. It implies that the net impact of the stimulus on GDP since 2008 has been a mere 9 cents for every deficit dollar spent. Buying dimes with dollars is bad business, government-funded or not.

So much for Obama's nonsense in claiming a growth "multiplier" of 1.5 times for each dollar of deficit spending. On the evidence, the Keynesian multiplier is really a "divisor." And this cannot be dismissed as a sudden departure from past experience, as judged by the behavior of the labor market after the last three downturns, in 1991, 2001, and 2009. The multiplier effects have been negative each time, with no net employment growth for at least a year after the supposed recovery.

The most recent episode was the worst of all.

"No Policy Tools Left"

There is a distinction between Herbert Hoover and Barack Obama, namely that Hoover was "a Quaker who abhorred war" whereas Barack Obama is "a ruthless opportunist." In my estimation he is not above resorting to military aggression to divert public attention from sinking living standards.

Nothing that has transpired since Obama has taken office makes me any less convinced that he would stop at nothing in pursuit of power, including starting World War III, if he thought this would serve his personal ambitions.

That may seem a harsh judgment, but it is not unrealistic, in my view, especially in light of the widely believed view that World War II was responsible for ending the Great Depression. For example, the website of the Economic History Association flatly states: "The war decisively ended the depression itself."

Why World War II Ended the Depression

Why? Keynesians tend to recollect the six-fold increase in government spending, which saw the federal budget jump from just $9.5 billion in 1940 to $72.6 billion in 1944. Note that, partly because the war ended with the surrenders of Germany (May 7, 1945) and Japan (August 15, 1945), mid-way through the year, total nominal, federal spending in 1945 at $72.1 billion was marginally lower than in 1944.

I see several factors as responsible for ending the depression, in addition to the six-fold explosion in government spending. The most important is the fact that the destruction of European and Japanese industrial capacity left the U.S. economy as the last one standing. As Adam Smith explained, competition lowers profits. When your competitors' factories are left as smoldering ruins, and yours are intact, your profitability obviously rises. More profitable business means more employment at higher wages.

For another thing, you can't forget that the military draft and associated recruiting efforts put 16 million men and women into the armed forces working for peanuts. In 1940, the labor force of the United States included 53 million persons, or 40% of the population. Hence, the 16 million persons taken into the armed forces represented 30% of the total labor force.

No wonder unemployment dropped to less than one percent by 1944. The combat pay of the U.S. armed forces in World War II was 30 cents a day or less than $10 a month. In effect, the war effort helped achieve higher levels of employment by impressing millions into work at nominal wage rates.

At the time, consumers were not heavily indebted, so forcing 16 million persons into the armed forces at 30 cents a day did not immediately result in a cascade of bankruptcies, defaults and bad debts in the banking system — as it would today. In fact, household debt as a percent of the GDP bottomed out at just 12% during World War II (1944-45.)

This points to another element in the apparent magic of World War II in ending the depression. It encouraged and accelerated deleveraging of the private sector by enforcing austerity in living standards. In effect, the war became a forced savings program of sacrifice on the home front, involving rationing and mandated scarcity of consumer goods in the name of assuring victory in combat.

But in today's debt-ridden economy, 70% of GDP depends upon consumer spending. That is to say, it depends on consumers going ever more deeply into debt to buy what they can't afford. This hasn't worked very well, as it has taken up to $9 of new debt to produce one dollar of new income since the '90s.

Today's officially defined "labor force" comprises 62.8% of the population — some 92.6 million persons. If 30% of the current labor force were dragooned into the armed forces at token wages, consumption would plunge. Many millions would go bankrupt trying to service their debts on token wages. And the banking system would become even more hopelessly insolvent.

Don't forget, the banking system as a whole is currently operating on about 20-times leverage. This implies systemic insolvency if the banks realize losses on just 5% of their total assets. Of course, this doesn't mean that every U.S. bank would be insolvent if the system as a whole realized losses on 5% of assets (loans) outstanding. But if almost 50 million persons had their incomes reduced to pocket change, this would imply massive defaults. Credit card debt alone is $887 billion. If 30% of it went into default, that would imply losses of $266 billion to the U.S. banking system.

Total household debt, only 12% of GDP during World War II, makes up 70% of total GDP. Even poor people carry a lot of debt in the U.S. With the growth of subprime lending, that took center stage in the credit crisis that shook the world in 2008. It became obvious that debt default by subprime borrowers could have a devastating impact on the banking system.

According to the Federal Trade Commission, as of 1998, 10% of all car loans were made to subprime borrowers. The banks also face substantial losses from recent college graduates who discovered to their sorrow that falling salaries for entry-level jobs don't permit them the latitude to pay what are often heavy student debt burdens.

The average student leaves college with $29,400 in student loans, plus a substantial burden of credit card debt. Because of the increasing promotion of credit cards by colleges benefitting from kickbacks from card issuers for signing on students, many low income students have significant debt.

This just goes to show that another major war, capable of mobilizing Americans in the same way that World War II did, would have very different effects today.

Obviously, the potential for grave losses in the banking system would make impressing 30% of the labor force into the military at token wages economically devastating today.

For these and other reasons, the experience of World War II in ending depression would not likely be duplicated if Obama were to lead the world into another major war.

In saying this, it should not be forgotten that conditions are hardly propitious for a six-fold increase in government spending for other reasons. Such an increase in the federal budget today would be impossible without Mugabe-style inflation. It would result in an annual budget of $24 trillion. Remember, current Treasury figures as of January 2015 show net tax receipts of just $1 trillion since October 2014. To raise total spending to $24 trillion annually implies a deficit equal to 83% of outlays. Far from stimulating the economy, it would destroy what remains of American prosperity.

I have no confidence that Obama fully understands this. The fact that he faces a politically disastrous situation "with no policy tools left," as Eric Sprout optimistically puts it, is ominous for peace.

I say "optimistically puts it" because Sprout clearly is not considering war as a policy tool to mobilize the economy, or justify cracking down on dissent and financial repression.

Obama's Campaign of Financial Repression

Obama's fascist disposition has already found eager expression in his efforts to increase financial repression. Almost every piece of legislation passed at Obama's behest includes some stealth provisions to make it more difficult or impossible for Americans to protect their wealth or escape from the inevitable financial collapse that will be the consequence of Obama's policies.

Coming on top of a provision that requires anyone buying gold worth more than $600 to report the seller to the IRS by filing a form 1099, Obama's "financial reform bill" will further curtail the financial freedom of Americans by restricting electronic transfers of money, among other things.

The 2,300 pages of this new law are full of what will be unpleasant surprises to most. Even the law's chief architect, Senator Chris Dodd (D-CT), admitted "No one will know until this is actually in place how it works."

It contains sweeping passages that grant the Administration arbitrary powers over your finances, in ways that not one person in a thousand comprehends. For example, the "Financial Reform Law," allegedly meant to forestall future credit crises, mandates that if you spend $600 or more buying office supplies annually at Staples that you may have to file a 1099 and possibly even withhold 20% of your purchase price and send it to the IRS. Again, to quote Sen. Dodd, his bill "deals with every single aspect of our lives."

Debtism Not Capitalism

Obama has shown that he will go to practically any length in support of the prevailing ideology of power in Washington. That is not capitalism, but rather debtism (the idea that prosperity depends upon the U.S. economy taking on ever-greater amounts of debt).

In current circumstances, with the private sector half-heartedly trying to deleverage and shed debt, this means the federal government under Obama will continue with its whole hog nationalization of the liabilities of the banking system. The bad debt of the U.S. private sector, under the philosophy and practice of "debtism," is destined to be added to the U.S. national debt. Those who initially contracted the debt may default, but their obligations will be perpetuated as your liabilities in the National Debt if you are a U.S. taxpayer.

Obama's Next War?

If Obama does succumb to the demagogue's temptation to seek to cure the depression with another major war, where will he fight it?

In a certain sense, of course, the answer is unknowable. He has enough arbitrary power to make war wherever the whim moves him. But some clues are on the table for analysis.

The U.S. government's indulgence of its prerogatives of power in issuing the world's reserve currency point to one aspect of John Flynn's prophetic passage quoted at the top of this chapter that is slightly out of focus. He wrote of "the industry of war and preparation for war which will become our nation's greatest industry."

As the country fell into the grip of debtism, however, it became clear that "the industry of war and preparation for war" comprise our nation's second greatest industry, subsidiary, though complimentary to what is actually our greatest industry, the manufacture of money.

We were able to manufacture paper, and by slapping some ink on it, create assets at virtually no cost that could be traded for valuable raw materials like oil and consumer products required for the "good life," as imagined by contemporary consumers. No country has ever enjoyed so great a competitive advantage in any sphere as the U.S. has in manufacturing money since the early 1970s.

As we have explored in previous analyses, there is a perverse feature of trying to engineer prosperity in an economy addicted to debt, namely that it requires an ever-escalating debt stimulus to sustain the illusion. We have seen how the number of dollars of new debt required to gin up one dollar of GDP growth rose asymptotically from just $1.50 in the 1960s, before Nixon repudiated the Gold Reserve Standard, jumping to as high as $9 in the past decade.

This unfavorable arithmetic underscores the need for recycling an ever-escalating stash of U.S. dollars from abroad to finance the U.S. debt bubble. So long as the dollar has remained the world's reserve currency, re-cycled dollars from the trade deficit have flooded into the U.S.

From 2000 to 2010, the world's holding of U.S. dollar assets has ballooned by almost $10 trillion to $15.3 trillion. That was equal to 108% of U.S. GDP in 2010, up from 60% of U.S. GDP just a decade ago. In other words, the U.S. has exported an average of about $1 trillion annually in fiat money to the rest of the world over the past decade.

The demise of the Gold Reserve Standard in 1971 led to the substitution of U.S. dollars as reserve assets of creditor countries.

These countries that collectively hold trillions of U.S. dollars and U.S. government debt denominated in dollars have become de facto accomplices in preserving the reign of the dollar as the world's reserve currency. If they contribute to scrapping the greenback, they will lose the purchasing power commanded by their trillions of dollars, as well as face the resentment of their publics for having traded valuable raw materials and manufactured goods for what could prove to be little more than scrap paper.

Under these circumstances, perhaps it is not a coincidence that the "Axis of Evil" countries identified by President George Bush, whatever else they were doing, were busily undermining the status of the U.S. dollar as the world's reserve currency. They were challenging what U.S. Rep. Ron Paul calls "dollar hegemony." All were busily working to convert their dollar reserves into euros.

Saddam, OPEC and the U.S. Dollar

While it turned out that Saddam's supposed weapons of mass destruction (WMDs) were non-existent, his attempt to undermine U.S. dollar hegemony was not. He was guilty, although the U.S. never mentioned Saddam's infraction against U.S. dollar hegemony in the "bill of particulars" justifying the war.

From November 2000, Saddam had begun to price "oil for food" contracts in euros, a currency that was then just coming into existence. The U.S. invasion and occupation of Iraq put an end to that currency apostasy. Thereafter, all Iraqi oil contracts have been priced in dollars.

Saddam Hussein knew the crucial importance in the debt-based economy for maintaining the dollar as the world's reserve currency. Iraq was a founding member of OPEC. Saddam was involved in an important way when the petrodollar standard was first cobbled together almost 40 years ago.

A little history: Saddam first rose to power in a 1963 CIA-backed coup, in which he was assigned to head the Al-Jihaz al-Khas, the clandestine Ba'athist Intelligence organization. Saddam leveraged control of the secret police to rise to power.

On June 1, 1972, the Ba'ath Party of Saddam Hussein nationalized the Iraq Petroleum Company (IPC), provoking unrelenting British and American hostility. IPC was owned by British Petroleum, Royal Dutch Shell, Standard Oil and a number of other western oil companies. You will remember that Saddam also tested the U.S. pledge to defend the oil-producing states by invading Kuwait to seize that country's tremendous oil reserves.

In effect, the U.S. let Saddam get away with it, as he was left in power after his army was driven out of Kuwait. He decided to play the remaining geopolitical card in his hand by dumping the dollar when the opportunity arose.

Saddam Hussein was overthrown and hanged, not because of his unsubstantiated backing for Al Qaeda (Saddam detested religious fanatics like Osama bin Laden), nor because of Saddam's crimes against his own people (he was a ruthless despot), but because he priced oil in euros, thereby threatening to undermine the U.S. dollar's status as the world's reserve currency, with potentially dire consequences for the U.S. banking system and the whole debt-based economy.

As Richard Benson reported in the Prudent Bear on August 11, 2003:

> In the real world… the one factor underpinning American prosperity is keeping the dollar as the world reserve currency. This can only be done if the oil producing states keep oil priced in dollars, and all their currency reserves in dollar assets. If anything put the nail in Saddam Hussein's coffin, it was his move to start selling oil for euros.

How right Benson was. Literally. Note that Saddam wasn't even executed until December 30, 2006. Benson's analysis was prophetic.

For another early analysis of the Iraq invasion as a petrocurrency war, see "The Real Reasons for the Upcoming War With Iraq: A Macroeconomic and Geo-strategic Analysis of the Unspoken Truth."

Analyst William Clark concludes:

It would appear that any attempt by OPEC member states in the Middle East or Latin America to transition to the euro as their oil transaction currency standard shall be met with either overt U.S. military actions or covert U.S. intelligence agency interventions.

Remember this. It is a crucial clue to the next war that Obama may decide to wage.

After the successful invasion and overthrow of Saddam, the U.S. immediately sought and received approval from the UN in resolution 1483, which granted control over Iraq's oil revenues to the provisional Iraqi authority installed during the invasion. They were promptly switched from euros back to dollars.

The "Margin Call From Hell" on a 30% Profit

Note that Saddam's petro euros had appreciated almost 30% against the dollar by June 4, 2003, when the dollar reconversion took place, making the switch all the more urgent from the U.S. perspective. It was already becoming evident to many in OPEC that the U.S. dollar had seen better days. A more general shift to euro pricing would have undermined the U.S. debt-based economy.

The semblance of prosperity that prevailed during the Dot.com boom and the U.S. Sub-Prime boom was crucially dependent on the continued recycling of the U.S. trade deficit into the U.S. banking system, especially from OPEC countries. This brought in capital to bid for U.S. assets, including Treasury bonds, making it immeasurably easier to fund the yawning U.S. budget deficits, while permitting Americans to continue to live beyond their means.

Iran, the second oil producer after Saudi Arabia, also started moving away from the dollar during the first Bush Administration. In 2002, the National Iranian Oil Company and the Central Bank of Iran began converting their dollar assets into euros. As of 2003, Iran made a tentative decision to accept only euros for oil payments from EU and Asian trading partners. As of 2007, more than 50% of Iranian oil sales were settled in currencies other than the dollar.

In February, 2008, just before Bear Sterns went broke, the Iranian Oil Bourse began trading petroleum priced in currencies other than U.S. dollars, including Iranian rials (IRR) and Russian rubles (RUB), as well as euros.

As the Prudent Investor wrote in 2005 when plans for the Iranian Oil Bourse were announced:

> Steering away from the almighty commodity, currency and commodity currency — the U.S. dollar — can have a deeper impact on the U.S. economy than a direct nuclear attack by Iran. The permanent demand for dollar denominated paper stems to a good part from the fact that until now almost all resources of the world are quoted in it.

The George W. Bush administration, especially in the person of Vice President Cheney, with his background as Chairman and CEO of Halliburton Company, evidenced a lot of sensitivity to oil pricing.

It is not unfair to conclude that Bush and company leveraged the war on terror in directions that protected the role of the U.S. dollar as the world's reserve currency. This provided a continued inflow of capital to support the metastasizing debt economy in the U.S.

Also note that, while the Taliban undoubtedly made enemies in the U.S. government by harboring Osama bin Laden, they also did not win any friends by blocking the construction of Unocal's central Asia gas pipeline, which had to cross Afghan territory. In case you have ever wondered where Hamid Karzai, the long-time, Afghan President got his leg up for the position he held, the simple answer is the Karzai was Unocal's man in Kabul. A report in Counterpunch in 2002 explained:

> Unocal executive John Maresca addressed the House Subcommittee on Asia and the Pacific and urged support for establishment of an in-vestor-friendly climate in Afghanistan, "… we have made it clear that construction of our proposed pipeline cannot begin until a recognized government is in place that has the confidence of governments, lend-ers and our company." Meaning that Unocal's ability to construct the Afghan pipeline was a cause worthy of U.S. taxpayer dollars.

> Maresca's prayers have been answered with the Taliban's replacement. As reported in Le Monde, the new Afghan government's head, Hamid Karzai, formerly served as a Unocal consultant. Only nine days after

Karzai's ascension, President Bush nominated another Unocal consultant and former Taliban defender, Zalmay Khalilzad, as his special envoy to Afghanistan.

The Bush Administration was well disposed to the interests of big oil, especially in the person of Vice President Cheney. Barack Obama, while not an oil man, is the big bank's man. Just look at his contributions from the 2008 campaign. He was the candidate from Goldman Sachs, whose executives donated nearly $1 million to Obama, one of the best investments they ever made. Every penny was returned to Goldman and the other bulge bracket Wall Street and big commercial banking firms that Obama has bailed out.

Obama put the bank's fair-haired boy, Timothy Geithner, president of the New York Fed, in charge of the Treasury, where no opportunity to advance the banks' interests was neglected. Given the desperate financial ratios of U.S. government finance discussed earlier in this chapter, and the 20-1 leverage in the U.S. banking system, you can expect to see a parade of crises in the years ahead.

Earlier in 2010, a crisis in Greek government finance, of no certain origin, precipitated a run on the euro, resulting in a reflex rally in the dollar and an up-tick in the prices of U.S. Treasury obligations paying invisibly low rates of return.

Does this imply that U.S. intelligence agencies played a covert role in precipitating the Greek crisis? No, the CIA did not write the rules that established an unsustainable retirement culture in Greece, where government employees were once paid for 14 months of work each year, and then retired in middle age with 96% of their top pay.

But the U.S. financial ratios are now worse than those of Greece in some respects. And there has been no U.S. Treasury funding crisis — partly because the Greek crisis came first.

As the de-leveraging of the private sector drags on, or actually achieves significant debt reduction — and the double-dip becomes more pronounced, you can expect ever more desperate interventions from future administrations.

Unfortunately, I think it is not unlikely that a future president will be tempted to launch a larger war, possibly with Iran, under the misapprehension that this will decisively end the depression itself.

The breakdown of hegemony has always led to conflict. But this is the first time that a hegemonic power has faded since the advent of nuclear weapons. The risks are large.

Global power is shifting at an accelerated speed unless something drastic happens to deflect the trends, the "submerging" (formerly advanced) economies will change places with the emerging economies. This kind of change cannot happen incrementally, smoothly or without pain.

Keep your thinking cap on, as John Malone does in the *New York Observer*:

The billionaire John Malone gave a little-noticed interview to *The Wall Street Journal* from Allen & Co.'s annual Sun Valley conference. Asked about the biggest risks to Liberty, his media conglomerate, Mr. Malone said his concern was this country's survival. "We have a retreat that's right on the Quebec border. We own 18 miles on the border, so we can cross. Anytime we want to, we can get away.

His wife is more concerned: She's already moved her personal cash to Australia and Canada. "She wants to have a place to go," said Mr. Malone, No. 400 on this year's Forbes list of the richest people in the world, "if things blow up here."

CHAPTER  11

Cabo. It's Over:
Why Prosperity As We Knew It
Could Be Gone For Good

B elo Horizonte, Brazil: It is not hard to see where Belo Horizonte, the third largest city in Brazil, got its name. I went there to explore private equity opportunities which abound in Brazil. In the process, I spent two days in the high-rise office of a friendly Brazilian tycoon, with views overlooking all of Belo Horizonte.

And the views are quite spectacular, even those of the mountains that surround the city. They look like everyday green hills you see in backgrounds everywhere, but are special.

Why?

They are comprised of hundreds of millions, perhaps billions, of tonnes of 30% to 80% pure iron ore. In 2010, a dry metric tonne of iron ore (67.55% pure) was worth $167. Multiply that by hundreds of millions, not to mention billions, and you are talking about real money.

The mountains overlooking Belo Horizonte could be bulldozed and taken to the blast furnaces and rendered into metal with little or no further refinement. It is a rich city that can afford the luxury of a backdrop worth billions of dollars. Some of the world's richest unused iron deposits act rather nicely as the frame for Belo Horizonte.

Belo Horizonte could be loosely described as the "Pittsburgh of Brazil," because it is the center of the Brazilian steel industry.

Yet any comparison with Pittsburgh short-changes Belo Horizonte. Unlike Pittsburgh, Belo Horizonte is still muscular and growing. Founded only in 1897, it is a much younger city than Pittsburgh, has a much younger population, and boasts a growing rather than receding economy.

Pittsburgh, by contrast, was founded in 1758. By the middle of the 20th century, it was an industrial powerhouse. No longer. Its population has halved since 1950, when the city had 676,806 residents and its steel mills were still running.

Belo Horizonte is a metropolis of five million. It has not decayed into a depot for dispensing insulin and other meds to a sick society. As you may know, health care is now the dominant business of Pittsburgh.

The idea that Belo Horizonte is young and muscular compared to Pittsburgh is not entirely metaphorical. A study at Carnegie Mellon University showed, astonishingly, that 28.4% of the population of Pittsburgh is "grossly overweight." By comparison, only 11% of the people of Belo Horizonte are overweight.

Sometimes you can get a more accurate perspective on home from a distance. The continued growth of Brazil's steel industry is probably an important informing condition for the future prosperity of Belo Horizonte. But, as far as I can tell, this is not a matter of very wide interest at the moment. The big news during my visit was a Brazilian re-run of the O. J. Simpson saga.

It involves an arrogant soccer star named "Bruno." I would not expect you to know Bruno, whose Christian name is Bruno Fernandez Souza. Like many Brazilian soccer stars, "Bruno" can be identified simply by his first name. He was the captain and, until recently, the most popular player for Flamengo, Brazil's most popular soccer club.

Like O.J., Bruno's name and athletic prowess no doubt earned him some benefit of the doubt after police were called to investigate the disappearance of a beautiful, 25-year-old model, Eliza Samudio, a young woman who not incidentally was Bruno's former girlfriend and the mother of his child. She met Bruno at a party in 2009. Bruno allegedly pursued her and they had a three-month relationship that culminated in her pregnancy. She later disappeared and was feared dead.

A subtext of the alleged crime is that Bruno is married, and attempted to bully Samudio into having an abortion. She told police that Bruno kidnapped her after she became pregnant, put a gun to her head, and forced her to swallow Cytotec, an illegal abortion drug. Before letting her go he told her to meet him at an abortion clinic the following day. She didn't. She carried her son to term.

Bruno then allegedly became more threatening when Samudio pressed him to take a paternity test after the birth of "Bruninho" or "little Bruno." Local TV was full of replays of Eliza's taped accusations of violence and threats from Bruno. She made a composed and credible witness.

I wondered what this beautiful young woman saw in Bruno, who reminds me so much of O.J. Simpson. Similarly, I had wondered what O.J.'s late wife, Nicole Brown, saw in him. I suppose it reinforces the cliché that fame and fortune are great aphrodisiacs. It was no doubt an attraction Nicole Simpson lived to regret. And, if the confessions by Bruno's associates are credited, Eliza's involvement with Bruno was the biggest mistake of her life.

The big question in Belo Horizonte was "will Bruno get away with murder?" At the time, I didn't know. There are certainly differences between the U.S. and Brazilian court systems. Emblematic of those differences are the contrasting depictions of the personification of Justitia, or Lady Justice.

You've probably seen these representations. In our tradition, they show a stolid matron, blindfolded, and sometimes carrying scales in her left hand and wielding a two-edged sword. If the artist's model for familiar versions of Lady Justice were put on a bathroom scale, she would weigh in between 175 lbs. and 200 lbs. Nothing sexy about her in my opinion.

The Brazilian version of Lady Justice, by contrast, is a maid, not a matron but rather a beautiful young woman. Imagine a supermodel sporting a blindfold. She is meant to be weighing justice impartially, but it would not be hard to see her as a beauty in bondage, about to submit to kinky sex.

Just as O.J. was ultimately accused of murder, Bruno eventually found himself under arrest, along with half a dozen of his friends and accomplices, on suspicion of having murdered and dismembered Eliza Samudio. Several of Bruno's associates have confessed. They told a gruesome tale of kidnapping Samudio, strangling her, dismembering her body, feeding the severed parts to dogs and burying the leftover remains in concrete.

The parallels with the Simpson case were driven home by extensive TV coverage of a caravan of armored police vehicles slowly driving up the BR 040, the freeway that links Belo Horizonte to Rio de Janeiro, with Bruno and his accomplices in tow.

I found myself wondering, as I did more than 20 years ago when O.J. Simpson was accused of murder, how he had managed to screw up so badly.

Simpson, like Bruno, had everything going for him. He was a poor boy who had made good. He had wealth, fame, a beautiful wife, and yet he managed to lose it all in a breathtakingly short time. As the song "Summer Wages" said, "And the years are gambled and lost, like summer wages."

On March 8, 2013, a Brazilian court sentenced Bruno to 22 years in prison for kidnapping, assaulting and murdering Eliza Samudio.

While there was a chance that Bruno could find a crevice in the Brazilian justice system through which to escape prison, it seems his great run of good fortune is over.

"Cabo" is the word in Portuguese for "it's over."

Cabo

If you think about it, the theme of an arrogant athlete gaining riches and fame and then squandering it is an apt metaphor for the disappearing prosperity of the United States. We not only became a nation of middle-aged slobs, athletes gone to seed; we also blew through our inheritance of wealth and prosperity.

The big story of the next few decades will be the demise of U.S. prosperity. It is a story that many will refuse to believe, as the jury refused to credit the idea that O.J. Simpson had murdered Nicole.

Still, I think it would be a huge mistake to carry over the mid-twentieth century assumption that the U.S. economy will necessarily afford Americans a superior standard of living compared to what enterprising people will earn elsewhere.

"It's over." For many reasons.

In a certain sense, it has been over for a long time, as the United States ceased to earn its way decades ago. The U.S. has been leveraging past glories for the past four decades. As Bill Clinton told an audience in New York in placing Goldman Sachs in context, "There is a bigger problem here... too much of our growth was in finance ever since we went off the gold standard."

Precisely. The move to fiat money led directly to greater wealth concentration and the demise of real income growth.

It also drove a fierce perversion of ethical economic policy involving financial institutions deemed "too big to fail." These lumbering giants of finance were permitted and encouraged to leverage their capital at a ratio of one hundred-to-one to make whole hog bets on subprime mortgages, guaranteed by the U.S. government on the preposterous premise that residential real estate could never decline in value.

When the limit of leveraged buying was finally breached and the subprime bubble burst, the trillions of dollars in explicit and implicit Federal guarantees, bailouts and backstops were triggered, socializing the losses at the expense of taxpayers.

The banks and other insolvent financial institutions were not only bailed out directly, but were invited to fatten their balance sheets by borrowing hundreds of billions from the Treasury/Fed at nearly zero interest. Think about this.

They then deposited these funds at the Federal Reserve, or bought Treasury obligations on which they earn 3-4%, reaping billions in guaranteed income by borrowing Federal money for free and getting paid a wide interest margin by the Fed/Treasury.

Yes, too much of what passed for prosperity was due to leverage and the bigger problem remaining is that most of what you have been promised and worked for, including that great retirement you imagined, to quote that song by Steve Earle, "has been gambled and lost like summer wages."

Most Americans won't be able to retire. You will have to work until you drop to pay interest on the National debt that has exploded to bail out big banks. To whom will that interest be paid? To foreign governments that have lent real money to the Treasury and, yes, to the big banks themselves, of course, who have been given Federal money for free to buy Treasury obligations that you have been indentured to pay.

The old feudal arrangements between the aristocracy and the serfs lacked the pure, breathtaking exploitation that has been packed into the fiat money system by your elected representatives.

Put simply, due to chronic "deficit attention disorder," politicians have assumed that the good credit of the United States was infinite. It isn't. But they have managed to see that its exhaustion was employed to bankrupt you rather than the big banks who gambled away your prosperity.

The American way of life is over, at least in so far as it can be realized in the United States. Paul Krugman notwithstanding, the U.S. faces the greatest solvency crisis the world has ever seen.

The U.S. national debt plus the present value of unfunded Medicare, Social Security and prescription drug benefits come to a sum in excess of $205 trillion. That is more than the total world GDP, far more than the total wealth of the world.

I am going out on a limb to forecast that this debt will never be paid. It will be settled by repudiation. Either by outright default or currency devaluation in an orgy of printing press money.

Attempting to pay would be unpleasant, but not necessarily insuperable, if the U.S. could grow out of it. But, based on historic patterns, this is unlikely. A great part of U.S. wealth capitalizes income streams that were themselves dependent upon the continued expansion of leverage.

Since leverage ought to contract for decades ahead, the result to be expected is for U.S. wealth to shrink drastically in the face of staggering liabilities.

In short, U.S. wealth is destined to decline as far as O.J. Simpson's reputation.

According to Rogoff and Reinhart in their comprehensive study of debt crises over the centuries, "This Time is Different," housing price declines have averaged roughly six years, while the downturn in equity prices has averaged about 3.4 years following systemic banking crises. On average, unemployment rises for almost five years. We have a long way still to fall.

If we date the beginning of the current Great Contraction systemic banking crisis to early 2008 with the collapse of Bear Stearns, it would be a remarkable departure from the historic norm for the March 2009 market low to have been the ultimate bottom for the stock market.

It would be still more remarkable for a sustained economic expansion to magically pick up where the massive dose of stimulus and bailout spending petered out.

This has decidedly negative implications for the ability of Americans to shoulder the staggering national debt, along with more than $100 trillion of unfunded liabilities.

In 2005, U.S. housing wealth totaled $27 trillion. By 2010, it had fallen to $21 trillion. At that point, I would expect a further write down in U.S. wealth by additional trillions, as stock market valuations reset to reflect much lower annual GDP growth. More on that below.

Remember, when Great Britain fell from world hegemony after World War I, real British GDP growth averaged just 0.7% annually until the mid-century.

A repeat of that pattern of growth reduced to a crawl is entirely possible in light of the decline in annual economic growth in Japan following the collapse of their credit bubble in 1989.

Notwithstanding repeated "stimulus" programs stretching over two decades, annual Japanese GDP growth fell from an average 5% in the 1980s to invisibly low rates in the past decades.

In the process, equity price multiples in Japan have fallen from 100 down to 15. GDP growth has plunged to one-sixth its average in the '80s, and EPS multiples have fallen accordingly. But even a 15 multiple may be too high if the country is unable to achieve even 1% average GDP growth rate for the foreseeable future.

Not only does Japan face severe demographic problems that promise to constrain growth, but it also faces the requirement for fiscal austerity to remedy one of the world's worst problems of sovereign indebtedness.

Note that one of the informing factors in the collapse of Japanese growth has been a drastic deceleration of bank lending. In spite of invisibly low Japanese Overnight Call rates for the past 15 years, the 10-year compound growth of Japanese M2 has fallen from almost 10% to about 2%.

If anything, the collapse in bank credit outstanding in the U.S. since the Great Contraction began in 2008 augurs for even weaker U.S. GDP growth in the years ahead. The broadest measure of liquidity, real M3 (which includes M2 plus long-term time deposits in banks) has been plunging since late 2009. As reported by John Williams at Shadow Government Statistics, it is down by 8%, the sharpest drop on record.

The reason that real M3 is plunging is that the extension of short-term credit to consumers and to businesses continues to contract rapidly. Overall consumer debt, including auto loans, personal loans and student loans has declined in 18 of the 20 months following the collapse of Lehman Brothers. Meanwhile, Commercial and Industrial loans are down by about $400 billion since the Great Contraction began. And Total Commercial Paper outstanding has plunged by about a trillion dollars since the peak in 2007.

This is contractionary. Investors who expect the U.S. economy to perform in the future as it has during recent decades will be sorely disappointed. Remember that de-leveraging does not consist of a single plunge in economic activity followed by a rebound. It involves a series or sequence of events in which outstanding loans are not rolled over, and therefore the finance supporting of various aspects of economic activity recedes over a long period, with contractionary consequences. The only result to be expected is declining activity — slower economic growth or no growth at all.

Since a high portion of our apparent prosperity in recent years was a function of a credit bubble, which cannot be reflated, it is no surprise that Obama's so-called "recovery" engineered with trillions in bailouts and stimulus is falling flat.

A return to "normal" would require still more leverage, as millions of individuals with little or no collateral would otherwise be unable to match their consumption levels from the sub-prime bubble. That won't happen. We'll see a continued slowdown in spending and the erosion of all types of collateral, leading to continued crises in the U.S. banking system, greater credit constriction, and a tighter squeeze on income and growth.

For example, note that U.S. banks are now carrying a record load of muni bonds in their portfolios, just as states and localities are going belly up in the deepest budget crisis since the Great Depression.

I think it could ultimately be worse than the Great Depression, and the long-term slowdown in growth could be as bad or worse than that suffered by Great Britain after it fell from hegemony after World War I. Real Growth averaged 0.7% in the U.K. It could be more like that in the U.S. for decades to come, implying falling P/E ratios in the stock market and a massive loss of wealth.

While the systemic banking crisis, the Great Contraction, began in 2008, I see the secular downturn as having begun in March 2000, with the collapse of the dot-com bubble. As I explore below, that is when U.S. GDP growth went into a stall.

The Sub-Prime Bubble did seem to take the credit expansion to extra innings, but the P/E ratios of 1999, 30.5x the S&P 500 Index, reflected GDP growth of 3.3% during the 1990s. If the collapse in U.S. growth rates is no worse than that experienced by Great Britain when it fell from hegemony, and

U.S. real growth averages seven-tenths of one percent in the years to come, as a rough approximation that would presumably deflate p/e ratios to something like 6.5 times earnings.

When U.S. GDP growth is disaggregated to GDP real growth per capita, or it is adjusted for money supply growth, U.S. GDP growth has been negligible during the 1990s and the bubble years after 2000.

From the FSK blog:

> GDP was $5484.4 billion in 1990 and $13194.7 in 2006, for a GDP growth rate of 140.6%. M2 was $3176.6 trillion in January 1990 and $6705.8 trillion in January 2006, for a growth in M2 of 111.1%. In other words, the actual GDP growth rate from 1990 to 2006 was only 29.5%, an annualized rate of 1%. This is a far cry short of the official government statistics.

Falling income is still the prospect for Americans. It has been falling since the end of the dot-com boom in 2000. And it is destined to go lower, until the superior standard of living enjoyed by the average American is no longer superior.

In terms of per capita GDP Growth, the U.S. has fared worse even than Japan as it has attempted to emerge from its 20-year-old Lost Decade. U.S. per capita GDP growth in the last decade was lower than Japan's. The apparently better U.S. GDP performance is mostly due to population growth stoked by illegal immigration.

But even illegal immigration has fallen sharply. The year 2008 was the first year since the 1930s when more persons left the United States than arrived. A reasonable extrapolation is that the increment to GDP growth generated by the influx of immigrants, legal and illegal, will grind to a halt in the decades to come. The collapse of the construction industry will adversely affect the demand for day laborers, and protectionist legislation to reserve ever scarcer jobs for natives will dissuade immigrants from coming to the U.S.

The other result to be expected, as outlined elsewhere in this volume, is intensified financial repression as the solvency crisis begins to bite. You can expect that any wealth you have will be confiscated to meet the unpaid bills racked up by generations of politicians.

This argues for getting your money out as soon as possible.

It also implies a significant regime change is in store in the intermediate future. The current fiat money system is headed for collapse, probably before the end of this decade. Navigating the chaos will be difficult.

Sometime before the crack of doom, leaders are going to realize that sticking with fiat money implies obliterating the accumulated wealth of the world.

This entire system is going to collapse. Like the career of O.J. Simpson, or his Brazilian counterpart, Bruno, it is over.

CHAPTER 12

The Herbert Hoover of the Democratic Party Stumps the Misery Index

"This State had about 200,000 cars in 1929. It has a million cars now. They weren't built in this State. They were built in Detroit. As this State's income rises, so does the income of Michigan. As the income of Michigan rises, so does the income of the United States.

A rising tide lifts all the boats…"

— John F. Kennedy, Speaking at Heber Springs, Arkansas, October 3, 1963

A "rising tide may lift all boats," but a receding tide seems counter-metaphorically to be sinking all but the largest yachts. One of the themes we have explored is the slowdown of the once advanced, now "Sick" Economies. My conviction is that secular — rather than merely cyclical — factors are inhibiting economic growth in the advanced economies, even while the emerging (middle income) economies retain a greater scope for growth. Below, I explore more of the consequences of de-growth, particularly in the United States.

Bill Bonner's Backhoe

Among other things, it seems likely to me that the political feedback from a continued growth stall is likely to be far more adverse in the United States than in emerging economies where living standards for average people can continue to advance. One of my favorite illustrations of this point was provided by my friend Bill Bonner and the saga of his backhoe that brought a major surge of growth at his Argentine ranch. Prior to his arrival, all the work at a ranch larger than Rhode Island was undertaken with somatic energy — human and animal muscle power. Bill sets the scene:

I've seen with my own eyes what machines can do. On the ranch I bought in northern Argentina, there were no machines when I came on the scene in 2006. Men and horses did all the farm work. Then the two big workhorses — Percherons — died.

I was faced with a decision. Bring in modern machinery? Or continue doing things as they had been done for the last 400 years? (Horses first reached the Calchaqui Valley, where the ranch is, after the Spanish arrived.) I bought two tractors…and a backhoe. The latter has been busy almost every day — clearing fields, repairing roads and digging foundations. The gauchos are very attached to it now; they look at it as if they were castaways watching the approach of a rescue ship.

This machinery has vastly increased output — just as you would imagine. They're now plowing faster … working more land … irrigating more fields. Productivity is increasing quickly. Output is growing fast. And I still have the potential to put more fossil fuel to work (I need to get a bigger truck and one more tractor). The ranch is like an emerging market. At least, I hope it is!

Bill's backhoe illustrates how well-understood recipes for mechanizing work with exogenous energy, applied through simple equipment like tractors and backhoes, can readily increase income for unskilled workers at an Argentine farm.

So long as oil is available at economical prices to fuel the tractors and backhoes, incomes in Bill's valley in northern Argentina can continue to rise.

When the peasant's income goes up, he buys more clothing in stores, gets a better pair of boots, and his wife scrapes together a few centavos to buy mascara. Their purchases increase the tax take for the government. Given the vote-buying proclivities of governments everywhere, democratic or otherwise, it is only a matter of time until the higher level of economic growth fostered by Bill's backhoe and others like it leads to the construction of more rural schools, the hiring of teachers, and the pavement of more roads.

As their incomes rise and living standards increase, Bill's gauchos are likely to be in a good mood. Nothing is guaranteed, but so long as he doesn't gratuitously insult and alienate his neighbors, they are unlikely to form an angry mob and burn down his house. There is a direct and unmistakable connection between his investments in new technology (new to that area that is) and economic advances that have made their lives easier, and raised their incomes.

The very fact that Bill Bonner is a foreign millionaire presiding over a vast, semi-feudal estate in a remote province of Argentina makes it less likely that his Argentine tenants and neighbors would imagine that he is obliged by some principle of justice to invest in the mechanization of their lives and thus promote a continued growth in their living standards. He comes and goes all the time. It is only too obvious that he might one day go and not return. Even if some Peronist thug in the government in Buenos Aires successfully conspired to steal his ranch, this would only be annoying and inconvenient, rather than devastating, for Bill.

In a world full of political hazards to fortune, Bill Bonner had the sagacity to internationalize his finances years ago, so his assets are not entirely hostage to the whims of Barack Obama. Or to put it more informatively, he has achieved "financial escape velocity." He is free to deploy his capital in any jurisdiction on the globe, based solely on his judgment of the highest likely return. He is free to invest, as in his Argentine ranch, in the highly leveraged growth arising from the displacement of muscle power by hydrocarbon energy.

A hint of the fantastic boost to productivity that hydrocarbon energy provides compared to the muscle-powered "organic economy" was offered by energy analysis Tim Morgan. He offers a compelling example. Put one gallon of gasoline in a car; drive it until the fuel runs out and then pay someone to push it back to the starting point. As stated by Tim Morgan in "Perfect Storm: Energy, Finance, and the End of Growth," this "illustrates the huge difference between the price of energy and its value in terms of work done."

It is a stark illustration. A (U.S.) gallon of gasoline equates to 124,238 BTU of energy, which in turn corresponds to 36.4 kWh.

In the book, "Life After Growth," author Tim Morgan states:

> Since one hour of human physical labor corresponds to between 74 and 100 W, the labor-equivalent of the gasoline is in the range 364 to 492 hours of work. Taking the average of these parameters (428 hours) and assuming that the individual is paid $15 per hour for the strenuous and tedious activity, it would cost $6420 to get the car back to the start-point. On this rough approximation, then, a gallon of fuel costing $3.50 generates work equivalent to between $5,460 and $7,380 of human labor.

Jeremy Grantham, in "The Beginning of the End of the Fossil Fuel Revolution", suggests a similar benchmark that underscores the productivity boost provided by hydrocarbon energy as compared to somatic energy (muscle power):

Just imagine, for example, that you had to cut your winter wood supply in a hurry and you had to choose between paying your local labor a respectable minimum wage of, say, $15 an hour or filling your empty chainsaw with a gallon of gas. One of my sons, a forester, tells me he could cut all day, 8 to 12 hours, with a single gallon of gasoline and be at least 20 times faster than strong men with axes and saws, or a total of 160 to 240 man hours of labor. For one gallon! So for this task an estimate of value of $2,400 to $3,600 a gallon would be about right.

If you are still not convinced, Tim Morgan's "Perfect Storm" invites you to employ "workers pedaling dynamo-connected exercise bicycles to generate the energy used by electrical appliances in a typical Western home." He guesses, and so do I, that the cost of powering the home that way would be many magnitudes higher than "the average electricity bill."

These cost mismatches reflect the fact that human muscle power is very inadequate in comparison to the work that is done for us by fossil fuels on a daily basis. These examples also highlight the huge margin for economic growth in areas of the world where hydrocarbon inputs have heretofore been inadequately adopted.

From Bill Bonner's standpoint (and possibly yours, too), there is not only a margin of higher profit to be earned from the higher growth potential of developing economies, but also a penalty of degrowth to be avoided in the sick economies where per-capita energy inputs are falling. This all means that less useful work can be done, and it is reflected in the real bills return of 0% per annum, as well as in exponentially mounting costs of income re-distribution. Luckily for Bill, he is not on the hook for the untold trillions of unfunded liabilities of the U.S. government.

Demagoguery and the "Misery Index"

In my view, one of the crucial consequences of de-growth in advanced economies, like the United States, is the adverse political turn it implies as the majority suffers falling living standards. This means all sorts of mischief that is barely imagined in advance as demagogues, like Obama, inevitably thrash about for policy expedients to disguise or cushion the impact of falling income on infatuated groups of their supporters.

This was on prominent display in the 2012 U.S. presidential election.

Speaking of which, I was wrong. I forecasted a Romney victory in that election, mostly on economic grounds. I felt that the plunge in real income and the surge in inflation during Obama's first term would make him the "Herbert Hoover of the Democratic Party." Not quite.

Herbert Hoover prided himself on introducing accurate statistics to the national dialogue about the economy. Obama's contributions to statistics lie in another direction.

The so-called Misery Index, an indicator created by economist Arthur Okun, (Chairman of the Council of Economic Advisers under Lyndon Johnson), is calculated by adding the unemployment rate to the inflation rate.

Heretofore the worst reading on the Misery Index — 21.98 — occurred in June 1980 under Jimmy Carter. If you were to consult official statistics, you would see that the worst reading on the Misery Index under Obama occurred in September 2011 with a high of 12.97. But look more closely.

The Carter era statistics do not measure the same variables as those promulgated under Obama. If inflation under Obama were calculated by the same methodology that was employed during the Carter Administration, the September 2012 inflation rate would have been two to three times higher.

Now consider the unemployment rate. In Carter's day, so-called discouraged workers, a.k.a. the long-term unemployed, were counted in the unemployment rate, as they still are in Canada. But not in the U.S. under Obama. Shadow Government Statistics (SGS) calculates an alternate unemployment measure that adds back the long-term discouraged workers into both the labor force and the unemployment count. In September, ahead of the 2012 election, the SGS alternate unemployment rate was 22.8%.

In other words, the real unemployment rate under Obama alone was greater than the total Misery Index under Carter.

When measured by statistical methodologies commensurate with those employed in Carter's day, a more accurate tabulation of the Misery Index under Obama in September 2012 was 32.4 — almost 50% higher than its previous all-time high of 21.98.

Recognizing this, I had forecasted a Republican triumph in the presidential election of 2012. I reasoned that since the economic discomfort measured on the Misery Index was real, its effect on the behavior of the electorate ought to be the same, whether or not it was reflected in widely reported headline economic statistics, or only in footnotes followed by connoisseurs of the fine print like me. Apparently, I was wrong.

Exit polling among voters on Election Day showed something I would not have expected. As the *New York Daily News* reported, Obama "won reelection Tuesday in large measure because growing numbers of Americans believe the economy is improving."

If you wonder why politicians set out to deceive you, just look at the 2012 election results. Apparently, the bogus statistics had more credibility with many voters than they had with me. By and large, voters who favored Obama believed the carefully cultivated conceit that the economy was recovering. This was notwithstanding the fact as reported in the *Washington Post* that many voters believed that inflation was a big problem. Some 37% of voters cited inflation and rising prices as "the biggest economic problem." So, in that sense, I was correct in forecasting that the escalating cost of living would trouble the electorate, even though the official consumer price index rose by only 2% year-over-year.

This leads to another puzzle highlighted by the 2012 presidential election.

While voters were not hoaxed about the reality of inflation, contrary to all past political experience, they tended not to blame Obama for rising prices. By a majority of 53% to 38%, the voters blamed former President George Bush as more responsible than Obama for the economy's problems. Even 12% of Romney voters suggested that Bush was more to blame than Obama for the weak economy.

Evidently, Obama achieved a feat that eluded Jimmy Carter and Herbert Hoover. He persuaded voters that his predecessor was to blame for their economic woes, and he managed to tar his challenger as less likely to succeed in correcting problems than he.

This is where the puzzle gets interesting. The fact that the voters did not hold Obama responsible for delivering a Misery Index that far exceeded what was experienced under any of his predecessors could mean that they doubt that anyone could have done better. Or it could also mean that the presumption behind the Misery Index is mistaken. Perhaps issues of affinity and voter identity play a larger role in voters' decisions than Arthur Okun thought.

When Carter sought reelection against Ronald Reagan, Reagan famously claimed the allegiance of millions of working class, "Reagan Democrats."

His 1980 presidential campaign brochure advised that "strong leadership in economic policy means lower taxes, more jobs, and less inflation."

The brochure went on to say that:

> Gov. Reagan has an economic program for America that will work because it's a comprehensive program. A program that recognizes the interrelationships and complexity of our economy… One that combines the wisdom of leading American economists with common sense.

The 1980 Republican campaign connected with voters with an economic plan that seemed credible in the circumstances. Reagan and Carter faced an electorate that was 88% white; only 12% black and Hispanic. The Asian-American vote was too small to measure.

Reagan won, capturing 56% of the white vote, 14% of the black vote, and 37% of Hispanics. 55% of men voted for Reagan, but only 47% of women. Among union households, 45% backed Reagan (the so-called "Reagan Democrats.")

The Republican campaign in 2012 lost the argument over the economy, even as it failed to connect with the growing array of hyphenated Americans.

Despite the fact that the majority of the electorate saw the nation on the wrong track, with an undeniably weak economy, exit poll interviews showed that 54% approved of the way Obama was doing his job. And the electorate was almost evenly split on the question of whether Obama or Romney could do a better job to improve it.

In other words, Romney totally failed to persuade voters that he had a more convincing plan to deal with their problems.

Normally in American politics, voters blame economic distress on the incumbent. The incumbent is the issue, not his challenger. In this election cycle, Obama's campaign succeeded in making the challenger an issue. I was surprised at how successfully Obama's camp was able to define Romney as an unsympathetic personality who would pose a threat to many if he had taken office. Even my own daughter refused to vote for him on the grounds that he was "anti-woman."

If the 2012 presidential election had been held a century ago, Romney would have won in a landslide. He would have taken 59% of the white vote and a large majority of men. Indeed, the last candidate who took almost 60% of the white vote, George H. W. Bush in 1988, won a 425 electoral vote landslide over Michael Dukakis.

No longer. In 2012, whites comprised only 72% of the U.S. electorate, with 28% accounted for by "people of color." Obama won overwhelming majorities among that category. I was not surprised that 19 out of 20 African-Americans cast their ballots for Obama. That is also what happened in 2008. I was mildly surprised, however, that the participation rates among African-Americans were higher than usual. Many Republican strategists and pollsters were banking on the fact that participation rates among Democrat-leaning minorities would tail away in 2012 as they had in 2010. In fact, voting among people of color increased by two percentage points from 2008.

I was dumbfounded that three out of four Asian-Americans voted for the incumbent. Apparently, the results were driven more by demographics and group affinity than by economic interest.

Asian-Americans are generally a successful, high-income group. In fact, their median income is higher than that of white people. Other things being equal, they are less likely to be found among the 47% of the electorate famously labeled by Romney as considering themselves "victims." Yet the anti-immigrant posture of the Republican Party drove almost three-quarters of the overachieving, high-income Asian-American community to vote for Obama.

Clearly, identity politics has trumped economics when high-income hyphenated American groups vote like poor people.

It is something of a small miracle that Romney's share of the Latino vote was higher than his portion of the Asian-American vote. In spite of his inflammatory suggestion that immigrants brought illegally as children to the United States by their parents should "self-deport" themselves, Romney's share of the Latino vote dropped by only 13%.

The most obvious take away from the election is that the Republican Party and its presidential candidate were tripped up by changing demographics.

Conceivably, if Romney had been a better candidate and better advised, he might have minimized the demographic liability with a shrewder selection of his vice presidential running mate. Florida Sen. Marco Rubio on the ticket would have almost certainly brought Florida's 29 Electoral College votes into the Republican camp.

And a Latino on the ticket could have bumped the Republican percentage of the Hispanic vote closer to the 40% garnered by George W. Bush in 2004. In addition, 13% of Latino electorate would have been a swing of 1,575,000 votes — enough to make Romney the winner of the popular vote and probably enough to tilt some closely contested states like Virginia into the Republican tally.

Another conclusion — that I suspect is yet to be demonstrated by events — is that voters of any and all ethnicities, who have fond desires to treat Washington as a wishing well from which they can enjoy easy answers to life's predicaments, are destined to be disappointed in the coming years. All the fantastic hopes and promises of political campaigns are destined to collide at the dead end of declining growth.

Romney suffered many embarrassments in the 2012 presidential campaign. By having lost, he spares himself the added embarrassment of proving that there are not millions of jobs to be conjured up by "talking tough with China."

Nobody knows how to rekindle the kind of robust economic growth the United States enjoyed in the middle of the last century.

Ethnic affinities and sexual politics aside, we probably face several more disappointing presidential terms before this unwelcome lesson can be learned.

CHAPTER  13

Outsmarting Buridan's Ass

"The idea of the future being different from the present is so repugnant to our conventional modes of thought and behavior that we, most of us, offer a great resistance to acting on it in practice."

— Lord Keynes

It must have been an inside joke: the decision by the U.S. National Intelligence Council (NIC) to invoke John Maynard Keynes as a prologue to its forecast of what the world will be like in 20 years.

Global Trends 2030: Alternative Worlds must have given rise to lots of giggles among CIA operatives in Langley.

Before I return to considering the ironies entailed in the NIC resting its telescope on the shoulders of Keynes, it might be useful to recap. Throughout this book, I've examined newly fashionable arguments about why the advanced economies had more or less stopped growing, even before the collapse of Lehman Brothers triggered the onset of the Great Recession.

As John Maynard Keynes' quotation at the beginning of this chapter implies, people in general are hardly eager to explore the unpleasant implications of change.

Nonetheless, change is coming, whether we decide to prepare for it or not.

Taking a cue from the National Intelligence Council, I will also venture some ideas about how the world will change over the next 20 years.

What Happens if the Slowdown Continues?

The crucial issue on the table for your consideration is what happens if the growth slowdown persists? I think it's very unlikely that the U.S. system, along with those of many other formerly advanced economies (the "Sicks" as I call them) could survive the end of growth.

As I explore below, the actual budget deficit of the U.S. government, calculated according to Generally Accepted Accounting Principles (GAAP), was $6.3 trillion in 2014. The U.S. has never grown fast enough to balance a deficit of that magnitude. But a growth stall implies a world of trouble.

I expect that a hyperinflationary depression will likely occur in the U.S. within a decade. The optimist in me would like to think this will not be an installment in a new Dark Age. But that is an issue that involves all sorts of complications better explored later.

Meanwhile, let's return to Keynes' analysis of why the "idea of the future being different from the present is so repugnant to our conventional modes of thought and behavior." The piece from which the Keynes quote is taken begins, "The future never resembles the past — as we well know. But generally speaking, our imagination and our knowledge are too weak to tell us what particular changes to expect."

Lacking knowledge and imagination, we assume "for psychological rather than rational reasons," that "the future will resemble the past."

This is precisely what the National Intelligence Council has done — given us a linear extrapolation of well-established and well-recognized trends — like China overtaking the U.S. as the world's leading economic power by 2030. They've also extrapolated a trend to predict that half the world's population will live at a middle-class level of affluence. The seemingly plausible extension of well-established trends among the BRICS and other emerging economies presupposes a tremendous strain on resources and soaring commodity prices.

As all-star investor Jeremy Grantham emphasizes in his argument against expecting a resumption of 20th century growth rates, the whole supply infrastructure of commodities, including energy resources, metals, food, and water, would have to be hugely expanded to support billions more people at the lifestyle that the middle classes of advanced economies have heretofore enjoyed. He doubts, as I do, that these resources could be forthcoming without startling price rises across the board. As the cost of living a middle-class life soars, the result to be expected is that tens of millions of people in the once advanced, now sick economies would be priced into poverty.

Hence, unless it is true that "the future never resembles the past," we can make a better guess of what lies in store than Buridan's starving ass playing "Eenie meenie miney mo" over two equally succulent bales of hay. (Another "inside joke," this time mine, referring to Keynes' essay of 75 years ago, where he compares the dilemma of an investor required to choose among alternative views of the future to the paradox of Buridan's Ass, a poor creature that hypothetically starved to death unable to choose between alternative meals).

Note for those who only know Keynes for his advocacy of deficit spending, he is interesting for another reason than being "the defunct economist" to whom "madmen in authority" are most likely to be enslaved. Almost uniquely among famous economists, J. M. Keynes was a spectacularly successful investor; the George Soros of the 1930s.

Keynes is also important in intellectual history for his contributions to understanding the economics of rationality. Before the advent of "neural-economics," Keynes was one of the foremost authorities on the way investors think about the economy. His 1921 book, "A Treatise on Probability," is considered a major contribution to the economic rationality debate, and covers a number of technical aspects of probability, including treatment of problems of non-rankability, non-measurability, and incommensurability, along with what Keynes called "non-numerical probabilities."

Given his undoubted eminence as an authority on economic rationality, Keynes' views on forecasting took on a special weight.

Keynes thought that "we have before us a large number of alternatives, none of which is demonstrably more 'rational than the others'…"

Ironically, while Keynes believed that we generally lack the knowledge and imagination to forecast the future conditions that should inform investment valuations, he did believe that "a small minority of the participants in stock markets" are shrewd enough to successfully estimate, not what a security is intrinsically worth, but what prospective buyers are likely to think it is worth. This is a consequence of the fact that while the future may not actually be like the past, people will dependably expect it to be.

So the Keynes comment at the top of this chapter suggests that, while we may be unable to forecast how the world will actually change, we won't be far off in guessing that conventional people under the sway of "habit, instinct, preference, desire, will, etc." will project that it won't change much and act accordingly.

Keynes' view that the innate conservatism of the human mind prejudices most people against entertaining the possibility of an alternative future explains a lot.

For one thing, it helps make sense of the sometimes huge, schizophrenic gap between underlying economic reality and consensus views of such. Hence, the otherwise puzzling fact that politicians of all factions and parties seem to devote great effort to the collection and dissemination of bogus economic statistics.

Peddling Bogus Recovery as the Genuine Article

For example, I have been amazed by the success with which the Obama administration peddled a patently bogus "recovery" as the genuine article.

The heart of this Great Deception is the phony baloney claim that the U.S. economy suffered only a short, 4.3% peak-to-trough drop between 2007 and 2009 and has since recovered. Not so.

A hint that this deception is unconvincing is encapsulated in the common term used to describe the allegedly short and shallow downturn: "The Great Recession."

That term, so obviously at odds with official statistics, found currency because it fits the underlying reality of a deep downturn from which no recovery has occurred, and none is forthcoming. Hence, the forecast from all-star investor Jeremy Grantham, whose GMO firm manages $104 billion, suggests that there will be no recovery until 2016.

Or 2022?

Grantham is an optimist compared to Bill Gross and Mohamed El Erian, formerly the co-CEOs of the $2 trillion PIMCO funds. They have advised clients to expect no recovery until 2022. Clearly, these prominent investors have around-the-clock access to official government statistics that purport to show that a recovery began back in 2009. They don't believe it, and neither should you.

Funny thing is, even if you are not one of the world's more successful money managers, chances are, you don't. As CNBC reported in its "All-America Economic Survey 2012," released on September 25, 2012, "Americans, by overwhelming margins, believe the economy is worse now than it was four years ago when Obama's term began."

In pure logic, that implies no recovery at all.

But of course, public opinion is not necessarily synonymous with pure logic.

Part of the reason it is difficult to parse public opinion for its logical implications, much less its political implications, is that the Great Deception that disguises economic reality is a multi-layered deceit, much of which commands bipartisan support. For example, both major parties have connived at the underreporting of unemployment. Richard Nixon, who was not called "Tricky Dick" for nothing, tried to get the Bureau of Labor Statistics (BLS) to underreport unemployment by fiddling the seasonal adjustments. He failed. Obama has succeeded in that Nixonian trick, with the result that up to 80,000 jobs a month are brought forward from previous reports through the magic of "concurrent seasonal adjustments" that revise each month's in ways that are incoherent from month-to-month.

The unemployment numbers are mostly fiction. But our politicians' mutual sleight of hand in dealing with inflation has caused greater confusion about the true state of the U.S. economy.

So-called "hedonic" adjustments lower the cost of living index, supposedly to reflect the higher quality of goods. But these quality adjustments are only taken in one direction. When Häagen-Dazs reduces the size of its standard tub of ice cream by 2 ounces, this is not treated as a 12 1/2% increase in the cost of ice cream. When furniture manufacturers replace solid wood with fiberboard and veneer, the cost of living index does not rise to reflect the lower quality furniture components.

Quality adjustments for government statisticians are strictly a one-way street. They are applied only to lowball inflation, not to bring it properly into view. With unfunded liabilities for entitlements like Social Security and federal pensions that are indexed to inflation stretching as far as the eye can see, many lawmakers in both parties turned a blind eye to statistical sleight of hand that understated inflation, thereby saving trillions in cost-of-living adjustments.

Equally, "Homeowner's Equivalent Rent" was a convenient device for disguising the impact of the greatest housing bubble in world history on the CPI. Housing accounts for a major portion of monthly outlays by most consumers. Indeed, housing costs notionally comprise about a third of the CPI. But note: by 2006, the peak of the housing boom, only 40% of homes were affordable for families earning the median income. You might think this would have been reflected in a surge in the cost-of-living index. Wrong. The house "price-to-rent ratio," usually synonymous with the "owner's equivalent rent" data published by the BLS, is often viewed by economists as an indicator of a housing bubble. When housing prices rise much faster than rents this is seen as an indicator that housing prices are overly inflated. Naturally, a government intent upon disguising inflation prefers to measure housing costs according to the generally lagging rental value. As John Krainer and Chishen Wei reported in an October 2004 analysis for the Federal Reserve Bank of San Francisco, "Current prices are high relative to rents. More precisely, house prices have been growing faster than implied rental values for quite some time: currently, the value of the U.S. price-rent ratio is 18% higher than its long-run average."

Obviously, the real cost of living was skyrocketing. But not as officially reported in the CPI. The Homeowner's Equivalent Rent gimmick helped disguise the impact of soaring housing costs on consumer pocketbooks by including only the gain in rental value, which was known to dramatically lag the real costs of owning a home as real estate prices skyrocketed.

Understated inflation is a crucial feature of the Great Deception in the age of Obama. As I have pointed out, if U.S. consumer inflation data were collected and reported on the same basis as they were during the Carter administration, year-over-year inflation in September 2012 would have been 9.6%. For simple reasons of arithmetic, unrealistically low, official inflation not only means lower cost-of-living adjustments for beneficiaries of entitlements, it also means overstated real growth.

The official, September 2012 Consumer Price Index (CPI-U) showed that the annual inflation rate grew from 1.7% to 2.0% — just 20% of the "real" inflation rate as it would have been measured before politicians plotted to disguise the greater part of soaring living costs. Obviously, if inflation were still measured in the more exacting way that it was during the Carter administration, the difference between inflation of 9.6% and 2% — 7.6 percentage points of statistical fudge — would not be overstating real GDP growth, real retail sales, and real household income. By changing the way that inflation data are compiled and reported, the government not only saved trillions that otherwise would have been paid cost-of-living adjustments for Social Security recipients and other pensioners, it also painted a rosier picture of real economic growth than is justified by the underlying reality.

A closer look at the composition of the U.S. economy shows that a major part of the U.S. private sector — almost 14% — disappeared between 2007, the start of the officially measured recession, and 2009, when a recovery allegedly began. Private economic activity plunged by $1.3 trillion while the measurement of the total GDP remained deceptively stable because the collapse in private activity was covered over by a $1 trillion surge in government spending. Hence the deceptive impression that the economy shrank by only $300 billion, or just about 2%.

The actual situation was far more ominous. Almost 14% of the U.S. private sector had disappeared — a loss that was papered over by an unsustainable surge of $1 trillion of government spending from an empty pocket.

Of course, you might make the mistake of supposing that consideration of the economy is less deceptive and more realistic where runaway deficits are concerned. Wrong. The presentation of the deficit itself is another installment in the Great Deception. For one thing, the noisy debate over deficit reduction in Washington focuses only on the headline "cash deficit" of the U.S. government. If you listen to politicians' speeches and read the newspapers that give credibility to their lies, you could come away with the false impression that the financial picture of the U.S. government is improving. Witness the headline from an October 12, 2012 article in *The New York Times*: "Federal Deficit for 2012 Fiscal Year Falls to $1.1 Trillion."

A narrowing deficit sounds like good news. But it is merely more deception. Executives of a public company who pretended that their financial picture had improved by reporting a decline in their "cash deficit" equivalent to that in Washington would be subject to prosecution and imprisonment for criminal fraud. The SEC requires that the accounts of public companies be kept according to Generally Accepted Accounting Principles (or GAAP standards).

Examine federal finances from that perspective, and you see not a falling deficit, but an exploding, runaway deficit enlarged from an average of $5 trillion for every year since 2004 to a staggering $7 trillion for fiscal year 2012 — roughly half of GDP. Meanwhile, what passes for economic growth added $165.13 billion to federal receipts. Revenues grew at a smidgen over 2% of the growth rate of the net present value of liabilities, which now stands at approximately $90 trillion, according to John Williams of Shadow Government Statistics. (Prof. Laurence Kotlikoff says that the current sum of explicit debts and unfunded promises nets out at $211 trillion). But who's counting? Either amount is greater than the total "GDP" of the world.

And more to the point, particularly if you are an American, the $90 trillion tally for the net present value of U.S. government liabilities is 50% greater than the total wealth of Americans. Think about that. Obama's Czar of Middle Class recovery, Prof. Larry Summers of Harvard University, pegs the total wealth of Americans at $60 trillion. This means that, implicitly, you are broke. And so is every American. The U.S. government could confiscate and tax away every penny of wealth owned by you and other Americans, and it would still be $30 trillion short of balancing its accrual deficit.

The annual GAAP Accounting of the finances of the U.S. government provide something of a proxy determining for the growth rate required to avoid total, wipeout insolvency. Before Obama, the GAAP deficit had been running at approximately $5 trillion per annum, and more recently at about $7 trillion. This now amounts to about 50% of the $14 trillion U.S. economy. The Congressional Budget Office (CBO) estimates that economic growth will add $105 billion to federal receipts — or 0.021% of the growth in liabilities.

Or, to look at it another way, last year's federal tax receipts rose by $165.13 billion, a gain presumably attributable to the dwindling momentum of economic growth. Not much compared to the $7 trillion deficit in GAAP terms.

It does not take a genius to realize that, when liabilities are growing by almost 50% of GDP annually, and the underlying economy is creeping along with real growth at 1.5%–2%, that paying those liabilities from growth or higher taxes is a fantasy.

That implies a far worse budget picture than the honorable members of Congress entertained in their deliberations over the Fiscal Cliff.

Both major parties have connived at the misreporting of economic statistics. In particular, they have joined in a mutual sleight of hand in dealing with inflation that has caused untold confusion about the true state of the U.S. economy. Even many fiscal conservatives have winked at a succession of statistical gimmicks introduced over the years that have altered the way inflation is measured and reported.

Witness, for example, the suggestion forwarded by House Speaker John Boehner (and accepted by Obama), as part of the Fiscal Cliff negotiations, that the government resort to even more heavily gamed "Chained CPI" inflation reporting to reduce Social Security COLA (cost of living adjustments) by another $250 billion over 10 years.

The Great Deception

And this brings me to another implication of Lord Keynes' recognition that "most of us offer great resistance to acting [on the idea] of the future being different from the present."

That is not exactly a prediction from a master of investment psychology that the U.S. public is unlikely to "be realistic" and accept lower welfare state entitlements. But that is an unavoidable implication of Lord Keynes' insight. We struggle to understand what the future will be like and we find it repugnant that it will be different. Obviously, the fact that the net present value of U.S. government liabilities exceeds the total wealth of Americans by 50% proves that there is very little public appetite for facing reality.

As businessman Jim Rogers put it in a recent interview:

> In 1918, right at the end of the First World War, the U.K. was the richest, most powerful country in the world… Within three generations, the U.K. was bankrupt. They couldn't sell government bonds. The IMF had to bail them out. So I suspect this will be the ultimate end for the U.S. The French went through it, the Italians went through it, the Spanish went through it — a lot of people have been in this situation before. They refused to accept reality, they go into a steady decline, and eventually the whole thing falls apart.

The exact route by which "things fall apart" is always "to be determined" as long as fiat money is created through the banking system.

That means that the surfeit of paper claims on the real economy can be obliterated through system price reversals. Deflation, in other words. As 2014 drew to an end, the power of the deflationary impulse was evident in plunging commodity prices, and associated debt distress. The 50% decline in the price of iron ore was mirrored by a 50% increase in the volume of non-performing loans in the Chinese banking sector since early 2013, much of it associated with zombie production of steel products, a sector plagued by enormous overcapacity. The question is whether the associated debts will be obliterated through deflationary default as a dollar rally continues, or by the inflationary emission of more fiat money.

It is rather like the debate about whether the world will end in fire. Or ice. The dynamic of deflation is powered by market adjustments. If the political process determines the outcome, it will be inflationary.

Let's take a closer look at where the political road will take you.

If you were to spend even an hour studying the history of hyperinflations, you could not miss the fact that governments throughout history have resorted to currency debasement to pay their bills when available revenues fell short of what was required. From 1980 through 1997, the price level in Brazil increased one trillion-fold due to monetizing budget deficits that never swelled as large in terms of percentage of GDP as those in the U.S. under Obama.

Other countries employing fiat money experienced devastating hyperinflation when runaway budget deficits were monetized. A common feature of these episodes was that they started slowly. In Germany, Austria, China, Turkey and even in Zimbabwe, the man in the street was slow to recognize the impact of currency depreciation when deficits were financed by creating money out of thin air.

As one of the more recent examples of "Quantitative Easing" taken to an extreme, Zimbabwe is interesting because it shows how slowly hyperinflation may develop in response to the monetization of runaway deficits, and then how drastically and rapidly the currency may collapse.

Zimbabwe began running large, chronic deficits and financing them with printing press money immediately after Robert Mugabe's forces overthrew Ian Smith and assumed power in the former Rhodesia in 1980.

Even though they ran large deficits in a chronic fashion, merrily printing money as they went along, measured inflation in Zimbabwe never rose above 15% — at least not for the first two decades. For a long time, they seemed to be getting away with it. Even a government run by an increasingly despotic Robert Mugabe could indulge in two decades of profligacy before anyone seemed to notice.

But notice they did. Eventually. Inflation rates remained relatively tame for two decades after the deficits began. But by November 2001, the monthly inflation rate had jumped to 200%. By April 2006, the monthly rate surged upward, as reported by Dr. Albert Makochekanwa in "Impact of Budget Deficit on Inflation in Zimbabwe," "with the monthly trend reaching 164,900.3% in February 2008."

A few months later, by July 2008, the inflation rate was 231.2 million percent. And by September 2008, the IMF estimated a hyperinflation rate at 489,000,000,000%. The record year of quantitative easing drew to a close with an inflation rate at 6.5 quindecillion novemdecillion percent. (65 followed by

107 zeros). Try pronouncing that astronomical number in a hurry. It is out of this world, but according to Johns Hopkins economics Prof. Steve Hanke, that was the cumulative inflation rate in Zimbabwe as of December 2008.

By all accounts, inflation was ludicrously high and ruinous. The Zimbabwe dollar, at long last, was so thoroughly discredited that it became a logistical nightmare to keep the denominations of currency rising fast enough to keep pace with the collapse in value of the money supply. There were not enough forests in the world to provide sufficient paper to have bought a dozen Happy Meals at McDonald's with $1 Zimbabwe notes. Denominations had to soar, not merely to save the forests, but to permit the public to physically carry enough cash to buy anything. As a reminder of what runaway deficits can do, I keep a Zimbabwean currency note for $100 billion in my wallet.

Luckily, Zimbabwe enjoyed its hyperinflation before the U.S. took to imitating Zimbabwe's fiscal policy. When hyper budget deficits led to hyperinflation of the Zimbabwe dollar, Zimbabwe adopted the U.S. dollar.

If you think about it, Keynes' views on "the continuity and stability of conventional behavior," (to use economist Bill Gerrard's phrase), help explain the advent and course of hyperinflation.

So long as the paper money produced out of thin air looks identical and shows the same denominations as the older, familiar bank notes, gullible people who expect the future to be no different from the past readily accept the rapidly inflating currency at old values. That is why the path to hyperinflation seems to be undertaken in slow motion, with people apparently unable to notice that they are actually racing down the road to ruin. Yet the sluggishness of perception works both ways. Once a currency is finally discredited, it is all but impossible to restore.

This is why it might be wise to begin planning now to prepare for the ruin that Obama's policies promise.

CHAPTER 14

The End Looms for the "Something for Nothing" Society

"Unfortunately, we can't print oil."

— Ben Bernanke

Here is a frightening thought: Suppose society had to live within the straitjacket of what it actually earned. And further to that, suppose you actually had to pay for the good and not-so-good things society demands from government, rather than passing them on for others to pay with taxes or to children and grandchildren in the form of an exponentially growing national debt.

That would entail a drastic change from current practice. It implies the end of "pay-as-you-go" retirement schemes like Social Security. To keep it solvent, the U.S. would need much larger cohorts of young workers and an average growth rate of 8% or higher. Neither of those things is going to happen. The nanny state that offered citizens a promise of meeting all of their urgent life needs — that formerly would have been supported from savings — was a faulty construct that has outlived its time.

Stand back and take a look. Wherever you turn, stories from around the world are variations on the same theme. Populations are growing indignant over the looming prospect that the age of "something for nothing" is drawing to an end. That is what the European debt crisis is all about. And this was in the news in the U.S. as "Occupy Wall Street" protesters cried out for income redistribution and make-work jobs.

Angry Greeks crowded into Syntagma Square in Athens to bellyache that foreign investors have tired of subsidizing their indolent lifestyles.

They consider it an outrage that German taxpayers decline to foot the bill for early retirement at an average of 94% of working income. With government employment comprising up to one third of total jobs in Greece (according to *The New York Times*), rioting public employees felt badly used by the fact that some benefactor, somewhere, was not stepping in to pick up the tab for all the cushy jobs that couldn't pay their way.

Closer to home, Occupy Wall Street protesters chanted that "education should be free, like air and water." In public parks across the United States and Canada, unemployed protesters erected base camps for organized shouting at passersby through electrified megaphones. "We are the 99%. Tax the 1%!" they yelled.

Note the not-so-subtle insistence on something for nothing. According to figures from the Internal Revenue Service, the top 1% of income taxpayers have recently paid more than 40% of all income taxes, an amount greater than the bottom 95% of filers combined. This isn't good enough for Occupy Wall Street. Apparently, they require a system in which the top 1% pay the bills for everyone, including the 4% of the income distribution, with adjusted gross incomes between $166,210 and $358,423 (2014 figures).

Talk about marginal tax rates. If Occupy Wall Street got its way and the top 1% had to foot the bill for the top 2% through the top 4%, as well as the bottom 95%, the marginal burden on earning the last dollar would be incredible. It would soon flush into the open the unhappy arithmetic of insolvency. There simply aren't enough super-rich people to pay the ever-escalating demands for "something for nothing."

No Such Thing as "Free" Services

The "tax the rich" calls are not so much coherent fiscal policy as social pathology that reflects the deep bewilderment of a large segment of the populations of the United States and European countries. These are people who believed all the bunk they have been told. They have taken to heart the fond delusion that the nanny state can lavish money and/or services on them for free.

A moment's reflection shows that this is impossible. There is no magic wand that could conjure up an education as free as "air and water." And even so-called free water is not without cost.

Someone must foot the bill for the infrastructure of pipes, pumps, chemicals and aqueducts that transports water from municipal and regional sewer systems, cleans it inadequately, and then returns it to your taps. Not since Marcus Agrippa, the protégé of the Emperor Augustus, repaired three of the city of Rome's aqueducts and built a new one at his personal expense, along with 700 cisterns, 500 fountains, and 130 distribution tanks in the year 33 AD, has there been any such thing as water being provided free as a gift.

A study from 2011 suggests that a huge surge in the incidence of prostate cancer in men over the past 40 years is related to the growing use of birth control pills among women. This underscores the risks involved in providing inadequate investment in water purification infrastructure.

You see, women using birth control pills excrete estrogen hormones in their urine. Unfortunately, however, public water purification systems in the United States and other "advanced countries" do not remove hormones from the water when it is recycled from sewer systems. As a result, men drinking municipal water are dosing themselves with estrogen. This has the unwelcome effect of greatly increasing the risk of prostate cancer, the incidence of which has soared.

So "free" water is not free at all. The water from your taps is less health-ful than that which coursed through the pipes 2,000 years ago in the Rome of Marco Agrippa's day. If you want healthful water, you must drink from a source that does not include recycled urban sewer water. Unfortunately, truly clean water from deep, rural aquifers is difficult and costly to come by.

Slaves to Energy

The great illusion of the nanny state — that it could provide people with free benefits — was erected on the back of rapidly increasing energy inputs. As we have explored, living standards skyrocketed with a massive infusion of dense hydrocarbon energy, particularly following the launch of the world oil industry in 1859 by Col. Edwin Drake at Titusville Pennsylvania.

Of course, no one at the time understood the impact that a 4,000,000% increase in energy inputs would have on the economy. Witness the fact that within a year or two the United States was engaged in fighting a protracted and bloody civil war ostensibly to "end slavery." Clearly, the soldiers who embarked on this deadly struggle were unaware that the discovery of oil would soon make slavery a non-issue. When gasoline-powered tractors and harvesters could replace slaves, even in plantation farming, the enslavement of human somatic energy (muscle power) equivalent to 1/20 horse power per annum no longer made economic sense.

But while engines powered by oil antiquated chattel slavery, they provided an unprecedented stimulus to the growth of government and an increase in the predatory extraction of resources from the population. Federal government spending as a percentage of GDP rose almost 30 times over from 1850 to the present.

Oil power not only made government bigger and richer, it did so within the context of a dramatic increase in the rate of economic growth. Prior to the Industrial Revolution, economic growth was erratic — almost entirely a function of cyclically warmer weather. When weather turned colder again, economic growth receded with crop yields. The pilgrims who left Europe to colonize North America in the 17th century lived less well than the Romans of Caesar's time who enjoyed much warmer weather. Grapes and citrus trees grew in England as far north as Hadrian's Wall. (Yet another illustration of the fact that hysteria over Global Warming is a historical bunk.)

The long-term compounding of economic growth made possible by the dense BTUs extracted from coal and then oil represents a dramatic departure from all past history. By increasing the margin over subsistence, growth fueled by oil permitted a vast expansion of predatory government.

Unprecedented Debt Expansion

Rapid economic growth also facilitated a change away from commodity-based money to pure credit or fiat money that is created out of thin air by governments and banks. But at a price. That price is the interest paid on money borrowed into existence.

In practice, rapid growth proved to be closely aligned with the rapid expansion of debt. The crux of the issue was the fact that an elastic capacity to expand debt accelerated growth by seeming to transcend the necessity of saving before investing. With potentially rapid credit growth, resources for investment could seemingly be conjured out of thin air by the banking system forestalling the need to save by economizing on other spending to fund outlays. (Of course, Austrian economists have long argued that in the apparent triumph over the need for savings was an illusion. They contend that investment funded through credit expansion becomes mal-investment, a view that was reinforced when more than one trillion dollars was poured into an already overbuilt U.S. housing stock in the first decade of this century.)

A hint of the dynamic incompatibility of a commodity-based money like the gold standard and debt expansion is provided by the contrast of these two numbers:

1) The compound rate of growth of global gold production in metric tons from 1900 through 2010 was 1.17%;

2) The compound annual growth rate of the U.S. national debt from 1900 to 2010 was 8.28%. The National debt, a proxy for debt in general, expanded more than seven times faster than gold production.

Because the debt was compounding from a very low level in 1900, and gold was relatively overvalued in its 1933 revaluation to $35 an ounce, there was sufficient "slack" in the system to permit a large measure of deficit spending in the U.S. prior to the 1960s.

But as the deficits from the Vietnam War and Lyndon Johnson's Great Society accumulated, the average spot price of gold began to poke above the official fix at $35. By 1968, it averaged $39.31. At that point, the gold reserve standard began to exercise a restraining influence on debt growth. CNN's David Frum, a remorseless Keynesian, explains why in his review of the impact of the gold standard in restraining deficits during the Great Depression:

> But why did decision-makers make so many bad decisions? The short answer is that they were trapped. Almost all of the right decisions (as he imagined them) would have ballooned the U.S. federal budget deficit. As budget deficits expanded, investors would inevitably worry that their dollars might lose value in the future. They would demand to trade their dollars for gold at the fixed price of $20.67 to the ounce. Under the rules of the gold standard, the U.S. government would be obliged to sell. As long as the deficits continued, the U.S. government would lose gold. Threatened with the exhaustion of its gold supply, the government felt it had no choice: It had to close the budget deficit.

In other words, what Frum does not like about the gold standard is precisely that it short-circuited the growth of debt at a much earlier point than is the case now. The gold standard helped prevent the fleecing of savers.

The Deindustrialization of the U.S.

In the decades after World War II, when energy inputs in the U.S. economy were rising rapidly, so was per capita income. But as discussed elsewhere, U.S. oil production peaked in 1970–71. This coincided with several crucial developments.

- Richard Nixon repudiated the gold reserve standard severing the last link between the dollar and gold. This set the stage for an 18-fold increase in the U.S. money supply from 1971 to the present.

- National Association of Securities Dealers founded the NASDAQ Stock market, which began trading in February, 1971 at an initial index value of 100. With it, they introduced the concept of the IPO for growth companies. As I write, the most recent NASDAQ closing value is 4944.16, an increase of more than 49-fold in 44 years. That is even higher than the 17-fold growth of the broad money supply since 1971.

- Meanwhile, officially measured inflation rose by slightly more than five times over as the dollar lost 82% of its value. This helps explain how the conversion to a debt society helped aggravate income disparities. The greatest portion of credit expansion was diverted into the inflation of asset values. Obviously, the minority of the population that owns stocks benefited disproportionately from a 25-fold increase in their value.

- The growth in real per capita income came to a halt along with the increase in per capita energy inputs. Per capita energy consumption stalled at about 70 million BTUs per head and has been fluctuating around that plateau since 1972. Perhaps not by coincidence, that was when the real income of production workers stalled out.

- Note that energy inputs and consumption per dollar of GDP have been sliding dramatically and are now less than half what they were in the early '70s.

Advocates of energy efficiency, ever eager to confuse the public, extol the benefits of declining per capita energy inputs in the United States. They miss the fact that, as energy use per capita has declined, so have real wages along with the genuine prosperity of the American middle class.

In fact, one of the simpler explanations for the "deindustrialization" of the United States is that manufacturing was priced out of access to energy, leading energy intensive industries to move overseas. The price-driven push for "energy efficiency" was a major factor in the outsourcing of manufacturing from the United States.

Financialization – The Ultimate in Energy-Efficient Profits

Equally, the increasing cost of energy was also a factor pushing the U.S. toward "financialization" where every effort was made to maximize profits through financial manipulation, which entails low energy inputs. This is why financial sector debt exploded by about 65% and financial market capitalization as a percentage of the S&P 500 shot up from around 7% as recently as 1990 to over 22% in 2007 on the eve of the Great Correction.

A Bleak Future Ahead?

I believe that before the still imaginary "deleveraging" cycle is complete, the market capitalization of financial stocks will fall within a range of 3%–4% of the total value of the S&P 500. This is a much lower value than what is forecast by most observers.

The lower numbers are justified, I believe. Here's why:

Firstly, I am both an optimist and pessimist about the U.S. capital markets. Currently, the U.S. has the deepest, most liquid markets in the world. I am optimistic in believing that U.S. capital markets will continue to function more or less efficiently, even as the frontiers of prosperity migrate elsewhere. As a matter of pure logic, the greater the percentage of S&P capitalization of economic activity outside the United States, the smaller the market cap of U.S. banks is likely to be as a percentage of the whole.

Secondly, as I look ahead I foresee that banks and other financial institutions, like insurance companies, will be severely strained by the collapse of growth in the advanced economies. They will be hard-pressed to achieve their investment benchmarks that were set at times in the past when economic growth was more rapid then it has been during the 21st century. Stagnation will also make it impossible for a great many debtors to meet the interest service on their obligations, much less repay principal.

I foresee a bleak future, not only for private debtors whose capacity to repay will be shattered by the end of the growth, but nonetheless many private debtors will prove to be better credits than sovereigns.

Remember, some companies can prosper even if a whole economy, in aggregate, does not. Firms like Apple, which holds more cash than the U.S. government, can pay its debts even if the government can't.

I expect that OECD sovereign debtors will prove to be worse credits than many corporations. The sovereign obligations are essentially call options on the future growth of economies over which particular governments hold taxing power. Contrary to expectation, that growth will not materialize, devastating a core asset base of the OECD banking and insurance institutions.

The result to be expected is widespread insolvency and the collapse in the value of collateral. As the eurozone crisis demonstrates, even sovereign debtors can go bust. With governments having run down their balance sheets, it is far from a sure thing that they will be able to step in and bail out banks swamped by the next wave of insolvency.

As long as the political system retains even a tincture of democratic checks and balances, it will be difficult to mobilize support from a sinking middle class for additional bank bailouts. Consider the following perspective from Kenneth Rogoff, author of "This Time is Different," and former chief economist at the IMF:

> Most of the world's largest banks are essentially insolvent, and depend on continuing government aid and loans to keep them afloat. Many banks have already acknowledged their open-ended losses in residential mortgages. As the recession deepens, however, bank balance sheets will be hammered further by a wave of defaults in commercial real estate, credit cards, private equity, and hedge funds. As governments try to avoid outright nationalization of banks, they will find themselves being forced to carry out second and third recapitalizations.

> Even the extravagant bailout of financial giant Citigroup, in which the U.S. government has poured in $45 billion of capital and backstopped losses on over $300 billion in bad loans, may ultimately prove inadequate.

I believe that before this crisis is resolved we will see a transformation of money and banking to a system centered on gold, that has the splendid characteristic of being a monetary asset that is not someone else's liability. The constraints on credit growth implied by a gold standard will make banking a much more boring business, with lower footings. This lack of leverage will inevitably find expression in the skinnier Price-to-Earnings (P/E) multiples.

Still another consideration that points to a relative shrinkage of the financial sector in the future of the United States is the fact that economic decline in the current depression will obliterate the cultural conditions conducive to debt. Bankrupt baby boomers will refocus their attentions toward savings and thrift rather than spending. Note that Q4, 2014 was the 26th consecutive quarter when households reduced debt — a record. This indicates that the culture of debt inculcated by the rapid economic growth facilitated by the historically transient surge of cheap oil in the economy has already begun to fade.

Emerging Markets Boom While
the West Drowns in Debt?

A somewhat confusing footnote about economic performance over the years, immediately following the Great Correction that began in 2007, is the fantastic difference in growth between the leading emerging (middle income) economies and the so-called "advanced economies" of North America, Europe and Japan.

Brazil, China and India grew, respectively, 30 times, 70 times and 48 times faster than the United States and infinitely faster than Europe and Japan through 2011. During that period, the European Union GDP shrank by 0.3%, according to data for the second quarter of 2011. Meanwhile, data over the same period showed that Japan's GDP fell by 5.2%, while the U.S. eked out a gain of just 0.6%. By contrast, China's GDP rose by 42.2%, India's by 28.6% and Brazil's by more than 17%.

Undoubtedly, some of the vastly superior performance of the leading middle income economies was attributable to Bill Bonner's backhoe (and the recipe it symbolizes for incorporating vastly more productive energy-intensive work). But as this decade has unfolded, it has seemed ever more apparent that the BRICS and other middle income economies have all collided with structural impediments to growth, that threaten to make them vulnerable to withdrawal from the QE punch bowl.

In the years since the Lehman collapse, $5.7 trillion (in U.S. dollars) poured into emerging markets, a development that we analyze more fully in Chapter 20. But a hint that QE was stimulating emerging economies more than the developed world was delivered in January, 2014, when widely articulated fears that the U.S. Federal Reserve would taper its QE program triggered a wide-spread selloff of emerging market currencies and assets.

The plunge in emerging market currencies was the flip side of the coin to a U.S. dollar rally. With the dollar having broken out of a multi-year range, it is creating a powerful short squeeze on emerging market borrowers who owe U.S. $5.7 trillion.

Consequently, there is a non-trivial risk that you will see more emerging market "risk assets" (investments financed by borrowed dollars) blow up. Oil and other plunging commodities could be just the beginning of a deflationary end game to a seven-decade debt expansion dating to World War II.

So the deepest stage of the coming depression may take its deepest toll on the BRICS and the other middle income economies that have enjoyed the most robust growth in recent years. If this happens, it will parallel the trajectory of the United States, the economy that grew most robustly in the 1920s, and suffered the deepest contraction among major economies after 1929.

Still, the vastly superior performance of the leading emerging economies in the wake of the Great Recession raises a crucial question for you and every thinking investor. Why? Why were Brazil, China and India able to register robust growth while the advanced economies stagnated or declined? In 2010, Brazil's GDP grew by 7.5%, China's by 10.8% and India's by 10.4%. What accounts for their huge performance gap over the U.S., Europe and Japan?

Various theories can be advanced. Policy wonks generally favor explanations that turn on policy differences. There are several from which to choose. One of the more prominently quoted is the Index of Economic Freedom published annually by the Heritage Foundation.

I am a convinced advocate of economic freedom, but it is far from obvious that these stylized rankings are accurate. As Swedish economist Stefan Karlsson argued in a paper for the Mises Institute in 2005, the methodology of the Index of Economic Freedom seems to be prejudiced to provide high rankings to OECD welfare states. Karlsson particularly criticized the high-ranking of Sweden as compared to China.

> For example, take Sweden and China. Which of these is the most free? On the one hand, Sweden has an enormous welfare state spending more than 55% of GDP and also has extremely powerful unions which have been given the power by the state to force companies operating in Sweden to obey their command, while China has public spending only about 20% of GDP and has no unions with any real power. Moreover labor and environmental laws are far more intrusive in Sweden than in China.

In short, economic freedom has many dimensions. It is far from obvious that Denmark is a freer country than the United States, or for that matter that the United States is freer than Mexico when many American cancer patients feel the need to travel there to undertake treatments that are permitted in that country but prohibited in the U.S. The cancer treatments can legitimately be considered a matter of "life and death." Yet the U.S. government denies Americans the right to enter into these transactions.

Whatever else it may be, that is not economic freedom.

In any event, the 2014 Economic Freedom Index rankings placed Brazil highest among the BRIC countries with a world rank of 118, followed by India at 128 and China at 139. Russia brings up the rear with a ranking of 143. Notably, all the BRIC countries were reported to have increased economic freedom over the previous year. And according to the World Economic Forum, Brazil led the globe in improving its economic competitiveness.

While economic freedom is a good thing, and it is certainly better to be seen as improving competitiveness rather than not, none of this goes very far toward explaining why the leading emerging economies have outperformed the "advanced" OECD economies by such a robust margin since the Great Correction began eight years ago.

A perhaps more compelling explanation is that Brazil, China, and India were much less lumbered with debt. Indeed, as economist Ranga Chand notes:

> The Great Recession of 2008-2009 that savaged the global economy and wiped out more than 50 million jobs worldwide has also blown a giant size hole in the government finances of countless countries. Public debt levels have shot up dramatically and are still rising especially in the developed economies. In the G7, the average debt level is expected to hit 112% of GDP this year according to the IMF, up from 85% in the pre-crisis year of 2007 and in the PIGS the ratio is projected to reach 105%, up from 57%. In stark contrast, the average debt level in the emerging BRIC nations, which has better weathered the global crisis, is expected to dip to 40% of GDP this year, down from 42% in 2007.

Debt: A Symptom of a Bigger Problem

The problem is not confined to the sovereign debt. The breakdown of income growth following the "peak oil" moment of 40 years ago was partially disguised by a massive increase in household debt. Adjusted for inflation, the average American man now makes more than $800 less annually than did a fully employed man in 1970. Meanwhile, however, household debt grew from a trivial amount to exceed U.S. GDP by the middle of the last decade. But, as indicated above, the attempt to disguise the collapse of income growth by compounding debt ultimately fails.

The fact that consumers in the old industrialized countries, like the governments of those countries themselves, are overextended in debt is not merely a problem, per se, it is also a symptom of a deeper problem — the decline of energy inputs. As analyst Gregor MacDonald put it:

It is highly unlikely that long-dated paper assets will ever regain their purchasing power against natural resources, because, while human innovation and technology will surely continue, the energy limit is only surmountable in small, incremental terms. Indeed, most of the revolutionary technology of the past 250 years has neither operated outside of cheap energy nor created cheap energy. Instead our technological era leveraged cheap energy... The advances made possible once humans started extracting fossil fuels, while likely to be repeated in humanistic terms, will not be repeated in industrial terms. Fossil fuels are not creatable. Their unique density made possible a whole range of laborious, constructive activities at a speed and scale that is not replicable.

A crucial, underlying reason for the rapid economic growth enjoyed by the leading emerging economies, while the old industrial economies stagnate or decline, is the fact that they are able to profitably increase primary energy consumption at prices that are uneconomic for the OECD countries. The old industrialized economies, as most prominently represented by the United States, Europe and Japan suffer from declining marginal returns across a large frontier of activities.

By contrast, the more dynamic emerging economies can profitably deploy energy inputs at much higher prices than the so-called advanced economies can afford. As you've no doubt learned, total primary energy consumption in Brazil, Russia, India and China has soared in the past decade. Brazil and Russia led the consumption growth with gains around 10% in 2009 through 2010. In Brazil total energy consumption has increased by about one third while 39 million Brazilians rose from poverty due to soaring economic growth over the past decade. During 2010, the growth of energy consumption in China and India declined from the pace of 2008–2009, but was sufficient to see China surpass the United States as the world's largest consumer of energy.

Crucially, as Gregor MacDonald advises:

100% of the new demand for global oil since 2005, mostly coming from the non-OECD, has not been met by new supply. Instead, in a world of flat oil production, the resources for the developing world have come solely from a reduction of demand in the developed nations. Global oil supply is now a zero-sum game.

As energy prices are bid higher, not only do the BRICs have the capacity to profitably pay for oil and coal, they're also much better positioned to utilize "alternative" and renewable energy sources. Two of the world's three largest hydroelectric facilities are in Brazil. The third is in China.

We have already taken advantage of the fact that an astonishing 84% of Brazil's electricity is generated by renewable, hydroelectric facilities. In a world without growth, the income realized from the profits from renewable energy in an economy that can still grow represent a much stronger credit than U.S. Treasury bonds or German Bunds.

For the first time since before the Industrial Revolution, you could be looking ahead to a world with a flat horizon of growth. That is to say, there may be none at all in the high cost OECD industrialized economies that are already suffering from declining marginal returns in many areas.

A surprisingly frank acknowledgment of this bleak reality was recently reported by China's vice Premier and head of finance, Wang Qishan. Wang said in the *Financial Times*:

> Now the global economic situation is extremely serious and in a time of uncertainty the only thing we can be certain of is that the world economic recession caused by the international crisis will last a long time.

Notwithstanding the glad talk about U.S. leading indicators looking up, Europe is already in a recession. And that makes a recession in the U.S. 86% likely. Only once in the past has one economy managed to escape the downturn experienced in the other. This is ominous news for those hoping for a return to "business as usual."

The "something-for-nothing" world as experienced in the United States in the second half of the 20th century is drawing to an end.

What happened in the United States has happened in other OECD countries. Japan is well and truly busted. Remorseless "stimulus" spending out of an empty pocket has brought the Japanese national debt to more than 210% of GDP. Japan's downturn is now in its third decade. Some of its many elderly retirees grew old waiting for recovery from the collapse in 1989.

Europe is equally sclerotic. Do you want to get a better grip on how sclerotic? Scour your dresser top and look behind the sofa cushions. Any loose change you find is worth more than all the economic growth realized in Italy since the end of the last century. That is right. Italy has realized not a single euro's worth of economic growth in this century. Yet its debt compounds year-to-year with no obvious remedy in sight. It is conclusively clear that Italy will be unable, under current terms, to grow out of its debt. The country is falling deeper and deeper into a debt trap with each year that passes. It is only a matter of time until Italy defaults on its debt. The same can be said of Germany, as well as Japan.

And yes, the United States, having abused the privilege of issuing the world's reserve currency, has run up the greatest deficits in the history of the world.

The time of "something-for-nothing" is coming to an end. It won't end well.

CHAPTER 15

The Worn-Out Status Quo

"Cheap energy keeps our cars and factories running. It leaves homeowners with money to repay their mortgages, and permits the long-distance transfer of goods needed for globalization…When economies of countries are able to grow rapidly, they can repay their debt with interest. But as growth wanes, it becomes much more difficult to repay debt, and many more defaults occur. Our debt-based financial system needs growth to continue. It is not a Ponzi scheme, but it has the same problem with not being sustainable without growth."

— Gail Tverberg, The Oil Drum

A reason that forward vision is obscured in current circumstances is that the status quo is shot. Worn out. There is no way it can survive in its present form. Yet this very self-evident fact adds a surreal element to America's political discourse. So-called "liberals" differ from conservatives only in the intensity of their fealty to the various features of an anachronistic industrial, welfare/warfare state.

America's most animated political debates are all about preserving the status quo. No one wants to hear or recognize that the status quo is shot. The older generations, in particular, were encouraged by politicians to treat the public till as a giant wishing well, where they could magically satisfy life's pressing needs — at someone else's expense. Social Security… Medicare… prescription drugs… they all represent trillions upon trillions of unfunded liabilities that would require the greater part of — if not the total of — the wealth of the world to satisfy. But this arithmetic means nothing to an infatuated electorate, whose members believe themselves to be entitled to maintain high standards of living, no matter what.

Why not? We've gotten away with it for so long.

Free Lunch, And More

For decades, Americans have managed to elude reality while capturing significant subsidies from the rest of the world. Investors and average citizens around the globe have underwritten as much as 8% to 10% of U.S. living standards.

It probably should go without saying that it is a rare circumstance indeed when a whole country can enjoy a "free lunch" daily at someone else's expense. I use this expression because it represents the classic example of an impossible treat. As they say, "There is no such thing as a free lunch."

In this case, however, the magnitude of subsidies from abroad far exceeds the entire annual lunch tab for everyone in the United States. According to the USDA economic research service, as of 2004, only 9.5% of income in the U.S. was spent for food consumed in all meals. In other words, subsidies from abroad pay for breakfast, lunch and dinner for all Americans. This is a ridiculous situation that cannot stand the test of time.

We have been subsidized from abroad, particularly by the two largest emerging economies — China and Brazil — with additional subsidies from Japan, the other BRICS and some OPEC countries.

U.S. Liabilities Should Scare You

In researching a previous book, I found that as of June 2014, the U.S. Treasury owes roughly $864 to each and every citizen of China and $1,202 to each Brazilian. And we owe other vast sums just about everywhere.

This is one example of the costs imposed on others by the remorseless exploitation of the U.S.'s ability to print the world's reserve currency — the dollar. The U.S. not only has a national debt exceeding 100% of GDP, but we have created unfunded liabilities in astronomical sums.

Professor Laurence Kotlikoff puts the total obligations of the U.S. government at $205 trillion. For reference, that is more than two times About.com's estimate of the world GDP — $87.18 trillion in May of 2014.

Bear this in mind, because it shows that it is completely implausible that tax increases could answer for unfunded liabilities that are triple the size of the world economy. (For what it's worth, this also suggests there will be hyperinflation in your future to extinguish out-sized dollar liabilities. Presumably, in decades to come, Americans will be as wary of promises of future benefits as Brazilians have been).

So what should you make of these numbers detailing total U.S. liabilities?

They are not closely guarded, top secret details that I wrested from the inner sanctums of the Treasury by stealth. As Prof. Kotlikoff emphasizes, these calculations are all based upon public data. While there could be some quibbles about the timeline on amounts owed and the present value of the liabilities, the broad outline is indisputable.

This underscores the conclusion that the American electorate is the most unrealistic in the world. I doubt there is a precinct in Athens where the voters are more determinedly deluded than the median voter in the U.S.

It should come as no surprise that American voters are unrealistic. Most of us have been told all our lives that "the United States is the richest country in the world." This may be sloppy accounting, but mostly it is nostalgia. Once upon a time — in the middle of the last century — the U.S. was the world's richest country and that, in turn, resulted in Americans enjoying more "pixie dust" in our political wishing well than the residents of any other country.

The U.S. Government's Pixie Dust

What do I mean?

I am talking about the huge surge of hydrocarbon energy that accelerated economic growth, as well as permitted a surge in the growth of the U.S. government from the middle of the 19th century onward.

The best analyses of pre-industrial economies show that an economy powered by human energy could generate only about one-twentieth of one horsepower per capita annually — not much. There was very little margin above subsistence for politicians to exploit. By contrast, industrial systems powered by hydrocarbon energy put tens of thousands of times more annual energy per capita to work in the economy.

As I detailed in my book, "Brazil is the New America," the advent of hydrocarbon energy multiplied per capita energy inputs in the U.S. economy by more than 4,000,000% from 1850 to 1990. That included an unprecedented 792-fold increase from 1890 to 1990. By contrast, biophysical economist Kurt Cobb reports that while human population rose 5.3 times from 1850 to 2010, overall human energy consumption rose 45-fold.

So the U.S. enjoyed a disproportionate share of the surge in hydrocarbon energy that fueled the growth of prosperity, and thus supported the growth of big government.

Notwithstanding the myth of "limited government" that is discussed so prominently at the surface of American political discourse, the huge surge in cheap energy inputs provided the "pixie dust" that turned the U.S. government into a popular "wishing well" for satisfying life's needs.

In the pre-industrial, "no growth" U.S. economy of 1850, government truly was limited. Its spending amounted to only 1.8% of GDP. By 1990, it had surged to 36% of GDP. By 2014, under Obama, it had mushroomed to 39%. The U.S. government has become the biggest, richest, most bloated government in the history of the world.

As the 20th century unfolded, voters were taught that this huge, bloated government of the "richest country in the world" could answer any and all of their life needs. And, so long as hydrocarbon inputs were surging, the economy grew rapidly and the government's capacity to bribe voters with free or subsidized goodies grew as well.

Politicians were able to deliver benefits that were more or less windfalls to those receiving them:

- Subsidies to buy houses through the FHA, Fannie Mae, Freddie Mac and 20 other programs.

- Subsidized or free higher education through the "G.I. Bill."

- Retirement benefits worth far more than the contributions to Social Security.

- Subsidized or free medical care through Medicare and Medicaid.

- Prescription drug benefits heavily subsidized to recipients.

- Free food through food stamps, now known as The Supplemental Nutrition Assistance Program (SNAP), and 17 other programs.

And don't forget, a big part of the status quo of big and wealthy government to which most American voters are addicted is the "make-work" military budget that provides job openings for ill-educated youths from small towns and rural America where employment is otherwise scarce.

Cheating the System

As long ago as the 1970s, the true underlying sentiment backing America's bloated military establishment found expression in the pro-Vietnam War button, "Don't knock the war that feeds you."

This reflects the nearly universal approval of government spending that voters think is of economic benefit to them. Even voters who must know in their hearts that no country ever became great or stayed great because of all the money it owed, are nonetheless remarkably complacent about cashing checks rung out of an empty pocket.

It is not immaterial that the number of permanently disabled Americans rises with the increasing difficulty of finding work. It is now quintuple what it was when I graduated from high school. Does anyone else think that the dramatic surge in the numbers grabbing disability pensions reflects an increasing willingness among Americans to "game" the system?

Is there any valid reason to suppose that Americans are five times more decrepit today than they were in the 1960s?

I think not. But it is easy to suppose that they are five times more ready to swindle the system than they were in the '60s. This is a symptom of moral rot layered over economic rot. Mitt Romney may believe that America's best days are ahead, but I don't. I can see no reason to presume that the U.S. economy will rediscover its capability for vigorous growth, especially when the "American Gospel of Wealth/Success" is increasingly playing second fiddle to entitlement through "poverty/failure." A dispassionate analysis of the facts on economic growth would lead to very different conclusions than those Romney felt obliged to voice.

Prepare for the Inevitable Collapse

The idea that America is about to surge ahead struck me as particularly vapid. Indeed, the recent theme has more to do with preparing for the inevitable collapse of the United States. To think in terms of "collapse" may seem exaggerated — but it isn't. Just as a bicycle is destined to topple over when it loses forward momentum, so too is the modern, advanced economy when it reaches stall speed.

The U.S. economy requires a lot more forward propulsion than it is getting. It incorporates a requirement for very rapid growth. How rapid? Faster than the world has ever seen from a large economy.

Even the Chinese growth rate would be inadequate to keep the U.S. solvent. Consider the implications of the annual U.S. accrual budget deficit (as officially reported by the U.S. Treasury). It is $6.1 trillion in a $15.6 trillion economy. In other words, the liabilities have been growing at a 39% annual rate.

Pause and think about that… GDP growth at the current stated annual rate of 2.5% won't cut it.

Liabilities are mushrooming almost 20 times faster than the economy grows. This inevitably implies declining marginal returns for a whole range of government functions.

In his important study, "The Collapse of Complex Societies," Joseph A. Tainter argues that, "Once a complex society enters the stage of declining marginal returns, collapse becomes a mathematical likelihood, requiring little more than sufficient passage of time to make probable an insurmountable calamity."

As I discovered in this book, the U.S. economy has been racing headlong into biophysical limits to energy conversion that make the indefinite continuation of exponential economic growth as we have known it in the 20th century a logical impossibility.

As an investor, you need to be alert to the conditions that are conspiring to pull the rug out from under the modern, advanced economy. In simplest terms, continuing, exponential compound growth is predicated upon the exponential compound growth of hydrocarbon energy, particularly oil.

The doctrine loosely known as "Peak Oil" is undoubtedly true, at least in its broad outlines. This is a matter of pure logic. As Kurt Cobb points out, "We simply cannot process more material than is contained in the entire biosphere." There is a hard and fast limit that cannot be exceeded.

Of course, the question is where the limit of crucial inputs falls. In the next chapter, we explore more dimensions of this problem in analyzing the advent of Peak Oil, marked by plunging Energy Return on Investment (EROI) in oil. It has dropped from one hundred-to-one in the 1930s to less than ten-to-one, according to some recent calculations.

Note that "Energy Return on Investment" should perhaps be more accurately known as "Energy Return on Energy Invested (EROEI), because the biophysical limits on energy conversion are ultimately set by energy itself, not by intermediate abstractions like money.

The classic example is that of squirrels gathering nuts. If the energy released to the squirrel from eating the nuts does not exceed the energy the squirrel expends to gather and chew the nuts, the squirrel does not have a bright future. In fact, the squirrel will die.

The human economy is more complicated than the squirrel economy. We don't traffic directly in nuts. When we think of investment, we tend to confuse ourselves by thinking in terms of money.

If you asked about "energy return on investment," you would probably get an answer expressed in terms of money. Today, that would be fiat money. Dollars in most cases are the currency of record for denominating transactions in oil and other commodities and natural resources.

The fact that fiat money accounting confuses calculations of energy return on investment does not alter the underlying logic. You can reasonably infer, since it takes increasing amounts of energy to find and produce a barrel of oil, that the commodity is growing more scarce.

Part of the delusion that the United States is poised to resume rapid growth is based upon hallucinations about supposedly fantastic expansions of U.S. oil reserves due to improved technology.

One email I received screamed, "This Oil Data Will Shock the World." It went on to report a 12% jump in U.S. oil reserves from 2009 to 2010, as if this were significant. It wasn't and still isn't. The gains in U.S. reserves are entirely attributable to expanding production from the Bakken Shale formation in North Dakota and the Eagle Ford Shale in Texas. This has led to projections of hundreds of billions or trillions of barrels of U.S. oil primarily in the Green River formation in Colorado, Utah and Wyoming.

Some have asserted that, since we are increasing access to the shale in North Dakota and Texas, that the Green River formation of roughly two trillion barrels of oil resources will soon, or someday, be developed.

This is highly unlikely.

Although the oil in the Bakken and Eagle Ford formations is being extracted from shale, it is not "shale oil," but light oil trapped in shale formations where it does not flow readily. Recent refinements in hydraulic fracturing, also known as "fracking," have allowed the oil to be produced.

Wild estimates that hundreds of billions of barrels of oil in these formations will soon allow the United States to achieve energy independence are reminiscent of the confusion between resources and reserves that plagued natural resource extraction in the late, not-so-great Soviet Union.

When the USSR collapsed, I immediately went there looking for opportunity. One of the first projects I delved into was a gold mining prospect that had been thoroughly drilled and mapped by Soviet geologists. For ideological reasons, however, they had never taken price into account in drawing the distinction between resources and reserves.

Resources vs. Reserves

"Resources" are at least trace amounts of some geological element. "Reserves" are resources that can be economically extracted in light of their price.

As any old Soviet oil geologist might tell you, there could be up to 400 billion barrels of oil resources in the Bakken formation. But the oil reserves — the portion that can be economically produced given known or foreseeable technology — is a tiny fraction of the total resource, probably no more than two to four billion barrels.

Likewise, the Eagle Ford formation is estimated by the Department of Energy to hold a reserve of 3.35 billion barrels. The use of fracking techniques to tap these reserves has perked up U.S. oil production.

But that infers nothing about the possibility of producing shale oil from the Green River formation. Shale oil is not light oil trapped in shale, like the Bakken formation. In fact, it makes the tar sands seem like light, sweet crude by comparison. Shale oil is kerogen, a solid more akin to coal in consistency than what you think of as oil.

To convert shale oil (kerogen) into a liquid that can be refined into a usable energy product is incredibly energy intensive. The shale oil rock must be heated to a high temperature. Imagine microwaving a mountain. Also, large amounts of water must be injected into the shale under high pressure — not an easy requirement to meet in the arid environment of the Green River formation.

Remember, water is an increasingly scarce resource, especially west of the Mississippi where the Ogallala High Plains fossil aquifer system — a vast, but shallow underground water reservoir — provides irrigation and drinking water for 82% of the population of eight states.

Water is not only essential for life, and therefore costly to divert for purposes of cooking shale oil, but is also heavy to transport. Water is much heavier than oil, which is why oil floats to the surface of water. In most cases, it is prohibitively expensive to transport water great distances.

This adds up to an extremely low potential energy return on energy invested in shale oil. The analysts who pretend to see a bright future of rising energy inputs from hundreds of billions or even trillions of barrels of shale oil are kidding you. This is like projecting a bright future for the squirrel that must run 100 miles to fetch an acorn.

Equally, the assertion that Obama's Energy Department is squelching shale oil development that could make the U.S. energy-independent is pure rubbish.

The 2012 Campaign

In this respect, it's interesting that Barack Obama feigned an understanding of how important energy is to reviving the U.S. economy during the 2012 Presidential campaign.

As a sometimes-resident of Argentina, I find his brand of demagoguery painfully reminiscent of the bunk that destroyed that once-prosperous economy. It is interesting that the big refinements in fascism over the past half-century seem to come in the realm of fashion rather than policy. Juan Peron favored jackboots. Obama is more comfortable in Nikes.

But, like Peron, Obama wants to burn down the Jockey Club. Obama demonizes the rich and pretends to represent the interests of the poor.

It is said by economists that if you want more of something, you subsidize it. Like Peron, Obama wants to subsidize poverty and failure.

Many Americans may not realize that when the 20th century opened, Argentina was the world's fifth-richest country on a per capita basis. As late as 1945, Argentina boasted the world's second largest gold reserves. Yet within a decade, the gold was gone. Thereafter, Argentina suffered bout after bout of hyperinflation that accompanied compound negative growth.

There is general agreement that a significant portion of Argentina's gold reserves was stolen by Dictator Juan Peron. But in a foreshadowing of the Obama administration, hundreds of millions of dollars' worth of Argentine gold were squandered backing Proyecto Huemul, a secret undertaking of Peron's designed to create "cheap energy in enormous quantities" from nuclear fusion.

Like Obama, who is notorious for his lavish backing of unreasonable solar energy projects with other people's money (think Solyndra, the company that took $500 million to money heaven), Peron squandered much of Argentina's wealth on futile "alternative energy" research. He offered German scientist Ronald Richter a blank check in support of a plan that was to have produced portable energy sources "in milk bottles" of one-half liter and one liter sizes.

Richter had proposed a similar project to the German government during the Second World War, but it was rejected. Peron was more eager and consequently wasted significant amounts of Argentina's gold reserve built up from large trade surpluses during the Second World War.

I suppose that makes a difference in comparison to Obama, who has no trade surplus to squander. That was gone long ago.

As we look forward, I doubt that Romney was right in projecting that America's best days are to come.

I just hope the next half-century does not prove to be as bleak in the U.S. as Argentina's became when the same policies were followed.

CHAPTER 16

The Lottery Ticket for Prosperity Built on Cheap Oil Has Already Been Cashed

"The world's problems will only be exacerbated by the dwindling supply of fossil fuels. Oil was in inherent oversupply from the discovery of the giant East Texas oilfield in 1930 until 2004. Since 2004 the price has risen threefold. What has supply done in response to this big price signal? Nothing. World oil production has gone sideways. Everyone who has an oilfield is producing flat out. They are not producing any more than they did when oil was a third of the price it is now — because they physically cannot. Production of conventional oil will soon tip over into decline."

— David Archibald, "Twilight of Abundance"

A McKinsey Global Institute study concludes that if America maintains the same level of productivity growth as it has enjoyed over the past half-century, income growth per capita for children born at the turn-of-the-century will be slower than for previous generations. Among the problems identified by McKinsey: the U.S. ranks low in energy efficiency.

Of course the U.S. ranks low in energy efficiency. As the pioneers of the world petroleum industry, Americans had so much access to such bountiful supplies of cheap energy that we unwittingly embedded the premise of cheap energy into the whole structure of our economy. It is now a giant edifice teetering on a crumbling foundation.

Our communities, transportation and business enterprises are legacy systems designed and installed when oil was cheap. In nominal terms, crude oil prices ranged between $2.50 and $3.00 from 1948 through the end of the 1960s. In inflation-adjusted terms, over the post war period the median for the domestic price of crude oil was $19.60 in 2008 dollars. That means that, from 1947 to 2008, oil prices have only exceeded $19.60 per barrel 50% of the time.

A Leading Indicator of Debt Default and Deflation

Over the decade before 2014, oil prices rose at a 15% compound annual rate. Ponder that while I marshal more data to illustrate in retrospect why that was an impossible situation. While oil prices were doubling every 4.8 years, growth in the developed economies was negligible. Both the U.S. and the developed economies as a group grew at an annual rate of just 0.3% from 2007 through 2010, when oil prices surged most. In other words, they were on a pace to double in 240 years. Obviously, the developed economies could not indefinitely afford to continue consuming all the oil they traditionally used while its price was compounding 50 times faster than their economies grew.

Indeed, the rise of the oil price was even more unsustainable than the data cited above would suggest. The weak economic growth of the developed countries was leveraged to declining absorption of energy, as exemplified by the United States, where U.S. energy use fell along with the rate of GDP growth. Historically, oil demand has grown at 75% of the trend rate of GDP growth. Extrapolating from past GDP growth trends implied a 23% increase in U.S. oil consumption from 2004 through 2013. It didn't happen.

The long-established normal growth trend was seemingly independent of price. Yet the fact that incremental differences in oil price did not deter demand said nothing about the effect of large swings. When oil prices rose sharply, the U.S. oil consumption trend from July 2004 through July 2013 turned negative to -1.5% per annum. Total U.S. energy use exceeded 100 quadrillion BTUs (quads) in 2004, when U.S. GDP grew at an annual rate of 3.8%. But it plunged below 95 quads thereafter, and has not recovered since.

The only thing that enabled the price of oil to soar while developed economies flat-lined was the extraordinary surge of growth of the BRICs and other emerging economies. In 2008, the BRICs accounted for two-thirds of world GDP growth. By 2011, they accounted for half of it.

Of course, economic growth and demand for oil, in the BRICs, as elsewhere, are intimately connected with credit conditions. Immediately following the 2008 financial crisis, the BRICs all loosened credit at the same time that the advanced economies launched massive bailout and stimulus programs, culminating in Quantitative Easing.

The first order effect of super-loose monetary policy was to amplify the growth impulse in the BRICs, as hot money from Europe, Japan and North America flowed into Brazil, Russia, India and China in search of yield. Later, protracted Quantitative Easing contributed to a growth slow-down in the BRICs. Each of them tightened monetary conditions in one way or another to counter the threat of "over-heating." This second order response, what *The Economist* described as "a striking slowdown in BRIC growth rates," coincided with flat oil production and prices between 2011 and mid-2014.

Narimen Behravesh, Chief Economist for IHS, warns that "there has been a sharp drop in GDP growth from BRIC countries." He sees a lot of vulnerability to a Chinese slowdown in that Chinese debt-to-GDP ratio more than doubled since 2007, and half that debt is in shadow banks like trusts, where you don't know where these are and how much bad debt there is.

The plunge in oil prices in the second half of 2014 promised at least a transient boost to growth, at the risk of a systemic deflationary reversal that could put the whole post-World War II debt build up in jeopardy.

The fall in oil prices did not reflect a fall in production costs. To the contrary: oil production faltered in the early decades of this century, even as capex soared after 2004, by nearly 11% a year. Total capital expenditures on upstream exploration and production totaling $4 trillion since 2005 have evidenced dramatically diminishing returns, with a decline in conventional oil production by one million barrels per day. We have seen a dramatic drop in Energy Return on Energy Invested (ERoEI), now amplified by a more dramatic decline in dollars returned per dollars invested in oil exploration and production.

Falling commodity prices in a world of easy money are ominous. If demand for necessities like oil and food is insufficient, it augurs ill for the satisfaction of the gigantic sums of debt that accumulated throughout the world economy since World War II. I expect the plunge in oil prices to be a leading indicator of a wave of debt defaults and deflation that could collapse history's greatest wave of credit expansion.

Cheap Oil and U.S. Prosperity

Because America was the richest and most developed country in the decades after World War II, we have a disproportionate share of the world's legacy systems that were designed and built when oil cost less than $20 a barrel in current terms. (When I first wrote this analysis, West Texas crude sold for $105.25 a barrel.)

This created a much greater hostage to fortune over oil prices for the United States than in rapidly emerging economies, which until recently used only trivial amounts of energy. India and China could better afford $100 oil than the U.S., Europe or Japan. They were incorporating it, at the margin, in systems designed at current prices. The U.S. cannot. Oil at $100 a barrel is five times as costly as our systems intended. Oil at $200 a barrel makes the United States insolvent. In particular, our housing patterns involving dispersed suburbs linked by highways would be extremely difficult and costly to retrofit.

And ironically, it may also be true that $50 oil also creates a U.S. insolvency crisis — as it jeopardizes the whole over-extended edifice of credit compounded since World War II.

The U.S. has already cashed the lucky lottery ticket it enjoyed as the first economy to amplify its repertoire of work with cheap oil.

As oil prices soared in the 21st century, the U.S. lost a decade of compounding growth. The February 2011 level of 108.3 million private-sector jobs was lower than 11 years earlier in June 1999 at 108.6 million jobs. The flat-lining of employment in the United States over the same decade, when broad stock market indices failed to rise for the first time ever, reflects the sensitivity of the U.S. economy to increasing energy costs.

I suspect that the ready availability of cheap energy was a greater factor in the rise of the U.S. economy than most people think. Much of the surge in prosperity that we tend to credit to the intelligence and hard work of our intrepid ancestors was really a gift of nature. More than the history books tend to tell us, our forebears leveraged plentiful, cheap BTUs sourced "from wood to coal" into rapid economic growth.

From Wood to Coal

In the first instance, English settlers in North America exploited the thick woods that stretched from the Atlantic seaboard far inland. Areas like Ohio and Indiana that are today largely open farmland were almost impenetrable forest when settlers first arrived. Ohio was said to have presented "the grandest unbroken forest of 41,000 square miles that was ever beheld."

Through the 18th and early 19th centuries, Americans enjoyed an advantage relative to Europeans because we could employ plentiful, cheap wood in building our economy.

Historian John Perlin explains:

> Cheap lumber and cheap fuel extracted from these forests made possible America's development from the Revolution to the Civil War into a powerful and prosperous nation. Such growth, though, took a terrible toll on the woodlands. By 1877, one observer reported in *The Popular Science Monthly* that "the states of Ohio and Indiana ... so recently a part of the great East-American forest, have even now a greater percentage of treeless area" than portions of Europe settled and cultivated for thousands of years.

The United States was doubly blessed with a large endowment of readily exploitable coal that became seamlessly available to fuel further and more rapid economic growth when the forests had mostly been chopped to the ground. The smooth transition from wood to coal was another blessing from nature. The U.S. not only had a large endowment of virgin forest, it also sported large coal deposits that were rapidly exploited. U.S. coal production grew logarithmically at a steady 6.6% per year from 1850 to 1910. Then the growth leveled off.

The famous geologist, M. King Hubbert, originator of the "Peak Oil" hypothesis, actually formulated his oil forecast by studying coal output in the U.S. Believing that no finite resource could support long-term exponential growth, he theorized that the production rate plotted versus time would show a bell-shaped curve, declining as rapidly as it had risen. At some point, the rate of production would have to peak and then decline until the resource was exhausted. Hubbert used his observation of U.S. coal production to predict peak oil. More on that later.

Before oil production could peak, it first had to begin.

The Original Petroleum Industry

The third phase of the extraordinary natural blessing the United States enjoyed where energy is concerned began to come into view in 1859 when Col. Edwin Drake discovered light sweet crude oil in a small northwestern Pennsylvania lumber town, Titusville. There were 16 lumber mills operating in Titusville when Col. Drake arrived. They were soon eclipsed as the stars of the Titusville economy.

Drake's first well pumped only 45 barrels a day but it was the beginning of the petroleum industry in the world. Titusville experienced a tremendous surge of prosperity as its population multiplied 40 times over. More oil was soon discovered. Within a few years, Titusville boasted the greatest density of millionaires per capita of any incorporated town on earth.

From that day in the summer of 1859 when Col. Drake's first well began to pump until 1971, U.S. production of light sweet crude continued to increase. So did U.S. prosperity. As the first nation to exploit petroleum, the U.S. soon became the leader of the world economy. Great Britain, the country that led the Industrial Revolution, lost its leading role in the carnage of World War I that began just one year after British coal production peaked in 1913.

The Shift from Coal to Oil and World War I

The advent of "Peak Coal" in Great Britain, along with the ensuing desperate scramble for oil fields between Britain and Germany, was a more fundamental cause of World War I than the assassination of the Archduke Ferdinand. Political assassinations have occurred at other times and places without triggering global war. But rarely do dominant global powers find themselves in major transition of energy sources.

The transition by the Royal Navy from coal to oil, instituted by First Lord of the Admiralty Sir Winston Churchill and Admiral of the Fleet, Sir John (Jacky) Fisher, was informed primarily by technical rather than geopolitical considerations. There were practical, military advantages of powering ships of the Royal Navy with oil that mirrored its advantages in the civilian realm.

Naval warfare analyst Erik Dahl wrote:

> Oil offered many benefits. It had double the thermal content of coal so that boilers could be smaller and ships could travel twice as far.

A pound of bunker oil contained 23,000 BTUs as compared to 12,000 BTUs in a pound of anthracite coal. Because the fuel aboard weighed less, greater speed was possible.

Erik continued:

> Oil burned with less smoke so the fleet would not reveal its presence as quickly. Oil could be stored in tanks anywhere on board, allowing more efficient design of ships, and it could be transferred through pipes without reliance on stokers, reducing manning. Refueling at sea was feasible, which provided greater flexibility."

Perhaps the most crucial advantage of oil-powered ships was enhanced speed. Again, quoting Dahl:

> In 1912, Fisher wrote to Churchill, "What you do want is the super-swift — all oil — and don't fiddle about armour; it really is so very silly! There is only one defence and that is speed!"

> The war college was asked how much speed a fast division would need to outmaneuver the German fleet. The answer was 25 knots, or at least four knots faster than possible at the time. Churchill concluded, "We could not get the power required to drive these ships at 25 knots except by the use of oil fuel."

In other words, the decision to convert to oil propulsion had a sound technological and military rationale, especially when oil was cheap. There was just one fateful drawback. Even after "Peak Coal" production was reached, Great Britain still had ample coal supplies, but on the eve of World War I, virtually no domestic oil was known in the U.K. BP did not discover the first commercial quantities of oil in Britain until 1939 at Eskring, Nottinghamshire.

A crucial reason why Britain faded as a world power is that it lacked oil. When the evolution of technology created unequivocal military advantages in shifting to a more energy dense fuel, the U.K. could ante up the money for oil-powered capital ships. But unlike the U.S. in the early 20th century, Britain had no oil of its own. Britain then was more dependent on foreign oil than the U.S. is today. The lack of ready access to cheap oil in the United Kingdom inevitably informed geopolitical maneuvering to secure oil fields elsewhere. Hence, World War I.

Note that Admiral Fisher predicted in 1908 that the UK would go to war with Germany in October, 1914. He based his prediction on the assumption that Kiel Canal would be completed then, enabling the German fleet to readily move from the Baltic to the North Sea. The Kaiser reportedly said, "I admire Fisher, I say nothing against him. If I were in his place I should do all that he has done and I should do all that I know he has in mind to do."

The British deficit in oil also retarded economic growth. As World War I was ruinously expensive, it cost Great Britain the greater part of its gold reserves and its overseas foreign assets. Thereafter, the British economy operated within the straitjacket of its export earnings. Unlike the recent situation in which the United States has borrowed trillions to fund imports of foreign oil, there was no group of creditors standing by to fund a yawning British deficit in petroleum trade. Consequently, the British economy employed oil more sparingly than did the United States.

In particular, the UK failed to share in the rapid development of suburbs that resulted from motorization in the U.S. The speedy adoption of automobiles and trucks powered the U.S. economy to average annual growth of 4.2% in the 1920s. Greater use of automobiles in the United States was linked to the adoption of assembly lines and higher incomes for blue collar workers. It also led to greater vitality of ancillary industries like home appliances and furniture where sales were stimulated by the growth of the new housing in the suburbs and satellite communities. Suburban building booms, of course, were second order effects of the growth of auto traffic over paved roads.

Notwithstanding the steep plunge in U.S. economic activity during the Great Depression, auto ownership was more than 400% higher in the U.S. in 1939 than in the UK. Almost 23% of Americans owned cars while only 5.4% of the British population drove.

The fact that U.S. suburbs and satellite communities were organized around automobile thoroughfares, built at a time of cheap oil rather than rail lines as in Great Britain, means that U.S. real estate could be subject to devastating losses as oil prices rise. The interstate highway system was designed when gasoline cost $0.30 a gallon. At $5 per gallon, many of the economic relationships capitalized into suburban real estate values will be obsolete. This is particularly bad news for California, the most car-centric state in the United States, where drivers in Los Angeles alone travel 300,000,000 miles per day.

A graph of rising U.S. per capita income directly traces the graph of rising U.S. domestic oil output. By 1950, petroleum had become the primary source of energy consumed in the United States. At that time, the U.S. accounted for 52% of world oil production. But the first shadows appeared on the energy-dense prosperity of the United States in 1956. In that year, a shrewd geologist named M. King Hubbert, then working for Shell Oil, interpolated a frightening conclusion from coal production data. Hubbert accurately predicted that U.S. oil production would peak about 15 years later.

This logistics model now known as the Hubbert Theory described, with fair accuracy, the progression to the peak and then decline of production from individual oil wells, oil fields, regions and countries (and now, the entire planet.) Hubbert foresaw the inflexion and tail off of cheap domestic oil in the early 1970s. He was right.

Peak Oil and Declining Money

In my view, it is no coincidence that 1971, the year of peak domestic U.S. oil production, was also the year when the United States started its descent into the thrall of "Debtism." In 1971, the old America went broke. Richard Nixon repudiated the gold reserve system, and put the U.S. on the road to becoming the greatest debtor nation in the history of the world.

Capitalism in the United States (as defined by the accumulation of capital in an economy based upon savings) came to an end when cheap domestic oil production tailed off. Our current system, one that I characterize as "Debtism," substitutes debt for capital at the center of economic life. The current depression is a direct consequence of the failed attempt to substitute global debt for cheap domestic BTUs as a recipe for sustaining prosperity. Put simply, governments can print money. But no one can print BTUs.

The U.S. did manage to continue increasing its aggregate consumption of energy dense oil, as population increased, with total domestic demand peaking at 21 million barrels a day — at the time the subprime housing boom peaked in 2006-2007. But strangely enough, the per capita consumption of BTU's in the United States stabilized at 1970s levels, and has remained remarkably consistent since then, even as real per capita income has stagnated.

As long as light sweet crude was available somewhere for purchase with easily manufactured dollars, we could forestall a collapse in energy density and continue to pretend that the United States was prospering. Note, however, that the money we created out of thin air was not just cranked off a printing press. It was borrowed into existence through a fractional reserve banking system that created liabilities to be repaid. The accumulated bills for years of living beyond our means in energy terms are still to be paid.

The Competition for Prosperity

As we went on our merry way using as much of the world's available cheap oil as we could borrow the money to buy, something else happened. Emerging economies like China, India, Brazil, Turkey, Korea and Mexico began to develop. People in those previously retarded economies started making money. As they did, they found something unsurprising. They preferred driving automobiles rather than riding bicycles and burros or just walking. Today, China has replaced the United States as the world's largest auto market. Brazil has replaced Germany as the world's fourth-largest auto market.

The growth of auto use in emerging economies implies skyrocketing oil use and prices. From now through 2020, world oil consumption is expected to rise by about 60%. The biggest part of that growth will be demand for oil for transportation. By 2025, some experts predict that half a billion cars will be added to the world's roads bringing the total to well over 1.25 billion from approximately 700 million today. Not only does this imply a lot of traffic jams and time lost looking for a parking space, it also predetermines runaway oil prices.

Indeed, the adverse acceleration in the cost of oil production, which in the final months of 2014 far exceeded the price of oil in all but long-lasting legacy fields, suggests that the experts' vision of another half a billion cars on the road within a decade is faulty. I doubt it will happen. You would be looking down the road toward gasoline prices of $8-$10 per gallon. Barring a technological miracle, I don't see an affordable way forward to doubling global consumption of gasoline. If it happened, it would imply a significant shift in relative income between residents of the currently wealthy countries and hundreds of millions of persons whose resources are presently too marginal to permit automobile ownership. In other words, if they are driving a decade hence, you may not be. (Or, at best, your cost for driving would skyrocket).

The two countries with the highest rate of growth in oil use are China and India, whose combined populations account for a third of humanity. In the next two decades, China's oil consumption is expected to grow at a rate of 7.5% per year and India's at 5.5%. (Compare this to a 1% growth for the industrialized countries).

Dramatically augmented demand in developing economies against a backdrop of dwindling production from the world's heritage oil fields spells higher prices. As Hubbert explained half a century ago, the first oil that was found was the cheapest and easiest to produce. As of 2010, the annual depletion rate of those cheap oil fields was about 4 million barrels per day of production. Even if that is exaggerated by a magnitude, it implies that by 2015 there would be 2 million fewer barrels of oil production per day to satisfy the surging world demand.

Expensive Oil Remains

Many quibbles have been advanced to challenge the theory of peak oil. Mostly, these relate to the question of whether the world is truly "running out of oil." Almost certainly those who argue that oil will not run out are correct. But this is a misleading truth.

What is happening is that the world is running out of the type of oil that fueled the prosperity of North America at a price that people could afford. Light sweet crude — the most desirable form of oil, as it flows easily and can be readily refined into gasoline — is rapidly depleting. The most famous varieties of light sweet crude, including West Texas intermediate, Brent oil from the North Sea and Saudi Light Crude, are being used up.

According to OPEC figures, annual output of sweet crude dropped by 2.6 million barrels per day from 2000 to 2004. While these figures aren't perfect because they don't completely integrate across the total production curve, it is incontrovertible that lighter more desirable varieties of crude oil have been replaced with heavier, more sulfurous heavy sour crude or synthetic oil such as that from the Alberta tar sands, which is extremely expensive to produce.

The original Saudi Light oil discovered at Dhahran in 1938 could be pumped profitably for three dollars a barrel. When oil was discovered at Spindle Top, in Texas, it sold for just three cents a barrel early in the last century. Today, the synthetic oil from tar sands costs $70 a barrel to produce. Perhaps more. There are 300 billions of barrels of difficult-to-extract oil in the Athabasca tar sands in Alberta and untold more billions of barrels in shale deposits in the American West. There are many more billions of barrels of petroleum under the ocean off the coast of Brazil.

It is true that there is oil in the world. The problem is that much of the oil that remains will be priced so high that you won't be able to afford to use it.

When oil costs $200 a barrel as it may, as high cost supplies are taken offline, how much driving would you be doing under those conditions?

You may not choose to completely scrap your car at those prices, but others will. They will have no choice. The average American drives about 15,000 miles a year. You have to assume that this is not merely joyriding. When gasoline costs $6, much less $10 per gallon, the jobs to which many Americans commute will no longer pay the tariff entailed in traveling to and fro. Whole suburbs and neighborhoods will go off-line.

When the oil from the Lucas Gusher in Texas sold at three cents a barrel, BTUs were priced at 193 million per dollar. True, the dollar was worth more then. But oil at $200 a barrel gets you only 29,000 BTUs to the dollar. Nominally, that is a 665,000% increase in the price of a BTU. While this is exaggerated because not much oil changed hands at three cents a barrel, the direction of the change is not in doubt. The radical falloff in the energy density of BTUs per dollar implies a continuing and perhaps precipitous drop in American living standards.

Prosperity will fall away as the return on energy investment falls.

I would guess that Sam Zell is right in predicting that American living standards are set for at least a 25% decline over the next couple of decades.

As we experience higher cost energy (or alternatively, deflationary debt default), you can expect to see a closure of the economy. Economic freedom will be curtailed. Globalization will be rolled back. The high price of bunker oil will effectively serve as a stiff tariff to refocus the production of heavy, relatively low value products like steel domestically. Some time ago, *The Wall Street Journal* reported that the world's longest containership, the Eugen Maersk, cut its cruising speed to 10 knots from its usual 26 knots. This reduced consumption to 100–150 tons of fuel daily from 350 tons, saving up to $5,000 an hour.

Talk about the retracing of prosperity. I expect to see the reintroduction of sailing ships for long-haul transport. The website treehugger.com has already begun to extol the promise of long-haul ocean freight under sail. If expensive oil requires container ships to poke along at 10 knots, they enjoy only an equivocal advantage over sail-powered freight. The largest sail powered vessel ever built, the Preussen, launched in 1902, averaged 13.7 knots in transit between Iquique, Chile and Hamburg.

The surge in fuel prices that will make bulk haulage costs go way up has other consequences. International steel companies that do not serve large domestic markets will suffer. So will shipping companies. There will be fewer Chinese goods at Wal-Mart. Hence; Wal-Mart will lose some of its competitive advantage. We will move backward toward a more local, closed economy.

You can see where this will lead. When oil gets to $200 a barrel, many suburbs and satellite communities will become uneconomic. Housing values that capitalize low energy prices will plunge. As real estate values are primary collateral to the U.S. banking system, you can expect a deeper systemic crisis to come. This deflationary pressure probably leads to a hyperinflationary response by the authorities. You will need to own physical gold and silver.

"Yes, we have no bananas"

Agriculture is highly energy intensive. Oil at $200 will lever up the cost of groceries and make your choice of food simpler and less exciting. Restaurant's margins will be squeezed as food costs rise. The quality of your diet will suffer, as there will be fewer internationally grown vegetables, fruits, meats and fish on your grocery shelves and in restaurants. You may have to go without fresh fish, avocados and out-of-season blueberries from halfway around the world.

If you want to get a view of the kind of food you will be eating, take a look at an old restaurant menu from the 1940s. Instead of Dover sole or fresh Alaska halibut flown in overnight, an exciting meal may once again consist of steak or even meatloaf with mashed potatoes and gravy.

As economic closure reduces productive efficiency, and energy prices rise, you can expect the economy to retrace aspects of its evolution. In many respects, the future may look like the past. Increasing transportation costs will negate much of the cost advantage of low-wage labor in China, Vietnam and other remote locales. An Increasing share of the products consumed will be produced locally and probably to a lower standard of quality. Most things that you will consume in the future will cost you more. As your standard of living falls, you'll have less spare cash to lavish on services. The prominent, financial services sector will be cut in half to approximately 4% of GDP.

The tertiary sector (services and the government) will necessarily shrink as a percentage of the economy, as more people are employed in goods making and farming. As the United States grows poorer, our trading partners will have less reason to finance our deficits, so they will stop doing it. Government spending will be forced back within the straitjacket of what a poorer public can actually afford. That means dramatically fewer government services and fewer entitlements, but within the context of higher taxes and more financial repression.

Another important implication: the United States will no longer have the wherewithal to police the world. I expect U.S. military spending to be slashed, but perhaps not until after we are embroiled in another major war.

Run Away from Home

The big question is: what can you do about it? Several steps are indicated. On the largest scale of life decisions, you might want to move to Canada or Brazil. Both are energy rich countries on sounder financial and fiscal footing than the United States. One of my grandfathers moved from Ontario to the U.S. early in the last century because he judged the relative prospects of the U.S. to be superior at that time. A similar assessment today would yield the opposite conclusion. Ontario derives all of its electric power from perhaps the world's richest endowment of hydro generators. The balance sheet of the Canadian government is far sounder than that of the United States. Canada's banks are solvent. Not a single Canadian bank failed in the Great Depression and Canada's banks are in even stronger shape today. (Of course, the 2014 oil plunge will stress Canada's banks as well as those in the United States, and not solely because the banks are exposed to debt from the oil sector. The cutback in capital expenditures in the oilfield will have widespread reverberations. Many high-paying jobs will be eliminated. Real estate values in oil-centric communities will take a hit. This will all feed back into the banking system.)

Brazil is also energy independent, and has the advantage of producing the most plentiful and varied array of foods of any country. Brazil is one place where food will not be an issue even under Little Ice Age conditions. With 60% of the earth's unused arable land and 15% of all the fresh water on the planet, Brazil is poised to grow. Both Canada and Brazil offer savers a far better shake than the United States.

Brazil is one of the few countries on the globe where nominal interest rates are higher than the inflation rate. Brazil also has a young population, so the burden of aging Baby Boomers on the economy will be far lighter than in North America. Another advantage of Brazil over Canada is that it is located at a safe distance from the United States. In the event that the U.S. becomes embroiled in another major war as our leaders thrash about for some solutions to intractable problems, less of the fallout is likely to reach Brazil.

Of course, if you do not wish to uproot your family or don't think you could afford to do so and you are only looking for portfolio recommendations, be guided by the logic of energy density and cost.

That suggests that you should invest in the most BTU dense energy options. Uranium is one power source that is denser in energy than oil. A pound of oil contains about 2.4×10^7 of Joules, while uranium contains 3.7×10^{13} Joules. (100 joules equal 0.0947 BTU.) While the recent Japanese experience led to prudent rules against building nuclear power plants over tectonic faults, the logic of BTU density will prevail. Nuclear power will be increasingly relied upon as oil prices surge.

Another attractive option for investment is thermal coal. Coal has a high BTU content and it is not subject to hysteria fanned by fears of a Chernobyl-style meltdown. Coal is still plentiful. While Hubbert made his prediction of peak oil in the U.S. to happen in the early 1970s, he and others employing his model have predicted that peak coal will be postponed until around the middle of this century, or later.

In due course, coal will be gasified, liquefied and otherwise modified to serve more of your energy needs. As the future retraces the past, coal will be a bigger investment theme.

Another energy source destined to be more widely used as a replacement for petroleum across the world is natural gas. One standard cubic foot of natural gas has 1.1×10^6 Joules equivalent. As you may know, natural gas is another form of oil that has been re-configured by subsurface temperatures. At depths beyond 15,000 feet, the subsurface rocks tend to be so hot that oil molecules are "cracked" into natural gas.

I envision much more adoption of natural gas across a wide spectrum of energy uses, including powering motor vehicles. It's already being done in countries like Bulgaria and Brazil. And in the U.S., UPS trucks, buses, and fleets are already powered by it.

The tanks required to fuel vehicles with natural gas are more voluminous than gasoline tanks, but they do provide an otherwise attractive option for fueling cars and trucks in an oil scarce world.

Finally, when oil prices bottom out and begin to rise, don't overlook the prospect of profiting from the return to expensive oil by investing in a company that has ample supplies of expensive crude and exciting prospects for their development.

Remember, before 1995 when the dot-com boom skewed historic investment statistics, the oil industry earned a higher rate of return on invested capital than any other industry. That was during a period when oil was less than $20 in current terms. If the modern world economy remains intact long enough to allow for extraction of high cost pre-salt oil, profits would overshadow anything seen in the past.

While the United States is clearly unprepared for a world of drastically higher oil prices, you are blessed with several options.

I encourage you to position yourself for the inevitable, before it's too late.

CHAPTER 17

The Coming Collapse of America

"Energy has always been the basis of cultural complexity and it always will be... our current and future investments in complexity requires an increase in the effective per capita supply of energy — either by increasing the physical availability of energy, or by technical, political, or economic innovations that lower the energy cost of our standard of living. Of course, to discover such innovations requires energy, which underscores the constraints in the energy-complexity relation."

— Joseph A. Tainter, "Complexity, Problem Solving, and Sustainable Societies"

Anthropologist and historian Joseph Tainter is the world's foremost expert on why societies fail. He has sketched out a thesis on the role of energy in the economics of problem solving. It is an argument of great importance for you in today's circumstances. It points toward some sobering conclusions that the mainstream media and even past presidential campaigns have relegated to the shadows.

One of the more crucial of these conclusions is that it is most unlikely that the United States will rapidly or painlessly recover the charmed position it enjoyed in the world economy during the 19th and 20th centuries. With the U.S. already suffering from declining, or even negative marginal returns from complexity, it is more likely to collapse than prosper.

The U.S. faces a future of static or declining energy inputs. Global oil production appears to have peaked, which translates into a falling standard of living.

Because our established bureaucracies and systems for solving problems will no longer be subsidized by readily available cheap oil, you will be unable to count on economic growth to paper over diminishing or negative returns from the provision of services that government provides. The fact that government is forcing resources to deal with minimal or negative returns does not make these investments sustainable.

Tainter explains that "once a complex society enters the stage of declining marginal returns, collapse becomes a mathematical likelihood, requiring little more than sufficient passage of time to make probable an insurmountable calamity."

Today, close observation of the economics of investments in complexity by government in the U.S. reveals unmistakable evidence of drastically declining or negative marginal returns in a wide range of endeavors.

The End of the Dollar's Global Dominance is at Hand. Or is It?

Put simply, with static or falling energy inputs, the U.S. is closer to collapse than almost anyone suspects. And, depending on whether the trillions in dollar debt are extinguished through deflationary default or hyperinflation, this collapse could forever sever the dollar's ties to the only thing keeping it credible — crude oil.

You are now enjoying the calm before an even bigger storm. Consider this your chance to prepare before the crisis deepens.

In his book, "The Collapse of Complex Societies," Tainter argues that "complex societies" are prone to declining marginal returns across a broad range of activities.

In other words, as problems arise, societies try to solve them by increasing complexity — solutions often imposed by government — in ways that involve higher costs over long periods. Stable societies tend to proliferate bureaucracies, raise taxes and deploy costly armies. As the cost curve evolves, it "may at first increase favorably, as the most simple, general, and inexpensive solutions are adopted," but then "society reaches a point where continued investment in complexity yields higher returns, but at a declining marginal rate." At this point "a society has entered the phase where it starts to become vulnerable to collapse."

Tainter defines collapse as "a rapid transformation to a lower degree of complexity, typically involving significantly less energy consumption." When "easier solutions are exhausted, problem-solving moves inexorably to greater complexity, higher costs, and diminishing returns."

Declining Returns in U.S. Health Care

Examples of greater complexity involving higher costs and diminishing returns are almost everywhere you turn in America. But these are problems with roots deep in the past. They are not a recent phenomenon.

For example, Tainter shows that the productivity of the U.S. health care system for improving life expectancy declined by 60% from 1930 to 1982.

The early '80s were even worse with startling jumps in costs in the U.S. health care system. Less productivity ensured that health care spending would suffer sharply diminishing returns.

Cross-national spending comparisons based on the Organization for Economic Co-operation and Development (OECD) data show U.S. health care costs per capita skyrocketing from around $1,200 in 1982 to $7,662 in 2012.

Over the same period, by the OECDs measure of healthcare success, the U.S. ranked dead last among 17 wealthy countries. The study included health indicators, such as life expectancy, self-reported health status, premature mortality, death from cancer, infant mortality and death from medical misadventure.

Even before Obama aggravated the problem of declining marginal returns by blowing another $1.75 trillion on health care without increasing the supply of services, the U.S. was spending far more than other rich countries.

In any standard economic situation, when you increase the demand of any one service, but do not have enough supply to handle it, that service becomes more expensive.

Health care represents one-sixth of the U.S. economy. When each additional dollar invested yields a diminishing or negative return, there is an urgent need, not for more costly complexity — such as the $1.75 trillion reorganization of the health care system — but for simplicity, such as advances in immunotherapy that help the body mobilize its own recuperative powers to defeat deadly diseases.

America's Expensive Education Failure

As occasionally reported in the media, even though the U.S. leads total annual spending on education, it ranks ninth in science performance and 10th in math, in a comparison with 11 other leading economies.

Furthermore, Bill Ponath argues in an article titled, "Um… the dog ate my report card," that "the United States is spending at least $20,576 per student in elementary and secondary schools." He reports this as an average of spending in all the U.S. jurisdictions ranging from $10,896 per student in Idaho to an astonishing $38,986 per student in the District of Columbia. In addition to state spending, the federal government is laying out $1,917 per pupil toward the total average of $20,576.

These numbers become startling in the context of the 2012 Program for International Student Assessment (PISA), which reported scores for 65 countries based on the administration of uniform tests to 15-year-old students in each country. The results showed that Shanghai, China came first, Singapore second, and Hong Kong, China third. Notably, the per capita education outlays in China were $1,326 annually, or just 6.5% of the U.S. level.

It should be obvious at this point that the U.S. is failing on education by wasting huge sums of money that yield diminishing (or even negative) marginal returns. And despite the sums being thrown to try to "correct" the problem, this strategy is not working.

Instead, half-baked opportunities are cropping up seemingly everywhere in an effort to "marginally improve" the education process in this country.

While some schools will do tremendously well, others will not.

The Most Expensive Military in the World

Health care and education are just two areas where politicians have increased complexity with economically ruinous results. In a competitive world, it is difficult to imagine how one supplier can stay in business when its costs are 15 times higher than competitors who are achieving better results.

Yet another area, which consumes a major part of the U.S. budget, is the military.

American authorities and bureaucracies are not always eager to present clear and easily-understood accounts of their spending. This is true in the case of U.S. military spending. Total reported Department of Defense spending for the fiscal year 2010, for example, was $707.5 billion. But this number does not paint the whole picture. Consider this:

- Outlays related to nuclear weapons, for example, comprised $21.8 billion of the Energy Department budget.

- Veterans' pensions took another $54.6 billion, under the budget of the Department of Veterans Affairs.

- Security outlays for the Department of Homeland Security entailed another $46.9 billion.

- At least one-third of the FBI budget, some $2.7 billion, was devoted to counter-terrorism, intelligence gathering and operations.

- The export of weapons to allies accounted for another $5.6 billion under the International Affairs budget of the State Department.

- A catch-all category, "Other Defense-related spending," spread among various agencies, was $8.2 billion.

- And last, but hardly least, interest on debt incurred to fight past wars and finance other military spending came to between $109.1 billion, to as much as $431.5 billion, depending on judgment calls about which debt should be included.

All told, military spending came to at least $1.03 trillion. If all debatable debt were included, the total could be as high as $1.42 trillion, or almost precisely double the widely reported Department of Defense budget of $707.5 billion for 2010.

And the U.S. accounts for approximately half of the total national security spending for the entire planet. But unlike the case of health care or education, it is much more difficult to determine the marginal returns from military spending.

World Military Spending

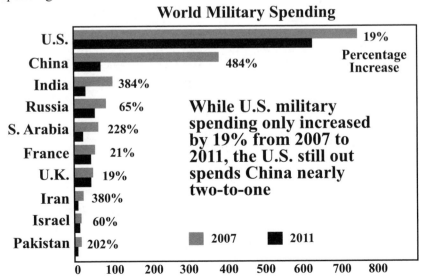

Nonetheless, educated analysis suggests there are declining (or negative) marginal returns for the trillion-plus the U.S. lavishes on military spending annually. Take for example, the failed war in Iraq or the Vietnam blunder.

The possibility that U.S. military outlays entail negative marginal returns, brings into perspective the success of the Al Qaeda "rope a dope" strategy of engaging the U.S. in conflict. As detailed in the September 8, 2011 *New York Times*:

> Al Qaeda spent roughly half a million dollars to destroy the World Trade Center and cripple the Pentagon. What has been the cost to the U.S.? In a survey of estimates by the New York Times, the answer is $3.3 trillion or about $7 million for every dollar Al Qaeda spent planning and executing the attacks.

The Times goes on to state that the total quote equals 20% of the current national debt.

The above examples from health care, education and military spending show that with economic growth stalled, growing numbers of Americans are experiencing negative returns from the complexity imposed on them by the U.S. government.

The remorseless desire of politicians to fix something by imposing increased costs that can only provide declining or negative returns brings to mind the parallels that Tainter drew with the collapse of the Roman Empire in his book.

Following in the Footsteps of Rome

Tainter points out that "as a solar-energy-based society which taxed heavily, the empire had little fiscal reserve." Consequently, when confronted with crises, Roman emperors often responded by resorting to debasing the currency and raising taxes. And while government grew, population declined as peasants could no longer afford to feed their families.

Tainter highlights a parallel that may inform the future evolution of our society:

> To avoid oppressive civic obligations, the wealthy fled from cities to establish self-sufficient rural estates. Ultimately, to escape taxation, peasants voluntarily entered into feudal relationships with these landholders. A few wealthy families came to own much of the land in the western em-

pire, and were able to defy the Imperial Government. The empire came to sustain itself by consuming its capital resources; producing lands and peasant populations. The Roman Empire provides history's best documented example of how increasing complexity to resolve problems leads to higher costs, diminishing returns, alienation of a support population, economic weakness, and collapse.

Obama's policies, enacted under similar conditions of declining and negative marginal returns, share strong similarities with those of the authoritarian emperors in the final years of the Roman Empire. As "the menacing specter of state bankruptcy" draws ever nearer, Obama enthusiastically embraces the old remedies: "reduction in the value of the currency and increased taxation." To a degree that few Americans yet realize, Obama has opted for financial repression to squeeze the population to the last drop.

However, one alternative is to leave the oppressed society.

Historically, as Tainter tells us, when a complex society is declining by garnering more and more negative returns, just as in the fall of Rome, the logical solution is not to make provisions for the payment of confiscatory taxes, but to move somewhere you may be able to escape them.

Financial Repression 101

This, indeed, is what a growing number of Americans have decided to do. Faced with financial repression at the hands of the Obama administration, a silent migration has been under way in which Americans are fleeing the U.S. at a rate of 742 per hour. While this rush for the exit has apparently escaped the notice of the mainstream news media, it seems to have attracted Obama's attention. He has decided to crack down with initiatives designed to make it more difficult for Americans to live abroad or even obtain passports for travel.

In the first instance, Obama has sought to deprive Americans of their civil right to open bank accounts outside the U.S. It is practically impossible to live anywhere in the world at a decent standard of living without operating a bank account. The Foreign Bank and Financial Account Report (FBAR) and the Foreign Account Tax and Compliance Act (FATCA) impose onerous and costly regulatory mandates on foreign banks that have American customers. These heavy-handed regulations seem to have achieved their purpose in bullying most foreign banks and financial institutions into rejecting U.S. citizens' applications and closing their accounts. Americans living abroad, even those who have never lived in the U.S., report great difficulty in opening and maintaining bank accounts.

Obama's next line of attack in his drive to block your potential lines of escape was to propose new regulations to make it more difficult to obtain a U.S. passport. Under these regulations, the application to attain a U.S. passport would be complicated with an incredible array of niggling questions.

Among other things, you would be required to "list your mother's residence one year before your birth." You would also be required to list your mother's place of employment at the time of your birth with the dates of her employment, the name of her employer and the employer's address. Good luck in assembling the information if your mother is dead.

But it gets more ridiculous. Here are other pieces of information you would need:

- Whether or not your mother received prenatal or postnatal medical care. If so, the name of the hospital or other facility, the name of the doctor, and dates of appointments.

- The circumstances of your birth, including names (as well as address and phone number, if available) of whomever was present at your birth.

- To list all of your residences inside and outside the U.S., starting with your birth until present.

- Current and former places of employment in the U.S. and abroad.

- All schools that you've attended inside and outside the U.S. along with dates of attendance.

- Full name, place and date of birth and citizenship of an array of your relatives — living and deceased.

And most astonishing of all is the proposal that would require men to specify details of their circumcision, if applicable. Mercifully, most of us cannot recall the details, but that ignorance might provide Obama's bureaucrats with an excuse to deny you a passport by saying you filed "an incomplete application."

Not content to overload the passport application with a battery of pettifogging questions that would be impossible for the average person to answer, the Obama administration has sought de jure powers to cancel your passport and thus prevent your escape from the fantastic burden of taxation that lies ahead.

A provision, "Revocation or denial of passport in case of certain unpaid taxes" in the recent highway bill would give the IRS the right to revoke your passport if it merely alleges that you owe $50,000 or more in taxes. If this provision — which already passed the Senate 74 to 22 — sails through the House, you can add the U.S. to the list of countries, like the late Soviet Union, North Korea, Cuba and East Germany, which are rightly called "police states" because they explicitly limit their citizens' right to travel.

No matter what transpires, it is all but indisputable that higher, even confiscatory taxes will be the downstream corollary to all the spending from an empty pocket that Obama is sponsoring today.

CHAPTER 18

Quantitative Easing Fails: Tomorrow's History Now

"Overall, the U.S. economy appears likely to expand at a moderate pace over the second half of 2007, with growth then strengthening a bit in 2008 to a rate close to the economy's underlying trend."

— Ben Bernanke, Testimony before Congress on July 18, 2007

Save your money. Don't buy the book. I can already tell you what Nobel Prize-winning Keynesian economists will write a few years from now when they do their appraisal summing up the policy failures that allowed the subprime crisis to morph into Secular Stagnation and Worldwide Depression.

They will claim that President Obama failed the country by spending too little money out of an empty pocket. Not enough deficit spending. However many trillions are spent, it is never enough.

They will deride helicopter Ben Bernanke, not to mention Janet Yellen, for failing to paper the economy with enough newly printed cash. The helicopter didn't fly high enough. Or low enough. Not enough inflation.

In short, they will repeat the same ill-informed arguments that are re-invented every time there is a major (or even minor) credit contraction.

As analyst Bob Hoye points out, the prescription for circumventing credit contractions doesn't amount to anything more original than the idea prescribed by Edward Misselden in "Free Trade, or the Means to Make Trade Flourish (London, 1622)." Note here that Misselden was not an advocate of what we know as free trade. Rather, what he meant by "free trade" was "freedom from competition." He favored a mercantilist policy of oligopoly and regulated trade, with easy credit all around.

Misselden wrote in the wake of early 17th century credit contractions originating in Germany and the Baltic States. The Ben Bernanke of his day, Misselden championed the ever-alluring but seldom successful strategy of countering credit contraction by creating more credit.

Much of the monetary history of the modern world has been driven by successively more desperate efforts to dismantle and minimize institutional checks on credit expansion. In this sense, the gold standard was being gradually vitiated for centuries before Richard Nixon abolished its last vestiges in August 1971.

At every stage of this downhill process, the Ben Bernankes of the world have thought that they could out-smart the credit cycle.

They never have.

QE's Shaky Start

It is often forgotten today that after 1929, the Fed — under prodding from Herbert Hoover — went wild trying to counteract the post-bubble contraction by flooding the system with credit.

George Harrison (not the Beatle, but the president of the Federal Reserve Bank of New York in 1929) overshot the previous limits on credit expansion by a factor of six. Because the dollar was still worth something then, the numbers were not as gaudy as those racked up by Bernanke in his aggressive programs to bail out the banks, but in relative terms, it was the same policy.

Obama could have saved time with his speechwriters by lifting whole paragraphs from Herbert Hoover's October 5, 1931 letter to George Harrison. In it, Hoover decried the impact of events in Europe in tightening domestic credit conditions…

> As I said last night, we are in a degenerating vicious cycle. Economic events of Europe have demoralized our farm produce and security prices. This has given rise to an unsettlement of public mind. There have been in some localities foolish alarm over the stability of our credit structure and considerable withdrawals of currency. In consequence bankers in many other parts of the country in fear of the possibility of such unreasoning demands of depositors have deemed it necessary to place their assets in such liquid form as to enable them to meet drains and runs. To do this they sell securities and restrict credit. The sale of securities demoralizes their price and jeopardizes other banks. The restriction on credit has grown greatly in the past few weeks.

Printing Money Doesn't Work

The irony is that Janet Yellen is liable to end up with the same bad reputation for parsimony and indecision with which Fed officials were tarred after 1929.

While it might seem that central bankers who can create money out of "thin air" would have no trouble in making good on their pledge to expand the money supply enough to forestall widespread bankruptcy and collapse in the wake of a credit bubble, in practice it doesn't prove that easy.

For one thing, they can create liquidity but they cannot create solvency. Their closest approximation to generating solvency has been to monetize stock indices, thus amplifying the assets of stockholders. But as John Hussman, Ph.D shrewdly observed in his Weekly Market Comment for November 24, 2014:

> Quantitative easing only "works" to the extent that default-free, low interest liquidity is viewed as an inferior holding. When investor psychology shifts toward increasing risk aversion — which we can reasonably measure through the uniformity or dispersion of market internals, the variation of credit spreads between risky and safe debt, and investor sponsorship as reflected in price-volume behavior — default-free, low-interest liquidity is no longer considered inferior. It's actually desirable, so creating more of the stuff is not supportive to stock prices. We observed exactly that during the 2000-2002 and 2007-2009 plunges, which took the S&P 500 down by half in each episode, even as the Fed was easing persistently and aggressively. A shift toward increasing internal dispersion and widening credit spreads leaves risky, overvalued, overbought, over bullish markets extremely vulnerable to air-pockets, freefalls, and crashes.

In other words, while quantitative easing or the outright monetization of stock indices may tend to raise prices during periods of calm, gains are vulnerable to being wiped out in the unbalanced environment of a bubble. In addition to the key factors canvassed by Hussman, another dynamic effect of super-low interest rates is to raise the capitalization of any given stream of income. While this tends to raise stock values as a first-order effect, it also gives corporate management a stronger incentive to slash expenses and downsize employment than to invest in growth (in what is already a condition of secular stagnation).

Quantitative Easing facilitates high stock prices. Low interest rates permit the payment of dividends and stock buy-backs with borrowed cash. Thus, stock prices can rise without top line growth in corporate revenues that entail an increasingly precarious imbalance. As the engineered prosperity of the few diverges from the straitened circumstances of the many, this also points to "free falls and crashes." And thus works against the desire to hold risk assets. So it is not merely credit spreads between safe and risky debt that make low-interest liquidity attractive. The social strains arising from Quantitative Easing point that way as well.

I wrote a book with Lord Rees-Mogg in the 1990s forecasting another depression. In "The Great Reckoning," we argued that the ability of government to forestall contraction was an over-bought illusion that would disappoint in the event.

This is proving true before our eyes.

Two of the policy initiatives aggressively undertaken by the Federal Reserve — Quantitative Easing (or the creation of new money to buy bonds) and the slashing of interest rates to near zero — both appear to have failed or backfired as stimulus.

Taken together, they appear to be insufficient in creating enough money to compensate for the trillions of dollars that have disappeared from the effective money supply due to the collapse of the Shadow Banking System.

The Shadow Banking System is comprised of non-depository financial institutions, both in the U.S. and around the world, including investment banks, special purpose investment vehicles, hedge funds, money market funds and insurers that played an increasingly crucial role in "funding infrastructure" of the economy after 2000.

It is little appreciated that the Shadow Banking System grew to be larger than the regular commercial banks, and thereafter contracted by more than $7 trillion. The broad measure of money that used to be known as M3 (no longer published by the Fed) continues to be calculated by Shadow Government Statistics (SGS).

The SGS compilations show continuing weakness in broad money, a deflationary phenomenon that is confirmed by the experience of small-business people and others seeking credit. Banks aren't lending enough to make up for the shrinking of the Shadow Banking System. But paradoxically, leverage is still expanding, particularly through the transfer of bad debt onto the public balance sheet, as government takes over private liabilities. As stated in the Geneva report *Deleveraging? What Deleveraging?* "the ratio of global total debt excluding financials over GDP (we do not have, at this stage, a reliable estimation of financial sector debt in emerging economies) has kept increasing at an unabated pace and breaking new highs: up 38 percentage points since 2008 to 212%."

The Fed's Hidden Bailout

The inflationary ambitions of the Federal Reserve are distorted by the same bias toward crony capitalism that contorts all the developed economies. The profitable franchise for the creation of money has been delegated to private banks. As you would expect, they use that extravagant privilege selectively to optimize their own profits. The Federal Reserve has permitted banks to essentially mint profits by borrowing from the Fed at an interest rate of 0.25%, then re-lending that money to the government at interest rates ranging from 1% to 3.4%. Naturally, the banks have had interludes of profitability on the basis of this incredible subsidy.

Ask yourself: could you make money if the government lent you billions at 0.25% and then let you turn around and finance its yawning budget deficits at interest rates 10 times or more higher than it charges to lend? Of course you could. A kindergarten class could make money under those conditions.

But the Federal Reserve has no better clue than the kindergarten class about how to reflate a credit bubble and re-launch a popular consumption orgy in a country where virtually no jobs have been created since the year 2000.

There were about 130 million jobs in the U.S. in 2000. Now there are only 141 million jobs. The population has grown by 36.7 million, but the number of jobs hasn't kept pace.

Even worse, the number of jobs that could support a middle-class lifestyle has been falling for decades.

As of March 2013, mid-wage positions accounted for 60% of the job losses in America, but only 22% of job growth.

The economy has performed worse than it did from 1920 to 1931.

How much did the average wage-earner gain from 2000 until now? Zero. As Bill Bonner, president of Agora Publishing, points out, inflation-adjusted average wages are stuck at $16 per hour.

Again, the closer you look, the worse the picture is. Between 1969 and 2009, the median wages of American men between the ages of 30 and 50 fell by 27%.

It is easy to talk about putting Humpty Dumpty back together again after his great fall. But much of the rising distress throughout the world economy is directly correlated to the too-clever policy of trying to counterfeit our way to prosperity through various QE operations.

Not for the first time in a credit contraction, the side effects of efforts to ramp inflation raise more questions than they answer. Putting aside the question of whether the indirect creation of money by private banks is an efficient and effective means of creating inflation, you then face the more basic issue of whether inflation is really an abracadabra that can magically revive contracting economies? I think not.

Three Ways Attempted Inflation Backfired

Fed officials reasoned that if they could cheapen the dollar through Quantitative Easing (QE), they would lift the burden of debt that is squashing the American economy and other advanced economies. In the event, however, Quantitative Easing had at least several unintended contractionary effects…

First, Quantitative Easing in the United States translated into "Quantitative Tightening" in the once rapidly growing emerging economies like Brazil, Russia, India, China, and similar countries such as Turkey.

The liquidity created by Quantitative Easing, along with the invisibly low yields on dollar investments and the freezing of rates at 25 basis points for years into the future, encouraged a massive flow of funds into high yielding emerging markets securities.

For example, the Japanese, who have suffered with Quantitative Easing for decades, shoveled hundreds of billions into high-yield Brazilian investments. The huge influx of hot money seeking better returns led to an overheating in Brazil, resulting in higher interest rates and other conscious steps to curtail Brazilian growth. These succeeded far more than Brazilian authorities intended.

Equally, Turkish authorities increased reserve requirements while lowering nominal interest rates in the hope of discouraging the influx of hot money from the U.S. and Europe.

In a sense, by promulgating QE, the Federal Reserve was applying the brakes to slow down countries like Brazil, India, China, Turkey, and Russia that were otherwise poised to account for a large portion of world economic growth.

As of mid-April 2014, the BRIC countries were struggling to contain inflation, courtesy of Quantitative Easing. Annual inflation reached 8.3% in India, 8.2% in Russia, 6% in Brazil, and 2.5% in China, according to official statistics. Each of the BRICs has taken measures to combat inflation and in the process has dampened growth.

The Quantitative Tightening exported by the Federal Reserve is poised to find expression as worldwide depression.

There are strong hints that China, which has been on a growth tear for decades, is settling into a hard landing. Zhu Min, Deputy Managing Director of the IMF, warns that there is a "large potential risk" that China and emerging Asian economies will "slow down too fast."

Growth in Chinese consumption of electricity — often considered to be the "true pulse" of China's economy — has been slowing since 2009.

Meanwhile, China's HSBC's Purchasing Manager's Index (PMI) for services showed contraction, while similar surveys showed Chinese manufacturing slowing or even contracting for most of 2013 and 2014.

The haunting similarities between the global slowdown now and the descent into a deeper stage of worldwide depression after 1931 are too obvious to miss.

Once again, an experiment in currency depreciation intended to end a post-bubble contraction washes out in greater market and political volatility.

A second (possibly) unintended contractionary effect of Quantitative Easing is the spread of social unrest...

The evident glee with which U.S. authorities viewed the prospect of devaluing the dollar encouraged a sharp rise in the prices of crucial commodities including food and energy. As a result of the surge in inflation, revolutions swept across North Africa and the Middle East in 2011. Chinese authorities, in particular, became nervous that protests against higher food costs would escalate into unrest even in that rapidly growing economy.

The higher cost of food not only ended a dictatorship in Egypt that U.S. taxpayers had forked out tens of billions to prop up over the decades, it also precipitated a slowdown in all the "advanced" economies as higher oil prices reduced spending by pinched consumers.

Of course, other factors have played a role in fueling the social unrest we witnessed a few years ago. For example, demand for commodities increased rapidly in developing nations during certain stages of Quantitative Easing.

Then there is the third unintended effect of Quantitative Easing…

Bill Gross, formerly of PIMCO, the world's largest bond fund, argued that the radical lowering of interest rates and the freezing of the yield curve with rates at invisibly low levels has actually destroyed leverage in the credit system. (This is another facet of the inefficiency of indirect efforts to generate inflation through the private banking system.)

Says Gross:

> To bring the point specifically to what occurred the past several months with a two-year Treasury extension and the conditional freezing of interest rates at 25 basis points for two years, you have that basically flat yield curve destroys systemic leverage…Credit is basically destroyed in the process of lowering and freezing interest rates.

In short, Gross argues that the Fed's attempts to shower the economy with indirectly created new money have backfired. The newly created money blew back into the helicopter and gummed up the engine.

Banks are holding the cash they have been given by the Federal Reserve and Treasury through numerous bailouts. At $2.7 trillion, excess reserves reached an all-time high on August 31, 2014. The Fed stuffed reserves into the system. But banks have their own balance sheets to worry about. They did not do a spectacular job of converting high-powered reserves into new loans. Small companies seeking credit have frequently been disappointed. Banks are reluctant to lend.

As a result, a global depression is gathering momentum. The authorities who long confidently proclaimed their ability to turn back the tide of depression with the magic wand of fiat money are now puzzled and hesitant. Debt levels throughout most of the world have reached a poisonous extreme.

The Tipping Point of Indebtedness

As Ambrose Evans-Pritchard wrote summarizing a study by Stephen Cecchetti of the Bank for International Settlements,

> Debt becomes poisonous once it reaches 80% to 100% of GDP for governments, 90% of GDP for companies, and 85% of GDP for households. From then on, extra debt chokes growth…

Cecchetti and his team at the Bank for International Settlements have written "The real effects of debt," the definitive paper rebutting the pied pipers of ever-escalating credit. "The debt problems facing advanced economies are even worse than we thought," he says.

Economies are beginning to reflect this reality by slowing down and falling back into a downturn as they did in the second phase of the Great Depression following the collapse of Credit-Anstalt in 1931.

Two Debt-Laden Peas in a Pod

The best way to think about the sovereign debt crisis in Europe is to compare it to the recent banking crisis in the U.S.

When Bear Stearns was allowed to go bust in March 2008 and then sold to JP Morgan at $2 a share… it signaled to investors that the government would allow irresponsible institutions to fail.

Just a few months later, Lehman went bankrupt too. And then the entire banking system in the U.S. changed forever.

These financial collapses happened in part because of the way banks were allowed to value the assets they held. As long as the bank held AAA-rated debt, they didn't need to have collateral put up against it.

AAA-rated debt was easy to come by. Not only did most sovereign governments hold that rating, but so did trillions worth of mortgage-backed securities. This gave banks an excuse to safely increase their leverage levels.

Some of these banks — which were supposed to invest responsibly — had leverage in excess of 50 to 1. With leverage that high, all it takes is a 2% drop in held asset values to wipe a bank out.

Bank	Assets	Shareholder Equity	Ratio
Deutsche Bank	€2,020B	€38.5B	52.0X
UBS	Fr2,272B	Fr42.5B	53.4X
Credit Suiss	Fr1,360B	Fr59.88B	22.7X
Fortis	€871B	€34.28B	25.5X
Dexia	€604B	€16.4B	36.8X
BNP Paribas	€1,694B	€59.4B	28.5X
Barclays	£1,227B	£32.5B	37.8X
RBS	£1,990B	£91.48B	21.7X

But as it turns out, this debt wasn't very safe. And as soon as the mortgage-backed securities started losing value, the banks ran into a huge funding problem.

As word spread through the street that banks were in trouble, a panic arose and we saw massive bank runs. This is what destroyed Bear Stearns. And it also caused the collapse of Lehman, and all the other bank failures that have happened since.

The situation in the EU isn't much different.

Thanks to the BASEL II accords, which dictate bank standards, European banks were allowed to hold sovereign AAA-rated debt with virtually no collateral to back it up. In other words, leverage rates are extreme.

How much debt are we talking about? According to the original European Stress Tests, the debt of the PIIGS (Portugal, Ireland, Italy, Greece and Spain) alone amounted to more than €1,147 billion. That's close to $1.56 trillion, which may not sound like much at first blush. But when leverage is as high as it is in Europe, a default on just 2% to 5% of that debt could lead to a massive banking crisis.

The most dangerous part about all of this isn't necessarily the leverage rates of the banks (even though they are bad). It is the prospect of a loss of confidence by investors and customers in their banks.

We have to remember that most of the time any given bank is fully invested. What they have "liquid" and available to customers is only a small percentage of their total liabilities (deposits). What this means is that, if even a few large depositors fear a banking collapse and withdraw their money, the bank could actually run out of cash and fall apart.

As you can see, this fear has driven up interest rates on the PIIGS for years now, and bailouts have not stopped this from happening.

An Obscene Tax That Hurts an Already Suffering Country

The problem with rising interest rates is that it adds an obscene sort of tax to any country that already has a debt problem. Just think about it: if a given country is already having trouble paying back its debt, how could a higher interest solve that problem?

It can't. And it won't.

As these EU members eventually enter default, the banking system in Europe will enter into a crisis mode. Banks will stop trusting each other and the entire funding mechanism will crash and burn.

This will most certainly destroy some European banks in the process.

2016: Still No Recovery

If, as I expect, there is still no decisive evidence of recovery by 2016, you can expect that this failure will only incite learned professors to fulminate more vociferously in favor of QE to monetize every pair of dirty underwear east of Cleveland.

No matter what they say, however, government can't print BTUs or food.

Unfortunately, the growth of jobs and income in the U.S. is closely correlated with energy output and the end of the gold standard in the 1970s, which turned the system decisively against the average person.

The Census Bureau recently reported that median income for males employed full-time had plunged to 1978 levels.

And this was supposed to be recovery. It isn't. It is depression. The "degenerating vicious cycle" Herbert Hoover lamented is fully in evidence. Every day, thousands of additional Americans fall into poverty. 46.2 million Americans are now poor. The U.S. government is helping to feed over 46 million Americans through food stamps. More than 65 million Americans are now on Medicaid.

But the government is broke, its credit downgraded, its credibility crumbling. What will happen once the social safety net inevitably frays and pulls apart?

The national conversation hasn't focused on that because it is too frightening.

What we have to keep in mind is that the globe is experiencing a balance sheet downturn; in other words, a depression.

It will not be brought to an easy, premature end by easy money or runaway deficit spending.

Given the current state of confusion about credit cycles, it will certainly take many years to complete the deleveraging essential to bring the global depression to an end.

That's why I suggest that, instead of fighting the forces of deflation gripping the world today, you use it to your advantage.

CHAPTER 19

How Quantitative Easing Destabilizes Economies

"Haven't modern shipping, modern agriculture, and modern industry given us a buffer of safety? Is it only that with more people and cash in the world than ever before, the losses from natural disasters will inevitably yield unprecedented numbers? No, a look at the interaction of climate and history over the past 15,000 years reveals another process at work more or less continuously over that span. In our efforts to cushion ourselves against smaller, more frequent climate stresses, we have consistently made ourselves more vulnerable to rarer but larger catastrophes. The whole course of civilization (while it is many other things, too, of course) may be seen as a process of trading up on the scale of vulnerability."

— Brian Fagan, "The Long Summer:
How Climate Changed Civilization"

Food prices hit an all-time high in January, 2011. According to the UN's Food and Agricultural Organization (FAO) "the FAO Food Price Index (FFPI) rose for the seventh consecutive month, averaging 231 points in January 2011, up 3.4 percent from December 2010 and the highest in both real and nominal terms" since records began. Note that prices exceeded the previously record levels of 2008 that sparked food riots in more than 30 countries. "Famine-style" prices for food and energy that prevailed early in 2008 may also have helped precipitate the credit crisis that then Federal Reserve Chairman Ben Bernanke described in closed-door testimony "as the worst in financial history, even exceeding the Great Depression."

The turmoil surrounding commodity inflation took center stage with more serious riots and even revolutions across the globe. Popular discontent was not just confined to "basket case" countries like Haiti and Bangladesh as in 2008. High food prices have roiled Arab kleptocracies with young populations and U.S. backed dictators such as Tunisia, Egypt, Bahrain and Yemen. Even dynamic economies have been affected. Indeed, all of the BRIC countries, except Brazil, witnessed food rioting.

The most overt unrest among the BRICs occurred in India, where food costs absorbed more than 25% of the typical Indian's budget before India's Food Price Index jumped by 15.57% on January 27, 2011. Indians were particularly incensed by a surge in the price of onions, a key ingredient in the food consumed by poor families. A government report at the end of 2010 confirmed the price of onions had risen to 85 rupees ($1.87) per kilogram from 35 rupees only a week earlier. Dismay over soaring onion prices incited major demonstrations against alleged government corruption.

While Indian protests mushroomed without grabbing attention on CNBC, an unassuming 26-year-old fruit vendor named Mohamed Bouazizi launched a revolution in Tunisia when he set himself on fire to protest the confiscation of his fruit cart and apples. His efforts to improvise a living had run afoul of stifling bureaucracy. Bouazizi became so furious and frustrated that he just "could not take it anymore." He adopted the extreme protest technique pioneered among Buddhist monks in Vietnam by Thích Quảng Đức almost half a century ago. Thích Quảng Đức burned himself to death on June 11, 1963 to protest oppression of Buddhists by the despotic Diem regime.

Mohamed Bouazizi was infuriated that corrupt officials had stolen his fruit wagon, along with his prized, new electronic scale. He became a martyr of the revolution that toppled the 23-year dictatorship of Zine El Abidine Ben Ali.

Bouazizi also inspired desperate advocates of regime change in Egypt, the world's biggest wheat importer, where three people set themselves ablaze igniting protests against the government. In Algeria, tied with Indonesia as the world's third-largest wheat buyer, three people were killed in clashes with police during rallies against high food prices. The government responded by purchasing as much as 800,000 metric tonnes of wheat a day in an effort to placate a public squeezed by rising prices.

Less than a month after the fall of Ben Ali, a similar popular uprising in Egypt toppled the 30-year authoritarian regime of Hosni Mubarak. A dictatorship that U.S. taxpayers had spent some $70 billion dollars to prop up was swept away.

The late Mr. Bouazizi, and the Facebook bloggers who organized resistance to Mubarak in Tahrir Square could never have subverted long-established dictatorships without the assistance of an important accomplice. More than Mohamed Bouazizi, it was Benjamin S. Bernanke who lit the fuse that set the world on fire. Much credit for fomenting the revolutions and turmoil sweeping the Middle East (and surely other countries to come) belongs to our own former chairman of the Federal Reserve. What the former Soviet Union, Al Qaeda, Hezbollah, The Muslim Brotherhood and associated bad guys could not do in decades of trying, Bernanke achieved in a twinkle through the magic of his Quantitative Easing project.

Bernanke's chaos must have caused a lot of sleepless nights in government palaces around the globe. Barely was the ink dry on the headlines heralding Mubarak's departure, when more rioting erupted in Algeria, Bahrain, Yemen, Libya, Jordan and Iran.

While Mr. Bernanke modestly declined the credit for destabilizing much of the world, close analysis confirms that he played a leading role. His QE2 program of counterfeiting trillions out of thin air has helped ignite a raging bull market with food and commodities. The fact that the U.S. dollar has been the world's reserve currency means that almost all commodity prices are denominated in dollars. As a matter of simple math, when the dollar goes down, the prices of commodities tend to go up.

Thanks to Bernanke's handiwork in conjuring trillions out of thin air, commodity prices rose faster than consumer demand.

For one thing, hedge funds, Sovereign Wealth Funds (SWFs) and other large investors, such as Calpers, the California employees' pension fund, staked out long positions in commodities in search of higher returns and to hedge against inflation. Vast amounts of easily stored commodities like metals have been tied up under cheap rental and financing deals, where the holders profit if prices rise faster than storage costs. QE has underwritten that speculation with easy money. The added bid from inflation hedgers amplifies the price of commodities at any given state of supply and demand.

Even commodities that can spoil, like wheat, can nonetheless be hoarded for limited periods. For less than 2/100th of a penny per day per bushel, speculators can hold wheat in storage elevators. The regulations of the Kansas City

Board of Trade for Hard Red Winter Wheat contracts state: "The maximum insurance and storage charge for regular elevators on grain delivered on futures contracts is established at $.00148 per bushel per day." Given that wheat prices doubled in 2010, anyone who paid to store a deliverable wheat contract probably walked away smiling.

Low Interest Rates Raise Commodity Prices — Or Do They?

During the 2008 run-up in food prices, the three major U.S. grain exchanges all sharply raised their initial and maintenance margins for trading grain futures. But Bernanke made commodity speculation more appealing by dropping interest rates to invisibly low levels. As Jeffrey Frankel, Harpel Professor of Capital Formation and Growth at Harvard, wrote in "The Effect of Interest Rates on Commodity Prices:"

High interest rates reduce the demand for storable commodities, or increase the supply, through a variety of channels:

- by increasing the incentive for extraction today rather than tomorrow (think of the rates at which oil is pumped, gold mined, forests logged, or livestock herds culled)

- by decreasing firms' desire to carry inventories (think of oil inventories held in tanks)

- by encouraging speculators to shift out of spot commodity contracts, and into treasury bills

All three mechanisms work to reduce the market price of commodities, as happened when real interest rates were high in the early 1980s.

A decrease in real interest rates has the opposite effect, lowering the cost of carrying inventories, and raising commodity prices, as happened from August 2007 to September 2008. Call it an example of the "carry trade."

In short, U.S. monetary policy unequivocally raised commodity prices in 2010, and following years — until 2014.

Adding to this witch's brew was the fact that "correlation traders" armed with sophisticated computer models have developed algorithms that tell them to purchase grains on future's markets when, for example, oil rises by 2% over its 30-day moving average, or rises more than Obama's poll numbers. The correlation traders may not be "inflation-hedgers" per se, but the correlations in the commodity market have mostly been to the upside during the past decade's astonishing bull market.

The drivers of this bull market in commodities were generally in plain view, without really being fully understood. The rapid development of emerging markets, especially the BRIC economies (Brazil, Russia, India and China) increased demand for basic commodities whose prices were heretofore determined mainly by swings in economic activity in the United States and other "advanced economies." Part of the impulse behind the rapid growth that made emerging markets expand to comprise half the world economy came from 20th Street and Constitution Ave. NW in Washington, D.C., where the Federal Reserve was creating $85 billion out of thin air each month to buy bonds. And thus keep interest rates low.

By starving investors for yield, Quantitative Easing set the stage for the infusion of massive amounts of capital into emerging markets. Emerging market borrowers took on $5.7 trillion in U.S. dollar debt. This was divided between $3.1 trillion in bank loans and $2.6 trillion in bond issues.

As Ambrose Evans-Pritchard observed in *The Telegraph* (2014), "Much of the debt was taken out at real interest rates of 1pc on the implicit assumption that the Fed would continue to flood the world with liquidity for years to come. The borrowers are 'short dollars' in trading parlance. They now face the margin call from Hell as the global monetary hegemon pivots."

Central Planning Flops Again

It is hard to review the actual effects of Quantitative Easing and not be struck by the wide gaps between the consequences of this policy and what its authors intended. Their attempts to "stimulate" recovery by massive intervention that suppressed price signals was a perverse bust. They sought inflation. They got deflation. Important commodities like oil, natural gas, coal, iron, copper, lead and tin plunged at double-digit rates in 2014. They sought to ease the burden of debt. They compounded it. They sought to depreciate the dollar. It soared in value. Not the least reason for the dollar strength were the misleading press releases from the Bureau of Economic Analysis and the Bureau of Labor Statistics citing massaged and manipulated statistics that grossly overstated the strength of the U.S. economy.

This fake recovery, culminating in the preposterously overstated claim of 5% annualized growth in the second revision to Q3 2014 real GDP, was more credible at a distance than it was to close scrutiny. Thus the appearance, if not the reality of robust economic growth in the U.S. that would necessitate a tightening of monetary policy by the Federal Reserve helped ignite a strong dollar rally that took the greenback to a five-year high.

Emerging market borrowers who owe trillions of dollars are exposed to gaping currency mismatches that could lead to a world of hurt as evaporating dollar liquidity not only impairs bank assets, but triggers some of the $192 trillion in exposure that U.S. banks have to interest rate derivatives, as well as their $31 trillion in foreign exchange exposure.

This "for instance" illustrates how massive, central planning-style interventions in markets inevitably come with a long tail of unintended consequences. Not only did QE spur more rapid growth in emerging markets that maintained more nearly normal interest rates, igniting episodic commodity booms with far-reaching geopolitical consequences, it also set the stage for systemic price reversals with both oil along with other hard and soft commodities and the dollar transmitting deflationary impulses.

Ostensibly, Quantitative Easing was to have counteracted deflation with inflation. It was to have stimulated the economy in the United States, not the emerging markets. And not the least important ambition of its authors was to rebuild the balance sheets of banks by giving them easy pickings for profits in the carry trade. In the event, it did not work that way.

As explored above, QE increased volatility in commodity prices, thereby increasing volatility in commodity derivatives with the risk that this would spread across asset classes and cause huge losses in interest rate derivatives to which U.S. banks are exposed to the tidy sum of $192 trillion, along with another $31 trillion of exposure to foreign exchange.

As of December 2014, Bloomberg's commodity index had dropped to its lowest level since 2009. The surge in the value of the dollar associated with the deflation in commodity prices has created a frightening mismatch between debts denominated in soaring dollars and emerging market borrowers whose income is denominated in sliding local currencies. These developments confound all the daydreams that inspired QE. Obviously, they also contradict the "recovery" narratives so loudly espoused by Wall Street and Washington. As recently as July 2014, Goldman's commodity strategist, Jeffrey Curie, proclaimed that "the long awaited global recovery appears to be getting on track, lifting commodity demand." Not so much.

Key Event: China Joins WTO in 2001

If any single event could be said to have triggered an explosion in commodity demand, it was China's accession to the World Trade Organization (WTO) in November 2001. After 15 years of negotiations, including bitter disputes and stand-offs over (what else?) agricultural subsidies, China gained full access to the world trading system. Chinese imports increased by a factor of 7 over the next 8 years. To put this in perspective, over the previous 8 years before China gained full access to the global trading system, Chinese imports had grown by "only" 2.8 times.

Note the tight correlation between Chinese imports and commodity prices since China joined the WTO.

As you know, there are several dimensions to the Chinese import story. A significant part of the Chinese imports relates to huge volumes of raw materials and commodities required to feed Chinese industrial production, and the ongoing, rapid urbanization of China. A significant amount of construction (and thus commodity demand) is required to bring the prosperity of the coastal boomtowns inland, where more than half of China's 1.3 billion people live.

For example, Bloomberg estimated that it required "at least 41 kilograms (90 pounds) of copper in electrical wiring and appliances" to outfit a new apartment for a single family in the central Chinese town of Daojiang in Hunan province. Multiply that by millions and millions and you could be forgiven for thinking you would end up with the commodity boom of all-time.

Another portion of imports is comprised of consumption goods, which the Chinese are buying to express their growing real income. You have probably read stories about the surging sales of Rolls-Royce automobiles (up 800% in China in 2010), expensive cognacs and Breguet watches (average price HK$1,000,000). But not all the imports that reflect growing Chinese wealth are luxury goods. For every bottle of Jenssen Arcana cognac (aged 98 years in Oak barrels) sold in China, thousands of times more money is spent laying the provision for future plates of sweet and sour pork.

Think that through. As the Chinese grow richer, they quite predictably demand more meat in their diet. China's hog population has now reached 440 million animals, more than seven times greater than the U.S. herd. Chinese hogs are growing consumers of grain, particularly corn. The expectation of having to feed these hungry hogs has led the Chinese to increase their purchases of U.S corn eight-fold.

More than a Demand Surge

What at first glance appears to be a simple demand surge driving prices higher is on closer examination partly a reaction to the provocatively inflationary monetary policy pursued by Bernanke, Yellen and Obama. The Chinese are not merely in the commodity markets acquiring goods for current use. They have done a tremendous amount of anticipatory and preemptory buying. Correlation traders take note.

The Chinese hog farmers who consume mountains of grain were also among the most important players in stockpiling copper in recent years. In 2009, London metals traders estimated that Chinese pig farmers had amassed more than 50,000 metric tons of copper — about 10% of world stockpiles.

"People who have nothing at all to do with the copper trade have been buying copper as a store of value, much like they would with gold," said Jiang Mingjun, an analyst at Shanghai Oriental Futures Co. (Part of the mysterious affinity of Chinese pig farmers for copper was the fact that they could use it to circumvent credit restrictions designed to slow the growth of the Chinese pig herd. The farmers could hypothecate copper to increase leverage in their operations when they could no longer borrow on the strength of their business plans.)

China is sitting on the world's largest foreign exchange reserves — an astonishing stash of $3.89 trillion, up from $212.2 billion in 2001 when China joined WTO. Having multiplied their reserves by more than 18 times in little more than a dozen years, the Chinese are not too happy with the prospect of sitting by and watching the U.S. inflate away the value of their hard-earned dollar holdings. They are well aware that the United States (which holds FX reserves of a paltry 0.88% of GDP) has no particular care for preserving the foreign exchange earnings of others. In fact, the Obama Administration has clearly indicated its desire to depreciate the dollar to facilitate greater sales of U.S. made products abroad. Luckily (or perhaps unluckily for the borrowers of dollars among Chinese companies), the dollar reversed its depreciation in a rally that recovered losses dating to 2009.

As of this writing, the Federal Reserve appears to have failed in its intention to depreciate the dollar through the inflationary policy of creating trillions out of thin air to monetize U.S. budget deficits. Even with nugatory interest rates earned on U.S. bank deposits and Treasury obligations, the Chinese pig farmers are probably only just beginning to regret their decisions to hold copper rather than greenbacks. Copper ingots have declined by 13.3% in 2014 after more than doubling in value since September 2009. Depending on their entry prices, the copper-hoarding Chinese pig farmers could have made a quarter of a billion dollars or more from copper in preference to holding U.S. dollars. But their profits are eroding as inflation turns to deflation.

This helps to explain the behavior of commodity prices, as well as one of the greatest wealth transfers in history — from Americans to everyone else — and then back again as the Chinese and others bet against the dollar by stockpiling commodities for future use, only to see the Fed's QE program trigger systemic price reversals that threatened to deleverage the system.

Oil and Food: The Central Importance of "Non-core Inflation"

Many Arab states have been at the forefront of hoarding grain in order to fend off popular uprisings like those in Tunisia and Egypt. While farming apparently originated in the Middle East about 10,000 years ago, the agricultural sector there today is severely limited because of water scarcity.

The region has been jolted by three waves of food riots in the past two decades, most recently in 2008. The world economic crisis temporarily rescued the situation then by rapidly deflating demand. But as Derek Headey, a researcher at the International Food Policy Research Institute (IFPRI), argues, the global financial crisis soon made matters worse because it "prompted a number of governments — particularly the U.S. — to pump money into their economies and lower interest rates. Together with a very weak U.S. dollar, these factors provide a macro-environment that is conducive to higher commodity prices, including higher oil prices, which also impact food process through production and transport costs."

As we reported previously, the impact of higher oil prices in the production cost of food is significant, as the "green revolution" is essentially an equation for converting petroleum into food. The energy intensity of food production may be poised to take a leap higher over the next quarter of a century if I am correct in thinking that we are living in the early stages of another "Little Ice Age."

QE lit the fuse that set the world on fire, with 44 protests and bloody riots against rising prices in just one week. The Fed's program to monetize yawning federal deficits led to a spike in food and commodity prices. As a result, prices have spiked even higher than in 2008. The United Nations' Food and Agriculture Organization reported that its worldwide food price index hit a record high in January 2011, having climbed each month since Bernanke announced QE2. Global food and commodity prices soared 28% in six months — but they don't want you to mistake that for inflation.

Bernanke (and now Yellen) operate on the absurd conceit that food and energy prices should be excluded from a calculation of Core Inflation. They may be able to hoax some people with that proposition, but I doubt that former presidents Zine El Abidine Ben Ali or Hosni Mubarak would be dull enough to exclude food and energy from an accounting of inflation.

Notwithstanding a surge in Food Stamp dependence in the U.S. that has led 46,670,373 Americans on to the roles, food costs still absorb a far lower percentage of the income of the typical American than in Tunis or Cairo.

The World Bank stated in a report on food security that "Arab countries are very vulnerable to fluctuations in international commodity markets because they are heavily dependent on imported food. Arab countries are the largest importers of cereal in the world [— more than 58 million metric tons in 2007 —] most import at least 50 percent of the food calories they consume."

It added that "of greater concern for Arab countries is that structural and cyclical forces are creating a system that is very sensitive to supply shortfalls and ever-increasing demand, making future price shocks very probable."

Malthus: Not Wrong but Early?

If you remember your footnotes from the history of economics, you will recall the storied work of Rev. Thomas Malthus, one of the pioneers of population studies. From "The Concise Encyclopedia of Economics:"

Noting that while food production tends to increase arithmetically, population tends to increase naturally at a (faster) geometric rate. Malthus argued that it is no surprise that people thus choose to reduce (or "check") population growth... Malthus was fascinated not with the inevitability of human demise, but with why humans do not die off in the face of such overwhelming odds. As an economist, he studied responses to incentives...

Malthus is arguably the most misunderstood and misrepresented economist of all time. The adjective "Malthusian" is used today to describe a pessimistic prediction of the lock step demise of humanity doomed to starvation via overpopulation. When his hypothesis was first stated in his best-selling "An Essay on the Principle of Population (1798)," the uproar it caused among non-economists overshadowed the instant respect it inspired among his fellow economists. So irrefutable and simple was his illustrative side-by-side comparison of an arithmetic and a geometric series — food increases more slowly than population — that it was often taken out of context and highlighted as his main observation. The observation is, indeed, so stark that it is still easy to lose sight of Malthus's actual conclusion: that because humans have not all starved, economic choices must be at work, and it is the job of an economist to study those choices."

In addition to the fact that the Arab homelands are generally arid, with little land suited to food production, also underlying their particular vulnerability are population growth rates among the highest on the planet. The population of the Arab world was 73 million in 1950. Now it has more than quadrupled to 389 million. The World Bank expects that to double again by 2050 — a suggestion that augurs ill for future oil exports from the Middle East given peak oil concerns.

On current trends, even Saudi Arabia's export capacity will be pinched by surging domestic consumption — a consideration of capital importance to anyone who takes a long-term "Malthusian" view of access to resources.

Saudi domestic oil and gas use was rising at an annual average of 5.9% from 2010 to 2015, far faster than population or GDP. A big part of the reason for the rapid growth in domestic consumption is that the Saudis, and, indeed, most Middle East oil producers, have been selling oil and gas to domestic consumers at "giveaway' prices. In spite of its small population, Saudi Arabia is the world's 15th ranked energy consumer, with 56% of its electric power generated by direct burn of petroleum.

This all becomes more important in the context of "bad weather" around the globe that has adversely affected crop yields and multiplied the mischief done by aggressive (some might think "belligerent") U.S. monetary policy in roiling commodity, debt and currency markets. The conventional view of weather disturbances is that they are down to man-made "Global Warming."

I think otherwise, and explain why in coming chapters.

CHAPTER 20

The Death Spiral of the Advanced Economies

"When I find myself on the side of the majority, I know it's time to find a new place to side."

— Mark Twain

In my view, anticipation of a "sustainable recovery," much less the U.S. leading a global recovery, is fantastic, in the true sense of the word. It magnifies fishy, fabricated statistics with a large lens of wishful thinking.

Indeed, given the increasing requirement for deleveraging in the heavily indebted U.S. economy, it could lapse into contraction again for no apparent reason. Something similar happened in Japan. Notwithstanding a quarter of a century of Keynesian pump-priming and lavish stimulus, the Japanese are still waiting for a "sustainable recovery."

The consensus view expecting a "sustainable recovery" ignores the fact that most consumers are stranded without income growth and liquidity. And remember that most of the employment growth in the U.S. since June 2009, the supposed end of the downturn, has been in part-time positions that pay an average of less than $20,000 a year.

The only good thing about these low-paying jobs is that at least they are paying jobs. The people taking them were most likely living off of unemployment benefits, or surviving with the help of their family with no income whatsoever.

But the bad thing about these jobs is that they won't be enough to grow the economy in a way that any average person could feel. If growth comes, it will be slow.

The big question government faces is this: How do you get a growing economy without income growth? There is no viable answer to that question, especially when fabricated money is raising the price of the goods Americans consume.

The Fed Hastens the Day of Reckoning

As you may know, the Fed's policies have resulted in erratic oil prices.

Barry Ritholtz points out, "Every penny at the pumps drains $1.5 billion out of household cash flow." But it is equally serious when oil prices plunge by more than 30% in six months, as happened after June, 2014. While lower oil prices gave American drivers a gift equivalent to a free, big Butterball Turkey at Thanksgiving, the plunge in prices reflects a strong deflationary impulse overtaking the heavily indebted world economy.

Deflation is a natural market reaction in an economy overburdened with debt. Debt drives production. Producers who require a certain amount of cash flow to service their obligations tend to sell as much as possible, whatever the price, often driving the price down below the cost of production. This has happened with oil. The world is so leveraged that it is vulnerable to systemic price reversals. Deflation in the oil market is particularly important because economic growth, credit growth and income growth are all leveraged to oil.

This is another example of how the Fed's Quantitative Easing (QE) strategy has hastened the Day of Reckoning. When the Fed heads first started talking about monetizing T-bonds to "stimulate growth," oil was selling at around $45 a barrel. It soon jumped above $100 — a price far above the ceiling at which real income growth for the vast majority of the population has ceased. In fact, there has been little, if any, broad income growth in the United States at any time when oil prices averaged more than $40–$50 (in 2012 dollars). Energy analyst Steven Kopitz, Managing Director of Douglas Westwood, has shown that the U.S. economy reliably sinks into recession when spending on oil and gasoline exceeds 4% of GDP, as was the case with oil at $104 per barrel.

In a U.S. economy thought to be 70% dependent on consumer spending, there was therefore little scope for growth in the recent past with oil prices near or above $100. Today, as I write, oil has traded down as low as $67.75 before settling at $68.90 a barrel, (after OPEC declined to cut production quotas — itself an evidence that the pretense of centrally-planned, administered prices tends to fall apart at crucial junctures). What has happened is an ominous systemic price reversal after years of remorseless QE.

QE was purportedly designed to stimulate world growth. Unfortunately, fabricating trillions in additional reserves for the banking system has had a far less stimulating effect than incorporating additional BTUs in the world economy.

It has been a decade since the U.S. economy grew vigorously. In 2004, when the American economy was growing by around 3.8%, total U.S. Energy use was about 100 quadrillion (quads) BTU. It has since fallen below 95 quads without recovering while GDP growth crawled along. (It is not insignificant that the data on BTU consumption are not politically fiddled in the same fashion that GDP numbers are manipulated. Hence, you have a clear view of one of two things: 1) You can see the continued lower absorption of energy in the U.S. economy as a more realistic, honest proxy for actual economic growth that in fact has not recovered since the Great Recession, or 2) More optimistically, you can see falling energy inputs as evidence of a great improvement in energy efficiency. I suspect the former.)

U.S. oil consumption per person employed has been decreasing at about 0.5% per year, along with percentage of the population with jobs. Has QE stimulated world growth so much that oil prices naturally more than doubled? And thereafter dramatically faltered with even greater QE? No.

The only thing the Fed has stimulated was a transient, "Hoteling Effect." Harold Hoteling was a professor in the Department of Geology at Stanford University. His seminal article, "The Economics of Exhaustible Resources (1931)," raised an important consideration for producers of oil. If you own oil wells, you have to decide whether to extract and sell the oil now or save it for sale later. If you produce and sell now, you can put the money in the bank, and it will grow because of the interest it will earn. Of course, thanks to the Fed's policy of driving interest rates to invisibly low levels to subsidize big banks, the interest earned on dollar deposits made by selling oil became nugatory.

By signaling its intention to further trash the dollar, the Fed reminded oil producers that they should not be in a rush to pump out valuable crude oil in exchange for rapidly inflating U.S. dollars. Consequently, oil prices shot up as oil producers and investors concluded that holding oil made more sense than holding U.S. dollar cash balances.

True, as far as it goes. But, of course, the Hoteling effect is negated when deflationary expectations supersede inflationary ones. Another negating factor in a highly leveraged world is the urgent need for cash flow to meet current obligations. When producers, particularly sovereign producers, are facing liquidity crises, they cannot afford to take a long view of asset optimization. They need cash now and will tend to sell as much oil as possible in an attempt to meet those cash flow requirements notwithstanding the fact that this depresses oil prices, or that they may earn less than the present value of future sales at a higher price.

The "Teeter-Totter Effect" of Unstable Expectations

Hence, there is a "teeter-totter effect" of unstable expectations arising from the dedication of authorities to manipulating the economy by manipulating fiat money. They aim for inflation in a context where market forces are tending toward deflation. Accurately anticipating whether the authorities will prevail over the market calls for delicate judgment, not only about monetary policy, but also about the often opaque geopolitics of energy. As Michael T. Klare spelled out in "Rising Powers, Shrinking Planet: the New Geo-Politics of Energy (Holt: 2008)," "There is an ever-present potential for confusion of normal price signals in energy markets because of geo-political snares and intrigues."

For example, there are hints that geo-political maneuvering has played a crucial role as a catalyst in the collapse of world oil prices. The story began, as investigative reporter Robert Parry detailed with U.S. Assistant Secretary of State for European Affairs Victoria Nuland, famous for her recorded and decidedly undiplomatic pronouncement: "Fuck the EU." Parry described Nuland acting as a "sorcerer's apprentice" in the overthrow of pro-Russian Ukrainian President, Viktor Yanukovych. In essence, the U.S. orchestrated a coup against Ukraine's elected government. This led to counter-measures by Russian President Vladimir Putin in seizing Crimea to secure control of Russia's only warm water naval port, while also providing backing for pro-Russian separatists in other areas of East Ukraine. Russia's countermeasures to the anti-Russian coup orchestrated by the United States, provoked another installment of countermeasures — Western sanctions designed to harm Russia's economy.

There have been numerous published reports indicating that the U.S. conspired with the Saudis to drive down oil prices because of the adverse effect this would have on Russia's economy. In these accounts, the Saudis were only too delighted to push oil prices down because doing so not only punished the Russians for supporting their enemy Assad in Syria, but also undermines the economics of tight oil production from shale formations in the United States. As President Obama is totally in thrall to the "Global Warming" lobby who oppose U.S. petroleum development, it is not impossible that he would have been willing to sacrifice the interests of oil drillers in North Dakota by driving the oil price down — while promising an increase in liquidity to consumers, perhaps even to counter the depressing effects of ObamaCare on consumer liquidity.

Consider this carefully. It underscores many imponderables you need to decipher to accurately foresee whether the coming collapse of the world's greatest ever debt bubble will involve a systemic deflationary collapse or hyperinflation. Surely, it is evident that the politicians lean toward an inflationary resolution of the insolvency dilemma. But equally, the economy is so highly leveraged that it is susceptible to systemic price reversals, as we seem to be witnessing in the oil market. So long as inflation is generated indirectly, through the banking system, there is always the lurking danger that the failure of debtors to pay interest on their obligation will trigger a deflationary collapse. This is what happened with the implosion of the Sub-Prime Bubble. The fact that leverage in the world economy has expanded by 38% since this narrow escape underscores the continuing vulnerability to deflationary collapse.

If and when the authorities move to direct inflation by outright monetary financing of fiscal deficits, as recommended by Lord Adair Turner, former chairman of the UK's Financial Services Authority, then you will see inflation. Lord Turner advises governments:

> … to deploy a variant of Friedman's idea of dropping money from a helicopter. Government deficits should temporarily increase, and they should be financed with new money created by the central bank and added permanently to the money supply. Money-financed deficits would increase demand without creating debts that have to be serviced.

At the first hint that Lord Turner's advice is being taken, you can safely conclude that the Advanced economies are all on the path to hyperinflation. From then on, you can expect prices to rise not from enhanced demand, but because of growing revulsion against the currency that is being trashed by the policy of the authorities.

Of course, Lord Turner's proposal for direct, unalloyed inflation has a major drawback from the perspective of the powers-that-be. Directly printing money and distributing it via helicopter, or through fiscal allocations, would unlikely be as rewarding from their perspective. Direct, rather than indirect inflation managed through the banking system would be less likely to concentrate the effects of the newly created funds in raising asset prices. Quantitative

Easing notoriously raised stock prices. On the other hand, money sprinkled from a helicopter hovering overhead might be more likely to find use in the purchase of goods and services.

Meanwhile, the result to be expected from this QE policy of indirect inflation is a renewed recession in the U.S. notwithstanding the benefits of lower energy costs in lifting consumer liquidity. Falling oil prices may be a leading indicator of a global downturn, as well as a lubricant of consumer income growth.

Quantitative Easing in U.S. Means Quantitative Tightening in Growing Economies

QE not only hastened the Day of Reckoning by distorting oil prices, it also put the brakes on the world economy by precipitating tightening moves in the BRICs and other growing economies. In other words, Bernanke slammed on the brakes to slow down Brazil, Russia, India, and China, along with other countries that are actually growing.

It is hardly a coincidence that all the BRIC countries have announced tightening moves in response to QE. By promising to flood the world with trillions spun out of thin air, the Fed flushed additional liquidity into the BRIC countries, where investment can earn an appreciable return, as compared to dollar balances in the U.S. that yield invisibly little.

As a result of the Fed's aggressive moves to trash the dollar, they have effectively reached out and slowed the only major economies in the world that were actually growing. The result to be expected, other things being equal, is slower growth worldwide in the years ahead. This seems to have been achieved — witness falling oil and other commodity prices. But forecasting when the Fed will raise interest rates is one of the least realistic predictions anyone could make.

The Fed cannot afford to drastically raise rates. For one thing, the weight of higher rates would crush the fragile illusion of recovery. More importantly, it would expose the insolvency of a bankrupt government that must come up with more than $6 trillion to cover GAAP deficits over the last year alone.

A Farewell to the American Dream?

As John Williams notes:

If the U.S. financial system were healthy and no longer at risk of collapse, banks would be lending increasing amounts of money into the normal stream of commerce, the money supply would be growing, and the Fed would not be monetizing federal debt. Instead, despite the Fed pumping extraordinary amounts of cash into the system, bank lending for consumer credit and commercial and industrial loans still is contracting month-to-month and year-to-year, due at least partially to impaired balance sheets at a number of banks.

Over the longer term, the American way of life as we have known it is doomed. I have explored how the perverse logic of "Debtism" drives the system toward sovereign insolvency and the risk of total collapse. Indeed, all the Advanced, cold climate economies are circling the drain in a death spiral.

It is crucially important for the success of your business and investments that you understand this and take precautions (by buying precious metals and gold stocks and getting some of your money out of the United States) to avoid being wiped out in the coming collapse. Here, it is worth repeating that the system that is doomed to collapse is not Capitalism but "Debtism," the evil cross-dressing impostor that has taken over almost everywhere with the triumph of fiat money.

It should hardly be necessary to emphasize that savings are the "capital" that forms the foundation of Capitalism. You cannot enjoy Capitalism without capital. Quantitative Easing and financial repression discourage savings essential to sustaining and renewing a Capitalist economy. With interest rates hovering near zero, it should not be a surprise that the savings rate in the U.S. economy hovers near zero.

The inherent logic of "Debtism" reflects a shocking lapse of ethics in economic policy. When money is borrowed into existence in a fractional reserve fiat system, people with larger balance sheets and collateral pocket more of it. Debtism almost necessarily concentrates an outsized percentage of income and wealth into the hands of a tiny group of the population.

Fiat money created out of thin air leads to a lopsided distribution of wealth that makes the middle class fall behind and the poor more poor.

In the final decade before Richard Nixon repudiated the gold link to the dollar that restrained the proliferation of debt, the bottom 90% of the U.S. income distribution collected 65% of the total income gains, while the top 1% pocketed about 12%. But during the run-up to the recent bubble burst, from 2002 to 2007, that relationship had reversed. The bottom 90% in the U.S. got just 11% of the income gains, with 65% going to the top 1%.

Debtism not only raises ethical questions about concentrating wealth, it involves important issues of generational equity. I believe it is wrong to structure a monetary system that implies a temporary flare-up of artificial prosperity to be enjoyed by favored generations, stoked by monetary expansion in a credit boom, followed inevitably by total collapse. We have already reached the snap-back phase, but are still in the slow motion prelude to total collapse.

The trailing generations that arrived too late to enjoy the boom financed by easy money inherit the diminished prospects and the unpaid debts, enlarged by bailouts and transferred to the national accounts when the bankers' losses are socialized, as they apparently must be to forestall collapse at any earlier juncture.

Note that this is not just a matter of fealty to Keynesian theory. It is almost dictated by the asymmetrical incentives surrounding fiat money, which is borrowed into existence in a fractional reserve credit system and extinguished when debts default.

A credit collapse morphs easily into total economic collapse because it tends to obliterate not only the over-mortgaged assets of the debtors and the capital of highly leveraged banks, but also assets of innocent counter-parties. When big banks go down, they become black holes that suck in everything they come in contact with. Watch what happens to the savings account balances of hardworking people when the president and Fed hyper-inflate the dollar.

Collapse: Then and Now

Twenty-five years ago, I gazed into my crystal ball and saw something ridiculous: the twilight of Communism and the death of the Soviet Union. At the time, this was considered so remote and unlikely that when I sought a book contract to spell out why the Cold War was about to end with the collapse of Communism, no publisher would take it. No major magazine would either. The only outlet for this heretical view was in the pages of Strategic Investment.

Seen in retrospect, it makes perfect sense that the Soviet Union collapsed. But Lord Rees-Mogg and I did not foresee its demise by tracking Soviet hard currency reserves. To the contrary. We looked at factors that once were both simpler and more complicated.

While most analysts make forecasts based solely on extrapolating from current trends, we developed our own theory of historic change that enabled us to forecast discontinuities or abrupt departures from existing trends. Our theory was based on close analysis of the state of nature or the logic of raw power. Most past theorizing about the state of nature treated it as an open-ended abstraction. Lord Rees-Mogg and I recognized that the state of nature was dynamic. We analyzed what we called the "hidden megapolitical factors" that determine the costs and rewards of projecting power, and thus the shifting dynamics of raw power.

Together, these factors comprise what political theorists call the "meta-constitution."

As a recent low farce in the Ivory Coast confirms (incumbent President Laurent Gbagbo was defeated in the election but decided to remain in office anyway), governments sometimes defy constitutions because they can. But no government can long defy the "meta-constitution," the unwritten rules of the state of nature.

In due course, all governments and populations inevitably conform to the meta-constitution because they have no choice.

We identified four largely hidden boundary forces that determine the scale at which power can be successfully exercised. They are:

- **Topography.** As exemplified by the rise of the first states on flood plains surrounded by desert, the "lay of the land" can play a crucial role in informing the incentives to submit to those who monopolize control of crucial resources, like water. Oriental Despotism of the kind practiced by the Egyptian pharaohs had its origins in the lay of the land. Without irrigation that could only be provided on a large scale, no crops would grow. Peasant farmers had no choice but to support the pharaoh or starve. On the other hand, democracy in ancient Greece originated because high value crops — wine grapes and olives — earned large profits for Greek yeoman farmers. Because they grew close to the sea on the Greek littoral, these crops could be carted to ships and cheaply transported to markets where they commanded a high price. A single Greek yeoman could produce a sufficient profit by farming a small plot to buy his own expensive armor. Because the Greek yeomen could defend themselves, they could not easily be enslaved.

- **Climate.** This, too, has been an important boundary force informing the exercise of power. "Climate change" stimulated the evolution of agriculture after the last Ice Age. But the most significant impact of climate in historic times has been felt with the impact of falling temperatures. Periods of cooling climate have frequently de-stabilized weak regimes, contributing to the collapse of Bronze Age civilization, and the fall of the Roman Empire, among others. The barbarian tribes that swarmed into Italy fled northern Europe to escape the terrible cold. And the Romans were too weakened to resist. In fact, it was so cold during the early Dark Ages that the Nile River froze. The spate of rebellions throughout the cold climate countries during the 17th century coincided with the advent of "The Little Ice Age" of plunging temperatures. A similar chill today would bankrupt the Advanced economies. Too bad "Global Warming" is a hoax. More on that below.

- **Microbes.** Disease plays another role in determining how power can be exercised. The conquest of the "New World" by Europeans after 1500 owed much to the fact that native populations were devastated by first contact with European endemic childhood diseases, like mumps, chicken pox, and measles. Equally, until the discovery of quinine, white troops could not invade malarial areas of Africa because the mosquitoes imposed devastating casualties.

- **Technology.** By far the largest factor in determining the costs and rewards of projecting power in recent centuries has been technology, particularly weaponry. When offensive capabilities are high, the ability to project power at a distance predominates. Jurisdictions tend to consolidate and governments get bigger. At other times, like now, when defensive capabilities are rising, there can be a gross disparity between the costs to small groups of attacking and disrupting global systems in comparison to the costs of combating them. It is telling that the Yemeni terrorists, who sent bombs (disguised as printer cartridges) to Chicago, spent just a few hundred dollars, while obliging Western governments and freight courier companies to lay out billions in counter-measures. This makes it more costly to project power outside of core areas. Empires tend to collapse and big governments break down.

We found insights into how the world would change by analyzing the factors that influence the costs and rewards of projecting raw power. In our view, the microchip was fatal to the Soviet Union. It reduced scale economies and decentralized decision-making in every form of endeavor. This made central planning and the totalitarian state as an economy-wide holding company obsolete.

Equally, I have come to believe that the current megapolitical background is almost as inimical to the survival of the developed economies with their expensive welfare states as it was for the late, not-so-great Soviet Union.

A little-noted consequence of the substitution of Debtism for Capitalism in the Advanced economies is the fact that it has linked homeowners, consumers, corporations, and governments in an artificial daisy chain of dependence. Fiat money that is borrowed into existence enlarges the scale of debt and creates a de-facto "command economy" under the control of big banks with central bankers orchestrating all-important decisions from behind the curtain, like the Wizard of Oz. On current evidence, Yellen is no better at central planning than the functionaries at Gosplan who drove the Soviet Union into the ground.

Mal-investment stimulated by artificial credit expansion squanders the reserve capacity of the economy, and the artificial compounding of scale in economic decision making greatly increases the risk of total collapse. Remember, as Gregor Macdonald suggests, the U.S. and other Advanced economies have incurred so many future obligations, including debts and unfunded welfare commitments, that when they fail to grow at a minimum rate, they are "essentially running backwards." I have not calculated the precise rate of growth that would be required to escape the solvency abyss, but it must be at an almost Chinese level, one that hasn't been seen in the U.S. for many decades.

The legacy institutions of advanced industrial society are vulnerable, as incomes for the majority are stagnant or falling. Historically, this has been a leading indicator of systemic collapse. As changing technology has undermined the meta-constitutional foundations of existing institutions, society has rendered itself ever more crisis-prone by marginalizing resources and deferring the recognition of costs. Obviously, the U.S. will not grow at even the 7% rate required to stabilize the national debt-to-GDP ratio. When you consider that off-balance sheet liabilities are many times greater than the official debt, the U.S. is "running backwards" towards the solvency abyss at a rapid pace.

Hence, the report by Professor Laurence Kotlikoff, discussed elsewhere, showing that the unfunded obligations of the United States government, have ballooned to $205 trillion, or some 12 times the official debt. This fantastic sum, calculated from Congressional Budget Office figures and implicitly endorsed by the International Monetary Fund, is greater than all the wealth of the world. As Prof. Kotlikoff says:

> We have 78 million baby boomers who, when fully retired, will collect benefits from Social Security, Medicare, and Medicaid that, on average, exceed per-capita GDP. The annual costs of these entitlements will total about $4 trillion in today's dollars. Yes, our economy will be bigger in 20 years, but not big enough to handle this size load year after year.

The U.S. government is insolvent. Broke. It cannot collect enough taxes to pay for its runaway spending and the promises of still more spending. And on current evidence, there are not enough willing buyers of Treasury debt to fund even the cash deficit, much less the accrual deficit.

Simulating Rather Than Stimulating Recovery

QE is not primarily about keeping long rates down. The real purpose is to fund runaway deficit spending and provide rhetorical cover for the Permanent Open Market Operations (POMO) that have employed counterfeit money to prop up the stock market. As we have previously reported, most of the gains in stock prices since the fall of Lehman Brothers have occurred when the Fed was injecting liquidity.

The Fed gives free money to the 18 Primary Dealers (big banks), and they, in turn, obligingly pour about half of it into the stock market. That's how stock prices surge even while individual investors are net sellers.

The stock market has surged not because of earnings prospects, but because the Fed has succeeded in monetizing the indices by flushing in liquidity. Note, that as a percentage of gross domestic product, corporate profits in 2013 were 10%. They have previously topped 9% in only two other decades — in 2006 and 1929. When you see perma-bulls on CNBC forecasting corporate profit growth ahead, remember the historic record. Profits are unlikely to rally dramatically from an all-time peak.

The contrasting impulses from weak fundamentals tugging stock prices down and heavy-handed efforts by the government to inflate stock values could make for extreme volatility. Be cautious in relying on the "Fed put." Prices could plunge on any overnight shock to the system.

The only thing likely to increase stock prices is more blatant manipulation by the Fed. Charles Biderman of the investment research firm TrimTabs has confirmed the role of the Fed in elevating stock prices. He recently announced on CNBC that, after two years of investigations into capital inflows into stock markets, he'd concluded that retail investors have quit stocks — and the only thing holding up the Dow today is manipulation by the Federal Reserve.

By monetizing stocks, the Fed has no doubt raised the household wealth of stockholders in the face of falling home prices, perhaps stimulating some consumer spending. But this manipulation has vitiated the usefulness of higher stock prices as a leading indicator of future economic activity. As I have written previously, it is a case of "simulating" a recovery more than stimulating one.

The bottom line is that the U.S. government is thoroughly insolvent. It owes a lot of money that it cannot pay. Someday, probably sooner rather than later, the government will drag the U.S. economy into total collapse.

It is Later Than You Think

U.S. politicians have made an art form of ignoring arithmetic and paying no heed to the unpleasant realities of national finance. Notwithstanding the risks this poses, it has heretofore been politically impossible to confront insolvency, so annual budgeting and discussions of "stimulus" in various guises have taken on a stylized character, a kabuki dance of "let's pretend."

The financial crisis of 2008, however, brought the system so close to total collapse that the bailouts deemed necessary to shore it up were shocking to many members of the public. Hence, the Tea Party reaction, which contributed to a crushing defeat for the Democratic Party in the 2010 elections. Still, I doubt that the new Tea Party Republicans are going to support a bailout… at least, not outright. In a measure of "compromise," they may wind up voting "yes" on a new state bailout, so long as a "Republican" backed initiative sees the light of day.

Either way, any money that is approved will likely be a lot less than most states are clamoring for.

That's why the next way-stop on the death spiral of the U.S. economy may be a headline crisis in the finances of state and local governments. This will result in another notch up in unemployment as previously sacrosanct government jobs are axed. Look around. It is already happening.

Collapse of States and Localities

CBS reports that, across America, state and local government employee pension plans are $1 trillion in the red. This is an instructive but probably optimistic estimate. My former father-in-law, a full professor of economics at Stanford, calculated that California alone is a half-trillion dollars in the hole. Recent reviews suggest that New Jersey's public pension hole is $100 billion. New York State's multiple pension systems are $196 billion underwater, according to the Manhattan Institute. So three big states account for approximately $800 billion in unfunded liabilities. And it would be amazing to me if the other big states, Texas, Florida, Michigan, Pennsylvania, Georgia, Ohio, and Illinois, plus the 40 others, were only a combined $200 billion in the hole.

Unfortunately, a comprehensive total of unfunded state pension liabilities cannot be calculated without resorting to research compiled by outside groups. The Government Accounting Standards Board (GASB) allows states to hide a big portion of their pension liabilities off balance sheet. TruthinAccounting. org explains:

> Because the GASB allows for a 40 year amortization of pre-GASB 27 underfunding and a 30 year amortization of benefit enhancements, the amount included as the Annual Pension Costs on the financial statements is usually considerably less than the amount the actuaries calculate is needed to adequately fund the pension systems. We are fortunate that the GASB does require the actuarial unfunded pension liability to be disclosed in the Required Supplementary Information. This may allow sophisticated users of the financial reports to approximate the true pension liability owed by some states.

> For example, as of June 30, 2007 the Illinois Statement of Net Assets includes a Net Pension Obligation of $14 billion. Information about the state's true pension liability is found on page 135 of the Illinois CAFR within the Required Supplemental Information on the Schedule of Funding Progress. This schedule shows three years of actuarial information for each of the five pension plans. To calculate the total pension liability, the Institute had to add together the actuarial unfunded liability for each of the pension plans. The total liability was $40 billion. This means GASB 27 allows $26 billion of Illinois' true pension liability to be kept off balance sheet.

Sounds bad. But wait. The updated facts are even worse. An NPR report aired March 24, 2010 concluded that Illinois' unfunded pension liabilities had ballooned to "a staggering $77.8 billion." So you can assume that the total unfunded pension liability of all the states together is considerably greater than one trillion dollars. The Day of Reckoning looms.

As it draws nearer, more government employees will lose their jobs. And still others are going to lose a big portion of their juicy benefits packages.

State pension plans across all the states may, at some point, cease to exist altogether... or change drastically. In fact, that's what needs to take place if these states ever plan on meeting their fiscal goals. But the crises in state government funding and hints of deeper crises to come flutter in and out of focus, without ever leading to decisive resolutions.

The Death Throes of the E.U.

Of course, the United States is not alone in facing a Day of Reckoning. All the Advanced cold climate economies are heavily indebted, with fragile, probably insolvent, banking systems.

In this respect, Australia and Canada seem to be a little less bankrupt than the rest. But both countries are in the midst of housing bubbles. Australian consumers are indebted on a par with Americans. A few maverick analysts, like Nicole Foss, forecast a 90% collapse in Canadian real estate. I don't think this is as likely as many of the other alarms I explore in this book, but Canada's economy is hostage to U.S. prosperity and Australia's is hostage to China's. No one should be surprised if even Canada and Australia collapse as the world economic crisis unfolds. That said, the biggest solvency problems outside the U.S. loom in the E.U. If the European Union were treated as a single economy, it would be the world's largest. A banking or sovereign debt meltdown could trigger the second down-leg of the Greatest Depression in history, just as the European banking crisis of 1931 sank the world into the deepest phase of the Great Depression.

Already, Greece, Spain, Portugal and Ireland have slipped into the solvency abyss, precipitating multibillion euro bailouts financed by Germany and the rest of the E.U., along with the IMF. In addition, a rescue fund totaling €750 billion was launched to dispel fears of a European collapse.

The prospects for Europe are bleak. All you need to do is look closely at the frequent "entitlement riots" that are common in European countries. The populations of these countries have planned their lives around all the expensive promises that politicians lavished on them during the heyday of the Industrial epoch. Times have changed. And these anachronistic promises are now unaffordable.

Europe is no longer earning its way, but Europeans are unprepared to accept the austerity (read lower benefits and higher taxes) required to reduce the yawning deficits that all the Advanced countries face.

It is important to distinguish between a liquidity crisis and a solvency crisis. A liquidity crisis is a temporary inability to pay. The debtor is sound enough to service the debt. In such a case, you might have a good reason for a bailout.

In a solvency crisis, the debtor lacks the capacity to service and re-pay the debt. Piling on additional debt only worsens the insolvency.

The European bailouts that allegedly helped Greece, Portugal, and Ireland resolved nothing. Anyone with a functioning brain can see that piling on more debt actually compounded their insolvency. They were already buried in debts they could not pay.

Let's remember as well that the PIGGS, Belgium, and other bankrupt sovereigns have been exploiting the euro and BIS reserve rules that permitted banks to hold the debt of E.U. governments without setting aside any reserves whatsoever.

These debts are destined for default. A minimum 30% haircut will be required for the PIGS to have a realistic opportunity of digging out of the hole. That 30% haircut implies a $660 billion loss for investors, including $370 billion for U.S., German, and British banks.

The interdependence of European sovereigns and banks creates a major hostage to fortune that belies the impression that Germany is a strong country that is not exposed to sovereign risk. The euro is in even more danger than the dollar, and it could unravel almost without notice. Unfortunately, the credit endorsement of the apparently more stable nations that this distinction implies is weakly grounded, particularly when it comes to France.

Why is France supposed to be more solvent than southern Europe? France runs a bigger budget deficit than Italy. It has high, chronic unemployment and has been a slow growth country for decades. Also, the French are among the most stubborn practitioners of the "entitlement riot." The French will no more welcome the austerity that is coming their way than have the Greeks.

Sovereign and banking insolvency are now intricately entwined in the "Advanced" countries. Even without any additional adverse shock, one or more of the weak Eurozone debtors could go under in the years ahead. The failure of even the weakest European sovereign could quickly cascade into complete systemic collapse. Look out below.

The systemic collapse of Europe will turn attention toward the dollar and the inevitable slide of the U.S. into the solvency abyss. That's when inflation will accelerate into hyperinflation as the U.S. dollar collapses, destroying purchasing power while precious metals skyrocket higher.

34 million Unemployed in Current Depression?

Investors are slowly working their way towards the realization that the "Old Normal" that inelegantly described the world economy before 2008 is not coming back. The "recovery" such as it was in the U.S. has been possible because of unsustainable runaway deficit spending, financed by creating trillions of dollars out of thin air to cover over the $1.3 trillion collapse of the U.S. private, economic activity that disappeared with Lehman Bros. years ago and has not come back.

The United States has not only failed to recover from recession, it is fully in a silent Depression with a capital "D."

At best, the U.S. has "bottom-bounced," as trillions in household wealth were obliterated and millions of middle class jobs disappeared, never to be seen again. In fact, as *The Wall Street Journal* noted in July 2009:

> The job losses are also now equal to the net job gains over the previous nine years, making this the only recession since the Great Depression to wipe out all job growth from the previous expansion.

This is another indicator to the thinking investor that we are in the midst of a Depression. Iterations of happy talk about "green shoots," encouraging Christmas sales, or sustained recovery aside, when you realize that practically all the net jobs created in the U.S. over the past decade have been wiped out, it implies that the unemployment rates reported by the government are a joke.

The Bureau of Labor Statistics has worked assiduously to kick as much sand in your eyes as necessary so that you can't see the true dimensions of the unemployment problem. Chief among their statistical tricks has been to define the unemployed out of the workforce in order to reduce the headline unemployment rate. As a result, officially measured workforce participation in the United States has plunged.

Unemployment has not kept pace with population growth. Under normal conditions, an increase in population would require an equivalent increase in jobs in order to keep the unemployment rate stable. But notice the statistical sleight of hand that has hidden more than half of the unemployment problem. Despite an increase in the U.S. population, the U.S. has about the same number of jobs it had in 2001. Therefore, the true unemployment rate is much higher than reported.

The U.S. economy has gone into reverse, as living standards retrace in the first installment of what threatens to be a long-term contraction in American wealth. More than 47 million Americans are now on food stamps, a fact that spares everyone the spectacle of soup kitchens in every town and village, as happened in a more innocent time during the Great Depression.

Still, most Americans remain oblivious. Millions are misled by remorseless lies about the "sustainable recovery." Few are prepared for the drastic write-down in living standards that will happen when the inevitable occurs and the U.S. dollar is finally dethroned as the world's reserve currency.

This will raise the cost of all commodities in a hyperinflationary collapse. Americans will no longer be able to exchange paper money or electronic versions of fiat money created out of the thin air with other countries in exchange for valuable natural resources like oil and manufactured goods of every description.

In the not-so-distant future, general living standards in the U.S. will be reduced to those of a Third World country. Get ready for it. The evidence of the last century suggests that even large economies can regress to a startling degree. China suffered negative compound growth from 1900 through 1950. By mid-century, Chinese living standards had regressed to those of the year 1500.

Of course, if you seek out projections of global GDP in 2020 and the decades to follow, you will see estimates that the U.S. will continue to enjoy a superior per capita living standard for half a century into the future. But those projections are based on previous growth rates, with increments to account for expected population change. In other words, the U.S. is projected to retain a superior living standard mainly because it has recently enjoyed high living standards.

This all assumes relative stability in the credit cycle as well as the meta-constitution. I doubt that can be expected. Unless the envisioned uptick in economic activity materializes in the face of falling liquidity, which would represent a radical departure from all previous times when M3 growth turned negative year-over-year, the U.S. can expect another down-leg in the relatively near future. This is also implied by the gyrations in oil prices that spiked above $100 a barrel, then plunged by one-third.

As GDP has been sustained, to date, by an ultimately unaffordable expansion of government, financed by trillions borrowed from abroad and more trillions conjured out of out of thin air with fiat money, current U.S. living standards are unsustainable. Sometime in the years to come, you can expect another sharp down-leg in the economy.

Advanced Economies in Peril

The U.S., like other Advanced economies, finds itself in a death spiral. We are already circling the drain but I believe most people are blind to this. Part of the story is told by the very word "Advanced" that we use to label the wealthier cold climate economies where people have tended to enjoy the highest living standards over the past couple of centuries.

"Advanced" is a complicated word with different meanings and connotations. "Advanced placement" is a good thing if you are a student of physics. It implies enjoying a head start in learning. On the other hand, "Advanced" sometimes indicates a bad thing — as in "Advanced Alzheimer's disease."

I fear that the prosperity of the Advanced economies has peaked in relative terms. Most of the surprises from now on are likely to be unpleasant ones. In particular, I believe we are destined for a rude shock where the price of food in cold climate economies is concerned.

In fact, I fear we are likely to see climate change of the most unforgiving sort. Not the "global warming" that has been drilled into our heads as part of establishment efforts to tighten control over global energy use, but global cooling in the form of another "Little Ice Age" that could result in a devastating surge in food and heating costs.

While in strict logic, you do not need to understand solar physics to recognize that the anthropogenic global warming promotion is a lot of blarney, bear with me.

There could be far-reaching investment advantages from gaining better perspective on the natural processes that modulate the solar cycle.

I will discuss this in great detail in the next chapter.

It may often seem as though the effects of playing along with establishment lies and deceptions is relatively benign. To pilfer a phrase from ObamaCare architect Jonathan Gruber, the government believes it can tell "stupid" voters anything it wishes to achieve its ends.

And it does.

If the employment numbers are lies and economic growth is only a fraction of that portrayed in official statistics, so what? The system seems to creak along anyway. Even if the deficit is understated by trillions, and the national debt is unpayable, it has heretofore seemed merely a trivial footnote. The system has seemed more robust then the consequences of the many lies that comprise the Age of Deception.

But not all lies are benign. If solar physicists are right about what looms ahead, we could experience the greatest crisis in history as protracted crop failures multiply food prices at a time when there are billions more mouths to feed than ever before.

This could write down living standards in the way that the solar cycle seems to have precipitated the Bronze Age Collapse in the 12th century BC, and toppled the prosperity of the Roman Empire into the Dark Age.

CHAPTER 21

You Have Been Deceived About Global Warming

"Nobody is interested in solutions if they don't think there's a problem. Given that starting point, I believe it is appropriate to have an over-representation of factual presentations on how dangerous it is, as a predicate for opening up the audience to listen to what the solutions are…"

— Al Gore (justifying lies about global warming)

Not since Chicken Little warned that the sky is falling has there been more baseless geophysical hysteria than the current furor over "global warming."

If you remember that cautionary childhood tale, you'll recall that its moral comes in two parts. Firstly, it is a warning not to believe everything you hear. The secondary moral is even more critical in current circumstances. When you have an atmosphere of hysteria, you need to be particularly alert, lest some clever fellow like Foxy Loxy turn the hysteria surrounding the imagined crisis to his own ends.

In case you've forgotten the gory details, Foxy Loxy cashed in "the sky is falling" hysteria by eating Chicken Little's infatuated supporters, Henny Penny, Cocky Locky and Goosey Loosey.

While you are not about to be eaten, you are vulnerable to one of history's great power and money grabs now being orchestrated in the name of fighting "global warming."

It is only a matter of months until Foxy Loxy opens another of the interminable, United Nations climate conferences with the objective of ramming through a "Climate Change Treaty" that will drastically reduce your standard of living while handing hundreds of millions or even billions of dollars to Al Gore.

Nah. Don't believe it?

I realize that I just warned you not to believe everything you hear. So I expect you to be skeptical when I tell you that people like Al Gore are making a fortune out of the global warming hysteria that makes AIG bonus payments seem like pocket change.

Believe me, however: The propaganda for global warming is more than just hot air. It involves a grab for billions, even trillions of cold cash.

Here is a brief outline of the facts:

Blood and Gore

As a U.S. Senator, then as Vice President of the United States, Al Gore helped funnel billions of your tax dollars into research (a.k.a. state propaganda) supporting his pet project for combating global warming.

After he left office, in 2004, Al Gore co-founded Generation Investment Management (GIM), a hedge fund devoted to "green" investments.

Former Goldman Sachs golden boy David Blood joined Al at GIM.

Together, "Blood and Gore," as they like to call themselves, called on all their wealthy friends in Washington, Wall Street and Hollywood and raised $5 billion.

With $5 billion of private capital in hand, and billions more in taxpayer funds being dispensed to support Climate Change "alarmism" every year, the groundwork was in place for what will one day be seen as the biggest rip-off in history.

An Inconvenient Truth

Once the money was raised, Al went to Hollywood with an idea for a movie.

In the lavish hotels of Beverly Hills, he pitched his idea for a documentary about global warming to his infatuated friends.

By December 2004, the film started shooting. "An Inconvenient Truth" was finally released in 2006.

Al then traveled the world promoting the movie with the best-financed promotion of intellectual hysteria in history.

He pushed hard the idea that an "end of the world/the sky is falling" scenario would occur if governments didn't act immediately to drastically curtail carbon emissions.

Gore booked pricey speaking engagements to show off his charts and graphs… quoted "experts"… and asked philosophers and religious leaders to save the planet from global warming.

<u>But he said nothing about how he and his business partners were set to profit handsomely off his global warming scam.</u>

Al was greeted by huge crowds the world over.

His film won two Oscars. And he was given the Nobel Prize for his scare tactics.

The Media Falls Hook, Line and Sinker

Rather than debate global warming, the mainstream media parroted every word out of Al's mouth and completely ignored his conflicts of interest. And that wasn't all they ignored.

They totally dismissed the arguments of scientists and other critics who disputed the contention that higher concentrations of atmospheric carbon were necessarily the cause of marginally warmer temperatures experienced in the last quarter of the 20th century.

Think about it. The underlying proposition of the global warming hysteria is that scientists can forecast global temperatures a century or more from now to an accuracy of 1/10th of a degree Celsius. How is this possible when they can't forecast temperatures to within an accuracy of five degrees, five days from now?

The obvious mathematical implausibility of long-term climate forecasts from tiny atmospheric changes should have invited a lot of rigorous investigation of "the sky is falling" themes of the warm-mongers. But apparently it didn't. Until recently.

You've heard the old adage, "he who pays the piper calls the tune." By and large, the government was paying the piper, and it was made clear early on that the basis for receiving large grants (now running at about $5 billion a year) was to underscore alarms about a climate calamity.

H.L. Mencken explained the dynamic reasons for this before Al Gore was born:

> The whole aim of practical politics is to keep the populace alarmed — and hence clamorous to be led to safety — by menacing it with an endless series of hobgoblins, all of them imaginary.

Gore himself has admitted that he thinks it is justified to lie in the service of convincing people that there is a global warming crisis. Of course, he stated his confession more diplomatically or perhaps in a more mealy mouthed way, as support for "an over-representation of factual presentation on how dangerous it is." Gore stated in an interview for *Grist*:

> Nobody is interested in solutions if they don't think there's a problem. Given that starting point, I believe it is appropriate to have an over-representation of factual presentations on how dangerous it is, as a predicate for opening up the audience to listen to what the solutions are…

Of course, it is easy for Gore to be enthusiastic about his solutions. They mean a fortune for him.

If you're like most people, you probably don't spend much time parsing differential equations. Truth be told, not even the Rev. Al Gore, Nobel Prizewinner that he is, can follow their intricacies. But as detailed below, that hasn't stopped him from pocketing a cool $100 million from a flawed differential equation worked out in 1922 by the "stepfather of global warming," astrophysicist Arthur Milne.

In a better world, it would not matter to you whether an astrophysicist, who has been dead for almost 70 years, incorporated a blatantly unrealistic assumption into a differential equation about the atmosphere. In this case, it does matter because climatologists are still using Milne's flawed equation purportedly to prove that carbon dioxide emissions, along with other "greenhouse" gases, will turn the earth into a furnace.

Milne's calculations of the behavior of atmospheric gases included the assumption that atmospheres are infinitely dense. Even as a simplification that is more than a little over the top.

In fairness to Milne, he was by no means a "warm-monger" like Gore. Milne's research into radiative equilibrium and the structure of atmospheres was part of a larger argument he had with Einstein over the General Theory of Relativity. Milne was not much interested in terrestrial atmospheres. His equations were focused on stellar atmospheres.

Hungarian scientist Ferenc Miskolczi, an atmospheric physicist and former researcher with NASA's Langley Research Center, who was forced out because NASA did not like his objections to the Al Gore thesis of global warming, has a lot to say about the defects of Milne's equations.

"Runaway greenhouse theories contradict energy balance equations," Miskolczi states. So Miskolczi re-derived the solution, this time using the proper boundary conditions for an atmosphere that is not infinite.

NASA refused to release his results. Miskolczi believes their motivation is simple. "Money," he says. Research that contradicts the view of an impending crisis jeopardizes funding, not only for atmosphere-monitoring projects, but all climate-change research. Currently, government funding for climate research tops $5 billion per year.

Miskolczi resigned in protest, stating in his resignation letter:

> Unfortunately my working relationship with my NASA supervisors eroded to a level that I am not able to tolerate. My idea of the freedom of science cannot coexist with the recent NASA practice of handling new climate change related scientific results.

Dr. Richard Lindzen, Alfred P. Sloan Professor of Meteorology at MIT, agrees with Miskolczi's view that the earth's climate does not amplify global warming because of greenhouse gases. To the contrary, Lindzen declares:

> … warming as may arise from increasing greenhouse gases will be indistinguishable from the fluctuations in climate that occur naturally from processes internal to the climate system itself.

These conclusions are supported by research published in the Journal of Geophysical Research by Steven Schwartz of Brookhaven National Labs, who gave statistical evidence that the Earth's response to carbon dioxide was grossly overstated. It also helps to explain why current global climate models continually predict more warming than has actually been measured.

The equations also answer thorny problems raised by current theory, which doesn't explain why runaway greenhouse warming hasn't happened in the Earth's past.

Of course, you can't expect any of these qualifications to impinge on the enthusiasm of global warming cultists for imposing draconian limits on carbon emissions. Witness this nonsense…

350: The Most Important Number in Your Life?

According to the environmentalist website, www.treehugger.com, "The most recent science tells us that unless we can reduce the amount of carbon dioxide in the atmosphere to 350 parts per million, we will cause huge and irreversible damage to the earth."

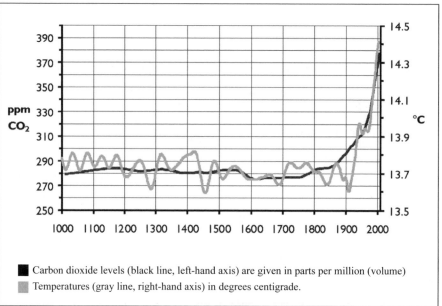

Carbon dioxide levels (black line, left-hand axis) are given in parts per million (volume)
Temperatures (gray line, right-hand axis) in degrees centigrade.

©Hanno/Wikimedia Commons

CO2 levels were 20 times higher than todays

I don't suppose that anyone at www.treehugger.com could begin to explain why holding carbon dioxide at 350 parts per million (a bare chemical trace) is crucial to preventing "huge and irreversible damage to the earth," in light of the fact that scientific studies have shown that atmospheric carbon dioxide in past eras reached concentrations that were 20 times higher than the current one. If that did not cause "huge and irreversible damage to the earth," why would 95% lower concentrations pose any danger now?

That, of course, is merely a rhetorical question.

Your role in this scam is not to think too deeply, but listen to what the media tell you.

Another of their recurring themes is the suggestion that the polar ice caps are melting. They say this over and over. Even when the evidence doesn't support their conclusion.

Arctic Ice Cap Grows by 520,000 Square Kilometers

In fact, the government's own surveys of Arctic Sea ice compiled by the National Snow and Ice Data Center (NSIDC) show that it has grown by 520,000 square kilometers since 2010. That's an area 1½ times the size of Texas.

Scientists don't consider this a recovery because they say the growing ice cover is thinner than it was at some points in the past. Right.

While the politicized U.S. agency pretends that Arctic Ice is getting thinner, a team of Canadian and German scientists flying over the ice, measuring its thickness with the latest electromagnetic equipment, found exactly the opposite, that the ice was "thicker than expected," as you would infer from the fact that the summer melt stopped 520,000 square kilometers short of its 2010 low.

It turns out that ice is melting… in Western Antarctica, where there is substantial volcanic activity. But at the same time, parts of Eastern Antarctica, four times the size of Western Antarctica, are cooling and gaining ice. By September 2014, the Antarctic ice cap had set a new record high of 16.8 million km. That is more than 600,000 km² greater than ever recorded since 1979 when satellites began tracking sea ice. At that time, CO_2 in the atmosphere was 336 ppm. Now it is 400 ppm, and the Antarctic ice is growing rather than melting.

Note that forecasts and alarms about melting snow and disappearing glaciers in Antarctica have been equally distorted by the mass media.

Years ago, when NASA scientist Marco Tedesco found evidence of increased summer snow melt in Antarctica, NASA put out loud press releases highlighting this information, which seemed to buttress alarms of global warming.

But NASA has remained totally mum about more recent evidence reported by Tedesco and his co-author, Andrew Monaghan, in the journal Geophysical Research Letters, reporting a record low snowmelt during a more recent austral summer.

According to space borne microwave observations for 1980–2009, the Antarctic snowmelt during austral summer 2008–2009 was the lowest ever recorded. The Antarctic Ice cover is now 30% greater than its average over the past 30 years. And, of course, the "ship of fools" tale of global warming alarmists who sailed to Antarctica hoping to "discover and communicate the environmental changes taking place in the south," is too comic to forget. While they intended to highlight damage to Antarctica allegedly done by man-made global warming, their ship was frozen in place after Antarctic Sea Ice hit record levels in 2013.

Compared to the remorseless dishonesty of claims about the melting of the polar ice caps, the hyping of "green investment" by the major media is almost measured and responsible.

Major print media mentioned green investing 3,485 times in 2006 — a 70% increase from the previous two years.

And going green became a cultural movement...

Paris dimmed the lights on the Eiffel Tower... Solar investments became hot — even for oil companies... Evangelicals preached the gospel of "creation care."

And scientists who disputed Al's claims risked losing their jobs and having their reputations smeared. For example, Princeton physicist Dr. William Happer was fired by Al Gore as director of Energy Research for the U.S. Department of Energy after he testified before Congress in 1993 that the scientific data did not support widespread fears about the dangers of the ozone hole and global warming.

Then-Vice President Gore sent a message to other scientists by firing Happer.

Happer said:

> I was told that science was not going to intrude on public policy... I had the privilege of being fired by Al Gore, since I refused to go along with his alarmism. I did not need the job that badly.

Unhappily, some other scientists feel they do "need the job," and depend upon government grants to fund their research. Unlike them however, Happer was not muzzled by strong hints that government wants scientists to support concerns about carbon dioxide in the atmosphere. To the contrary, Happer continues to sharply criticize global warming hysteria:

> I have spent a long research career studying physics that is closely related to the greenhouse effect. Fears about man-made global warming are unwarranted and are not based on good science.

Dr. Happer views climate change as a predominantly natural process.

> The earth's climate is changing now, as it always has. There is no evidence that the changes differ in any qualitative way from those of the past... Computer models used to generate frightening scenarios from increasing levels of carbon dioxide have scant credibility.

Richard Lindzen, an Alfred P. Sloan Professor of Meteorology at M.I.T, explains how Al Gore and company have manipulated scientists with a combination of money and intimidation to create the impression of authority for ill-founded global warming claims. (This analysis was presented as a keynote address on March 8, 2009 at the second International Conference on Climate Change.)

In candid moments, even some of the government scientists who conjured up the scare stories admit that they were playing fast and loose with the facts in the service of political goals. Witness this comment from Stephen Schneider of the National Center for Atmospheric Research:

> On the one hand, as scientists, we are ethically bound to the scientific method, in effect promising to tell the truth, the whole truth, and nothing but-which means that we must include all the doubts, the caveats, the ifs, ands, and buts. On the other hand, we are not just scientists but; human beings as well. And like most people we'd like to see the world a better place, which in this context translates into our working to reduce the risk of potentially disastrous climatic change. To do that we need to get some broad based support, to capture the public's imagination. That, of course, entails getting loads of media coverage. So we have to offer up scary scenarios, make simplified, dramatic statements, and make little mention of any doubts we might have.

If you believed scare stories about global warming, you have been deceived.

Al has almost everyone scammed. Even conservative giant Newt Gingrich wrote a book demanding action on global warming.

Everyone was buying the hype.

Al's plan was working perfectly...

Cap and Trade

Once Democrats seized control of the House, the Senate and the presidency, there seemed to be no stopping Al's last act.

You see, while he was touring the world, promoting his movie and scaring everyone about the world heating up, his banker friends back in New York and London were very busy…

… Busy buying up shares in green energy companies all over the world. And laying the groundwork to profit handsomely from carbon taxes.

And they've already made a heap of money in the process.

Bloomberg reports that Al's net worth jumped from $2 million to $200 million since he left office.

But Al's biggest profits are still to come.

Al has been calling for a laundry list of heavy-handed regulations and carbon taxes since Obama came to power…

Gore wants a freeze on greenhouse gas emissions, a ban on new coal-fired power plants, tough new fuel efficiency standards for vehicles, carbon taxes and timetables for reducing greenhouse gases.

But his favorite policy idea is "Cap and Trade." And I'll show you why in just a moment.

Cap and Trade means Washington will place a "cap" on the amount of carbon dioxide emissions that the economy can create.

If companies go over their allocated limit, they must buy a carbon credit from a company that emits less carbon than its allocated limit… or pay a hefty fine.

As I explain below, Cap and Trade as originally proposed would have made Al Gore a billionaire.

The problem is that Cap and Trade would cost you and every other American wads of money.

According to the Heritage Foundation, the version of the Cap and Trade bill that passed the House of Representatives in 2009 would have immediately reduced U.S. GDP by $161 billion dollars.

That is roughly $1,870 for every family of four in America.

In my view, however, this estimate is laughably conservative, as it more or less supposes that Al is right and the world will get warmer.

The costs of repressing carbon dioxide emissions would be much higher if climate takes a turn in the direction I expect and the earth gets colder. More on that below.

Remember also that Cap and Trade imposes an arbitrary and unnecessary burden of "carbon accounting" on every business in America. Not only would every business have to purchase "carbon offsets" through Al Gore's carbon exchange, it would have to audit its carbon emissions to prove that panting employees have not discharged more carbon dioxide into the atmosphere than they have paid for.

Another ghastly cost for the economy that would be imposed along with Cap and Trade would be validation of the effort by scavenging plaintiffs' attorneys to sue every industrial company and utility in the United States for damages associated with bad weather. Consider this from *The Wall Street Journal's* Law Blog on October 19, 2009:

> For years, leading plaintiffs' lawyers have promised a legal assault on industrial America for contributing to global warming.
>
> So far, the trial bar has had limited success. The hurdles to such suits are pretty obvious: How do you apportion fault and link particular plaintiffs' injuries to the pollution emitted by a particular group of defendants?
>
> Plaintiffs' lawyers were gloating after a favorable ruling from the Fifth Circuit in New Orleans, which is regarded as one of the more conservative circuit courts in the country.
>
> The suit was brought by landowners in Mississippi, who claimed that oil and coal companies emitted greenhouse gasses that contributed to global warming that, in turn, caused a rise in sea levels, adding to Hurricane Katrina's ferocity.
>
> The central question before the Fifth Circuit was whether the plaintiffs had standing, or whether they could demonstrate that their injuries were "fairly traceable" to the defendant's actions. The defendants predictably asserted that the link is "too attenuated."

You can be sure that a lot more "attenuated" links will be asserted if Congress were to dignify the far-fetched connection between carbon emissions and bad weather by passing Cap and Trade.

Cap and Trade would also increase your electricity bills by up to 90%. Maybe more, if utilities lose jury trials and have to pay Katrina damages to Mississippi farmers and similar shakedowns to every street vendor from New Orleans and those disadvantaged by similar storms, like Hurricane Sandy.

It could even cost you your job!

According to *U.S. News and World Report* (July 6, 2009):

> The government is going to be directly responsible for the destruction of millions of jobs if the bill passed by the House becomes law — anywhere from a net loss of 0.5% of total jobs over the first 10 years, according to the liberal Brookings Institution, to 3 million by the year 2030, according to the industry-backed Coalition for Affordable American Energy.

That may be bad for you, but it would have made Al Gore very wealthy indeed. It could turn him into the world's first green energy billionaire.

Al Gore's Trillion-Dollar Monopoly

So why has Al been such a huge promoter of Cap and Trade?

It's simple.

He owned 10% of the exchange that would have handled every single carbon credit traded. That's why the Cap and Trade bill and the Copenhagen Conference were so important to culminating Gore's scheme.

If laws and international treaties with the effect of law bound the whole world to trade carbon credits, Gore's carbon exchange would have been worth untold billions.

The Chicago Climate Exchange collapsed and shut down in November, 2010. Al's "Blood and Gore" Generation Investment Management lost money, but collected $18 million in consolation from the sale of the soon-to-fail business to the Intercontinental Exchange, in May of 2010.

It must have been a big letdown compared to what they expected with the passage of Cap and Trade. That market would have huge.

Bigger than the New York Mercantile Exchange. Maybe even bigger than the NASDAQ.

According to *The New York Times*, carbon "will be the world's biggest commodity market, and it could become the world's biggest market overall."

A report by New Energy Finance put the value of the carbon market at $1 trillion a year by 2020.

But this non-market barely even exists.

All the banking big boys want to get their greedy little fingers in this pie.

See, until a few years ago, exchanges were private companies. But that's all changed. Now they're publicly traded cash cows that get a small slice of money each time a trade is made.

And early investors in these exchanges can cash in big.

Consider CME group, the largest futures and options exchange in the world. Early investors could have bought shares for $41 dollars back in 2003.

Over the next five years, the exchange surged in price, giving investors 15 times their money.

I bet you wish you could have gotten in on these profits back then...

Who wouldn't?

A $5,000 investment turned into $85,000... just like that.

Al Gore lost out on his Cap and Trade scheme to become a billionaire at your expense. But don't cry for Al. The rest of his global warming scam still provides him an opportunity with more upside potential.

Why?

Because Gore has big investments in alternative energy that could only be profitable with lavish subsidies from you and other taxpayers. As Carol Leonnig reported in the Washington Post:

> Fourteen green-tech firms in which Gore invested received or directly benefited from more than $2.5 billion in loans, grants and tax breaks, part of President Obama's historic push to seed a U.S. renewable-energy industry with public money.

And, of course, Al came tantalizingly close to pocketing billions from Cap and Trade. A law that would have inflated the carbon offset values, which collapsed to a nickel a ton in 2010, before the Chicago Climate Exchange shut down, actually passed the House of Representatives.

But had Cap and Trade been signed into law, much less reinforced by a global treaty, every single company in the United States would've had to join Gore's Climate Exchange.

That means 470 companies would have ballooned to hundreds of thousands overnight.

Such is the majesty of the law.

If Al Gore gets his way, he will become a Green Economy billionaire, while you and other investors are carried away on a tide of red ink.

More on this in just a moment…

First, I want to tell you about something called the Maunder Minimum. It proves that carbon emissions have little to do with global warming.

You see, for all the hype, global warming is hardly a proven science.

Yes, the climate is changing. Climate is always changing. It has changed a lot over the past 10,000 years. It is a lot warmer now than it was at the end of the last Ice Age.

But it is also colder than it was 1,000 years ago. When the Vikings first went to Greenland, it actually was green. Believe it or not, they grew grain there. As late as 1300 AD, 3,000 farmers lived on 300 farms there. But then the climate got colder and eventually it became too cold for crops, starving the Nordic farming settlements out. By the end, the few remaining farmers were all dwarfs due to malnutrition.

Based on historic records and the indisputable evidence that the earth has been both much hotter and much colder in the past, there is no logical basis for the supposition that solar output is stable and constant from year-to-year.

To the contrary, there is evidence of considerable cyclical variability in the sun's warmth. This explains much more about climate than do fluctuations in minute concentrations of so-called "greenhouse gases."

If you ask yourself why the Ice Ages ended and why the Medieval Warm Period petered out in generations of cold, wet summers… you are on the path to understanding the dynamic of climate today. Not surprisingly, it's closely linked with variations in the energy output of the sun itself.

By the second quarter of the 17th century, astronomers were carefully observing the heavens. Among the key measurements they recorded were daily records of sunspots — the visible manifestations of magnetic storms on the sun. It turns out that sunspot activity is closely correlated with the sun's total energy output.

When there are lots of sunspots, the sun produces more energy and temperatures on earth rise. When sunspots recede, the earth gets colder.

In the 17th century, the sun plunged into a 70-year period of almost total spotlessness known as the Maunder Minimum. The sunspot drought began in 1645 and lasted until 1715. During that time, also known as the "Little Ice Age," temperatures plunged. It was the coldest period in the last millennium. Some of the best astronomers in history (for example, Haley, who discovered the famous comet) monitored the sun and failed to count more than a few dozen sunspots per year, compared to the usual thousands.

The summer of 1693 was so cold that millions of people in France and surrounding countries died of starvation. Equally, there were crop failures in Scotland in eight of the last nine years of the 17th century. That's one of the reasons that Scotland joined England in the Treaty of Union to form the United Kingdom in 1707. The English growing season also shrank by five weeks in the late 17th century, but some grain could still be grown at lower altitudes whereas food production in Scotland was almost totally frozen out.

In Norway, total grain harvests late in the 17th century were only about two-thirds of what they had been in the year 1300. The failure of Norwegian crops from 1680 into the 18th century was a prime reason for the great growth of merchant shipping there. Coastal farmers whose crops failed turned to selling their timber and to constructing ships in order to transport these timbers themselves.

If you've ever been on a cruise, chances are you sailed with a Norwegian crew who were sent to sea by the Maunder Minimum.

Meanwhile, Al Gore's late 20th century crisis of global warming just so happened to coincide with the 20th century solar maximum, an historic high in sunspot activity. What a coincidence.

But not to worry. It's all over now. Sunspot activity has plunged. And global warming seems to have vanished with it, except as a political cause.

The period from January 2007-through September 2009 showed the sharpest drop in worldwide temperatures in recorded history. (Note that this flatly contradicts the forecasts of the CO_2 warm-mongers. According to the global warming alarms, average global temperatures should have increased by 0.2 degrees Celsius.)

Temperatures are now back to what they were in the 1980s, the Arctic icepack grew in the past two years, and the Antarctic icepack continued to increase, as it has steadily done.

The moral of the story is that there is no need for you to fret about warming in your future. Even if you live on the coast, you won't have to swim to work.

But you may need some thicker blankets.

Global warming is a hoax. Only the money that will be made out of this scam is real.

In all probability the world will continue getting colder in the immediate future. Timo Niroma, the late Finnish expert on sunspots, flatly declared that the era of global warming is over. He projected that the period between now and 2300 will be another "Little Ice Age" with a repeat of the Maunder Minimum. Brrr.

Niroma has closely studied sunspot cycle lengths since the 17th century, cycles that he correlated to the Jovian year. As the largest planet in the solar system, it would stand to reason that Jupiter's orbit could create perturbations in the sun.

However, Niroma did not base his forecast of a colder climate solely on cyclical patterns. Among the reasons he emphasized for his forecast of deepening cold — the clear trend toward diminishing solar output.

Bill Livingston and Matt Penn of the National Solar Observatory (NSO) in Tucson, Arizona report that the magnetic strength of the sunspots irrespective of their amount has linearly declined since at least 1990.

Equally, Niroma pointed out that the brightness of the sun has dropped a whopping 6% at extreme UV wavelengths since the solar minimum of 1996. Sunspot activity has plunged below that associated with the Dalton minimum that led to bitterly cold temperatures and "the year without a summer" in the early years of the 19th century.

The furor over global warming is misplaced. As part of the research I did into the hidden factors that drive history for the books I wrote with Lord Rees-Mogg, we found evidence that climate fluctuations have destabilized civilizations throughout history. By far, the most destabilizing climate changes are those that involve cooling of the earth.

A major reason for the collapse of the Roman Empire was colder weather that drove the barbarian German tribes south looking for food and warmth. Global warming is just another name for good weather.

No Need to Worry About Global Warming

What you really have to worry about is not global warming, but global cooling. The danger is when the weather gets colder, as it did in the 17th century, during the Maunder Minimum.

I have followed Dr. Timo Niroma's work with interest. Obviously, I cannot independently confirm his forecast that we are now headed into either a Little Ice Age or, even worse, a Big Ice Age. Unlike Al Gore, I do not pretend to be an expert on climate. But I do tend to recognize a contrarian investment opportunity when I see one.

With the whole world focused on global warming, especially since the December 2009 treaty in Copenhagen, there has probably never been a more wide open field for spectacular returns on a contrarian play.

> "No matter if the science is all phony, there are collateral environmental benefits… Climate change [provides] the greatest chance to bring about justice and equality in the world."
>
> — Christine Stewart, Minister of the Environment of Canada, 1997-1999

> "Even if the theory of global warming is wrong, we will be doing the right thing — in terms of economic policy and environmental policy."
>
> — Tim Wirth, while U.S. Senator, Colorado.

> "Oh I takes de gospel whenever it's pos'ble
> But wid a grain of salt."
>
> — Porgy and Bess

If you think the U.S. and Canadian economies have trouble now, wait until much of North America is buried again under glaciers a mile or two deep as it was in the last Ice Age.

The fact is that what happens when sunspot activity declines is something that can't be ignored or dismissed.

If we do enter even a semblance of an Ice Age, it will trigger the greatest social crisis in history, as even an apparently minor fall in average global temperatures could have a devastating effect on growing seasons in temperate latitudes. Millions and millions of people would die.

Experts believe that average global temperatures fell by 2 degrees Celsius or less in the Little Ice Ages associated with the Spörer Minimum of 1400-1510 and the Maunder Minimum of 1645-1715. This does not sound dramatic, but it meant a sharp drop in summer warmth in higher latitudes in the Northern hemisphere. A decline in global temperatures of a couple of degrees Celsius can precipitate an increase in food prices of 800%. A bankrupt world could not afford to feed itself if growing seasons dramatically contracted at higher elevations and higher latitudes. When the number of frost-free days contracts below 60, it is generally not practical to sow cereal crops.

With all the hot air coming from Al Gore and company, you probably haven't even noticed colder temperatures in recent years.

Even changes that fall far short of the advent of an Ice Age can have devastating economic consequences in a world accustomed to temperature inflation. The end of the medieval warming period (warmer than the present) was a matter of dire consequences in mainland Europe where crops failed year-after-year and millions of undernourished people perished through starvation and epidemics, culminating in the Black Death.

Note also that cold spells tend to have persistent cultural effects. The fact that Little Ice Age conditions eliminated the cultivation of grapes in Northern Europe precipitated an apparently permanent shift to beer-drinking.

The Doomsday Book census of England in 1085-6 reported the existence of 42 vineyards, mostly owned by nobles to provide wine for their dining tables. By the end of the 14th century, the decline in global temperatures was enough to wipe out wine production in England. Beer and ale became predominant for reasons of climate. In cold, wet weather, stored grain spoiled too readily to be kept in unprocessed form, so beer brewing came into vogue as a technologically efficient way of storing vulnerable grain for later consumption. And beer had another advantage. It could be brewed from barley, a short season crop.

The preference for wine in the everyday diet was preserved among the wealthy who could afford to import wine, and among the population in general in Southern Europe, where climate did not become too cold for grape cultivation.

You see, contrary to what the "warm-mongers" suggest, life has mostly gotten better when temperatures have risen. Thankfully, it did get warmer after the Black Death. With a few instructive exceptions, it has mostly been warmer since 1500 than it was in the late Middle Ages, but not as warm as the Medieval Warm Period.

Though Al Gore and his pals have figured out how to profit spectacularly from his pet theories that burning hydro-carbon fuels releases too much atmospheric carbon, humans unfortunately have little or no capacity to regulate the earth's thermostat by manipulating atmospheric carbon. This is important to bear in mind when you consider the investment consequences of another Little Ice Age.

Greenhouse Gases Mainly From Natural Sources

As explained by Geocraft.com, about 99.72% of the so-called greenhouse effect is attributed to natural causes — like water vapor and trace amounts of gases that are not caused by people. Total human contributions to greenhouse gases account for only about 0.28% of the greenhouse effect, just a little more than a quarter of 1%. Man-made carbon dioxide (CO_2) comprises only about 0.117% and other man-made sources, including methane, nitrous oxide, carbon monoxide and other miscellaneous gases contribute another 0.163%.

In other words, eliminating human activity altogether would have little impact on carbon levels in the atmosphere, and even less on climate change. Even if we wanted to, we could not up-regulate temperatures in the face of a deep solar chill by emitting more CO_2. Of the 186 billion tons of CO_2 that enter the earth's atmosphere each year from all sources, only a little more than 3%, or about 6 billion tons, are from human activity. Approximately 90 billion tons come from biologic activity in the earth's oceans and another 90 billion tons from such sources as volcanoes and decaying land plants.

Further to that, at 400 parts per million, CO_2 is only a trace element of earth's atmosphere. It comprises less than 4/100ths of one percent of the total gases present. Compared to former geologic times, earth's current atmosphere has only a bare trace of CO_2. In the Paleozoic Era, atmospheric CO_2 was present in concentrations up to 20 times higher than current readings of 386 parts per million.

Unfortunately, if we needed to raise the earth's temperature in order to save millions from starvation, we would have no idea how to do so. The only route forward would be to attempt to adjust to the celestial forces that govern the sun's dynamo.

If you'll permit me to rant and rave for a moment, the prospect of a coming Ice Age underscores the folly and evil involved in Al Gore's program of phony research into global warming. In recent decades, the U.S. government has wasted untold tens of billions on bogus climate research which amounted to little more than bribing scientists to add credibility to Al Gore's semi-religious conviction that human activity is imperiling the planet. In a real climate crisis, almost all of the U.S. government's research would be utterly useless, as we have been paying supposed experts to come to bogus conclusions.

Unfortunately, it is all too plausible that our climate could rapidly revert to Little Ice Age conditions. For one thing, the earth has been in an Ice Age for most of the past 750,000 years. This suggests that more frequently than not, the sun fails to provide enough radiative energy to keep the earth from freezing.

Notwithstanding all the bellyaching about global warming, we are technically in an Ice Age now, as there are extensive glaciers covering most of Greenland and Antarctica, as well as other smaller glacial formations in Patagonia, on the South Island of New Zealand and at high elevations and high latitudes in the Northern Hemisphere. We have enjoyed an intermission from advancing glaciers, known as an "Interglacial period" during all of recorded history, but that is a short interlude in geological time.

The past temperate interglacial periods like the current one, known as the "Holocene" interglacial, have tended to last for relatively short periods of about 11,500 years. Our current interglacial has persisted for about 11,400 years, which means it is due to end relatively soon. Unfortunately, based on the evidence that an Ice Age is the baseline climate of the earth, it is more probable than not that any major climate change would involve the world getting colder.

Furthermore, the evidence of cyclical patterns in the waxing and waning of Ice Ages also points to the possibility that we could rapidly revert to a period of glaciation. Dr. George Kukla, of Columbia University argues that variations in the earth's orbit around the sun largely inform Ice Age cycles.

He states:

> I feel we're on pretty solid ground in interpreting orbit around the sun as the primary driving force behind ice-age glaciation. The relationship is just too clear and consistent to allow reasonable doubt.

… It's either that, or climate drives orbit, and that just doesn't make sense.

Some evidence suggests that the return to glaciation can happen as rapidly as one year. In 2008, German scientists reported that a Little Ice Age known as the "Big Freeze" 12,800 years ago took hold in just one year, more than ten times quicker than previously believed. Rather than a gradual cooling over a decade, Europe plunged into the Big Freeze.

An abrupt shift to cold, stormy conditions plunged Europe almost instantly into an Ice Age during the Younger Dryas less than 13,000 years ago — a very recent period on a geological scale. Dr. Achim Brauer and his colleagues at the GFZ (GeoForschungs Zentrum) German Research Centre for Geosciences at Potsdam analyzed annual layers of sediments, called "varves," from a German crater lake. Each varve records a single year, allowing annual climate records from the region to be reconstructed. From one year to the next, an Ice Age began.

Evidence of a dramatic fall-off in sunspot activity suggests a serious risk of this happening again.

I know that politicians assure you that there is no such danger — because carbon dioxide emissions from human activity are purportedly poised to turn the earth into a hothouse.

Unfortunately, this is a blatant lie, upon which you cannot depend to stay warm in winter. For that, you will need fuel.

As evidence accumulates that global warming has not transpired as predicted, Gore and his minions have shamelessly recast their campaign as one to combat "climate change." Al doesn't want to risk the billions he has at stake on the chance that people will look past all his "hot air" to focus on the thermostat and realize that the world has been getting colder, notwithstanding his elegant, computer-driven syllogisms.

Global Warming? Ice Age?
What's the difference?

In case you missed it, Obama's White House science czar, John Holdren, has predicted that one billion people will die in "carbon-dioxide induced famines" in a coming new Ice Age by 2020.

Talk about brazen "double think." Holdren published two books in the 1970s in which he set out completely contradictory theories on the impact of CO2 on global cooling. Holdren and Ehrlich argued in their 1973 book "Human Ecology: Problems and Solutions," that the main effect of carbon-dioxide-induced global warming "might be to speed up circulation patterns and to bring arctic cold farther south and Antarctic cold farther north." Just how and why mixing hot and cold air under warming conditions could lead to an Ice Age is a matter that they cannot explain.

In "Ecoscience: Population, Resources, Environment," last revised in 1977, Holdren, together with co-authors Paul and Anne Ehrlich stated that "a man-made warming trend might cancel out a natural cooling trend."

Equivocating, contradicting himself, and making plainly ridiculous leaps without scientific basis, Holdren forecasts disaster, no matter what. He based his prediction on a theory that human emissions of carbon dioxide would produce a climate catastrophe in which global warming would cause global cooling with a consequent reduction in agricultural production resulting in widespread disaster. Got that?

It is key to answering the most important IQ test in history. It will determine whether the great majority of Americans are stupid enough to sign away what remains of the superior living standard we have enjoyed in the service of a global power grab designed to make Al Gore and his Wall Street buddies richer while millions are reduced to poverty under the weight of draconian carbon taxes.

Holdren is right about one thing, however. A return to Ice Age conditions, or even a marginal Little Ice Age cooling, would devastate food production. If the current plunge in solar activity as measured by sunspots and other indicia of solar radiation leads to the same drop in global temperatures experienced in the 17th century, when growing seasons in Europe suffered, the world will have a serious challenge in feeding itself.

Human population is now ten times higher than it was in 1700. Feeding all these mouths under Little Ice Age conditions is no easy task. Food prices would soar, as food output in Europe, Canada and the United States plunged.

Note that the temperature gradient between winter and summer in the American grain belt averages about 59 °F. If winter temperatures persist erratically into spring, or return early before the harvest, the result could be a collapse of the growing season.

This is what happened during the last Dalton Minimum, in 1816, the so-called "year without a summer," when diminished sunspot activity, combined with volcanic pollution from the eruption of Mount Tambora, led to a sudden onset of Little Ice Age conditions.

The greatest effect of the cold was felt in the Northeastern U.S., New England, the Canadian Maritimes, Newfoundland, and Northern Europe. In times of "normal" solar radiation, late spring and summer temperatures in the Northeastern U.S. and Southeastern Canada average (day and night) about 68–77 °F and rarely fall below 41 °F. Although there are occasional May flurries, summer snow is an extreme rarity.

In May 1816, frost killed off most of the crops that had been planted, and two major June snowstorms devastated crops in Eastern Canada and New England, causing many human deaths and precipitating a mass migration out of New England. (If you own property in the northern part of the U.S. or in Canada that you intend to sell within the next few years, you might want to take a lesson from the past and try to sell it before all the potential buyers realize that the climate has taken a long-term turn for the worse).

While obviously some crops were brought in at lower latitudes in 1816, grain prices skyrocketed eight-fold. The result was the last major subsistence crisis in the Western world, with malnutrition, starvation, epidemic, and famine.

Europe, still recuperating from the Napoleonic Wars, suffered from acute food shortages. Food riots broke out in both the U.K. and France. Grain warehouses in many locations were looted. The violence was worst in Switzerland, where the government declared a national emergency to combat unrest precipitated by famine. A BBC documentary, using figures compiled in Switzerland, estimated that fatality rates in 1816 were twice those of average years.

The evidence that widespread unrest accompanied Little Ice Age conditions in the past in countries as well-mannered as England, France and Switzerland is a strong hint of what you can expect in North America when temperatures plunge. Social unrest and the declaration of "states of emergency" would probably make it complicated to move to warmer locales. The government might even impose a "windfall profits taxes" on oil and natural gas companies.

You can be sure that politicians will seek to deflect public anger over a climate reversal.

They will pretend that the cause of the crisis lies in human activity, rather than in the dynamo of the sun, and the complicated patterns of changing orbits of the earth around the sun.

Another hint from "the year without a summer" comes from China, where the cold weather killed trees, rice crops and even water buffalo, especially in northern China. Unusually low temperatures in summer and fall devastated rice production in Yunnan province in the southwest, resulting in widespread famine. Fort Shuangcheng, now in Heilongjian province, reported fields disrupted by frost and conscripts deserting as a result. Summer snowfall was reported in various locations in Jiangxi and Anhui provinces, in the south.

On this evidence, it is suggestive that China would probably be a big buyer in food markets at the outset of Little Ice Age conditions.

If grain production in Canada, Europe and the U.S. fell short, what other countries could take up the slack? Answer: Not many.

Just about the only major agricultural producer that would not likely be devastated by Little Ice Age conditions is Brazil. According to the U.S. Department of Agriculture, Brazil is already the world's leading agricultural economy as measured by profitability. U.S. farmers currently grow more crops. But because of our crazy-quilt of farm subsidies, much of the U.S. farm output is unprofitable. In Little Ice Age conditions, Brazil could literally be the world's breadbasket.

As you probably realize, the equator passes through Northern Brazil. The temperature gradient between winter and summer in Brazil is, on average, less than the difference between daytime and nighttime temperatures.

In other words, if winter temperatures lasted into spring or arrived early in the autumn, there would be serious crop failures throughout the Midwestern United States and in other temperate latitudes. Late or early winters in equatorial Brazil would have little or no effect on growing seasons. But there may be a risk that disturbances in wind patterns in the upper atmosphere could disrupt rainfall. But the Amazon basin starts as the most well-watered region in the world. Hence, my conclusion that Brazil is just about the only leading agropower where growing seasons would not be adversely effected by the return of a Little Ice Age.

In addition to Brazil, Eastern Bolivia, Paraguay and parts of Argentina would probably become more attractive in comparative terms because the growing seasons there would not be wiped out by erratic cold. Some African countries could also pick up some slack in food production. Kenya lies close to the Equator. Zimbabwe was formerly a food-producing country. In a starving world, I would expect some drastic action to improve the productivity of Zimbabwean agriculture. Someone would make it worthwhile for Mrs. Mugabe to divest the stolen farms she has been mismanaging.

You could also expect to see the business of "hot house" farming get a boost. If food could no longer be grown outdoors in North America, there would be efforts, no doubt subsidized and screwed up by government, to bring farming indoors. Some of the empty factories and abandoned strip malls in Detroit and in the Northeast of the U.S. and southern Canada would no doubt be fitted out with artificial lighting and heated to a degree required to grow food. While there are a few firms piddling around in this area, I know of none that has developed sufficiently to be an attractive receptacle for investment.

An adverse climatic shift implies a drastic drop in living standards, a climatic deflation, including a plunge in the sale of air conditioners, and a general fall in discretionary income.

The current depression has already wiped away a full decade of progress in industrial production. The "recovery" in production, such as it has been, has leveled off at a low-level plateau of activity that has wiped out the last 10 years of growth. As John Williams of Shadow Government Statistics notes, "Despite the near-term gains (as will tend to become evident as inventories are worked off in the months ahead), the series generally still is bottom-bouncing."

A Little Ice Age would mean a multi-decade plunge in real living standards, perhaps wiping out most of the progress since World War II. It would mean the final end of U.S. economic predominance, already long frayed; probably the death of the dollar; a big surge in gold; and a fall in demand for other non-essential commodities.

Another side effect might be to restore the reputation of genuine science, in preference to the Al Gore version of "political science," the neo-scholastic heir to medieval "natural philosophy" that seems in many respects to be a throwback to the pre-Copernican medieval superstition that insisted upon making humans and the earth the center of the universe. But to my knowledge, while the Ptolemaic astronomers insisted that the earth was the center of the universe, none of them ever insisted that human action could arbitrarily change the climate. In those days, that was the province of God.

And yes, climate change in the form of a Little Ice Age would grant Ms. Stewart's — Christine Stewart, former Minister of the Environment of Canada, 1997-1999 — wish to bring about "equality in the world."

There will be a lot of equality in subsistence poverty.

CHAPTER  22

The Coming Dark Age

"Future generations will wonder in bemused amazement that the early 21st century's developed world went into hysterical panic over a globally averaged temperature increase of a few tenths of a degree and, on the basis of gross exaggerations of highly uncertain computer projections combined into implausible chains of inference, proceeded to contemplate a roll-back of the industrial age."

— Prof. Richard Lindzen, Alfred P. Sloan Prof. of Meteorology at MIT

One of the more pernicious consequences of Al Gore's trumped-up fuss about global warming is its effect in shrouding all questions about climate in a deep fog of political correctness. Thanks to Gore and his accomplices, rational discourse on climate has been stifled. But if you are among the few whose "climate-brain" has not been lobotomized by overexposure to Al Gore's terror of good weather, it may not be too late for you to prepare for an unexpected and potentially devastating climate change in coming decades that could precipitate a new Dark Age.

For a better perspective on the real risk that climate change poses to economies, you need to forget almost everything you may think you know about the history of climate and its impact on civilization. Unless you studied geology or you share my gamey taste in reading, you are liable to have internalized something like Al Gore's cartoon view of climate — that it was stable and benign until humans happened along and began to change it.

Wrong.

Climate is dynamic, always changing, and almost entirely outside of human control.

Even during the Holocene period, which began about 12,000 years ago, when climate became extraordinarily favorable to human habitation, there have been centuries when climate took a turn for the worse and our ancestors faced a heightened challenge to survive. Looking back, most of these periods of climate lapses (protracted colder periods) are known variously as "the Dark Centuries," "the Greek Dark Ages," "The Bronze Age Collapse" or just the "Dark Ages."

Over the longer term, the Earth's climate has been anything but benign. For most of the past 100,000 years, the areas of the Northern Hemisphere, including Great Britain and the most industrialized areas of North America that were the most economically advanced through the 20th century, were buried beneath tens of millions of cubic miles of ice. Where Chicago, Detroit, Glasgow and Stockholm now stand, glaciers more than a mile deep buried everything in sight.

The Discovery of Our Ice Age Past

After the study of geology was launched by James Hutton at the end of the 18th century, researchers in Europe began combing the landscape for evidence of past climate change. They found a lot. By 1825, numerous observant naturalists found evidence that northern Europe had formerly been covered by ice.

The first advocate of this view to be taken seriously was Louis Agassiz, a Swiss native who moved to the United States and taught at Harvard. While researching Nova Scotia and the Great Lakes, Agassiz found compelling evidence of several glacial intrusions. So while Agassiz's coining of the term "die Eiszeit" for a single Ice Age seemed sensational in 1837, by 1900, scientists studying the Alps identified at least four major Ice Ages.

Their calculations (now outdated by more recent research) showed that over the last 600,000-to-1,000,000 years there had been four glacial periods lasting 50,000 years apiece, separated by warm interglacial periods ranging from 50,000 to 275,000 years in length. In other words, the evidence revealed that the Earth regularly cycles between warm and cold periods.

But the story was really more complicated than that. As William J. Burroughs wrote in "Climate Change in Prehistory:"

> The possibility of rapid and frequent changes from intense glacial cold to relative warmth seems not, however, to have entered this orderly version of events.

By the very nature of things, it was difficult — if not impossible — for researchers to draw an accurate picture of the past by studying only features of the landscape visible to the naked eye. Simply put, the waxing and waning of ice sheets obliterated much evidence of past climate resulting in "no identifiable buildup of deposits" of vegetation and animal residues.

A much more accurate picture of climate history came into focus beginning in the 1950s when scientists began to assess a variety of proxy data, such as tree rings, pollen records, ocean sediments and ice cores. A signal advance occurred in 1955 when Cesare Emiliani published his analysis on the properties of fossil shells of tiny sea creatures. He was able to show that, instead of just four Ice Ages punctuated by lengthy interglacials, there had been seven glacial periods since then, occurring every 100,000 years or so.

While Emiliani's findings were initially controversial, they were reinforced by evidence from pollen records, ocean sediments and ice cores from Greenland and Antarctica that confirmed, in Burroughs' words:

> ...beyond any shadow of reasonable doubt that the climate of the last million years has been dominated by periodic variations in the Earth's orbital parameters that have resulted in an Ice Age is occurring roughly every 100,000 years.

Of particular interest, an important core drilled on the ice sheet of Antarctica by a European team covered a continuous record of over 730,000 years, encompassing eight Ice Ages. As Burroughs said:

> It shows that cold conditions prevailed for much of the time, especially during the last 400,000 years, and were interspersed by much shorter warmer interglacials. This pattern was clearly a global phenomenon as the same features are evident in the results from ocean sediment cores in the tropics.

> Since around 400,000 years ago, the pattern has been broadly consistent. Each Ice Age ended rapidly, then after an interglacial that lasted only around 10,000 years, the climate slipped back into glacial conditions.

In other words, the current Holocene episode of benign climate has already lasted as long as the typical interglacial warm period over the past 400,000 years. If the known pattern of past interglacials repeats, you could expect another relapse into full-fledged, glacial conditions beginning at almost any time.

I am not so bold as to suggest that another Ice Age is just around the corner. I hope it isn't.

But it's not as unlikely as you might suspect, judging by the hysteria over global warming. The timing of the ultimate end of the Holocene interglacial period is inherently unpredictable because of the scale of the cycles involved. Not only is there a 100,000-year elliptical cycle that interacts with a 41,000-year axial tilt cycle, there is also a 23,000-year precession or "wobble" cycle. And overlaid on these is the most active and complex cycle of all — the approximately 1,500-year solar-driven cycle. Climate physicist S. Fred Singer believes this cycle is particularly important as it "drives most of the Earth's climatic change during interglacial periods like this one."

To make pinpointing when a new Ice Age begins even more complicated, the 1,500-year warm/cold cycle is not precisely a 1,500-year cycle. It is a 1,470-year (plus or minus 500 years) cycle that is a composite of the 87-year Gleissberg cycle and the 210-year DeVries-Suess cycle. A 2001 study by Hollger Bruan et al. of the Potsdam Institute put it this way:

> Because they are close to factors of 1,470 years, the 210-year cycle and the 87-year cycle of the sun could combine to form a period of 1,470 years and thus explain the climate cycle of the Ice Age.

Strikingly, the 1,500-year solar cycle is in evidence both during big Ice Ages as well as warmer periods. Broadly speaking, the warmer phases of Ice Ages and cold spells during interglacials reflect the overlap of the 1,470-year solar cycle over the longer astrophysical cycles that reflect the Earth's position in the solar system as well as the solar system's position in the galaxy.

Jan Veizer, a geologist at the University of Ottawa, and Nir Shaviv, an astrophysicist at the Hebrew University of Jerusalem, published an interdisciplinary study in 2003 that concluded 75% of the earth's temperature variability in the past 500 million years can be attributed to changes in bombardment by cosmic rays as we pass into and out of the spiral arms of the Milky Way. They summarize:

> ... our approach, based on entirely independent studies from astrophysics and geosciences, yielded surprisingly consistent picture of climate evolution on geological time scales. The global climate possesses a stabilizing negative feedback. A likely candidate for such a feedback is cloud cover.

So much for carbon dioxide as a driver of climate.

Ominously, experts on the shorter, Gleissberg cycle of solar activity (an 87-year cycle often thought to be "an amplitude modulation of the 11-year Schwab Cycle") have been warning for decades that a new Little Ice Age could settle over the earth by 2030. Here is what the late Dr. Theodore Landscheidt, founder of the Schroeter Institute for Research in Cycles of Solar Activity in Waldmuenchen, Germany wrote in 2003:

> Analysis of the sun's activity in the last two millennia indicates that, contrary to the IPCC's speculation about man-made global warming, that we could be headed into a Maunder minimum type of climate (a little Ice Age).

> The probability is high that the minimum around 2030 and 2201 will go along with periods of cold climate comparable to the nadir of the little Ice Age, and La Niña's will be more frequent and stronger than El Niño's through 2018.

> We need not wait until 2030 to see whether the forecast is correct, however. A declining trend in solar activity in global temperature should become manifest long before then. The current 11-year sunspot cycle 23 with its considerably weaker activity seems to be the first indication of the new trend, especially as it was predicted on the basis of solar motion cycles two decades ago. As to temperature, only El Niño periods should interrupt the downward trend but even El Niño's should become less frequent and strong.

> I (Landscheidt) have shown for decades that the sun's varying activity is linked to cycles in its irregular oscillation around the center of mass of the solar system (the solar retrograde cycle). As these cycles are connected with climate phenomena and can be computed for centuries, they offer a means to forecast phases of cool and warm climate.

Dr. Landscheidt, a connoisseur of solar cycles, believed their quasi-periodic nature suggests a coming plunge in temperatures. He wasn't alone. Dr. Habibullo Abdussamatov, head of space research at St. Petersburg's Pulkovo Astronomical Observatory, also predicts another Little Ice Age:

> Observations of the sun show that as for the increase in temperature, carbon dioxide is "not guilty"... and as for what lies ahead in the coming decades, it is not catastrophic warming, but a global, and very prolonged temperature drop.

In short, contrary to what Nobel laureates Al Gore and Barack Obama have told us, students of solar physics warn of a coming drop in global temperatures.

And although you won't read about it in *The New York Times*, or hear about it on CNN, no less an authority than NASA even harbors some politically incorrect experts who suggest that solar irradiance patterns point to the imminence of another Maunder-style solar minimum (a Little Ice Age).

This is doubly interesting. For one thing, if you are one who was inclined to be skeptical about my contrarian forecast of a coming cooling trend, the fact that any scientist at NASA's National Solar Observatory could break ranks and lend credibility to forecasts of declining solar irradiance should make you think twice.

Equally, because NASA is a government agency that depends upon the whims of politicians for its continued funding, you can expect heads to roll because someone made the mistake of hiring scientists like Matt Penn and William Livingston, who have the temerity to put scientific honesty ahead of political correctness.

"Striking Suddenness"

As Burroughs reports, one of the conclusions implied by close study of past climate is that "the striking suddenness of many of the changes came as a surprise to many climatologists."

Over the longer term, the climate of the world has been much more variable than the clement weather to which we have become accustomed during the last 12,000 years.

An important feature of the benign climate of the Holocene is that outside of the tropics, the Holocene climate showed much less variance than the previous 60,000 years. "Variance" is a term of art in climate study that measures the disruptive potential of fluctuations in climate. This is calculated by computing the squares of the difference in climate measurements over a decade compared to a smoothed version that removes periodicities shorter than 200 years.

What these data show is a drastic drop in variance by a factor of five to 10 over the past 10,000 years, compared with the previous 50,000 years. This feature of low variance is an important characteristic of the generally benign Holocene climate in which civilization emerged and advanced.

Even though there were periods lasting thousands of years between 40,000 and 60,000 years ago when temperatures averaged over centuries in the North Atlantic were not drastically lower than during the Holocene, their variance from year-to-year was three to four times greater. Broadly speaking, larger deviations in weather have a bigger disruptive influence on human activities.

For example, there is good reason to doubt whether agricultural civilization could ever have found its legs with the high climate variance experienced prior to the Holocene.

Thinking about the impact of climate on human prosperity provides the useful antidote to the climate hysteria promoted by Al Gore and company. Generally speaking, most life forms on Earth, including human beings, thrive in relatively warm conditions. Ten thousand years ago, near the beginning of the Holocene period, the human population of the earth was only about five million. Today, it is about seven billion. In "The Long Summer: How Climate Changed Civilization," Author Brian Fagan noted that:

> Civilization arose during a remarkably long summer. We still have no idea when, or how, that summer will end.

While humanity thrived, by and large, over the "Long Summer," there have been several important interruptions as the shorter solar cycles impinged on the good weather with sometimes locally devastating cold spells. These cold spells have frequently been experienced as Dark Ages — periods of devolution, decay and acute systemic crises often accompanied by political as well as economic collapse.

The First Proto-Dark Age

One of the first cold spells of the Holocene occurred before civilization was sufficiently formed to be affected in the full range of ways spelled out below in my summary of the characteristics of Dark Ages.

Here I am thinking of the mini Ice Age of 6200 to 5800 B.C. that marked the end of the Holocene Optimum, a period that marked the high point in Northern Hemisphere temperatures following the last Ice Age.

When this mini Ice Age struck, farming civilization was still in its embryonic form. A significant detail is that fields were rain-fed, meaning that freelance farmers, much like their hunter-gatherer ancestors, faced less compulsion to affiliate with a political organization as complex as those which would later come to control the hydraulic systems of Oriental despotisms. A typical early farming village, according to Fagan, would have "covered a hectare or so at most." Among the larger and most impressive early Middle Eastern farming communities was the walled village of Jericho of Biblical fame, which covered four hectares. (The current thinking among archaeologists is that Jericho's famous walls were originally erected for flood control and only accidentally came to have military significance.)

In that faraway time, farming was too young and the social structures organized around farming villages too rudimentary to adequately reflect all the facets typical of Dark Age devolution. There is no evidence of any rulers whose palaces could be sacked and burned. There was not as yet an elaborate division of labor to implode.

There was no evidence of a rigid theocracy whose principles could be abandoned and whose priests could be slaughtered.

There were no great empires to fall, no great metropolises crammed with monumental buildings that could crumble into disrepair as the city was de-populated like ancient Rome.

The first Proto-Dark Age predated writing, so there could be no reversion to illiteracy, as would happen later.

Equally, metallurgy had not been invented.

Yet, strangely, even in those primitive times, there was considerable long-distance trade of Obsidian blades from Anatolian farming villages, as early as 8300 B.C. These obsidian artifacts could be traced to individual Anatolian villages of origin by their unique trace elements.

The early farming communities had taken enough shape so that the impact of the suddenly colder weather could find expression in the form of a mini Dark Age, a prototype for other, more famous phases of stagnation and devolution to come.

Fagan put it this way (remember as you read this that drought in the Near East is more commonly associated with colder air that alters circulation patterns):

> The mini Ice Age of 6200 to 5800 B.C. was a catastrophe for many farming communities between the Euxine Lake and the Euphrates River. Month after month, a harsh sun baked soils that were no longer fertile. Dust cascaded out of a cloudless sky, lakes and rivers dried up, and the Dead Sea sank to record low levels. Farming society shrank or evaporated in the face of unrelenting drought. Then they turned to sheep farming as they resorted to the classic famine strategy habitat tracking moving to areas less affected by drying and cooling, where they could eke out a living off their herds.

As would be the case with later Dark Age episodes, this first Proto-Dark Age precipitated economic reorganization, including presumably population losses (although there is no dependable census recording the population of these embryonic farming communities before the mini Ice Age hit).

There is evidence of significant migration and the permanent abandonment of the land. In this case, the early farmers moved away from areas of rain-fed agriculture to warmer, river-fed fields along the banks of the Tigris and Euphrates rivers.

Again, quoting Fagan:

> Then in 5800 B.C., the good times return. The Atlantic circulation switched on; the moisture-laden Mediterranean westerlies abruptly resumed. Within a few generations farmers expanded from their places of refuge into a warmer and better watered landscape throughout the Fertile Crescent to the banks of the Tigris and Euphrates rivers.
>
> Some farmers founded settlements far downstream, where the two great rivers entered a floodplain of sluggish channels and innumerable streams. Here was abundant water, easily diverted into storage basins and onto fields. All the farmers needed to do was to build simple levees and canals. By 5800 B.C. small agricultural communities dotted the landscape of southern Mesopotamia… Within three thousand years, the tiny hamlets of 5800 B.C. had become some of the earliest cities on earth. Urban centers like Eridu, Nippur Ur, and Uruk were surrounded by green patchworks of heavily irrigated fields and labyrinths of narrow canals. Cities arose here… The city was a different entity from the village, not just larger in size but requiring more economic specialization and much more centralized social organization than smaller-scale societies. The scale of operation led almost inevitably the still larger political entities, to city-states, and eventually empires, loose over large areas.

Dark Ages have been few in number during the "Long Summer." Yet they share predictable features of a retrograde development of society. As space restrictions prohibit me from exploring them chronologically, I have distilled the following summary which should help inform an intelligent perspective about how to prepare for the coming Dark Age.

11 Traits of a Dark Age

Among these common features:

1. **Societies under stress from colder climates tend to regress to lower levels of "complexity"** in terms outlined by Joseph Tainter. As declining

marginal returns beset economies, this means political collapse and the substitution of simpler, less costly forms of social organization for existing institutions. This is perhaps most famously exemplified by the fall of Rome.

2. **Economic depression and disruption of trade** feature prominently in the historic record. Dark Age downturns make the Great Depression seem like a garden party. For example, as Bryan Ward-Perkins wrote in "The Fall of Rome: And the End of Civilization," "mass archaeological evidence now available... shows a startling decline in Western standards of living during the fifth to seventh centuries. This was a change that affected everyone, from peasants to kings, even the bodies of saints resting in their churches. It was no mere transformation — it was decline on the scale that can reasonably be described as 'the end of a civilization.'"

3. The unwinding of trade ties frequently leaves producers of specialized and luxury goods without a market, resulting in a **contraction in the division of labor**.

4. Ominously, past Dark Ages have frequently entailed **extensive population losses, with astonishing examples of de-urbanization**, particularly in core areas. As Brian Fagan suggested,

> The moment when people moved into cities and towns, into larger settlements from which they could not move and which depended on humanly managed farming landscapes, they stepped over a threshold of far greater vulnerability to sudden climatic change than ever before. Now there was no middle ground between prosperity and collapse.

This was evidenced during the Greek Dark Age (also known as the "Bronze Age Collapse"), when population losses between the 12th and 11th centuries B.C. are estimated at more than 75%. Only one out of every four persons survived. The same pattern repeated itself throughout the ancient Middle East. After 1206 B.C., almost every city between Gaza and Pylos was violently destroyed or abandoned, including Hattusa, capital of the Hittites, Mycenae, Ugarit, the early city state and others. In ancient Egypt, crop yields plunged after 1200 B.C., leading to a 24-fold surge in grain prices by 1130 B.C. Egypt's population plunged and did not recover to the 1200 B.C. level until about 500 B.C. Later, in the next Dark Age, the population of the city of Rome fell from over one million persons in 367 A.D. to fewer than 30,000 by the end of the 10th century — a breathtaking 97% decline. Constantinople suffered a large, though less drastic, population drop of 70%.

5. **Decline in social stratification and repudiation of elites** go hand-in-hand with economic devolution, depopulation and de-urbanization. This was a particularly prominent feature of the Greek Dark Ages. The Athenian general Thucydides later spoke of his country during that period as "without commerce, without communication by land or sea, cultivating no more acreage than the necessities of life demanded, destitute of capital, building no large towns or obtaining any form of greatness."

The same pattern repeated itself throughout the Near East and Eastern Mediterranean, where archaeologists have unearthed evidence of widespread violent convulsions as famished peasants revolted against elites. The Palace of Nestor at Ano Englianos was destroyed along with 240 settlements occupied by the palace administration and the ruling elite. Similarly, palaces and fortifications were burnt to the ground at Athens, Corinth, Mycenae, Tiryns, Laconia and Messenia. In Crete, the palace of Knossos was torched. Having spent their fury on their overlords, as Fagan wrote, "The populace scattered into small, self sufficient villages."

The pattern repeated itself in most of the adjacent lands. Hattusa, capital of the Hittite Empire, was destroyed by fire in 1180 B.C. Babylon was sacked in 1157 B.C. Iconoclastic French archaeologist Claude Schaeffer showed that almost every major settlement in the near East, from Troy to Ugarit, along with all communities on the trade routes from Syria to Egypt were destroyed. While there was no direct urban destruction in Egypt, after the colder global climate reduced inundations of the Nile, the ability of the pharaohs to command allegiance dried up with the river. Around 1182 to 1151 B.C. during the reign of Ramses III, surging food prices led craftsmen and workers for the royal tombs in the Valley of the Kings to go on strike after their food rations went unissued.

6. The repudiation of elites during Dark Age famines was also associated with a **collapse of religious principles** and sometimes the emergence of new religious principles during Dark Age transition periods. A part of the requirement for complex social structures to manage the irrigation systems of oriental despotisms such as those in Egypt and Mesopotamia was the emergence of an autocratic theocracy. The theocracy got the attention of the peasant farmers because they would have been only too aware of the impossibility of moving off into the desert on their own to grow a crop watered by rainfall. The theocracy held the peasants' allegiance so long as their irrigation systems could dependably produce the crops. Under normal Holocene climate conditions, the regular inundation of the Nile was as close

to a sure thing as you can find in nature. The farming was very productive, supporting "as many as 760 to 1,520 people per square kilometer." Equally, cuneiform accounts report that yield-to-seed ratios of 30-to-one were the norm for irrigated fields in southern Mesopotamia and ratios as high as 50-to-one were sometimes achieved. So long as the irrigation systems delivered a timely flow of water, they reinforced the authority of the theocracy that claimed to intervene with the gods on behalf of the farmers. But woe to the priests when climatic stress brought drought that wiped out the crops. Burroughs points to the drought that apparently destroyed Mayan civilization (more than a millennium before their long calendar ran out last year) during the global Dark Age in the eighth century A.D. He highlights "gruesome evidence of the slaughter of priests and their families."

7. An almost axiomatic consequence of a reversal of the division of labor is **the loss of specialized arts and skills, including the loss of literacy**. This was certainly a notable feature of the Greek Dark Ages, when pottery and the other decorative arts, along with literacy, practically disappeared. Of course, the very idea of the European Dark Age originated with Petrarch in 1330 as a rather arch commentary on the low quality of literature written following the fall of Rome. Ward-Perkins points to a somewhat more complicated collapse of skills associated with the contraction of markets in the Dark Age. He reports, "almost all archaeologists, and most historians, now believe that the Roman economy was characterized, not only by an impressive luxury market, but also by a very substantial middle and lower market for high-quality functional products."

Ward-Perkins goes on to lament "the almost total disappearance of coinage from daily use in the post-Roman West" in what was not a recession… with an essentially similar economy continuing to work at a reduced pace. Instead what we see is a remarkable qualitative change, with the disappearance of entire industries and commercial networks. A number of basic skills disappeared entirely during the fifth century, to be reintroduced only centuries later. The economy that sustained and supplied a massive middle and lower market for low-value functional goods had disappeared, leaving sophisticated production and exchange only for a tiny number of high-status objects. In short, unlike the Greek Dark Ages when luxury goods almost entirely disappeared, during the post-Roman Dark Age some of the only trade to survive was in luxury goods for an elite market. In a future issue of Strategic Investment we'll explore more closely how the next Dark Age may unfold and will try to decipher whether we are likely to veer closer to the Greek or the Roman-style Dark Age.

8. Another feature of past Dark Ages are **mass migrations or habitat tracking** as displaced and desperate people move away in hope of finding prosperity elsewhere. Typically, societies lose population not only to starvation and disease but also outmigration. It is not a coincidence that Germans call the cold period we generally refer to as the Dark Ages as "the Völkerwanderungen," or the "folk wandering time" because Europe was invaded then by so many migrations of famine stricken, displaced people looking for a more benign climate in which to reside. Such migrations have been a common feature of Dark Ages in the past. In general, these migrations have overwhelmed the best efforts of political authorities to resist them. But it is not for lack of trying. The ruler of the ancient Sumerian city-state Ur sought unsuccessfully to keep out migrating Amorites by building a wall 180 km long.

9. Mass migrations during Dark Ages are sometimes punctuated by **the rise of piracy and attacks by marauding vagrants**. Perhaps most famous of these menacing Dark Age hordes were the mysterious "Sea People" of the Bronze Age collapse who destroyed several well-established empires and city-states, and then menaced Egypt in two massive invasions. William Burroughs explains:

> The Sea People were probably part of a great migration of displaced people. The migration may well have been the result of widespread crop failures and famine relating to the climatic change occurring at the time. They were, however, an efficient military force: aggressive, well-armed and ruthless raiders. Their successful progress appears to have focused on attacking capitals and cities important to administration. In these cities they destroyed government buildings, palaces and temples, while leaving residential areas and the surrounding countryside untouched. They appear to have first destroyed Mycenae, then moved on to Troy, which they laid waste around 1250 B.C. They then moved into the Levant and on to Egypt where they met their match in two battles.

In short, think of Hells Angels on foot. In spite of being called "Sea People," they did most of their damage marching over land.

10. Not incidentally, one of the common features of Dark Ages is that they coincide with **the emergence and spread of diseases and pandemics**. Obviously, diseases can do more damage when they attack starving people with weakened immune systems. When the deadly bubonic plague was introduced to Byzantium it killed about 200,000 persons in the first four months, about one-third of the people in Eastern Europe soon thereafter,

and ultimately half the population of Western Europe. As David Keys explores in "Catastrophe," weakened by "Justinian's Plague," the Byzantine Empire soon lost many of its provinces to an assault by the military missionaries of Islam.

11. As perhaps best exemplified by the Greek Dark Ages (or Bronze Age Collapse leading to the Iron Age), **Dark Ages are periods of transition when society is reorganized, often focused around different technologies**. The fact that iron weapons, although inferior to bronze weapons, were far cheaper figures to have been a factor in the growth of the hoplite infantry of yeoman farmers that took power from the smaller, aristocratic armies of bronze-armored chariot warriors. Another factor that favored the transition to iron-based military technologies was the fact that iron was plentifully available locally, while the manufacture of bronze weapons was dependent upon long-distance trade of tin from mines in the Badakhshan region of Afghanistan. (A partial exception was Egypt. Egyptian bronze was an alloy of arsenic, a fact that may help explain why Egyptian forces were able to turn back invasions by hordes of sea people who overwhelmed other empires and city states whose forces were outfitted with bronze weapons fabricated with Afghan tin). This meant that bronze weapons were harder to manufacture when the upsurge in piracy by the Sea People disrupted imports.

Looking ahead to the technological transitions likely to be associated with the reorganization of society in the coming Dark Age calls for delicate judgment. But it entails issues that may be of capital importance going forward. For example, it strikes me as obvious, in light of the probability that trade networks will be radically disrupted, that one of the technologies we have focused on — 3D printing — could be more important than it first seems. It would potentially afford a way for isolated individuals and communities to custom manufacture replacement parts to preserve the comforts of life against the dangers of a catastrophic collapse of living standards in the coming Dark Age.

Meanwhile, I close by emphasizing that, although you can make predictions about quasi-periodic phenomena like climate cooling, the specific expression of the collapse of complex societies are mostly matters of conjecture.

I believe that the prospect of such a collapse in the foreseeable future is sufficiently high to make this thought exercise a useful one.

CHAPTER 23

A Contrarian Take on Our Fair Weather Civilization

"Knowledge of the past helps to anticipate the future."

— Thucydides

My hunch that the world could be at the threshold of a coming Dark Age is a Contrarian opinion with a capital C.

Take note.

If the accuracy of forward vision depends upon a view being widely shared, then the advent of a new Dark Age would have to rank as one of the more startling developments in history.

Talk about Black Swans.

For every million persons worried about global warming or Iran getting a nuclear bomb, there may be one who frets about the prospect of a coming Dark Age. But the Dark Age is far more frightening.

At one level, thinking about these deep drivers of history may seem remote from the factors that weigh on a choice of ETFs (Exchange-traded funds) or growth stocks. But I found with my own investments that Big Picture thinking can pay handsome dividends.

With the help of my friend and colleague, Charles Del Valle, we've expressed how lucrative Big Picture investing can be.

Yet, there are few other developments that could have such far-reaching consequences as a new Dark Age. It would pose unprecedented challenges to the survival of billions of people. And no experts of whom I am aware are even thinking about this problem.

I say this recognizing that I am hardly the first to contemplate the possibility of "the end of the world as we know it." Here, I am not thinking of science fiction or survivalist screeds, like "Surviving the Economic Collapse," or "When All Hell Breaks Loose: Stuff You Need to Survive When Disaster Strikes."

Thinking specifically about Dark Ages is relatively limited.

Other than historic texts like "The Inheritance of Rome: Illuminating the Dark Ages 400–1000," by Christopher Wickham, Chichele Professor of Medieval History at the University of Oxford, Dark Ages are not a popular subject for thought exercises. I have been able to locate only three contemporary books that suggest that we could be at the threshold of a Dark Age. They are "Dark Ages America: the Final Phase of Empire," by Morris Berman; "Dark Age Ahead," by Jane Jacobs, and "The Recurring Dark Ages: Ecological Stress, Climate Changes and System Transformation," by Sing Chew.

Let us consider what they have to say.

Prof. Berman and the late Jane Jacobs are better prose stylists than Prof. Chew. "Dark Ages America" and "Dark Age Ahead" are fluent, easy reads, while "The Recurring Dark Ages" is turgid and stuffed with jargon and noun-phrases, like this:

> In this subsequent volume to World Ecological Degradation, given the above set of sequences, the focus will be to deliberate on other non-anthropogenic factors conditioning a social system crisis by continuing our historical examination of the Culture-Nature relationship that was started in World Ecological Degradation.

I confess I harbor a strong prejudice against any thesis expressed in such bad writing. Bad writing normally betrays bad thinking. Berman and Jacobs have a much better way with words. The trouble with their work, however, is that they tell you little about what causes a Dark Age or how they can be distinguished from any generally unsatisfactory episode in history.

Fundamentalist Voters Cause Dark Age?

Prof. Berman lists four characteristics of Dark Ages, the foremost of which appears to be "the Triumph of Religion over Reason."

He sees this as having been evidenced by "the re-election of George W. Bush, and the prospect of long-term Republican hegemony over American politics." Setting aside his crude partisan tilt and the now questionable projection of Republican hegemony, the notion that religion triumphs over reason during Dark Ages mistakes cause and effect in the face of historical evidence. It is not changes in the intensity of religious expression that cause Dark Ages, but rather that Dark Ages cause changes in the intensity and nature of religious expression.

One of the prominent features of many Dark Age episodes is the violent repudiation of received religions. Archaeological evidence in Mesoamerica, for example, points to the gruesome murder of priests by starving peasants who treated recurring crop failures as the equivalent of contract fraud by ruling theocracies. On the other hand, it is easy to imagine that the prospect of starving to death in Dark Age famines would have encouraged lots of prayers and religious supplication by frightened people.

To cite another example, evidence suggests that the famines in the sixth century A.D., post-Roman Dark Age, were global. The Annals of the Western Wei reports that 70% to 80% of the population died in the Shaanxi province of China. Meanwhile, in Japan 60% of the population was said to have "starved of cold."

Japan's Shinto clans complained that the recently introduced practice of Buddhism was at fault for offending Japan's native gods. Mortality rates were so high "that the…danger of extinction" in the country was said to be, "owing absolutely to…the Buddhist religion." Consequently, the Emperor banned Buddhism, and Buddhist religious artifacts — including a brand new temple — went up in flames.

Meanwhile, the advent of the Dark Age in post-Roman Western Europe led to the collapse of adherence to traditional Roman deities. No one today worships Jupiter, the leading Roman God who embodied just rule before Constantine embraced Christianity. (But note, Roman elites continued worshipping traditional deities after the official embrace of Nicene Christianity.) The collapse of Rome also effectively ended the worship of Mithra, the Christlike God of the Roman legions. As other religions were eclipsed, Christianity was established through the continent.

None of these experiences suggest that the waxing of religious conviction could have been an informing factor in the climate disruptions that caused crop failures and thus economic and demographic collapse.

"A Crazy Dame" Laments Educational Shortfalls

Jane Jacobs, a largely self-taught "crazy dame" who had a major impact on urban economics as a critic of city planning and urban renewal, was not at her best when tackling the prospect of a new Dark Age. Her discourse, "Dark Age Ahead," is full of interesting detail and lively writing, but, like Prof. Berman's "Dark Ages America," offers little coherent insight into what constitutes a Dark Age and why one might be on the horizon. Indeed, Jacobs appears to labor under the illusion that sub-optimal behavior is at fault for the transition from normal economic growth into Dark Age conditions. She states:

> The purpose of this book is to help our culture avoid sliding into a dead end, by understanding how such a tragedy comes about, and thereby what can be done to ward it off and thus retain and further develop our living, functioning culture which contains so much of value, so hard won by our forebears. We need this awareness because, as I plan to explain, we show signs of rushing headlong into a Dark Age.

If my thesis is correct, namely that Dark Ages are periods of devolution triggered by adverse shifts to a colder climate, then it is nonsense to think that a cultural choice, such as weak educational attainment, is the cause of these catastrophes.

No one chooses to shorten growing seasons and confront famine and pestilence under conditions of economic collapse.

No urban real estate investor wants to see his town devolve into a squalid, backwater village.

There is no historic record of any people at any time clamoring to supplant the local state, however expensive and predatory its laws, in favor of the arbitrary exactions and oppressions of warlords.

Equally, Dark Ages are not caused by bad taste in music. The fact that a disconcertingly large portion of the American population cannot locate the United States on the world map may say a lot about challenges of contemporary education, but it poses no threat of mass starvation or the decimation of the population by disease.

Before the Roman legions were withdrawn from Britannia (modern Great Britain) around 410 A.D., the Roman governors distinguished between civilized Britons, who adhered to Romanitas, and uncivilized barbarian tribes that mainly resided north of Hadrian's Wall, whom the Romans called Picti, who were stubbornly illiterate as a matter of principle, clung to their native Celtic religions and tattooed their bodies. While I generally share the Roman distaste for tattoos, I don't for a moment suspect that the decisions by young women to adorn their ankles and backs with subcutaneous graffiti contribute to the prospect of a new Dark Age.

This brings me to Prof. Chew's "The Recurring Dark Ages." While almost entirely devoid of literary charm, this book can at least be commended for seeking a comprehensive explanation for the Dark Ages in history. Unfortunately, Chew offers yet another behavioral explanation for Dark Ages. He contends that they are caused mostly by ecological degradation. Consider his thesis in his own words:

> It is my belief that Dark Ages (as historical events and as a theoretical concept) are critical crisis periods in world history over the course of the last 5,000 years when environmental conditions have played a significant part in determining how societies, kingdoms, empires, and civilizations are reorganized and organized. Therefore, Dark Ages are significant moments for human history. They are periods of devolution of human communities and as such from the perspective of human progress, a period of social economic and political decay and retrogression. However, Dark Ages are significant moments for human history. They are periods of the restoration of the landscape, which are a consequence of the slowdown of human activities. In short, Dark Ages rejuvenate Nature but are bad for Humans.

Crazed Shoppers Cause Dark Age?

Chew's attribution of Dark Ages to "ecological exhaustion and stress" is more convincing than Prof. Berman's suggestion that a Dark Age is brought on by crazed shoppers. He cites the death of an unfortunate woman in Florida who was trampled to death by "a frothing mob" in 2003 while standing in line at a Walmart to buy a DVD player on sale.

I cannot even begin to imagine how Berman's conception of a Dark Age brought on by crazed shoppers could illuminate the fall of Rome and the Dark Age that followed, much less the Bronze Age Collapse from 1200 B.C. to 700 B.C.

The major weakness of Chew's argument is that he fails to recognize that the driving force behind the various Dark Ages was natural climate change, rather than human influence. Some 60 pages of his book are devoted to a confused exercise in paleoecology — the analysis of pollen data. Through this method, Chew purports to show that Dark Age episodes are brought on by human efforts to over-exploit the environment.

To say that his treatment of pollen counts leaves much to be desired is an understatement. His pollen interpretations clearly exaggerate human influence on the environment. For example, Chew arbitrarily treats evidence of plantago pollens in any context to be a measure of human-induced deforestation — even in Greenland during the first millennium B.C. — an area that was practically uninhabited at the time. Of course, pollen counts wax and wane for reasons other than human activity in felling trees.

More broadly, Chew's treatment of pollen data is confused in a more profound way. In a statement that contradicts common sense, and indeed contradicts his own pronouncement that "Dark Ages rejuvenate nature but are bad for humans," Chew states, "The shift from predominantly forests to grasslands in terms of proportion occurred during periods of Dark Ages."

Huh?

While it is certainly possible to imagine that a future Dark Age could precipitate widespread deforestation due to a breakdown in world energy trade, this would hardly have been the case during past Dark Ages when economies were dominated by human and animal muscle power, rather than intense use of liquid hydrocarbons.

During the 20th century, as Vaclav Smil points out, "a roughly 17-fold expansion of annual commercial energy use (from about 22 to approximately 380 ExaJoules) produced a 16-fold increase of annual economic output, from about $2 to $32 trillion in constant 1990 dollars."

By implication, a breakdown in world energy trade on a scale similar to trade disruptions evidenced in past Dark Ages would precipitate rapid deforestation as people struggled to cushion an abrupt drop in energy inputs — by switching to "renewable energy" — in other words, burning their furniture and any other wood they can get their hands on.

The whole basis of Chew's otherwise inexplicable thesis that ecological degradation causes Dark Ages is a bogus correlation between possible deforestation and Dark Age episodes.

Even if Prof. Chew's excursion into paleoecology were not overtly confused, his insistence that the prime cause of past Dark Ages was anthropogenic ecological degradation rather than natural climate variation is manifestly untrue. It is only slightly less silly to propose that farming and grazing inevitably degrade the environment so drastically that food production collapses, than to suggest that a handful of Eskimos deforested Greenland in the millennium before Christ.

The missing element in his equation is the fact that colder (and sometimes dryer) climate depresses agricultural output. Given warmer weather and optimum growing conditions, the productivity of most farmland can be sustained indefinitely.

Prior to the Industrial Revolution, human alterations of the environment were more or less limited to clearing land. Hence, deforestation, Chew's favorite measure of environmental degradation. Al Gore would probably be more bothered by increased greenhouse gases due to the digestive processes of cattle, sheep, goats, and camels. A 2008 U.N. study showed that animal burps and farts contributed 18% more greenhouse gas emissions to the atmosphere than exhaust from all human transportation.

That factoid notwithstanding, there is little warrant for assuming that human influence on the natural system has always and inevitably led to environmental degradation. For one thing, there are literally thousands of habitats, biomes and eco-regions spread across the globe. The UN's Food and Agricultural Organization (FAO) lists 12 major thermal zones determined as part of its effort to map Global Agro Ecological Zones.

In most of the local ecologies in which agriculture has been practiced, in some cases for thousands of years, investments in the land laid the groundwork for sustainable food production. I believe that close analysis shows that ecological degradation could not be the ultimate cause of systemic collapse leading to Dark Ages.

But let's give degradation its due. Irrigated Mesopotamian farming practice has been a "poster child" for Chew and other partisans of the view that "accumulation" or profit-seeking inevitably leads to environmental degradation. No less an authority than the formidable Jared Diamond (author of "Guns, Germs, and Steel: The Fates of Human Societies") argues that the Fertile Crescent in Mesopotamia provides a cautionary example of ecological degradation attributable to human actions. Diamond writes:

> Deforestation led to soil erosion, and irrigation agriculture led to salinization, both by releasing salt buried deep in the ground and by adding salt to irrigation water. After centuries of degradation, areas of Iraq that

formerly supported productive irrigation agriculture are today salt plains where nothing grows.

Irrigation: Better Than Cannibalism?

This would seem to be one of the few instances where local environments have become unsuited for farming after long-term exploitation. But look more carefully. As Brian Fagan outlines in "The Long Summer: How Climate Changed Civilization," natural climatic change was the driving force behind adaptations that only eventually became unsustainable.

He writes:

> Ironically, Ur and its ancient neighbors were born of human responses to earlier climatic changes. They were, to some degree, a product of climatic stress... About 3800 B.C., the climate became suddenly drier, a trend that affected southwestern Asia and the Eastern Mediterranean region for well over 1,000 years. Solar insolation, the rate of incoming light at the Earth's surface, declined throughout the world, a phenomenon well-documented by radiocarbon dated tree rings and lakebed cores from southwestern Asia and as far away as Southern California. Such changes are due to alterations in the Earth's angle to the sun, which determines the amount of radiation that reaches the surface. Almost immediately, the southwestern monsoon with its summer rainfall weakened and shifted to the south. The rains faltered, began later and ended much earlier. Now the summer flood arrived after the harvest. The summer inundations were far smaller than earlier floods reflecting sharply lower rain and snowfall in the Anatolian highlands... For generations, people had relied at least partially on rainfall to nourish growing crops. Now they were dependent on irrigation alone. Food surpluses vanished and gave way to shortages.

> The hungry villagers had few options. Their fate was tied to their carefully irrigated lands, now parched and cracking in the harsh sun. Archaeological surveys tell us that many people simply abandoned their villages. We can imagine them destitute, desperate, wandering aimlessly across the landscape in search of food.

In other words, the intensification of irrigation farming in Mesopotamia, which in the very long run led to salinization of the soil, was a forced choice precipitated by exactly the kind of climate deterioration that has always precipitated the Dark Ages of the past.

A global shift toward colder weather had especially adverse effects in Mesopotamia, an arid area sensitive to disturbances in ocean currents and those in the upper atmosphere, because it lies in a junction where three separate weather systems collide. As often happens in areas of marginal rainfall, colder climate meant drought. Fagan calculates that as rainfall receded, overall moisture declined by 85%. So to say, as Chew does, that "societal relations with the natural environment" had "become exploitative and unsustainable" is, at best, half-right. It was mainly the natural environment that changed to make rainwater farming impossible.

By the standard of decision-making in the modern political economy, where the scale for judging success is the time between now and the next election, the Mesopotamian turn toward fully irrigated farming was a fabulous success. It worked for more than 5,000 years. That was certainly a preferable solution to mass starvation as a response to the failure of rainwater farming caused by a colder, drier climate.

And to put it in better perspective, ask yourself, "Will there be farming in Iowa in 5,000 years?" And if there isn't, would this prove to future generations of ecologists that current farmers in Iowa caused the next Dark Age by exploiting and degrading the land? Rhetorical questions, to be sure, but they highlight the unbalanced judgment that is central to overwrought concern about ecological degradation.

That said, yes, irrigation farming in Mesopotamia eventually did become unsustainable. But that happened thousands of years later. As Sandra Postel, in "Pillar of Sand: Can the Irrigation Miracle Last?" reports:

> Mesopotamian society reached its zenith between the third and seventh centuries A.D. under the rule of the Sassanians… They planned and invested in a series of bold water schemes that expanded irrigation to nearly all the arable land in the region. Archaeologists estimate that the area under cultivation by late Sassanian times totaled some 50,000 km², 40% more than Iraq's total irrigated area today.

A practice that worked for more than 5,000 years is not a luminous failure in the catalogue of civilization. The fact that a once Fertile Crescent is today an Infertile Crescent is hardly an indictment of a survival strategy precipitated by climate deterioration more than five millennia ago.

Equally, it is a stretch to claim that ecological degradation precipitated Dark Age collapses when the archaeological evidence shows that the system not only flourished, but also reached "its zenith" during the Dark Age that coincided with the fall of Rome.

Irrigated farming in Mesopotamia survived for millennia notwithstanding the fact that it was extremely labor-intense. The Tigris and Euphrates carry huge amounts of silt at flood level — as much as three million tons a day. Consequently, the irrigation works had to be cleared of silt almost continuously. This involved a lot of work, as documented by the fact that Alexander the Great put 10,000 men to work for three months to clean and repair just one diversion canal on the west side of the Euphrates.

Furthermore, as the upper layers of soil became sterile after thousands of years of inundations because of the salt deposits, these had to be peeled away to expose the more fertile soil underneath. The process of stripping away the dead soil broke down after the Arab conquest in the seventh century A.D. because of the high death toll associated with recurring slavery during the worst of these — a 14-year slave uprising from 869–883 A.D. Without adequate maintenance and repair, the system eventually broke down completely about 500 years ago.

Whether irrigation farming in Mesopotamia was cause or consequence of an adverse Dark Age climate change, neither Chew nor anyone else has cited any compelling reason to suppose that severe ecological degradation would lead to abrupt, synchronized collapses in the productive potential of numerous societies in different ecological niches spread over the whole globe. However, such simultaneous collapses have been well documented.

The coincidence of synchronous economic and social collapse across the globe during past Dark Ages is just what should be expected if the driver of collapse is an adverse climatic shift to colder weather that affects everyone.

As archaeologist David Keys details in "Catastrophe," there is compelling evidence "that a dramatic cooling of temperature took place in A.D. 540." Tree ring data from South America suggest that 540 had "the coolest summer of the past 1,600 years." Historical chronicles along with paleo-ecological evidence confirm a coincidence of extremely cold weather across the globe in the late 530s to 540s A.D.

A chart of European Oak growth incorporating data provided by dendrochronologists from Ireland to Poland shows "a substantial dip in 536 and an even greater decline in tree growth in 539 and 540. The ring width in A.D. 540 represents one of the three lowest growth years of the past 15 centuries.

In some of the tree ring chronologies... Tree growth in 539 was the lowest in 1,500 years."

A similar analysis of pine tree growth in northern Finland, compiled at the University of Joensuu, shows that temperatures appear to have dropped abruptly in 536 and again in 539, reaching a low point in 542. Meanwhile, China was hit by frost in July 537. And "The History of the Southern Dynasties" records that "in August in Qingzhou there was snow that ruined the crops."

A review of the record, clarified by the availability of ever more detailed paleoclimatic data, shows that periods of cooler temperatures in the past were associated with declining agricultural production. This is hardly a startling revelation. Anyone with even a hint of a green thumb knows that colder weather curtails growing seasons. But this has consequences. When food is less plentiful, prices rise, in turn contributing to a series of dire social effects, including famine, war, economic and political collapse, pestilence and population decline.

Dr. David Zhang of the University of Hong Kong has shown that war has been far more prevalent throughout the world over the past millennium in periods of colder climate rather than mild. Zhang also documents the fact that colder climate is associated globally with population collapses. His research confirms that cooling, when it occurred, engendered disastrous effects on Europe and China synchronously. He reports:

> Socio-economic fluctuations were the same in terms of their macro-trends, turning points, and isolation magnitude. Besides, those fluctuations were in a successive order and corresponded to the temperature change.

Zhang has shown, beyond a doubt, that Dark Ages could not be attributed to local religious fervors, local educational deficiencies, or local ecological degradation. Indeed, they could not have been precipitated by any purely local cause at all, as they were felt simultaneously at widely separated locations across the globe.

According to the U.N.'s Food and Agricultural Organization, there are 51 Global Ecological Zones in Europe, ranging from Subtropical Caucasian mixed hornbeam-oak forests to Arctic polar deserts, while 30 different GEZs are spread over China, from the Tropical Leizhou to the Boreal Daxing'anling. Presumably, if these different ecological zones expressed a very similar response to colder weather, its impact must be robust.

Looking Ahead

Could such a shift to colder weather happen again? Al Gore notwithstanding, anyone who reviews the record of past fluctuations in climate could only conclude that the answer must be "yes."

Climate is not static.

Change has recurred for as long as the Earth has existed. There is no reason whatsoever to expect that process to come to a halt now. Both on a macro and a micro level, the world is in jeopardy of a shift toward colder weather. It is well understood that Ice Ages have prevailed for most of the past million years. Our current warm "interglacial" interval, the Holocene, has already lasted some 12,000 years, about the average for recent "interglacial" warm spells. The penultimate interglacial warm period, the Eemian, which was as much as five degrees Celsius warmer than the current climate, came to a sudden end, and a new, full scale Ice Age began with a transition period perhaps as short as a decade.

It is also notable that evidence from Greenland ice cores shows that the warm Eemian climate was interrupted by mini Ice Ages, that lasted as long as a few thousand years. Similar, though shorter episodes of colder climate during our current Holocene Epoch are what I contend precipitate Dark Ages.

Early I talked about Dr. Habibullo Abdussamatov, the Russian Heliophysicist who believes that the 19th Little Ice Age of the past 7,500 years will begin next year. He writes:

> The earth as a planet will henceforward have negative balance in the energy budget which will result in the temperature drop in approximately 2014. Due to increase of albedo and decrease of the greenhouse gases atmospheric concentration the absorbed portion of solar energy and the influence of the greenhouse effect will additionally decline. The influence of the consecutive chain of feedback effects which can lead to additional drop in temperature will surpass the influence of the TSI (total solar irradiance) decrease. The onset of the deep Bicentennial minimum of TSI is expected in 2042 ± 11, that of the 19th Little Ice Age in the past 7,500 years in 2055±11.

It is noteworthy that Dr. Abdussamatov speaks of a return of Little Ice Age rather than Dark Age conditions. His work is full of references to the Little Ice Age, an interlude of colder climate that lasted from the 14th into the 19th century. He also frequently refers to the Maunder Minimum, which marked the coldest phase of the Little Ice Age during the 17th and early 18th centuries when total solar irradiance (TSI) as measured by sunspots was at a minimum.

The stress imposed by significantly colder weather was manifested in many similar developments to those that characterize past Dark Ages. "History in the Headlines" has catalogued "numerous trends and events climatologists and historians have chalked up to the Little Ice Age..." Among them:

Great Famine

Beginning in the spring of 1315, cold weather... decimated crops and livestock across Europe. Class warfare and political strife destabilized formerly prosperous countries as millions of people starved... According to reports, some desperate Europeans resorted to cannibalism during the so-called Great Famine, which persisted until the early 1320s.

Black Death

Typically considered as an outbreak of the bubonic plague which is transmitted by rats and fleas, the Black Death wreaked havoc on Europe, North Africa and Central Asia in the mid-14th century. It killed an estimated 75 million people, including 30% to 60% of Europe's population. Some experts have tied the outbreak to the food shortages of the Little Ice Age which purportedly weakened human immune systems while allowing rats to flourish.

Manchu Conquest of China

In the first half of the 17th century, famines and floods caused by unusually cold, dry weather enfeebled China's ruling Ming Dynasty. Unable to pay their taxes, peasants rose up in revolt and by 1644 had overthrown the Imperial authorities. Manchurian invaders in the north capitalized on the power vacuum by crossing the Great Wall, allying with the rebels and establishing the Qing Dynasty.

Witch Hunts

In 1484, Pope Innocent VIII recognized the existence of witches and echoed popular sentiment by blaming them for the cold temperatures and resulting misfortunes plaguing Europe. His declaration ushered in an era of hysteria, accusations and executions on both sides of the Atlantic. Historians have shown that surges in European witch trials coincided with some of the Little Ice Age's most bitter phases during the 16th and 17th centuries.

Thirty Years War

Among other military conflicts, the brutal 30 Years' War between Protestants and Catholics across central Europe has been linked to the Little Ice Age. Chilly conditions curbed agricultural production and inflated grain prices, fueling civil discontent and weakening the economies of European powers. These factors indirectly plunged much of the continent into war from 1618 to 1648…

French Revolution

As the 18th century drew to a close, two decades of poor cereal harvests, drought, cattle diseases and skyrocketing bread prices had kindled unrest among peasants and the urban poor in France. Many expressed their desperation and resentment toward a regime that imposed heavy taxes, and provided themselves with relief by rioting, looting and striking. Tensions gave way to become the French Revolution of 1789, which some historians have connected to the Little Ice Age.

For more grim details see "The Little Ice Age: How Climate Made History 1300–1850," by Brian Fagan.

Another volume with engrossing details of distressing human reactions to suddenly colder climate is "The Curse of Akkad: Climate Upheavals that Rocked Human History," by Peter Christie. He reports, "About one million people are believed to have been burned, hanged, strangled, drowned, or beheaded for witchcraft…" in Europe during the Little Ice Age.

These episodes of starvation, plague, war, mass psychosis and political upheaval would fit comfortably into any history of the other Dark Ages. So why, you might ask, does this relatively recent episode of climatic stress not rate designation as a Dark Age? There is always the possibility that in some future history, it may. Meanwhile, I suspect that the answer lies in the fact that the predominant economic power at the end of the Little Ice Age, the United Kingdom, did not collapse like Rome, but emerged from the crucible of climate stress as the first nation to undergo an Industrial Revolution. Rather than succumbing to peak wood, the British economy adopted new technology and a higher BTU energy source, coal, which led to unprecedented economic growth, thus providing a vivid counterexample to the fall of Rome.

Equally, you would look in vain for a news report stating that a new Dark Age began on March 15. There has never been such a report. There never will be. There is no entity that measures Dark Age regressions with a false precision comparable to the way the National Bureau of Economic Analysis measures U.S. economic accounts, calculating GDP, along with the start and stop dates for economic expansions and recessions. If I am correct in suggesting that there could be a new Dark Age ahead, no one will confirm it to you. You will only know it by its effects.

You can expect widespread declines in agricultural productivity in the years to come as the climate cools, bringing higher prices for food and overcoats. And much more. In a marginalized world, with seven billion mouths to feed, a turn to colder weather will leave a large fraction of the world starving, with destabilizing effects that will make the "Arab Spring" seem like a tea party.

Governments of food importing countries will collapse first, followed by apparently more stable temperate zone regimes. This could lead to a sequence of famines; the mass migration of bands of marauders; war; social unrest; new plagues; and political collapse.

Until recently, I supposed that the welfare state might expire in the throes of bankruptcy simply because it no longer paid. But the record of history suggests a more complex accounting requirement for devolution and collapse.

Governments seldom fall solely because they are insolvent.

In the absence of a severe shock to the system, they operate with the advantage of an added margin of "credit" — in the heads of citizens who recall their glory days and have not yet updated their expectations in keeping with now diminished prospects of bankrupt systems. More often than not, the precipitating catalyst for collapse is an adverse shift in climate. Stress surges associated with a turn to a colder climate frequently overwhelm socioeconomic systems without a sufficient reserve capacity.

As Professor Zhang's comprehensive study of the past millennium confirms, the greater correlation with wars and collapse is change to a colder climate. Since the advent of agriculture, it is difficult to find even one instance of a socioeconomic system that was destabilized by warmer weather.

With the United States, the EU, Japan and practically all "advanced" temperate zone economies operating with chronic deficits, the prospects for navigating major crises in the next few decades cannot be good.

Consequently, as you plan your life and investments, you would do well to take into account the fact that we live in a fair weather civilization that is destined to collapse with the fall of the first summer snow.

CHAPTER 24

Adventures In the Fourth Level of Survival Mode: Navigating the Terminal Crisis of the Post-Constitutional United States

"So I started a new world, testing out the new terrain. I eventually got a portal built. The second I entered the Nether, I had a swarm of pigmen attacking me. Getting in radius of 5 blocks seems to cause them to always attack. I'm not even threatening them. Does this happen to anyone else?

The Nether is dangerous enough as it is, we don't need undead swines from Hell attacking us on sight."

— oCrapaCreeper, Minecraft Forums January 6, 2012

Beware the Swarms of Hostile Zombie Pigmen

If you have not had a teen living at home with you in the last few years, the allusions to "Minecraft" and the comments from "oCrapaCreeper," (the NSA knows who he is) may be a bit mysterious. Permit me to decipher.

"Minecraft" is a video game that is quite unlike most of the popular offerings of which you may be aware, such as "Call of Duty," an action-adventure first-person shooter game and "Assassin's Creed," another example of pixelated mayhem in the context of a detailed story line. The "Assassin's Creed" game turns on a rivalry, illustrated in hyper-realistic animation, between two secret societies of medieval origin — the Assassins and the Knights Templar. (For more details of the pre-computer history of the Assassins and the Knights Templar see "Secret Societies of the Middle Ages" by Thomas Keightley, London: 1837.)

In place of photorealistic graphics, "Minecraft's" blocky images seem to have been inspired by Lego. "Minecraft" is an open-world game in which the players determine their own goals rather than having them informed by a plot chosen by the game designers. Core play involves building structures and landscapes with computer-aided design (CAD). One of my boys was so taken with "Minecraft" that he has decided to become an architect when he grows up.

My teenage son, Nate, describes "Minecraft" in terms of the libertarian latitude it provides gamers to be inventive in their own way:

> I feel that "Minecraft" is literally a person's own world in which they can do whatever they please. If they want to build a huge skyscraper they can. If they want to mine for diamonds they can. If they want to do nothing but run around and kill the pigs, cows and sheep, they can. I think people find "Minecraft" appealing because in real life you can't do whatever you want, but in "Minecraft," they can. This applies in "Minecraft" more than other games, where the player has to follow a strict path.

Helen Lewis of *The New Statesman* wrote in the *Financial Times*, "Minecraft, like Lego, is a game of imagination — and the long, slow process of turning your imagination into reality."

Reading what "Minecraft" can tell us about the new reality that looms ahead may be one of the best ways for an old fogey to prepare for it.

"That is no country for old men."

I probably would not have given more than superficial thought to what video games were if it were not for the fact that teenage boys (sometimes with an eight-year-old accomplice) turn my home into a video game parlor every weekend.

As a baby boomer, I am too antique to enter the video gaming world on my own. But I am not so oblivious that I fail to notice the pride and delight my boys have experienced in their various "Minecraft" constructions.

This inspired me to think more closely about video games. But before I delve into the implications of "Minecraft" in survival mode, permit me to address the stereotyped disdain that video games commonly evoke among those who have reached middle age or older.

A 2013 survey conducted by Common Sense Media reported "a whopping 75% of polled parents say they think violent video games contribute to violence." Meanwhile, Mothers Against Videogame Addiction and Violence, (MAVAV), went so far as to campaign against a Wendy's kids' meal promotion featuring Nintendo Wii. MAVAV frets that the Wii operating system is more dangerous and addictive than other video game platforms because "by moving one's hands and limbs one is actually acting out with one's own body the violent behavior."

More generally, MAVAV contends:

> Video game addiction is without a doubt, becoming this century's most increasingly worrisome epidemic, comparable even to **drug** and **alcohol abuse**. All the while, the video game industry continues to market and promote **hatred**, **racism**, **sexism**, and the most disturbing trend: clans and guilds, an underground video game phenomenon which closely resembles **gangs**. <u>Parents NEED to be aware of the hidden dangers</u>.

Whatever. My wife agrees, but I find these frets overwrought, especially in light of the fact that there is not even a semblance of scientific evidence that video game play increases violent behavior. I grant that the case against violent video games seems plausible. And I am uncomfortable with games that involve gratuitous violence portrayed in a hyper-realistic way. But where does one draw the line?

I could hardly dispute that there is violence in "Minecraft," much less in other video games. But rather than throw a conniption about it, I think it more useful as a parent and a citizen to understand it in a broader context. Yes, there is violence in video games. Perhaps it would help to consider them as pixelated fairy tales?

Think about it. There is often extreme violence in fairy tales, and paradoxically, perhaps the more extreme, the better. That may be precisely why we are not overwhelmed by the violence. It is so extreme it is unreal.

Beyond the Disney Version

Have you ever read "Hansel and Gretel"? Did it disturb you, or did you cheer when Gretel got behind the witch and pushed her into the oven? I did. Cheer, that is. But that didn't lead me to push anyone into an oven.

When you re-run the story of "Hansel and Gretel" in your mind's eye, don't waste your time with the Disney version, circa 1987. Most of the drama and terror have been edited out. Consider the original, as published by the Brothers Grimm in 1812. In that version, a "great dearth" had fallen on the land, and the poor woodcutter "could no longer procure even daily bread." Now when he thought over this by night in his bed, and tossed about in his anxiety, he groaned and said to his wife, "What is to become of us? How are we to feed our poor children, when we no longer have anything even for ourselves?"

"'I'll tell you what, husband," answered the woman, "Early tomorrow morning we will take the children into the forest to where it is the thickest; there we will light a fire for them, and give each of them one more piece of bread, and then we will go to our work and leave them alone. They will not find a way home again, and we shall be rid of them."

It is unequivocally clear in the original that the woodcutter's wife is also the children's mother. It is her idea as the mother that the parents should save themselves from starvation by abandoning their children deep in the woods where "the wild animals would soon come and tear them to pieces." I don't know about you, but I find that more disturbing than any video game.

Hansel and Gretel's mother is not the kind that Hallmark celebrates. In later versions of the tale (it was revised continually over the next half century until the final Grimm edition — number seven in 1857), details were modified to make the story less shocking.

Perhaps an early 19th-century version of Mothers Against Violent Accounts prevailed on the Brothers Grimm to change the wicked mother into a wicked stepmother, as they similarly did in revising "Snow White," whose wicked mother was also hyphenated into a "step-mother."

No matter. Edits notwithstanding, it is still a violent tale of the sort that led John Updike to describe fairy tales as the "television and pornography" of an earlier age. Maria Tatar, the author of "Enchanted Hunters: The Power of Stories in Childhood," who presides over the program of folklore at Harvard, assures us of the virtue of fairy tales, even when they are brimming with violence. She says, "It's often surreal — it's burlesque — it's carnivalesque." But that is part of what allows you to "let your imagination run wild... You can go in places that you'd be scared to go otherwise. You can say things that you were afraid to talk about."

It is not immaterial that "Hansel and Gretel" is a fairy tale that dates to one of the colder periods of the millennium — the Little Ice Age at the end of the Middle Ages and early modern times, when Europe experienced repeated subsistence crises. The strain on poor European families facing starvation at that time must have given rise to a lot of anxieties and heartache. Famine, child abandonment, even cannibalism were unhappily all-too-common. This is evidenced by the fact that there are at least 18 similar stories to that of

"Hansel and Gretel" that were told in many cultures around the world at that time. Among the first of these was "Nennillo and Nennella," published in Italy by Giambattista Basile in 1634.

These stories reflect the realities centuries ago when 50% of children died before the age of 10. Think what that means.

Under such conditions, it is hardly surprising that many parents, like the woodcutter and his wife, could be emotionally detached from their children. In 1980, the French economic historian, Jacqueline Hecht, surveyed a large range of literary evidence reflecting the emotional response of parents to the early deaths of their children. Her survey pointed to a major shift from an attitude of religious resignation bordering on indifference, to one of bitter sorrow as child mortality declined. This reflects what family historians have described as "the invention of parental love."

When child mortality is low, parents tend to invest more emotionally and economically in each child, while having fewer children. Chances are, most children today, even those whose parents permit them to play the most violent video games, enjoy more parental love than the poor offspring of poor woodcutters who clung to a precarious existence a couple of centuries ago.

All of this is linked back to a crucial question asked by historians Carlo A. Corsini and Pier Paolo Viazzo, namely whether the impact of lower child mortality on parental love could have also worked the other way around after child mortality began to abate because of economic progress:

> Certainly one of the historian's most fascinating and important tasks is to try to determine whether, and to what extent, the rate of infant mortality decline was influenced by the parents' growing awareness that their children had both the possibility and the right to survive the dangerous first months and years of their life.

So not only were children more deeply loved because they lived longer, as life expectancy improved some may have lived longer precisely because they were more deeply loved.

Be that as it may, back in the dark days of the Little Ice Age, when mortality was high, children were not oblivious to the perils they faced. This was made explicit in the "Hansel and Gretel" tale when the children overheard their parents discussing plans to "be rid of them." Even without that deft eavesdropping, however, the peril to children in times of dearth would have been too obvious for them to ignore.

Hence, the antidote to anxiety — "Hansel and Gretel," a violent fairy tale in which terrible things happened to the predator in the woods. The telling of this allegory made the struggle to grow up easier, by disassociating the danger to the children from the possibility that poor parents might abandon them for economic reasons. One need only consider the shocking rates of female infanticide in India and China today to see that in early modern Europe the deliberate disposal of children by parents was probably a bigger issue than we care to remember. A four-year study in South India showed that "72% of all female deaths were due to femicide," the outright murder or intentional neglect of the health of young girls.

"Hansel and Gretel" tells us that "the godless witch" who threatened the children "was miserably burnt to death." This contributed to the happy ending for the good boy and girl by punishing the would-be cannibal, and setting the stage for the children to take the witch's jewels back home to their parents as spoils of their adventure. This, of course, resolved the family crisis by removing the economic motivation for the parents to abandon their children.

No doubt, stories like "Hansel and Gretel" helped generations of anxious children face their fears. And they did so in a fashion that was more effective and easier to approach than it would have been for parents to directly assure children that they did not intend to feed them to cannibals in the woods. A fantasy removed from reality can be more effective than a dispassionate analysis in creating a "safe place" for children. As Maria Tatar suggested, fairy tales have the "power to change us — not least by frightening us into imagining alternate realities."

"Hansel and Gretel," like most tales from folklore, is a "children's story" in the sense that it has been told to children. But it was not a tale told by children. That is where an open world video game like "Minecraft" is different. Fairy tales were sometimes violent fantasies told by adults to children to allay their anxieties about life. But seldom have older generations gained as much information from what children told them.

Some of the self-conscious messages proclaimed by young people today seem like self-parody — as for example, the quasi-hysterical demand for "trigger warnings" on college course offerings, to protect dainty sensibilities from exposure to off-label "racism, classism, ableism, sexism and heterosexism." But we can't be too hard on them, as the whole generation suffers the lingering effects of fiscal child abuse on an unprecedented scale. In the words of Herbert Hoover, "Blessed are the young for they shall inherit the national debt."

Little wonder that some of today's unconscious messages from the young are worth heeding. The often-violent content of open world video games reflects the pixelated anxieties of children about the straightened prospects of American life, anxieties that can tell us a lot if we pay attention.

New Anxieties Tackled in New Terms

One can make all sorts of inferences from "Hansel and Gretel" and other fairy tales. They represent a significant cultural departure from more directly allegorical morality plays, like The Interlude of Youth, where a conspicuously healthy, indeed, rich, Youthe cavorts with Ryot, Lechery and Pride in a debauche of abundance. Youthe seems to be without a care in the world. He brags:

> I am the heyre of my fathers lande
> And it is come into my hande
> I care for no more."

Such morality tales were larded with theological messages for earlier generations of young people. Tales like "Hansel and Gretel" will not give you much of a tutorial in Christian theology. But read closely, they can tell you a lot about economic history.

Heretofore, however, there has been no way to directly discern what the themes of children's fantasies and gameplay tell us about the present state of the economy and its likely future. But as my son Nate explains, "'Minecraft' is literally a person's own world in which they can do whatever they please."

Among the things they please to do is building their own maps or landscapes and "Mods," or modifications to the game that permit emergent gameplay. Minecraft multi-player servers offer players a wide range of games and competitions, including many that resemble the game described in Suzanne Collins' dystopian novel, "The Hunger Games," set in a post-apocalyptic North America. The best-selling novel describes an annual contest in which one boy and one girl from each of twelve districts of impoverished, subjugated people is selected by a despotic government in the wealthy Capital to compete in the ultimate reality TV spectacle — a televised fight to the death.

The "Hunger Games/Survival Games" customized on "Minecraft" reflect its status as "a game of imagination." But it is well-suited to host "Hunger Game"-style competitions because "Minecraft's" creative freedom is constrained, as in life, by a requirement to eat. While creating structures and "maps," "Minecraft" players in "Survival Mode" must feed themselves by scavenging the landscapes they create and exploit. Players have a hunger bar that drains when they go unfed. Certain strenuous activities, such as sprinting, cannot be undertaken when the hunger bar is at low ebb (six or lower). Players also have a health bar, which is slowly depleted when they fail to eat food in-game. When playing in the most difficult level of "Survival Mode," the players' health will keep draining until they eat something or starve to death.

It is only a matter of time until *The New York Times* best-selling author Lauren Oliver's grim "Panic" game is echoed in a "Minecraft" "Mod." The novel, inspired by Grimm fairy tale #4, "The Story of the Youth Who Went Forth to Learn What Fear Was," is set in a poor, dead-end town in New York State where the fondest dream of high school seniors is to get out. They compete in a dangerous ordeal from which just one winner emerges with a ticket to a better life.

It is also notable that when played in "Survival Mode," players of "Minecraft" must defend themselves and their creations from attack by an array of menacing creatures including "creepers" (suicide bombers that explode causing death and damage), giant spiders, skeletons, and "Zombie Pigmen," who seem to be embodiments of the menacing agents of the State.

These are the analogues to the witches of the Little Ice Age — personifications of contemporary anxieties — obviously informed by the perceptions of young people that they are trapped in a dead-end economy from which there is no visible escape. This is a far cry from what America used to mean, as expressed by Herbert Hoover early in the last century:

> In no other land could a boy from a country village, without inheritance or influential friends, look forward with unbounded hope. My whole life has taught me what America means.

Today that is only a quaint memory.

With this in mind, revisit the thoughts of Harvard folklorist, Maria Tatar:

> This savagery we offer children today is more unforgiving than it once was. And the shadows are rarely banished by comic relief. Instead of stories about children who struggle to grow up, we have stories about children who struggle to survive.

From the American Dream to
the Post-American Nightmare

Even if we don't see it ourselves, the millions of children who play "Minecraft" have already gotten the message that they no longer live in the imagined community that we knew as "the United States of America." When I was their age, we talked seriously of "the American dream," and "the land of the free; the home of the brave." Today, I doubt that many young people take such vocabularies to heart as a guide to what they expect in their future. They are not only separated by generations from us Baby Boomers, but also by completely different conditions of life.

They may still hear old fogeys of my generation nattering on about prospering in "the richest country on earth." But the America they know, perhaps better than we do, is the most thoroughly bankrupt landscape on the globe.

Americans Without a Job – Up by 27 million

As documented throughout this book, we live in an economy of deceit. While the government's propaganda of "recovery" trumpets a supposed improvement in the job market, the unvarnished numbers tell a different story. The ranks of Americans without a job have swollen by 29 million since the year 2000, and businesses in the United States are being destroyed faster than they are being created.

Serfdom Reinvented

For Americans in the 18-29-year-old age group, full-time employment has proven elusive. In June, 2013, only 43.6% of that entire demographic segment had a job. Note that some that did find employment and many that didn't are indentured with $1.111 trillion of student loans. In 2013, 53% of recent college grads were jobless or underemployed. Many are indentured for life to pay high interest student loans that cannot be discharged even in bankruptcy. Think about that.

No wonder the U.S. federal government is now thought to receive less support than King George III did at the time of the American Revolution. Student loans are merely the most extreme expression of the culture of neo-feudal debt bondage that characterizes the waning years of the U.S. imperium.

Ominously, the ratio of what men in the 18-to-29-year-old age bracket earn today is at an all-time low compared to earnings of the general population. This is confirmed by a precipitous drop in labor force participation rates. Almost 18% fewer persons aged 16-24 were in the work force in 2014 than at the turn of the century.

The bleak job picture for young people in America not only helps inform the fascination with alternative realities embodied in video games, it also illuminates why so many young adults in America are living with their parents. According to a Gallup Poll in February of 2014, 29% of all U.S. adults under the age of 35 are living with their parents.

This represents a reversal of one of the 20th century's more important demographic trends — the tendency of young people to leave their parents' home after high school and form their own households. It was a development predicated upon high and rising incomes that helped sell a lot of refrigerators and more than a few ugly sofas.

But the high and rising incomes we took for granted in the middle of the 20th century have ceased to rise. Indeed, they have plunged. As reported by Michael Greenstone and Adam Looney of the Hamilton Project:

> … for most of the past century, a good job was a ticket to the middle class. Hitched to the locomotive of rapid economic growth, the wages of the typical worker seem to go in only one direction: up. From 1950 to 1970, the average earnings of male workers increased by about 25% each decade. And these gains were not concentrated among some lucky few. Rather earnings rose for most workers, and almost every prime-aged male (ages 25 – 64) worked.

> Over the past 40 years, a period in which U.S. GDP per capita more than doubled after adjusting for inflation, the annual earnings of the median prime-aged male has actually fallen by 28%. Indeed, males at the middle of the wage distribution now earn about the same as their counterparts in the 1950s! This decline reflects both stagnant wages for men on the job, and the fact that, compared with 1969, three times as many men of working age don't work at all… The reality is that the relative income of a large portion of working Americans has sharply declined is indisputable.

They go on to report:

> … the median wage of the American male has declined by almost $13,000 after accounting for inflation in the four decades since 1969… Indeed,

earnings haven't been this low since Ike was president and Marshall Dillon was keeping the peace in Dodge City.

Little wonder that many young people are lost in the fantasy worlds of video games. I would contend also that the enormous success of the "Hunger Games" franchise, along with the popularity of "Minecraft," foreshadow another instance of life imitating art.

I don't pretend that young people are consciously aware of the many measures of decline I have outlined for you. It is a challenge, even with the help of Google, to parse through the abundance of disinformation and propaganda that pour forth from official channels to obscure what you need to know.

Equally, people are not as stupid as the government might wish. Young people, in particular, are less susceptible to the often deceitful blandishments of the establishment because their consciousness is not conditioned by recollections of a time, generations ago, in the middle of the last century, when the American economy and Empire were in their heyday. If the American dream promises that every generation will live better than the previous one, it was far easier to credit that when it was actually the experience of your parents and their parents before them. But as this has not been true for the majority of Americans during recent decades, young people may have a more open mind about the future than do we fossils. They see that the grand narrative of American life no longer describes their reality.

CHAPTER 25

"Don't Know Much About History" Toward the "Fourth Revolution"

"When world reserve currencies are replaced and major empires die, it is not the end of the world but history shows it will be the end of the world we've known for much of our life in the United States."

— Ron Holland, The Daily Bell

Here is the factoid of our times: the United States squandered trillions of dollars and the lives of 5000 Americans to create the Iraqi army that threw down its weapons and ran when faced by Sunni fanatics. If your perception is not curdled by regret, it should by now be obvious to you that the American imperium faces the Breaking Point. I say this in light of the many analyses we have canvassed that underscore the fact that we live in a bankrupt system. The status quo is doomed not only in Iraq, but globally.

If you are on top of the news, you may think that the U.S. national debt is $17.5 trillion. But this is wrong, not simply because any figure I could site is rapidly antiquated with the Federal government adding $2.2 billion per day to the national debt, saddling future generations with debt bondage. That is true, but it isn't the worst of the problem.

As Professor Laurence Kotlikoff has detailed, the true fiscal gap facing the U.S. government is in the range of $222 trillion. Drawing on CBO figures, he explains it this way:

> What you have to do is look at the present value of all the expenditures now through the end of time. All projected expenditures, including servicing the official debt. And you subtract all the projected taxes. The present value of the difference is $222 trillion.

For perspective, the funds required to meet this staggering liability net out at roughly 10% greater than the total wealth of the world. That assumes that you credit a calculation by the McKinsey Global Institute, as reported in *The Atlantic*: "The $200 Trillion World: Who Owns All the Wealth?" My guess is that McKinsey is as likely to be right about such an extraordinary guesstimate as anyone.

But you only need to eyeball it to realize that America's politicians have promised vastly more than they can deliver. While there is no definitive accounting of total world wealth, the fact that the "present value of all the expenditures" the government has promised to pay from "now through the end of time" (an undoubtedly optimistic estimate) could arguably exceed the total wealth of the world, shows how insanely bankrupt the United States government is.

Needed: $20 trillion From Outer Space

Obviously, not even the most despotic police state could seize all the wealth of its citizens, much less all the wealth of other residents of the globe. But even if it could, that means we need only depend on a bit more than a $20 trillion infusion by friendly Transformers from outer space. It is so preposterous that it defies serious consideration.

Unless you think an interstellar mercy mission is headed this way from an advanced civilization with more respect for arithmetic than our politicians show, you have to conclude that the U.S. government is headed for the Breaking Point.

Needless to say, I doubt such a windfall is forthcoming. For one thing, there is the nontrivial challenge of how wealth could be ported across space.

It would obviously be idiotic to fill up giant spacecraft with trillions of dollars in printed (counterfeit) money, as this would add nothing to the sum of wealth on earth. (Fans of Quantitative Easing, take note).

Equally, there would be nothing gained by flying across space to deliver algorithms for "minting" Bitcoin, Namecoin, Dogecoin, Megacoin, FeatherCoin, Terracoin, or any of the other myriad cyber-currencies derived from algorithms. Further to that, the needed sums exceed the permissible expansion of the controlled supply cyber-currencies. Their value in dollars would have to skyrocket to fund a $20 trillion deficit.

An interstellar subsidy in the form of gold would at first glance seem more worthy of a long spaceflight from an advanced civilization. It would be quite a payload. Unfortunately, a quantity of gold sufficient to close a $20 trillion deficit in the wealth of the world as compared to U.S. obligations would more than double the world's gold supply. Best estimates are that only about 165,000 metric tons of gold have been mined through all of history. That is a bit more than 6.385 billion troy ounces, worth $8.222 trillion as I write, with the price of gold at $1,287.70. Therefore, $20 trillion worth of gold would be 15.531 billion troy ounces, or more than 400,000 metric tons. Quite a payload to be sure.

But would the import of 400,000 metric tons of gold by friendly Transformers really make the world wealthy enough to finance the U.S. government's extravagant promises? Probably not. If the quantity of gold in the world were more than doubled, its value per ounce would certainly decline.

An advanced civilization would foresee that and come to a better solution for multiplying our wealth to rescue us from debt bondage.

How could they go about it?

Here is a possibility. Imagine a hologram of Michael Jackson. Instead of lip-syncing "Slave to the Rhythm" at the Billboard Music Awards, he could address a joint session of Congress, and reveal a formula for harnessing cold fusion or some other advanced technology for jump-starting the economy with ultra-cheap energy. As Joseph A. Tainter, the author of "The Collapse of Complex Societies," advises:

> Obtaining a new energy subsidy (through Empire-building or by exploiting a new energy source), can for a time either reverse a declining marginal curve, or at least provide the wealth to finance it.

Remember the claims that the United States went into Iraq for the oil? If so, we weren't able to grab very much of it. Perhaps an energy formula from outer space would go further?

But a $20 trillion energy subsidy, cleverly deployed by our fairy godmothers from outer space would avail little in the long run. As Lee Kwan Yew once told me, Singapore could only have become rich because it did not enjoy an endowment of oil wells. Easy money would only encourage feckless politicians and their feckless constituents to enlarge their ambitions and spend still more.

You do not need to don green eyeshade or waste time fretting about the discount rate that should properly be used to calculate the vanishing point at which the United States government disappears into insolvency. Accountants and economists could argue about the precise number of trillions by which the fiscal gap of the U.S. government should be measured. But no one who is the least bit aware of fiscal reality can doubt that the budget of the U.S. government is chronically and deeply in deficit.

The very fact of runaway deficits tells you something important. It is a meta-message about where the actual control of government lies. Not with voters, as proposed by civics book theory — but with its employees. As Frederic C. Lane outlined in his classic essay, "Economic Consequences of Organized Violence," in The Journal of Economic History, (1958), "treating governments as enterprises which seek to maximize profits" helps illuminate who controls the government. Differences in control determine the government's fiscal profile, and in turn determine how and whether the tribute collected by government contributes to economic growth. Lane lists three alternative possibilities, all of which were illustrated in the early modern world.

1. The first, widely discussed, but historically rare, is control of government by "its customers," the producers and consumers who pay the government for protection. Lane argues, and I agree that the notion that "We, the People," determine the expenditures of government is no more than a widely acceptable form of "wishful thinking." Lane points out that in the rare instances where customers did control the government, "as it is supposed to be in the theory of representative government," it would "take no tribute," and "it would lower the prices (taxes) charged for protection as fast as it was able to lower the cost." In other words, a government controlled by its customers would efficiently balance its budget at a low level of costs. But as Lane warns, more frequently than not, however, control of government has "been in the hands of a separate group or class pursuing distinct purposes of their own. In so far as they rationalized the economics of the violence-controlling enterprise, they pursued aims diverse from that of serving customers by maximizing the quality of their service and minimizing the price charged for it."

2. In a minority of cases, a government has been "controlled by a prince or emperor so absolute that he could be considered the owner." The owner's preferred fiscal policy, as a profit maximizer, would be to run a huge budget surplus. He would seek to keep prices (taxes) high, while minimizing costs. Lane comments, "From lowered costs, or from the increased exac-

tions made possible by the firmness of his monopoly, or from the combination, he accumulated a surplus, the kind of monopolistic profit which I am calling tribute."

3. The final alternative, rarely extolled in theory, but widely seen in practice among "advanced economies" is control of government by its employees. Lane observes, "A great many protection-producing enterprises were controlled by the upper ranks of the Army and police, in short, by their top management. In such cases we might say that their primary objective was preserving the life of the firm, and that maximizing size was more important than maximizing profits… When employees as a whole where in control, they had little interest in minimizing the amount exacted for protection and none in minimizing the large part of costs represented by labor costs, by their own salaries. Maximizing size was more to their taste also… When violence-producing enterprises were controlled by employees, they made little or no effort to minimize costs, and as a result a large part of total production was consumed in militarism." Because a government controlled by employees has little or no interest in minimizing its operational costs, the necessarily weak efforts by the producers and consumers who pay the government for protection to rein in costs achieve little. As Lord Rees-Mogg and I detailed in "The Sovereign Individual," "Where conditions impose strong price resistance, in the form of opposition to higher taxes, governments controlled by employees would be more likely to let the revenues fall below their outlays than to cut their outlays. In other words, their incentives imply that they may be inclined toward chronic deficits…" We also noted that the welfare state is a mechanism for ensuring employee control of government: "Since there were not otherwise enough employees to create a working majority, increasing numbers of voters were effectively put on the payroll to receive transfer payments of all kinds. In effect, the recipients of transfer payments and subsidies became pseudo-employees of government who were able to dispense with the bother of reporting every day to work." Government controlled by its employees is characterized by runaway spending and high fiscal deficits.

This is why the whole giant edifice of industrial big government cannot be reformed. The government cannot decide to downsize. As I endeavored to show in my graduate thesis at Oxford, the incentive structure of modern, big government dictates that it will almost always seek to grow and seldom, and only temporarily, to retrench. The politicians are no more likely to slow down their spending spree than a great white shark would be inclined to stop swimming.

As you may remember, great white sharks are "obligate ram ventilators," which more or less means they must swim constantly in order to keep breathing. Their movements are controlled by their spinal cord, not their brain, so there is no arguing with a great white shark. If they stop, they die.

Governments are not great white sharks. But they operate on similar principles. They are predatory. And they cannot stop.

Adam Smith's "Absurd Tax"

Because big government manifests declining marginal returns across a wide range of activities that do not pay their way, it cannot stand still. It must consume ever more resources, or die. Here, it is worth recalling Adam Smith's admonition that high profits can only be achieved for any length of time through government interventions that disrupt the operation of the free market. In this sense, The U.S. government is the embodiment of the "anti-market," Fernand Braudel's "contre-marche." As Smith warned, it has been captured by special interests, or "people who employ the largest capitals, and by their wealth draw to themselves the greatest share of the public consideration." That is a polite 18th century way of explaining why today's young people face such meager prospects. Their future has been ripped off by special interests that employ government to steal from you and the next generations, in Adam Smith's words, "by raising their profits above what they naturally would be, to levy, for their own benefit, an absurd tax upon the rest of their fellow-citizens." Perhaps the main bulwark against the free market is the manipulation of fiat money with Quantitative Easing, which suppresses interest rates and steals the savings of the middle class, while raising the wealth of the already wealthy.

It is an ever-more expensive proposition to thwart the market, which guarantees radically declining marginal returns to big government. It will require still more resources next year to achieve the same thing — or even less than it did this year. Big government as currently constituted cannot long endure. While it will not choose to downsize, it will have no choice.

The Fourth Revolution

This is why smart people, like John Micklethwait, editor of *The Economist*, and his sidekick Adrian Wooldridge, argue that those countries that will do best in the 21st century are those, presumably on the periphery, where the state can be shrunk and reengineered. That is the theme of their new book, "The Fourth Revolution: the Global Race to Reinvent the State." In their view, and I agree, it is not a coincidence that wherever one looks among the advanced economies, governments are "bloated, dysfunctional and distrusted."

If I have a quarrel with Micklethwait, and Wooldridge, it is that I don't think they have probed deeply enough for the causes of the dysfunction. They cite three "forces" which explain little: 1) failure to deliver, notwithstanding runaway spending, 2) global competition, and 3) an unrealized opportunity gap for the provision of better services by changing the nature of the state.

It is a matter of some interest that there are two books with the name, "The Fourth Revolution." In addition to the work by Micklethwait and Wooldridge, there is another "The Fourth Revolution: How to thrive through the world's transformation," by French analyst Jeremie Averous. I find it a matter of interest that authors coming from entirely different perspectives detect that the world is at the threshold of dramatic change in which, as Averous puts it, "Established institutions and elites will crumble and disappear."

Averous' work is all the more interesting because it is so naïvely framed. He correctly recognizes that a fourth phase in the evolution of human society is about to emerge, following the Hunter-Gatherer, the Agricultural and the Industrial economies. But his explanations of the past stages of human social evolution are so weak that his forward vision can only be attributed to intuition rather than a deep understanding of history. Averous says, for example, that the Agricultural revolution "was brought about by the invention of Writing," a ridiculous assertion. He seems to imagine that farming was launched by some wise men promulgating instructions about plant husbandry through a prehistoric version of an agricultural extension service.

In fact, nothing like that ever happened. Writing emerged after the Agricultural Revolution created surpluses that permitted occupational specialization, particularly in the violence-wielding enterprises that became governments. There is very good evidence that writing gradually evolved from the efforts by primitive accountants to record inventories of valuables — of which there were none during hunting and gathering times. And of course, in order for violence wielding enterprises to attain any size, kings required scribes to send their orders to distant generals, impose taxes, and praise them as close relatives to the gods. Written language was a by-product of the food surplus created by agriculture. But in no sense was the agricultural revolution "brought about by the invention of Writing."

Equally, Averous displays his naïveté in discussing the "changes" of The Fourth Revolution that "will shake societies." He tells us "that manufacturing will become subsidized," as agriculture is now. By whom? He says that a "new united governance body" will impose a "Universal Education Program...that is consistently followed" in all schools." More ominously, he imagines his new world government launching a program "to manage global atmospheric temperatures by injecting into the high atmosphere some components that would shield the sun's rays." Averous intuits that the digital revolution changes everything. But he is so in thrall to conventional thinking that he imagines this new world will give rise to an even bigger government that will continue the crony capitalist ways of contemporary big governments by subsidizing manufacturing and launching a global educational boondoggle.

I don't think so. Intuition is sometimes a great guide. But, to have your best shot at forward vision, you must analyze the deeper causes of change.

God Sides with the Big Battalions

As you know, I tend to look for explanations to megapolitical factors that define and alter the costs and rewards of projecting and resisting violence. The crucial fact about today's big governments is that they are megapolitical anachronisms. They grew in response to high and rising returns to scale in the mobilization of violence.

Starting in the era when Genoese capital teamed with Iberian monarchies to dominate the world, until recently the pay-off from deploying ever-"bigger battalions," to steal Voltaire's phrase from the 18th century, was "hegemony" or predominance for countries operating at an ever-larger scale. As you may remember, Napoleon, cycling Voltaire, famously observed, "God is on the side of the big battalions."

And so He seemed to be for most of the modern period. Never more so than on D-Day (the 70th anniversary of which has been celebrated), the greatest logistical undertaking in the history of warfare, when 11,590 aircraft and 6,939 ships, along with almost 200,000 personnel, were deployed in the decisive Allied Invasion of Normandy.

History tells us, as Giovanni Arrighi reports:

> ... each of the successive systemic cycles of accumulation that made the fortunes of the West has been premised on the formation of ever-more powerful territorialist-capitalist blocs of governmental and business or-

ganizations endowed with greater capabilities than the preceding bloc to widen or deepen the spatial and functional scope of the capitalist world-economy. The situation today seems to be such that this evolutionary process has reached, or is about to reach, its limits.

Arrighi also makes the important observation that each succeeding period of hegemony has been shorter than that preceding it:

> ... the development of historical capitalism as a world system has been based on the formation of ever more powerful cosmopolitan — Imperial (or corporate — national) blocks of governmental and business organizations endowed with the capability of widening (or deepening) the functional and spatial scope of the capitalist world economy. And yet, The more powerful these blocks have become, the shorter the lifecycle of the regimes of accumulation they have brought into being — the shorter, that is, the time that it has taken for these regimes to emerge out of the crisis of the preceding dominant regime, to become themselves dominant, and to attain their limits as signaled by the beginning of a new financial expansion.

The United Provinces superseded Genoese/Iberian hegemony; the United Kingdom superseded the Dutch; and finally, in the second quarter of the last century, the United States imperium eclipsed the British Empire. While the earlier hegemonic systems during the modern period all underwent "terminal crises," as Arrighi notes, "characterized by long periods of systemic chaos," these did not entail total collapse comparable to the fall of the Roman Empire.

Partly, this is because the scale of governance and enterprise was rising throughout the whole period dating back to the 15th century. As Joseph Tainter explains:

> Collapse occurs, and can only occur, in a power vacuum. Collapse is possible only where there is no competitor strong enough to fill the political vacuum of disintegration.

In each instance of past hegemonic transition since the 15th century, the scale of the new hegemonic system that replaced the old power was bigger still, so there was always a new predominant power "to fill the political vacuum of disintegration."

The scale of enterprise was also rising, so the high taxes collected for the "ever-bigger battalions" for a time seemed to pay their way. So long as the returns to scale were high and rising, increasingly big and costly governments were more tolerable then they would be in times of radically falling marginal returns implied when overgrown systems entail large diseconomies to scale.

This is precisely what has been in evidence lately. In the third quarter of the 20th century, as U.S. hegemony experienced its "signal crisis," the "bigger battalions" began to become less of an advantage and more a big burden. The returns to scale had fallen too much to be ignored.

A signal event was the invention of the microprocessor, patented by Intel in November 1971. Its Intel 4004 was a silicon-based chip measuring one-eighth of an inch long by one-sixteenth of an inch wide, containing 2,300 transistors. It had about the same computing power as the original ENIAC computer that weighed 30 tons, occupied 3,000 cubic feet of space and used 17,468 vacuum tubes. The Intel microchip accelerated a dynamic process of miniaturization that has been gathering momentum for decades. The impact of miniaturization on big governments and large business organizations has been increasingly subversive.

"The Decaying Power of Large Armies"

One of the more important consequences of miniaturization has been to reduce the scale at which groups can attain military effectiveness. As Moisés Naim documents in "The End of Power," based on his analysis of "The Decaying Power of Large Armies:"

> Al Qaeda spent about $500,000 to produce 9/11, whereas the direct losses of that day's destruction plus the costs of the American response to the attacks were $3.3 trillion. In other words, for every dollar Al Qaeda spent planning and executing the attacks, the United States spent $7 million.

This is by no means the only example of smaller and apparently weaker actors confounding larger and more expensive militaries in asymmetric conflicts. In his 2005 book, "How the Weak Win Wars: A Theory of Asymmetric Conflict," Ivan Arreguin-Toft documents a dramatic shift away from success of the bigger battalions in the decades since 1950. Whereas big governments with big militaries prevailed in more than 80% of asymmetrical conflicts during the 19th century — and notwithstanding Mussolini's ill-fated invasion of Ethiopia, continued to prevail almost two-thirds of the time through the first half of the 20th century — from 1950 through 1999, the weaker actor prevailed the majority of time in conflicts with a bigger, better funded military, such as the United States, as famously exemplified by the U.S. defeat in Vietnam.

This is exactly why Averous' projection of a "new united governance body" operating at a world scale is a fantasy. Rather than getting bigger still, government is destined to get smaller in the digital age.

The realignment of the tectonic plates of power has profound implications. It will turn the monumental edifices of big government to rubble. Brace yourself for an onslaught of "Creative Destruction."

"Creative Destruction"

As you may remember, "Creative Destruction" is the engine of progress lauded by economist Joseph Schumpeter. He spoke of the virtues of "the competition from the new commodity, the new technology, the new source of supply, the new type of organization — competition which commands a decisive cost or quality advantage and which strikes not at the margins of the profits and the outputs of the existing firms but at their foundations and their very lives."

While lauding "Creative Destruction" as the driver of innovation and economic progress, Schumpeter strangely thought that big business was better at innovation than entrepreneurs were. But his attitude needs qualification. He was a former banker and ardent advocate of fiat money who served as Finance Minister of Austria after the First World War. Perhaps because he was such a man of the establishment, it is not as surprising as it otherwise would be that he seems not to have considered that governments themselves might be subject to Creative Destruction due to competition from "the new type of organization — competition which commands a decisive cost or quality advantage."

That would be a logical expectation in an era when governments no longer pay their way. Indeed, that is the thesis of Micklethwait and Wooldridge's "Fourth Revolution." But Schumpeter did not anticipate it. He died in 1950, just as the era of big government had nearly run its course.

When governments outlive the megapolitical foundations that served as the basis of their competitive advantage, they tend to become bloated and predatory. Their first objective is to survive and, in most cases, they are only too willing to squeeze the population to the last drop and stomp out any vestige of autonomy or liberty that seems to stand in their way.

Big governments (and the U.S. government is the biggest and most costly the world has ever seen) are destined to sink on the shoals of fiscal bankruptcy. The U.S. government, being the world's biggest, is perhaps the most sclerotic, as well as the most hopelessly bankrupt.

It is also increasingly despotic, as often happens when Imperial powers find themselves on a downhill trajectory. The Roman Empire had its secret police, the Frumentarii, so named because they were ostensibly "collectors of wheat." But actually, they were collectors of secrets, secret police who roamed the land spying and eavesdropping on citizens, a job which is much more thoroughly and comprehensively undertaken by the NSA in modern America. It records every word you utter in a phone call and the texts of all your emails, pouring over them as the Frumentarii pried into the secrets of the private lives of leading Romans.

It was a terrible danger, even for the wealthiest aristocrat, if an off-hand comment in the Forum or marketplace that could be construed as unflattering to the Emperor — or even the rumor of such statements — reached the Frumentarii. That could lead swiftly to death and the confiscation of family fortunes. The Speculatores, special units of the Praetorian Guards, were dispatched to execute citizens reported to the Emperor by the Frumentarii. Even the wealthiest and most powerful Romans were victimized by this tyranny. For example, one of the wealthiest men of the ancient world, Tiberius Claudius Narcissus, who amassed the enormous personal fortune of 400 million sesterces (about $5 billion in today's money), was poisoned by Agrippina the mother of Nero, and the widow of the Emperor Claudius. Claudius, in turn, had condemned 35 Roman senators and confiscated their family fortunes. As Peter Turchin and Sergey Nefedov document in "Secular Cycles:"

> After the purges of Nero and Domitian, most of the old Republican noble families had disappeared... Under Trajan and Hadrian, only some 30 senators are known that still bore the names of the old Republican nobility... These numbers imply a 50% extinction rate for 25 years.

The information collected through NSA spying may not yet be leading to the assassination of important targets, but it apparently is being used for character assassination. Among the prominent victims was Eliot Spitzer, son of real estate tycoon Bernard Spitzer and former governor of New York, who was obliged to resign when information was leaked to the press in March 2008 indicating that Spitzer was a client of the Emperors Club VIP escort agency. Spitzer had apparently made himself obnoxious to some among the powers-that-be by prosecuting white-collar crime among the bankers on Wall Street when he was Attorney General of New York. The fact that Spitzer was independently wealthy and governor of New York made him a potential threat to the powers that be in the "Deep State." Information gathered by government spies was used to kill his career.

Another prominent victim of character assassination was Gen. David Petraeus, former Director of the Central Intelligence Agency. General Petraeus was forced to resign from his position as Director of the CIA on November 9, 2012, after an extramarital affair was reported, having allegedly been discovered in the course of an FBI investigation. The word is that the NSA leaked these details of Petraeus' private life from their vantage point spying on everyone. Why did the Deep State turn against General Petraeus? Perhaps because he was not a sufficiently gung-ho partisan of military intervention in every circumstance. He told the Margaret Thatcher Conference on Liberty in London that it would be a mistake for the United States to become re-involved militarily in Iraq. He said it would be unwise to offer military support if the political conditions were not exactly right — which they certainly would not be. "This cannot be the United States being the air force for Shia militias, or a Shia on Sunni Arab fight," said Petraeus.

As former NSA executive Bill Binney — who created the agency's mass surveillance program for digital information, recently explained:

> We are now in a police state, because the government is laundering data generated by mass surveillance, to go after people that — for whatever reason — the government doesn't like.

As was true in Roman times, no one is too prominent or successful to fall afoul of government spies. But the real burden of post-constitutional collapse is likely to fall, as it did with the collapse of the Roman Empire on everyday people pushed into debt bondage.

Tenney Frank, the prominent ancient historian and classicist of the early 20th century, detailed how misleading the prosperity of the early Roman Empire was as a guide to what was to come. Consider this from his book, "An Economic History of Rome (1927):"

> The Empire is world-wide and at peace. The seas are safe for commerce, and military roads, well-built and policed, run through all the provinces. There are no prohibitive tariffs or restrictive laws limiting the scope of industrial enterprise, and the state has no economic policy either helping or hindering business: men are at liberty everywhere to develop their resources and improve their capacity. The end of the century shows favorable balance is almost everywhere and the demonstration of wealth and stately public buildings and luxurious private houses becomes especially conspicuous in the reign of Hadrian.

During the downward slide of the Roman Empire, when conditions were being perfected for the Western world's first plunge into feudalism, the middle class of small farmers (80% of the Roman economy was based on agriculture), who had been the backbone of the Republic, lost their lands to oppressive taxation and debt bondage.

It was a process of immiseration that took centuries. But it accelerated sharply in the third century when agricultural productivity plunged due to colder weather. Of course, the tax obligations continued to be demanded as in former times, based on the historically higher productivity of farming during the Roman Warm Period. "The Cambridge Ancient History" summarizes:

> The system of small tenancies subject to the payment of a rent was in some cases simply the continuation of older conditions; elsewhere it arose since the native population was not forthwith enslaved but merely degraded to the condition of tenants or again native peasants who were heavily in debt were, it is true, deprived of their land but allowed to cultivate it on the payment of a rent.

The yeoman farmers who had formed the original backbone of the Roman legions became tenant farmers (coloni).

By the end of the fourth century, they had been reduced to serfdom, legally designated as "slaves of the land." The Emperor Theodosius I decreed:

> [I]n case it may seem that permission has been given to coloni, free from the ties of their taxable condition, to wander off and go where they will, they are themselves to be bound by the right of origin, and though they appear to be freemen by condition are nevertheless to be held to be slaves of the land itself to which they were born, and are not to have the right to go off where they will or change their domicile.

An enduring puzzle of Western civilization is what caused the granddaddy of all collapses — the fall of the Roman Empire. At last count, there were at least 210 theories explaining Rome's downfall, a devastating collapse that marked the end of the ancient world. Lest you think I exaggerate on 210 explanations of Rome's fall, these were collated by German researchers and recently re-posted by the University of Texas.

Of course, these explanations range from the sublime to the ridiculous — we have to be smart about interpolating them to today's circumstances because superficial similarities may mask profoundly different circumstances. And, (with apologies to Sam Cooke, dare I say it?) even some historians "don't know much about history." Among the more tenuous explanations are those blaming Rome's collapse on celibacy, "fear of life," female emancipation, gluttony, gout, lead poisoning, and "marriages of convenience."

I suspect the more pressing issue was the fact that predatory government, all by itself, without help from "gluttony and gout," much less "emancipated women" who married for "convenience," reduced most of the Roman population to the status of a sprawling proletariat at the service of a tiny elite of "potentiores." Those who controlled the state fought ceaseless wars, including civil wars to enrich themselves because, as economic historian Aurelio Bernardi put it: "Each war could become a new opportunity to augment the private fortunes of the potentiores. This explains in part why the barbarians were sometimes greeted as liberators from the invasions of the rich."

It was a protracted exercise in freebooting, undertaken at the expense of the balance of the population who sought to claw out a "hand-to-mouth existence." As Bernardi concluded: "The fall of an immense state that had lasted 1000 years was completed in the course of not much more than half a century." That is not a long time, about the length of the show we baby boomers have witnessed on the road to ruin.

How close are we to the "terminal crisis" of the U.S. imperium? I can't tell you for certain. As Giovanni Arrighi put it in his scholarly quest to answer the biggest question of the 21st century: "It is not easy to choose among the successive crises that mark the transition from one regime to another, the 'true' terminal crisis of the declining regime."

We do know that "signal" crises that have marked the shift to financialization in past hegemonic regimes have occurred between 40 and 70 years before the terminal crises. The signal crisis that marked the turn from primary investment in the material expansion of the world economy to financialization in the United States occurred around 1970, epitomized by Richard Nixon's 1971 decision to repudiate the gold reserve standard and open the way to unlimited issue of fiat money. It is not a coincidence that the average man in America has not gained a penny of real income in the intervening years.

The terminal crisis, the Breaking Point, could begin at any time, without notice. It may already have begun. Witness the first contemporary report of real GDP contraction since 2009. As John Williams of Shadow Government Statistics reports:

Underlying real-world economic activity suggests that the broad economy began to turn down in 2006 and 2007, plunged into 2009, entered a protracted period of stagnation thereafter — never recovering — and then began to turn down anew in the second and third quarter 2012... "Corrected" GDP... shows fourth-quarter GDP activity at 7.1% below the pre-recession peak of first-quarter 2006.

There are at least 50 video games set in ancient Rome, incorporating various degrees of historical accuracy. I have never played any of them and have no clue about what light they shed on this momentous collapse into the Dark Ages.

They may not say as much as the attacks by swarms of hostile Zombie Pigmen imply about the next great collapse, coming in the wake of the terminal crisis to a neighborhood near you.

Look out below.

CHAPTER 26

Planning for Life Beyond the Welfare State

"We hate our politicians so much that even if they tell us they lied, we don't believe them."

— Peter Newman

The Terminal Crisis, a.k.a. The Great Reckoning, is still to come.

Most people don't see it because they haven't grasped the nature of the change that is overtaking the world. Only the actual crisis itself — when the economy slips down into a deeper stage of depression — will convince the majority that the postwar prosperity is gone forever. Until then, the economic news will continue to be a rerun of the recent past, a concoction of fake jobs, and fake growth, calculated from fake inflation numbers, that taken together form no basis for a sustained upsurge of the kind that characterized the third quarter of the 20th century.

In previous chapters, I spelled out reasons to begin planning now for life beyond the welfare state. You cannot bank your future and that of your family on faltering, anachronistic institutions whose stability rests on a crumbling foundation of lies and financial repression. You cannot afford to ignore the potentially sweeping consequences of a terminal crisis of the welfare state.

Even if you do not intend to depend upon government transfer payments for survival for the rest of your days, you may need to take action now to assure that your assets are well-placed to outlast the turmoil ahead. No less an authority than Alan Greenspan has stated the problem you face: "The financial policy of the welfare state requires that there be no way for the owners of wealth to protect themselves."

He should know.

The $30,000 Annual Gift

If you are like 98% of our readers, you have some wealth to protect. You live in a rich country that had already undergone an industrial revolution by early in the 20th century. By living in the United States or another industrial country, you've been given a startling wealth advantage over the rest of the world. On a per capita basis, residents of Australia, Canada, New Zealand and the United States enjoy a startling advantage over the rest of the world. An OECD calculation, based upon the research of economist Angus Maddison, shows that residents of the leading English-speaking former settlement colonies enjoy an average per capita income of $36,400. Meanwhile, the rest of the world has an income (in 1990 international dollars) of $5,101.

Branko Milanovic, of the World Bank, published a detailed analysis of world income equality, "The Haves and the Have-Nots: A Brief and Idiosyncratic History of Global Inequality." He concluded that, contrary to Marx, global inequality is not:

> … being predominantly driven by class, it has changed to being almost entirely driven by location (80% of global inequality). Today, it is much more important, globally speaking, whether you were lucky enough to be born in a rich country than whether the income class to which you belong in a rich country is high, medium or low.

He goes on to point out that the poorest 5% of Americans enjoy higher income than 68% of the rest of the world. Perhaps more dramatic is the fact that:

> The richest people in India have the same per capita income as the poorest people in the United States… In the case of India and the United States, only about three percent of the Indian population have incomes higher than the bottom (the very poorest) U.S. percentile.

This gigantic income gap is a gift of history. While people living in the industrial countries still have far higher productivity than the rest of the world, and U.S. productivity is highest of all, this does not explain the whole of the income gap. A plumber in Nairobi works harder and often must be more inventive than a plumber in Manhattan. But he earns a small fraction of the New York plumber's wage. A bureaucrat in Chad is not necessarily less adept at pushing papers than his counterpart in California. He is paid less because the country in which he lives is poor.

Wealth Raises Income for Everyone

Much of the income gap between rich and poor countries, at least in many occupations, rests upon the differences in accumulated wealth. A Chadian bureaucrat would earn more money if Chad became richer. A bureaucrat in California would earn less if the state were impoverished. Contrary to the thinking that predominates in political circles, wealth creation does a great deal for society. It may do more to raise the long-term income of others when it is allowed to accumulate than when it is taxed away. Those who create wealth create a basis upon which people who need not be particularly clever or rich themselves can earn higher incomes. The wealthy man in Nairobi or Nashville is helping to raise the standard of living of the plumber and the bureaucrat there as well as himself.

Thanks to a lot of work in savings by our ancestors, and a few lucky accidents, you and I have the income we do. We enjoy a huge margin of grace, and inheritance of wealth equivalent to the annual yield on a 10-Year Treasury bond portfolio of about $1,317,900 at interest rates as of November 2014. Just by being born in a rich country, you received a bequest that is currently worth about $31,300 annually over the income you would now enjoy if you lived like the 85% majority of the Earth's population. That is a sobering thought. Or it should be.

No Monopoly on Prosperity

Yet the countries that for so long held a monopoly on the world's prosperity no longer do. This is one of the chief consequences of the collapse of communism and socialism. The revolution in attitude manifested in Deng Xiaoping's reforms in China and the collapse of the Soviet Union has added billions of low-cost competitors to world labor markets.

The peoples of emerging economies, particularly in Asia and Latin America, are no longer being as effectively prevented from prospering by their governments' idiotic policies. Countries that once scorned private investment as "imperialism" and "colonization" now welcome it with open arms.

This change of heart is all the more convincing because it is made as a matter of utter necessity. Even unrepentant Marxists like Fidel Castro have found that they have no choice but to open their economies to foreign investment and market incentives.

Competition Multiplies

This revolution in pro-wealth policies implies a rapid erosion of the artificial advantages enjoyed by residents of Western industrial countries and Japan during the Cold War. Our incomes will continue to remain high so long as our wealth remains high. But watch closely: All the Western industrial countries are rapidly running down their balance sheets, running massive budget deficits to finance costly welfare state programs that cannot pay their way.

Fake Deleveraging

Notice also that the dominant response to the 2008–2009 financial meltdown has been a fake. The 16th Geneva report on the World Economy (published September 2014 by the Centre for Economic Policy Research) reveals that the total of global non-financial debt, private as well as public, "has risen from 60% of national income in 2001 … to 215% in 2013."

The declining returns implied by the nationalization of bad debt pose the prospect of dramatically falling incomes ahead, particularly in the U.S. and the Eurozone. The U.S. has experienced similar stagnation to that witnessed in Japan and Europe, but the U.S. authorities have been somewhat more effective in disguising slowdown with fake statistics that report exaggerated growth and fake job creation, implying artificial stability.

When politicians squander the remaining wealth from the Industrial Age, incomes in North America, Europe and Japan could fall further than anyone now expects. Given the tremendous increase in competition from Asia and Latin America, it is unreasonable to expect that the currently rich societies will recover wealth once lost with the same ease with which it was accumulated in the first place.

Better Quality at One One-Hundredth the Cost

Technology has made it too simple for high-value production to be relocated almost anywhere. Essentially unskilled factory jobs, once monopolized by manual laborers in Western industrial countries, can now be learned in a few days' time in low-wage countries. Volkswagen pays its workers in China just one one-hundredth the wages and benefits it pays in Germany and gets a product which matches or exceeds German output in quality.

Little wonder that the Chinese economy has grown in recent years at such an astounding clip — averaging 15.8% in the 32 years from 1979 through

2010 with a peak growth rate of 36.41% reported in 1994. This happened while Western industrial countries and Japan have barely grown at all. Something similar can be said of other emerging economies of Asia and some in Latin America. Hong Kong, Singapore, Thailand, Malaysia, Chile, Colombia, Peru and Brazil have all grown much faster than the G7.

I expect that, over the long-term, growth in the emerging economies will continue to far outstrip that in the mature welfare states. By and large, the high-performance economies are not hobbled by costly entitlement programs. They are low-tax countries, with much lower total debt burdens. Because they have limited welfare costs, most have balanced budgets with national debts that are a fraction of those in the formerly advanced countries. The rapidly growing economies have little in the way of old-age public pensions. Chile and Peru have privatized their social security systems.

Services that are engrossed by government in the United States and most of the G7 countries are being privatized in the emerging economies. Brazil's leftist ex-president Luiz Inácio Lula da Silva pursued a program of privatizing highways, airports and other transportation infrastructure. Similar programs are underway in India. In a matter of a few years, China has gone from being a stagnant, communist economy to a place where the central government's share of the total economy is lower than in the United States.

You Haven't Seen Anything Yet

In 1985, when I began to warn in *Strategic Investment* of the coming collapse of Communism, few readers believed this likely. Fewer still felt the need to adjust their life strategies to take account of the changes we foresaw. Some may now wish they had. For those with careers in the defense industry, or businesses in areas dependent upon defense spending like California, early preparation might have avoided some losses.

But that is old news. There is a greater challenge to come. The demise of the welfare state will prove more difficult to work around than the death of Communism, not the least because it will happen in your own backyard. Now is the time to prepare.

I cannot pretend that the strategies outlined below are right for you. They may not be. Much depends on your age, private circumstances, temperament and abilities. Bear in mind that whatever you do must be something that interests and excites you as well as holds the promise of reward. And always remember, I could be wrong in the fundamental analysis. Check and recheck what I say against what makes sense to you.

Be Among the First Rather Than Last

Taking the caveats into account, there can be little doubt that the world is changing far more than most people have yet understood. The world we grew up in, with its apparent certainties, is gone forever. The Information Age is upon us, and that means more than just a growing use of more powerful computers. It means a revolution in lifestyles, institutions and the distribution of wealth.

You will not go far wrong in being among the perceptive few who first update their life strategies in keeping with the new realities. Notwithstanding the plain fact that nesting in one of the dominant political ecologies was key to earning higher income during the Industrial Age, the new megapolitical realities of the Information Age mean that, more than ever, a global approach may be your best route to building and preserving prosperity in the future.

If you will permit an obscure reference to antiquarian, political economy, the looming problem of overleveraged, bankrupt governments in jurisdictions that dominated the old Industrial Age, shows that it is time for a new take on David Ricardo's "equivalence theorem." As you may recall, Ricardo's "Essay on the Funding System (1820)," spelled out the idea that consumers should internalize the government's "budget constraint" when making consumption decisions. In other words, when the government is broke, they should set aside the funds required to pay their share of its obligations. But as we've shown above that consumers in the leading economies face a poisonous combination of secular stagnation and obligations to heavily indebted governments, one of the more rational responses is to migrate away from these implicitly ruinous obligations.

Now is the time to begin to think globally for these and other reasons:

1) Information technology has reduced the transaction costs of internationalizing your business life. It is now possible for individuals with just a few hundred thousand dollars to enjoy many of the same services and financial advantages of operating offshore that formerly could only be accessed by large corporations and families of great wealth. True, governments are eagerly imposing artificial barriers to globalization, but in the fullness of time, I expect these to be transcended by technology.

2) Most of the growth that will occur in the world for the perceivable future will occur in countries that were basket cases when I was a child. It will be far easier to compound your wealth if you can participate in growing

economies than if you must eke out all your gains from slowly growing or contracting economies.

3) Diversification is a protection against uncertainty. The period between now and the middle of the 21st century will be one of rapid and destabilizing change. No one can predict precisely how messy the death throes of the welfare state will be expressed. It is probable that one or more of the G7 countries will cease to exist in its present form by the year 2050. By diversifying your interests into different jurisdictions you increase your odds of surviving with something. Given the predatory U.S. tax and legal systems, money invested in offshore jurisdictions may be more secure against confiscation than it is at home.

In keeping with these principles, here is a checklist of strategies for surviving the terminal crisis of the welfare state:

1) Renew your passport as far as possible into the future.

2) Where possible, acquire multiple passports from various countries. Investigate which other passport you may qualify for, if any. Irish and Italian passports carry automatic entry into the European Community and are often easily obtained by persons of Irish and Italian descent.

3) Whatever your present line of work or study, assume that there is no single body of knowledge that will preserve a high-income job for you over your lifetime.

4) Seek to cultivate a second or third area of specialized knowledge even beginning as a hobby in areas that interest and excite you, so that you will have alternative areas of expertise to replace what is lost.

5) If you make savings and investment one of your specialized areas of knowledge, you will increase your wealth over the long run. If you can get compound interest to work for you rather than against you, it'll make you rich even if your job is not high paying.

6) Try to learn one or more widely spoken languages to widen your comfort zone for working and living abroad.

7) If you have many years of useful work ahead of you, think less in terms of a job and more in terms of inventing your own work. Try not to depend upon renting your time at a high hourly wage that puts you in competition with billions of others who subsist at a low standard of living. Seek instead to obtain a residual interest or profit share in some activity.

8) If you are still a student or have children or grandchildren whose career choices are ahead of them, you or they will have been told by everyone to specialize in the knowledge skills, like biotechnology and computer programming. However, it would be a mistake to neglect a broader, more old-fashioned liberal education. These skills will be more important as the world changes. If you can see the big picture, you will be able to adapt more successfully than someone who only knows a lot about one narrow specialization — which may end up being completely antiquated by the meandering of technology even if it seems the highest of high tech today.

9) Steer clear of dead-end occupations that package knowledge and services that will soon be displaced by information technology, such as accountant, pharmacist, travel agent, lawyer, etc. As transaction costs of global communications plunge, more and more formerly immune services will be open to low-cost competition.

10) Skills such as marketing, customer relations, and entrepreneurship may continue to be more rewarding. You will prosper if you can learn to package needed services in forms that eliminate transaction costs for customers and thus command premium prices. Examples: the caterer who plans a party, sends out the invitations, and arranges to recycle the leftovers; or the florist who contracts to decorate the hotel lobby with appropriate displays for each week of the year rather than merely filling orders.

11) Repair jobs, and hands-on services, such as plumbing, that cannot be displaced by information technology, are also likely to remain in demand as the urban depreciation crisis intensifies.

12) Activities that were once confined within a single corporation will break up into the spot market as "virtual corporations" continue to evolve. If you can package services to larger companies and make it easier for them to downsize, you will enjoy a booming business.

13) Think in terms of business relationships rather than business structures. The boundaries between occupations will break down, which will make good relations with honest people more useful. The advent of truly protected encryption will make all the valuable possessions of large impersonal organizations, from cash reserves to trade secrets, highly vulnerable to undetectable employee theft. Moral and trustworthy associates will be more important than they were in the era of large organization. Cultivate trusting personal relationships with winners.

14) If you have enough risk capital to consider starting or investing in a business, think about doing so offshore, possibly in a legal form in which your profits accumulate free of tax. In recent years, ex-patriot American entrepreneurs have achieved robust success in launching companies throughout Latin America.

15) As growth accelerates in formerly stagnant areas, this will dependably create a template for profitable plagiarism. Rising incomes in emerging economies will re-create opportunities initially seized decades ago in the United States, Canada, Australia, the UK and Japan when those economies achieved similar income levels. For example, land in areas where freeway exits are sited will be valuable locations for shopping centers.

16) If you are Chinese or Indian or have good contacts in those countries, try to become involved in areas that will benefit from growth there. Africa holds promise for the intrepid. Otherwise, focus on Latin America as the area of greatest opportunity. Brazil, Chile, Colombia, Mexico and Peru are growing rapidly and tend to look favorably upon North Americans.

17) Learn as much as you can about promising environments where you might like to live at a substantial discount to North American and/or European costs. Take advantage of educational trips to perspective destinations offered by the Sovereign Society.

18) Find one or more safe havens to which you and your family can withdraw in times of social unrest.

19) Accumulate physical gold and silver.

20) Devote some of your time and resources to trying to change the world in a positive way. This will help keep you balanced. It is part of the responsibility of wealth to use your energies proactively to improve life, including the life of your community, as much as you can.

There you have a very abbreviated outline of some strategic thoughts for positioning yourself and family for the Information Age.

CHAPTER 27

Poor Richard's Almanack Revisited

"Three-fourths of the demands existing in the world are romantic;
founded on visions, idealisms, hopes and affections; and the regulation of
the purse is, in essence, regulation of the imagination and the heart."

— John Ruskin, "Unto this Last"

Someday, between now and the crack of doom, many of the challenging, if not to say "gloomy" developments canvassed in this volume will have come to pass. This new day will eventually become a new year. Its start, like those that came before it, will be a time for taking stock; reviewing the past and previewing the new, and swearing out resolutions of the Ben Franklin sort. His autobiography is still the motherlode of hopes for improving life. Most of us are in his camp. We aim to tuck in our tummies and fatten our purses, while gravity and the calendar weigh-in for the reverse.

I think of this now because it bears directly on the prospects for the future. There is more of Franklin in all of us than a casual look at a $100 bill would reveal. He was the Founding Father of consumer confidence as well as a Renaissance man who invented the Franklin stove, bifocal lenses, the lightning rod, and the glass armonica. He published the first map of the Gulf Stream in 1769, 200 years before it was definitively tracked by a submersible. He also founded the University of Pennsylvania, the American Philosophic Society, *The Saturday Evening Post*, and the Philadelphia Police Department. He left a generous inheritance to his country, and an endowment to encourage the poor apprentices of Philadelphia and Boston.

Yet one of the little-known secrets of American history is that Franklin's success was due far more to his ingenuity in earning money than his discipline in saving it. The founder of *Poor Richard's Almanack* was not always a penny pincher himself. Indeed, Benjamin Franklin could be a lavish spender.

As Ruskin says, "regulation of the purse" is "regulation of the imagination and the heart." Franklin had a great imagination and a big heart. He was a man of appetites, which partly explains his considerable girth and his illegitimate son. Even in his 70s, Franklin was famous for entertaining the ladies of Paris. John Adams thought him a sloth and a lecher. Franklin also liked to indulge himself by going on shopping sprees. In that respect, if not in others, he was the archetypal American.

Benjamin Franklin would have felt at home in the shopping malls during the week before Christmas. Of all the founding fathers, he was the incarnation of consumer confidence. Franklin often went out on a limb, spending beyond his means because he was confident he could earn more money as needed. He was right.

Franklin could overspend without embarrassment because he was a genius. Whenever he ran shy of money, he earned more, conjuring up new sources of income as easily as he identified the jet stream or tested the heat-absorbing properties of colors. So easy was it for him to make money that he was able to retire by age 42. He lived for another 42 years, indulging his curiosity and ascetic philanthropies and supplementing his fortune as needed.

Franklin is the best example of a consumer with confidence that comes to mind. If everyone were as sure as he was of increasing his income to meet spending desires, then consumer confidence, as such, would not be worth measuring. Everyone would always spend to the limits of his imagination. But of course, this isn't the case. Most people are realistic enough to know that they are not enterprising geniuses of Franklin's caliber. This is why the wiser among us follow his advice, if not his practice, and pinch pennies when times are bad.

This also illustrates why good news that lifts sentiment stimulates consumer spending, as it has repeatedly. Sometimes, and not infrequently in recent decades, talk of recovery has been sufficiently persuasive to be self-fulfilling in the short run.

As a consequence of structural change in the current depression, there are many people without jobs or job security who nonetheless have the capacity to pick up their spending when their confidence gets a boost. For example, more than one million persons lost high-paying jobs with major corporations in the 1990s. As goodbye presents, the downsized employees received severance payments. The size of these packages varied, but some were in the hundreds of thousands of dollars and many were in the tens of thousands of dollars.

Only about 15% of those terminated, however, recovered their jobs. But because they had significant financial resources, unlike the unemployed of the past, those fired with severance packages did not show up on the unemployment rolls. They could live for months or even years while looking for other work. The degree to which they were willing to deplete their nest eggs at any given time was highly dependent on their confidence. And how closely they consulted *Poor Richard's Almanack*.

Hence, the importance of any passing factor that gives a boost to confidence. Economists have long recognized the "broken-window fallacy." It holds that developments like vandalism — for example, throwing a rock through an expensive plate glass window — or natural disasters, like hurricanes that increase demand for durable goods to replace those lost to storms, only appear to stimulate the economy. In fact, they are damaging.

Equally, lies and deceptions about economic strength that raise animal spirits and spur spending do more harm than good by depleting savings under false pretenses. Most of the millions of consumers who take on more debt when their confidence is falsely boosted will be likely to find that, unlike Benjamin Franklin, they cannot raise their incomes at will to pay for a spending spree.

The world for which Poor Richard's advice prepares us is the real world in which we live — a world of diminishing prosperity and uncertain prospects. Or, as Franklin put it, "For age and want save while you may; No morning sun lasts a whole day." He is not preparing us for an unbridled bull market, but an environment of marginal prospects, where the wise "plow deep while sluggards sleep." Franklin also advised to "work while it is called today for you know not how much you may be hindered tomorrow."

Franklin succinctly explained why his advice was mouthed by "Poor Richard" rather than "Rich Richard." He said:

> The Art of getting Riches consists very much in THRIFT. All Men are not equally qualified for getting Money, but it is in the Power of everyone alike to practice this Virtue. He that would be beforehand in the World must be beforehand with his Business. It is not only ill Management, but discovers a slothful Disposition, to do that in the Afternoon, which should have been done in the Morning.

Franklin, himself, may have been the confident consumer but his advice to us is more circumspect: "Buy what thou hast no need of and ere long thou shall sell thy necessities." And "The way to be safe is never to be secure."

As you plan ahead to the world anticipated in this book, bear in mind that I may be wrong in crucial respects, as most experts would gladly tell you. And even if I am not, you should draw comfort from the fact that I am unlikely to be more than half right. "Actual events play cat-and-mouse with our ideas," as poet Paul Valéry said. "They belong to a quite different species and even when seeming to bear out our preconceptions are never quite as we expected. Foresight is a dream from which the event wakes us."